D1352205

This book is to be returned on or before
the last date stamped below

ACLE LIBRARY
BRIDEWELL LANE
ACLE
NR13 3RA
Tel. No. (01493) 750693

	23. JUN 01	23. MAR 04
14. SEP	29. AUG NOV 01	17. APR 04
16. NOV 00	06. NOV 01	22. OCT 04
		25. NOV 04
		14. DEC 04
14. DEC 00	31. DEC 01	18. FEB 05
GREAT YARMOUTH	02. OCT 02	15. JUN 05
LIBRARY		29. JUL 0
(01493 844551		
21 01 VP		
13. MAR 01	04. DEC 02	18. AUG 05.
10. APR 01	04. AUG 03	05. OCT 0
17. APR 01	18. AUG 03	31. DEC 05.
	24. FEB 04	10. JUN 2006
		29. JUN 06

18 NOV 2008

NORFOLK LIBRARY
AND INFORMATION SERVICE

NORLINK ITEM

3 0129 026 559 527

♻ 100% recycled paper

The Doctor, the Detective
and
Arthur Conan Doyle

A Biography of Arthur Conan Doyle

Martin Booth

Hodder & Stoughton

NORFOLK LIBRARY AND INFORMATION SERVICE	
SUPPLIER	*farr*
INVOICE No.	C422011
ORDER DATE	15.8.97
	DGY

Copyright © 1997 by Martin Booth

First published in 1997
by Hodder and Stoughton
A division of Hodder Headline PLC

The right of Martin Booth to be identified as the Author of
the Work has been asserted by him in accordance with the
Copyright, Designs and Patents Act 1988.

10 9 8 7 6 5 4 3 2 1

All rights reserved. No part of this publication may be
reproduced, stored in a retrieval system, or transmitted,
in any form or by any means without the prior written
permission of the publisher, nor be otherwise circulated
in any form of binding or cover other than that in which
it is published and without a similar condition being
imposed on the subsequent purchaser.

British Library Cataloguing in Publication Data

Booth, Martin, 1944–
The doctor, the detective and Arthur Conan Doyle :
a biography of Arthur Conan Doyle
1. Doyle, Sir Arthur Conan, 1859–1930 – Biography
2. Novelists, English – 19th century – Biography
3. Novelists, English – 20th century – Biography
I. Title
823.9'12

ISBN 0 340 64897 X

Typeset by Hewer Text Composition Services, Edinburgh
Printed and bound in Great Britain by
Mackays of Chatham plc

Hodder and Stoughton Ltd
A division of Hodder Headline PLC
338 Euston Road
London NW1 3BH

Contents

List of Illustrations

Acknowledgements

I am indebted to the following people and institutions, without whom this book could not have been written: the Earl of Cromer, Penny Hext, Lord Kimball, Murray Pollinger, my agent Patrick Walsh, my editor Roland Philipps, Alex Booth, the University of Dundee, the University of Edinburgh, the University of Pennsylvania, Penn State University, the Humanities Research Center at the University of Texas, Somerset County Council Library Service (in particular the staff of the Langport branch library), Hampshire County Council Record Office, the British Olympic Association, News International Group the Royal Automobile Club, Stonyhurst College, the Royal Photographic Society, the British Film Institute, Dr. Kenneth McAll, Dr. Kenneth Keddie, Devon County Record Office, Marylebone Cricket Club, The New York Times, Portsmouth City Council, the British Medical Association, the Master of Foxhounds Association, the Territorial Army, Richard Lancelyn Green, Angus Health Trust, the National Rifle Association, the British Museum and the Imperial War Museum. Finally, my greatest debt of all goes to my wife and co-worker, Helen, whose astonishing sifting of a vast amount of research material was utterly invaluable.

Foreword

Early in 1986, I spent a month living in a small hotel in Naini Tal, one of the lesser-known hill stations in the Himalayan foothills of northern India. My room was spartan but comfortable, with a smoky wood-burning stove (it was bitterly cold at night), a substantial but creaking mahogany bed and a bookshelf upon which resided an oil lamp and a candle, for the electricity supply was at best unreliable and at worst dangerous, a box of American waterproof matches left behind by a mountaineer and three books proudly stamped with the hotel's rubber chop. The first was a Bible, the second was a copy of the Kama Sutra and the third was the collected stories of Sherlock Holmes. Of the three books, the latter was the most thumbed.

Sitting with a view of one of the holiest lakes in the Hindu religion spread before me, and a Bhutia shawl wrapped around me, I read the stories again for the first time since boyhood and, for twenty-minute stretches at a time, was transported. The breathtaking majesty of the lake was supplanted by the cosy interior of 221B Baker Street, a world of hansom cabs and tall hats, hell-hounds and speckled bands. I could almost smell the shag tobacco.

When I embarked upon this biography, Arthur Conan Doyle was a favourite author, a writer whose work I greatly admired. I had read *The Lost World* and *The White Company* as a twelve-year-old but, other than those brief trips into the Middle Ages and the Amazonian jungle in the company of Professor Challenger and pterodactyls, all I really knew of him was his creation of Sherlock Holmes and his conversion to spiritualism.

Once I set out on the journey through his life, however, I quickly came to the realisation that there was much, much more to him than I had ever perceived or, indeed, could have conceived. He wrote not only detective and adventure stories but horror and sci-fi, long historical novels, non-fiction (including seminal histories of the Boer War and the First World War), a massive corpus of journalism, the most comprehensive history of spiritualism and dozens of pamphlets in support of the wide range of causes with which he became involved. His knighthood, which I had always assumed to have been bestowed for services to literature, was actually awarded for patriotism.

Arthur Conan Doyle was a genuine polymath. Raised in poverty in Edinburgh, the son of a loving mother and a dipsomaniac father, he became immensely wealthy only to lose much of his fortune in the pursuit and furtherance of his religious beliefs. He was first and foremost a writer but he was also to be, over the years, a general practitioner, military doctor and ship's doctor, a war correspondent, a prospective parliamentary candidate (twice), a first-class county cricket player, a famous champion of victims of miscarriages of justice, an instigator of legislation, a family man and a devout spiritualist. A supporter of women's rights regarding divorce legislation, and the main force behind the rewriting of them to address their sexual inequality biased against the wife, he was also almost rabid in his hatred and condemnation of the suffragettes. As a determined anti-Roman Catholic, he stood up for the rights of Catholics. He was fiercely patriotic yet defended Roger Casement, who was executed for treason. Finally, although scientifically trained as a doctor, he believed in fairies. In short, he was a paradoxical character, an enigma, sometimes complex, at others naïve and simplistic. He was also dictatorial, doggedly stubborn, rejected all criticism and would never admit he was wrong about anything.

In the preface to his autobiography, he wrote, 'I have had a life which, for variety and romance, could I think, hardly be exceeded.' He was absolutely right.

Although a number of biographies of Sir Arthur Conan Doyle have been published, there has not been a full and detailed study for over twenty years, and several of those that have appeared have been either shallow, one-sided, or set out to denigrate him. Over more recent years, however, a number of studies have appeared dealing with specific aspects of his life. Owen Dudley Edwards, Geoffrey Stavert, Kelvin I. Jones, Michael Baker, Alvin E. Rodin and Jack D. Key, John Michael Gibson and Richard Lancelyn Green have uncovered facts about such subjects as Conan Doyle's childhood, his early life as a medical student and doctor, his involvement with the spiritualist movement and the true story of what really happened to his alcoholic father. To all of these writers, as well as to the previous biographers, this book must owe a considerable debt. Yet it also throws new light on Conan Doyle's life and work, presenting the new material with the old in the hope that the amalgam might bring a new generation of readers to this quite remarkable man who was, in essence, the first-ever blockbuster novelist.

When I came to leave Naini Tal, the proprietor of the hotel wished me *bon voyage* and apologised for the inconvenience of the dubious electricity supply. I complimented him upon the basic comforts of the room and he expressed a wish to have had more books, for I was an author and authors need books. I replied I had had more than sufficient with Sherlock Holmes.

'Ah, yes!' he exclaimed. 'Shur-luck Homes! You know he came to Naini Tal?'

'You mean,' I corrected him, 'Arthur Conan Doyle came to Naini Tal?'

'No, sahib. It was Shur-luck Homes.'

When I asked why he had come, the proprietor did not know. It had happened before the war, before he was born. His father had told him about it. It had something to do with solving the murder of a Rajasthani prince. I decided not to labour the point that Sherlock Holmes was a fictional character.

I know that Arthur Conan Doyle never visited India, never mind a small hill station in the Siwalik Hills, and no Sherlock Holmes story was ever set there. However, it is believed that, in the years after Sherlock Holmes fell over the Reichenbach Falls and went into hiding from Professor Moriarty's vengeful men, he travelled to, amongst other places, Tibet, where he had an audience with the Dalai Lama – and Naini Tal is on one of the ancient routes north to Lhasa.

In truth, both Arthur Conan Doyle and Sherlock Holmes have been to Naini Tal, if not in the flesh. And they are both, to the best of my knowledge, still there.

Martin Booth
Somerset, 1997

Note

For several decades, access to Sir Arthur Conan Doyle's private papers has been refused to biographers, due to an on-going and complicated legal dispute. All letters quoted in this biography, therefore, have been drawn from previously published records or material available prior to the withdrawal of the archives. Several early biographers were allowed access to the papers but the content of their biographies was, to some extent, controlled by the family who only permitted what they wished to see printed being released. Needless to say, when these papers are, once more, made available to biographers, then a thorough and much more comprehensive biography than this one may be written.

1

The Poor Relations

In the middle ranks of class-conscious Victorian England, the nobility were looked up to with a mixture of servile admiration and wistful envy. Fictional heroines sought noble husbands, books were devoted to heraldry and the tracing of one's lineage, and the family crests of even the least significant branches of the aristocracy were frequently purloined by commoners. Any family was deemed fortunate if it could irrefutably claim a distinguished ancestry and the Doyles, whose origins lay in what is today the republic of Eire, were no different.

A very common surname in nineteenth-century Ireland, Doyle has two distinct provenances. One root has it derived from the Old Irish word *dougal*,* meaning a dark stranger or foreigner: it was frequently applied to the descendants of Vikings and there was a famous Irish tribal chieftain called D'Oil who was probably of Viking ancestry. The alternative has it originating in the village of Pont-d'Ouilly on the banks of the River Orne, eighteen kilometres west of Falaise in Normandy.

From this stock sprang a number of branches that included a famous general, Sir John Doyle, who became lieutenant-governor of Guernsey and constructed the island's defences, Sir Francis Hastings Charles Doyle, barrister, commissioner for customs and one-time Professor of Poetry at Oxford, General Welbore Ellis Doyle, commander-in-chief of Ceylon, and Sir John Milley Doyle, who aided in the suppression of the Irish insurrection of 1794, was Member of Parliament for County Carlow and who was briefly imprisoned in 1823 for meddling in the struggle for the Portuguese succession. It is conceivable that the family could also count Foulkes D'Oyley, a crusader under Richard Coeur

*= DUBH GHAILL

de Lion, amongst their illustrious forebears and, through him, claim as distant antecedents such a diverse group as Thomas D'Oyly (or D'Oylie), a doctor and friend of Francis Bacon, Edward Doyley, who defended Jamaica against the Spaniards in the 1650s, and a variety of eminent theologians and scholars.

Whatever the truth of its origin it is certain that, by the fourteenth century, the Doyle coat of arms, consisting of a hart's head over the motto *Fortitudine Vincit*, was being attributed to an Anglo-Norman family called D'Oel which had settled in Ireland where, in 1333, Edward III granted lands in County Wexford to one Sir Alexander D'Oyly. By 1618, it was being used by a family called Doyle at Arklow in County Wicklow.

It is impossible to follow and document the fate of the Doyle family in Ireland. The turbulent life of that island, its civil unrest and insurrections, not to mention the persecution of Roman Catholics after the Reformation, have destroyed not only records but also family properties: the Doyle ancestors of Sir Arthur Conan Doyle, being of the Catholic faith, were deprived of lands and wealth by anti-papist legislation.

What is known is that, in 1668, the estates of one John Doyle were sequestered by the Duke of York and, in 1762, his grandson Richard, losing the last remnant of the family properties, a small estate at Barracurragh, on the banks of the River Bann in County Wexford, ten kilometres south-west of Arklow, travelled to Dublin where he established himself as a silk merchant. He appears to have prospered, raising a family that was to include some remarkably talented members. His grandson, John, who was born in 1797, trained to be an artist at the Dublin Society Drawing School under Gaspare Gabrielli, the Italian landscapist, and John Comerford, the miniaturist. Finding Irish artistic life limiting, he moved to London in 1817 where he established himself within a small but influential coterie of people who moved in high political, literary and artistic circles. Within a short time, he had developed a reputation for himself as a miniaturist and portrait painter who also became known for his pictures of horses. For ten years, from 1825, he exhibited at the Royal Academy. However, it was under the pseudonym of 'HB' that he became nationally famous as an astute, satirical political caricaturist in the mould of William Hogarth: he is today regarded as the foremost cartoonist of the Regency era. His penmanship was fastidious and detailed whilst his wit was as sharp as his nib and all the more subtle for being polite, unlike the unequivocally ferocious and blunt work of his contemporary, George Cruikshank, and James Gillray, who had died in 1815. Where Gillray and Cruikshank were a pair of blatant bulldogs who went for the throat of their subjects, John Doyle was far more gentlemanly and attacked politicians with a sophisticated, almost courteous wit which depended for its success as much upon intellectual as artistic prowess.

As a caricaturist, John Doyle was extremely secretive about his activities. He closely guarded his anonymity behind his pseudonymous initials. His cartoons, which appeared weekly, were widely distributed by his publisher, a man called Maclean with offices in Haymarket, but the original artwork was delivered to the printer by a go-between in a closed carriage. The engravers, etchers and printers worked in secrecy. It was thirty years before John Doyle's identity was publicly known.

Arguably the father of the modern political cartoon, John Doyle minutely observed those he lampooned, always on the look-out for small tell-tale details that showed a weakness or betrayed a character trait: and, being anonymous, he could often carry out his observations from close quarters. As an artist, he moved in high society, visiting the Prince of Wales and Queen Victoria and counting amongst his close dining acquaintances and friends the likes of Benjamin Disraeli, William Thackeray, Sir Walter Scott, Sir Edwin Landseer, William Holman Hunt, Sir John Millais, Thomas De Quincey and Charles Dickens. Those with whom he was intimate, however, ran an albeit unknowing risk: they were not beyond the reach of his satirical eye, and amongst those whom he lampooned were George IV, William IV, Queen Victoria, Robert Peel and Lord Palmerston. He even pasquinaded the nation's hero, the Duke of Wellington, for whom Doyle, a tall and austere man referred to behind his back by his sons as Lord John or Gov'nor General, was sometimes mistaken when walking in Regent's Park. John Doyle prospered. He bought an imposing house at 17 Cambridge Terrace, overlooking Regent's Park, and took a wife.

Marianna Conan was the sister of Michael Conan, foreign correspondent and arts critic for the *Morning Herald*, and came from a noble background in Brittany, her ancestors having fled to Catholic Ireland to escape religious persecution. Theirs was a devoutly Catholic marriage, for, like his wife, John Doyle adhered closely to his faith, considering his to be one of the families of the hierarchy of Anglo-Catholicism. He believed his faith was not merely a matter of tradition but something that gave him an inner strength: because of his family's historical persecution, and, in some respects, the continuance of it in predominantly Protestant Victorian England, he considered himself if not a cut above his peers, certainly apart from them. There ran in him, as may still be found in high-born Anglo-Catholics, a streak of religious arrogance that he rarely displayed yet which he nevertheless harboured.

Marianna bore him seven children: two girls, Annette and Adelaide (nicknamed Adele), and five boys called James, Richard, Henry, Francis and Charles. Francis, who was known in the family as Frank, shared his father's artistic talent, especially in the painting of miniatures, but he was never to live to realise it: he died, aged fifteen, in a typhoid epidemic, his sister Adele having succumbed to consumption before him. Marianna herself died young, John Doyle employing a part-time tutor called Street and a governess to raise his children.

He was, by all accounts, a good father. Austere he may have been, and strictly Catholic in the upbringing of his children, but he was also loving and involved himself with them. He coached them to draw and paint, encouraging them to be individuals and passing on to them a large share of his own artistic abilities.

For a while, John Doyle fared well but his substantially furnished family house in Cambridge Terrace, in one of the fashionable areas of London, not to mention his need to maintain his standard of living in order to keep up his position in society, proved a drain on his finances. He fell heavily into debt. The servants were dismissed, Annette becoming his housekeeper. John Doyle died in 1868 but his legacy of talent lived on in his children.

James Doyle, who was born in 1822, was the first. He was to become a scholar. Like his father, he was stern-looking, tall and lean with a dense black beard, his appearance earning him the nickname of The Priest. He inherited his father's artistic skills and was both a talented portrait artist as well as a caricaturist and painter of religious subjects. A genealogist, he wrote and illustrated *The Chronicles of England*, a historical study up to the beginning of the Tudors, and spent thirteen years producing *The Official Baronage of England*. Published in 1886, it was considered a standard genealogical source text by the College of Arms.

The second son, Richard, was born in 1824. Fondly nicknamed Dicky, he also had his share of artistic talent. Publishing his first caricatures at the age of fifteen, he went on to become one of the most important illustrators and cartoonists of the nineteenth century. Like his father, he paid great attention to detail and was a graphic artist of considerable skill. At the age of nineteen, he joined the staff of *Punch* magazine as a cartoonist and illustrator and, in 1849, was responsible for the famous portrait of Mr Punch that was featured unchanged on the cover for well over a century. However, the following year he resigned, surrendering a substantial annual salary of £800 on a point of principle: the magazine had criticised Anglo-Catholicism and poked fun at the Pope. Thereafter, he became a much-sought-after book illustrator. He provided the drawings for Ruskin's *King of the Golden River*, Thackeray's *The Newcomes* and some of the works of Charles Dickens: he was also particularly successful at illustrating fairy stories. His vision of the classical fairy image, of the little winged girl in a gossamer gown, is familiar to this day.

Three years later, the third son, Henry, was born. In what was almost a family tradition, he became a portrait painter and art critic. A close friend of Cardinal Newman, the central figure in the Oxford Movement and defender of Anglo-Catholics, he painted the murals of the Last Judgment in the Roman Catholic church in Lancaster. Made honorary secretary of the National Portrait Gallery in 1865, he was appointed director of the National Gallery of Ireland in 1869 and spent the rest of his life building up the collection, investing in painters whom he was sure would gain in reputation and buying judiciously: his most renowned purchase was made in 1883 when he paid £514 for Rembrandt's *Sleeping Shepherds*.

The last surviving son was called Charles Altamont. At the time of his birth, around 1832, Marianna was terminally ill and John Doyle was over fifty. Charles was, if not the runt of the litter, certainly the odd one out. As a child, he was prone to emotional outbursts and rages and, like many a younger sibling, he lived in the shadow of his talented elders. This is not to say that he was without talent. He had a distinct artistic bent but he lacked the astute commercial flair of the other artists in his family and, although he was like his father in that he was tall, with a long beard reaching well down his chest, Charles was not a forceful but rather a retiring man, always gentle and courteous with a quick but quiet wit.

In November 1849, perhaps wanting to establish himself outside the sphere of his clever brothers, but possibly also to relieve some of the pressure on the family income in Cambridge Terrace, he travelled north to Edinburgh where he was employed as an assistant to Robert Mathieson, the head of Her Majesty's Office of Works. It seems he might have gained the post through his father's influence. He would have preferred to have stayed in London but he was persuaded to go to Scotland because, he was told, the position had prospects. Charles went, hoping the job might be a temporary one before promotion took him back to England: he was to spend the rest of his working life as a civil servant in Edinburgh.

The Scottish capital was not as dull and dry as Charles had feared it might be. He was impressed by its buildings and the bustle of commerce, yet he was still homesick and wrote long letters to his family which he illustrated with sketches. The replies he received back must have increased his pining for home. His brother Richard regaled him with stories of literary dinners and parties, name-dropping everyone from Thackeray to Emily Brontë. Gradually, his optimism faded. He became cowed and unambitious. His brothers went from strength to strength whilst he just accepted his lot and plodded along. As time passed, he lost his desire to return to London or, as he once dreamed, to travel to find his fortune in the goldfields of Australia. When a chance at last arose to take up a post in London, he let it go.

Upon reaching Edinburgh and looking for lodgings, Charles was introduced to an Irish Catholic widow with two daughters, Catherine Foley, who took in lodgers as a means of supplementing her income. Charles gratefully rented one of her rooms.

Born Catherine Pack in 1809, she was the daughter of a Protestant landowner in Ireland descended from a major in Cromwell's army and remotely descended from the distinguished Percy family, the Dukes of Northumberland: a relative, possibly her uncle, was Sir Denis Pack, who had commanded the Scots forces at the Battle of Waterloo. She married an Irish Catholic doctor, William Foley, presumably embracing his faith. Why, upon his death, she went to Scotland is open to speculation: she may have been spurned by her father for taking to Catholicism and by her in-laws for being a Roman Catholic by convenience rather than conviction.

By eking out a small inheritance, renting lodgings and working part-time at a variety of jobs, Catherine Foley was able to keep bread on her table and educate her daughter, Mary, who was twelve years old when Charles moved in as a lodger. A plain-looking child, she was partly educated in France in order, it is thought, that she might gain a good grounding in Roman Catholicism, from where she returned as a lively and cultivated young woman.

How long Charles courted Mary is unknown but they were married on the last day of July 1855. She was seventeen and he was about twenty-three. After the wedding, they continued to live with Catherine who carried on accepting lodgers, advertising herself as a landlady offering accommodation to governesses. The other daughter, named Catherine after her mother, also lived with them and, in time, became a governess herself.

Two years after the marriage, Mary gave birth to a daughter, Anne Mary Frances, known in the family as Annette. She was the first of ten children of whom seven survived into adulthood. A second daughter, Catherine Emilia Angela, arrived in April 1858 but was dead before the year was out. In the meantime, Mary was pregnant again and gave birth to her first son on 22 May 1859 at 11 Picardy Place, a three-storey building close to St Mary's Cathedral, to which the family had moved and in which they rented a small apartment. His parents named him Arthur Ignatius Conan.

The choice of names was not fortuitous. Ignatius was selected because it was common practice for Catholic families to include a saint in a child's given names, and it may also be the case that the Doyles were being sentimental, for they were wed on St Ignatius' Day. The other two Christian names appear to have been picked to please the child's great-uncle and godfather, Michael Conan, who had moved to Paris in 1854 and was now Paris correspondent of the *Art Journal*. It is even possible that Arthur was decided upon by Michael Conan himself who, being keen on genealogy and heraldry, fascinated with the Arthurian legend and conscious of the family's Breton roots, may have wanted to give the child a certain romantic individuality and carry on a family tradition. As Michael Conan and his wife, Susan, apparently had no issue, the matter of keeping the family name alive may have been important to him.

There has been, for decades, a debate as to whether or not the name Conan was added to Doyle as a double but unhyphenated surname. Arthur was not the only child to carry it: Annette, who was also Michael Conan's godchild, did so too. For all of his adult life, Arthur was known as Arthur Conan Doyle, but he neither legally nor formally established a double surname. In official lists, such as the *Dictionary of National Biography*, he is most often listed under *D*, but in many other reference books he is frequently indexed under *C*. As a schoolboy, Arthur sometimes signed himself A.C. Doyle, so what seems most likely is that, as he reached adulthood, he took to using his third given name partly to perpetuate the family name, partly out of deference to his godfather, and partly to give himself a more imposing name. Plain Arthur Doyle hardly had a ring to it.

Not long after his birth, the family moved from Picardy Place. This was not unusual: the Doyles, like many other middle-class Edinburgh families, frequently shifted from one rented home to another, always on the lookout to improve upon their lot, to escape from disease that might be rife in one neighbourhood or from the stench of effluent. Nineteenth-century Edinburgh was not a healthy city and a substantial majority of the population lived in run-down town houses that had seen better days. Not quite ghettos or slums, some of the inner-city areas were nevertheless bleak, dark, noisome places in which the streets were unsafe at night and the sewers either non-existent or in poor repair.

More children followed and the strain imposed on Charles's salary, even though it was increased to £250 per annum, was considerable. The result was that the Doyles lived in a state of perpetual, if genteel, poverty. They were not without food, clothing or a roof over their heads yet there was little room for financial manoeuvre and the children rarely had any of the little luxuries a normal middle-class family might have expected.

To supplement his salary, Charles fell back upon his inherited artistic talent yet, unlike his brothers', his work was uncommercial and he was no businessman. Furthermore, he was caught in the cleft stick of being able only to paint in his spare time: he would have liked to have made his living entirely from his pen and brush but he could not because he had no means of obtaining a studio and his time was limited on account of his having to work in order to provide for his family. Despite these strictures, he did manage to earn around £80 a year from paintings and book illustrations, some of his commissions being put his way by his brother Richard. Conceivably, he could have earned more: he would on occasion give away paintings and seldom chased payment for money owed to him. With book illustrations and line drawings, he was somewhat more successful. At a time when photography was in its infancy, skilled artists were much prized by magazine editors to illustrate news stories. Charles worked as a sketch artist on criminal trials and produced a fair body of drawings for the famous *Illustrated London News* in addition to illustrating books of children's rhymes and fairy tales including *The Book of Ballads*, *Brave Men's Footsteps* and the seminal Waterston's Library editions of *Three Blind Mice* and *The Two Bears*. His illustrative style, the drawings delicate and detailed like his father's political caricatures, was well suited to the fantasies of children's stories, containing a certain whimsical, dark mystery occasionally tinged with a sense of the bizarre or even horror.

Charles Doyle's artistic activities served for more than to increase his income. They gave him an escape from the realities of life on the poverty line into his imagination: but this was beginning to alter. His images started to lose their light humour, turning grotesque, melancholic and macabre to such an extent that his paintings, with such titles as *An Oriental Dream* or *The Death Coach*, were no longer bought. His fascination for puerile fairies and elves was sometimes supplanted by supernatural, nightmarish visions containing monsters and evil figures.

It was hardly surprising that Charles Doyle's pictures should develop such a preoccupation with the morbid. He was a disappointed man. The job he had in the Office of Works had not proved to be what he had expected. Charles had thought, or been led to believe, that he would be employed primarily as an architect: although he had no formal training, his draughtsmanship was certainly of a sufficient standard. Indeed, he was involved in the designing of a number of structures including the great window of Glasgow Cathedral and the fountain at Holyrood Palace in Edinburgh. The greater part of his work, however, had him supervising building plans and acting as a senior clerk, more of his time than he wanted being spent in an office. Furthermore, his post carried a considerable responsibility which weighed upon him. Having come from a comparatively free-living artistic background in the cream of London intellectual society, to find himself tied to a desk in an office in Holyrood Palace must have been soul-destroying.

Compared with his creative father and brothers, Charles considered he was a failure. His rented home was impermanent, the spectre of abject poverty was always rattling the door handle and he felt inadequate: his childhood had been a far cry from that which he was providing for his own offspring. Rather than fight his circumstances, Charles accepted them and withdrew into himself, living in a world of misery and self-pity which his exile – as he saw it – in Edinburgh only heightened. Very gradually, the effects of his misery, the responsibilities of his dreary job and his large family began to break his spirit. He grew distant, lived in a defensive reverie and became a stranger to Mary and the children. His sadness was made all the more wretched by occasional visitors from London: even Thackeray called on him. Such visitations humiliated Charles who could not afford to wine and dine his callers in a fashionable eating-house: he had to entertain them in his shoddy accommodation.

It was inevitable that, as melancholy took a hold of his soul, he should lose his grip on his very existence. His office work became negligent and his paintings, when he bothered to sit down and work at them, were increasingly uncommercial. It is probable that he was never cruel or violent to his children or to Mary yet he was, in all but flesh, an absentee father who, when family life oppressed him deeply, would go off fishing.

The rod and line were not his only means of escape: he also retreated into the bottle and developed into an alcoholic. When his addiction was complete it is impossible to say, for he had started drinking, occasionally to excess, not long after arriving in Edinburgh. His penchant was Burgundy. It is safe to say that, in the early years of his marriage, he was a loving husband who did his best but that, in time, he simply caved in under the pressure.

For Arthur, Charles was a distant figure with whom he found it hard to relate. He saw his father's drinking and although, as a young child, he was unable fully to comprehend it, he disliked the casual aloofness and sloth it engendered. As he grew older, his father's attitude frustrated the boy, who was lively in both body and brain, and, as for many a son of a failed father, it strengthened his own resolve not to follow in the same footsteps.

Whether or not Charles and Mary argued or fought over the situation in which his drinking put them is unknown. It seems they must have although, in the true mould of a suffering Victorian wife, Mary must have given in to her husband, either out of devotion or with a silent reluctance and resignation.

It was, inevitably, Mary who bore the brunt of the strain of their poverty, and it was fortunate for her husband and children that, as he deteriorated and life grew steadily worse, she found an inner strength.

Quite what it was that brought them together in matrimony is a matter for conjecture, for they were as chalk and cheese. Where Charles was tall, she was only just over 1.5 metres high. He was a quiet, withdrawn, solitary and unworldly man, but she was intelligent, imaginative, charismatic and practical. Whilst he was serious, sometimes moody and pensive, with his long beard and troubled eyes, she was bubbly and gay. Not overly pretty, she was nevertheless an attractive woman with fair hair and grey, short-sighted eyes that caused her to peer at things as if intensely curious in them, which, in truth, she probably was, for she had an enquiring and lively mind. Her mouth was small and vaguely sensual, her hair often parted severely down the middle in the fashion of the day. In his autobiographical novel, *The Stark Munro Letters*, Conan Doyle described her as 'the quaintest mixture of the housewife and the woman of letters, with the high-bred spirited lady as a base for either character'.

As Charles slipped further from reality, it was Mary who kept things together: she wore both trousers and skirt. Like a heroine from a contemporary novel, she coped with her husband's moods and alcoholism, fed and clothed and loved her children, and did her very best for them, frequently at some sacrifice to herself. They might have lived in the shadow of poverty, but her children were always washed, combed and neatly dressed. She might not have been proud of her husband, but she was of her brood. She was also determined that her offspring should be educated, for, in the way of the Victorians, she knew that the only way out of poverty was through personal betterment and that meant a sound schooling.

For Mary, education was a broad slate. A romantic at heart, she was passionate about legends, history and, in keeping with the times, her own forebears, about whom she could make extravagant claims. It was as if, by claiming an illustrious past, she somehow mitigated her present condition: they might be poor but they had the stuff of greatness in them.

Through her mother's line, she claimed royal blood because, in the seventeenth century, when the Reverend Richard Pack, the principal of Kilkenny College, married Mary Percy of Ballintemple, heir of the Irish branch of the Percys of Northumberland, there was forged a link between her family and the Plantagenets. She asserted that the Foleys, her father's family, had been established at Lismore in County Waterford since Tudor times, but this does not imply they were of noble or even genteel stock. Foley was a common Irish surname derived from the Gaelic for the follower of a plunderer (in other words, a Viking or a pirate). For Mary, however, they were a band of dauntless adventurers.

To say the least, some of her claims were tenuous in the extreme, yet it was not snobbery which prompted her to regale her children with such tales. It was more a case that, as her husband took refuge in his fishing, his drink and his daydreams, so she escaped to her genealogical fantasies which bolstered her spirits when she was low: and they instilled in her children a certain pride, fascination and respect for their roots. As a Catholic, she might just as well have run for the comforting bosom of the Church but she was never that devout – indeed, she turned to the Protestant faith in later years – and preferred stories of chivalry to those of piety. What was more, through these stories, she could enjoy the company of her children, especially her adored Arthur.

That she doted upon Arthur is hardly surprising. He was her first son, and she had lost her previous baby within months of its birth. Yet there was probably more to her affection than this. In Arthur, she could have sought consolation for the shortcomings of her husband and brought some light into her otherwise dismal life.

For his part, Arthur absorbed her stories of knights and heralds, courage and honour, weaving them into his own childish tales of historical adventure: the world of jousting and suits of armour also provided him with a welcome escape into fantasy from his father's descent into dipsomania. In time, encouraged by his mother, he

developed the study of heraldry as a hobby and was fluent in its
arcane terminology, enjoying delving into genealogical tables which
his mother or his uncle, James Doyle, provided for him. It was also
through this shared interest that Mary implanted in Arthur the concepts
of morality and honesty that were to shape his character and govern
the rest of his life. He was brought up to follow noble values, to abhor
cruelty, to be modest and gentle, to fight injustice and never to whinge
at his lot as, no doubt, she suggested – and Arthur realised – his father
did. For all her attentions, she did not indulge him but, in lieu of his
father, set him an example by which he was able to judge and assess
the world around him.

Arthur's relationship with his mother was very close. To all intents
and purposes deprived of a father's love, the boy compensated by loving
his mother all the more. He hung upon her every word and it was to her
he turned for advice in all things. This is not to say he always followed
her suggestions or shared her opinion, but he respected it and, for the
whole of her life, she offered counsel and he usually listened to it.

Her maternal influence went well beyond interesting him in knights
of yore and the values of a romantic, chivalrous age. She also taught
Arthur to read and encouraged him to take to books, which he did
with a ready fervour. Mary was herself cultivated and well read, and
not just in the trashy fictional contents of the lending libraries. She
read widely for her own enjoyment and elucidation (and perhaps as
yet another means of escape), was rarely without a book within her
reach: Conan Doyle wrote of her as stirring porridge with one hand
and turning the pages of *La Revue des Deux Mondes* with the other,
the book held close to her face on account of her short-sightedness,
and discussing the writings of the Goncourt brothers whilst darning
socks, scrubbing or setting about her other domestic chores.

The debt the embryonic writer owed his mother was considerable
and one he readily acknowledged. In 1907, when Conan Doyle was
interviewed for the *New York World*, he conceded that he might have
inherited some of the necessary artistic attributes for dramatic effect
from his father, which would equip him for life as a writer, but that
it was from Mary he gained his physical looks and character and 'my
real love for letters, my instinct for story-telling [which sprang] I
believe, from my mother, who is of Anglo-Celtic stock, with the
glamour and romance of the Celt very strongly marked'. He stated
that he owed his first interest in literature to his mother's skill as a
storyteller and remembered her dramatic knack of 'sinking her voice
to a horror-stricken whisper when she came to a crisis in her narrative'.

He went on, 'I am sure, looking back, that it was in attempting to emulate these stories of my childhood that I began weaving dreams myself.'

It is beyond doubt that Mary Doyle was, in many respects, the most important single force and influence in Arthur's early life. Had she not nurtured him, given him the background and upbringing she did, his writing would not have contained a number of seminal aspects. Her sense of history, honour and fair play lies at the heart of so much of her son's fiction. In a postscript she wrote to the first biography of her husband published the year after his death, Conan Doyle's second wife, Jean, commented, 'My husband's mother was a very remarkable and highly cultured woman. She had a dominant personality, wrapped up in the most charmingly womanly exterior.'

Dominant Mary might have been but she was not domineering. She was forceful – she had to be in the circumstances – but she had purpose: her children were not going to fail. Certainly, she imbued in Arthur a determination to succeed.

For all the good Mary gave her son, and it was considerable, it has to be said that she also limited his horizons. A close mother-and-son relationship has its faults, for, no matter how well intentioned Mary may have been, a boy still needs a father. In effect, Arthur did not have one. He grew up with his mother's opinion, no doubt coloured by his view of how she coped with a drunken spouse and raised a family on £250 a year less the substantial amount that must have been paid to the vintners of Edinburgh, that women were superior. Men could fail, turn to drink or dope themselves on laudanum, become feckless and disloyal, turn into hypocrites (as she must have felt Charles had, for he was a far more pious Catholic than she yet he still allowed his family to suffer, stayed out all night and ignored their children), but women did not: at least, women of noble upbringing, even if in straitened circumstances, behaved otherwise.

As a result of his mother's influence, Arthur acquired a biased attitude towards women. They were, for him, either courageous and resolute personalities in command of the situation or creatures who were weak, victimised or dissolute and, therefore, in need of protection or moral guidance.

In June 1862, Catherine Foley died aged fifty-three. She had been ill for some time but her death still came as a shock. Her passing was Arthur's first encounter with death and, although he was only just three at the time, he remembered her as a 'white waxen thing' lying on the bed. Yet the shock of her death was more terrible than a corpse in the bedroom. Since her daughter's marriage, she had helped the family financially as well as being a spiritual anchor for her long-suffering daughter. With her gone, Mary lost a comrade-in-poverty and had to rely more upon Arthur for moral support.

Possibly as a result of losing Catherine's contribution to the house-keeping, the family moved to Tower Bank House at Portobello, an area of the city on the coast overlooking the Firth of Forth. Rents were lower there. It was a false economy. Charles had a greater distance to travel to his office at Holyrood Palace and frequently returned home late, the worse for the wine flask. Mary, now lonely and disillusioned with her husband, increasingly loved her son and became all the more determined to see him turn out well.

She not only told him stories of knights rescuing maidens from dragons but single-mindedly set about shaping his intellect. Not only had she taught him to read and write but, when he was eight, she started to tutor him in French, of which she had a good command. Arthur did not take to mathematics but he became an avid, quick and retentive reader. After devouring the contents of the family bookcase in the house, he started borrowing books from a nearby public library at such a rate that a special bye-law was ratified prohibiting readers from exchanging books more than once a day. Arthur was known to visit the library twice, occasionally thrice, in a day.

Books were more than a source of entertainment or knowledge. Writing in *McClure's Magazine* in 1894, Conan Doyle declared, 'I do not think life has any joys to offer so complete, so soul-filling, as that which come upon the imaginative lad whose spare time is limited, but who is able to snuggle down into a corner with his book, knowing that the next hour is all his own.' Clearly, a book was as much an escape from reality for him as the Arthurian legends were for his mother and a bottle was for his father.

At the age of six Arthur, encouraged by his mother, produced his first story. She provided him with a sheet of foolscap and, writing four words to the line, he created a tale about a man and a tiger, illustrating it in the margins. However, once the tiger had eaten the man or, more accurately, had somehow melded into him, Arthur found himself stuck for an ending.

Throughout her marriage, Mary Doyle had kept in touch with the Foleys in Lismore and, when he was about seven, Arthur paid them his first of several childhood visits, travelling to Ireland for a few weeks in the company of his mother and the other children. The trip may have provided Mary with a brief respite from the poverty and misery of her marriage and it is almost certain that the journey was paid for by the Irish relatives, for there was no way the Doyle finances could have stretched to such an extravagance. Little is known of these visits to County Waterford but they must have been welcome, for, despite his mother's attentions, Arthur's poverty-stricken childhood was not a happy one.

By the time he was eight, his father was utterly dependent upon alcohol. Drink did not seem to make Charles violent, either towards his wife or his children, but it did make him increasingly melancholic and plunged him into long periods of self-imposed despair verging upon the manic depressive. There was little Mary could do to get Arthur away from this pernicious atmosphere until an opportunity suddenly presented itself to her and she took it with gratitude.

How Mary came to be acquainted with John Hill Burton is unknown. A distinguished historian and Historiographer Royal of Scotland, Burton was born in 1809 and educated at Aberdeen before becoming articled to a solicitor and reading for the bar in Edinburgh. Passing the bar examinations, he was made an advocate but rarely practised law. Much respected as a bibliophile and man of letters, he wrote a vast number of reviews and journalistic articles as well as books and pamphlets for Edinburgh booksellers. His *History of Scotland*, published in 1853, was the most famous of his historical books, bringing him considerable local fame.

Burton's gregarious sister, Mary, owned a cottage called Liberton Bank in the village of Liberton about five kilometres to the south-east of the city centre, in what was then countryside, well away from the pollution and squalor of Edinburgh. Knowing of the Doyle family circumstances, Mary Burton offered to have Arthur live with her for a while and so, when he was either seven or eight years old, he was packed off into this comparatively idyllic setting. How long he lived in Liberton is unknown, but it was sufficient time for him to form a bond with John Hill Burton's sons, especially William, who was three years older than Arthur and one of his earliest and closest friends. The friendship between Mary Doyle and the Burtons went deeper than such an exchange of charitable favours. When Mary Doyle gave birth to her next child in 1866, she named her Caroline Mary Burton Doyle but the family called her Lottie.

One reason for Arthur's stay at Liberton Bank was to allow him to attend a local school called Newington Academy, at which he was enrolled as a pupil from the age of seven to almost nine: it is, therefore, fair to assume that he lived with Mary Burton for just under two years,

at least during the school term. It was a truly Dickensian Dotheboys Hall-type establishment ruled by a strict and hard master Conan Doyle was to describe many years later as a 'pock-marked one-eyed rascal' for whom the tawse, a leather strap used for beating miscreants in Scottish schools, was as close at hand as the stick of chalk. Arthur did not enjoy his time there yet the school toughened him up. He was frequently involved in fights with the other boys who were, by all accounts, an uncouth and belligerent rabble. One of his assailants was a boy of approximately his own age called Eddie Tulloch, the son of a Baptist minister. What the cause of their quarrel was is open to speculation but it might have been founded on the prejudice felt at the time by Scottish Protestants towards Irish Catholics. AND STILL
IS

By the age of eight, Arthur was an archetypal, sturdy product of a hard, urban Victorian childhood. The misery of his home life was now tempered with the knock-about and knock-down life of the streets and playground, his strong character being forged in the furnace of experience. Yet, for all his pugnacity, he was also not to forget his mother's values, and there is an anecdote of his fighting some of his peers because they mocked an old woman who lived in the neighbourhood: after Arthur's intervention, they subsequently left her alone.

He might come home with a bloodied nose but no sooner was he in the door than the nose would be buried in a book within the stories of which he would see his fictional heroes doing just what he had done in his own life. Thus it was that, at an early age, Arthur came to equate the physical with the intellectual: for him there was no dividing line between the word and the deed.

From Portobello, the Doyles moved to 3 Sciennes Hill Place in the Newington area of Edinburgh, less than two kilometres from the city centre and Charles's office. The house was subdivided into eight flats, the rent a third less than it had been in Picardy Place: clearly, with each move, the Doyles were going further down-market in their accommodation, as more of Charles's salary went on booze. What was worse, one of Charles's fellow clerks from the Office of Works lived only a few hundred metres away and it seems likely he may have been one of his pot-pals. On the other hand, the move and reduced rent might have served another purpose: by having fewer overheads, Mary might have been freeing up some of her precious money to send Arthur away to boarding school.

She was, by Arthur's eighth birthday, increasingly anxious to get him away from home. Charles Doyle's alcoholism was now so bad she feared it might have a long-lasting effect upon her son. There was, in her mind, only one course of action. Arthur must attend a public school and not the local George Heriot's or the Edinburgh Academy: wherever he enrolled, it had to be far away from his father. She was not a smotheringly possessive mother but she deeply loved her son and to admit to such an inevitability was a sharp tug on her heart and, in the circumstances, to let him go at such a tender age required an inordinate amount of maternal courage.

Quite how Mary thought she was going to pay for such an education can only be surmised. With every economy possible, she would not have had sufficient funds to meet the fees. It is feasible to speculate that Charles's brothers might have contributed towards their nephew's education and might even, as Catholics more devout than Mary, have suggested a few schools with religious foundations to which he might be sent. If Charles was at all interested in his son's schooling, he would almost certainly have insisted upon a Catholic education, for, behind his bottle, he was a pious man. Michael Conan may also have contributed and the Foleys might have given further limited financial assistance.

Whoever footed the bill, in 1868 Arthur Ignatius Conan Doyle, dropping his saintly name, left home for boarding school.

2

Stonyhurst, Feldkirch and Edgar Allan Poe

The choice of a school for Arthur was limited. There were only two good Catholic public boys' schools of repute in Britain, Downside School at Stratton-on-the-Fosse in Somerset, which was run by Benedictines, and Stonyhurst College near Whalley in Lancashire, which was operated by the Jesuits. Michael Conan, taking very seriously his godson's future, recommended the Jesuits saying that, as far as secular education was concerned, they were amongst the very best, although he also forewarned Mary Doyle of the fanatical aspects of the Jesuits' devotional teachings.

The fees were £50 per annum. Knowing of their potential charge's circumstances, the Jesuits offered Arthur his education for free on the condition that his parents agree to allow him to dedicate his life to a career in the Catholic Church. In other words, in the time-honoured tradition of monastic orders, they were, *de facto*, offering to purchase the boy for service as a Jesuit brother, priest or, at least, a professional who would give himself to the order.

Mary Doyle, no doubt somewhat sceptical of a church to which her errant husband professed a piety that allowed him to drink his entire family into poverty, refused. Conan Doyle was to be, in adult life, ever grateful to her for what must have been a difficult decision: £50 was a great deal of money to his mother.

Arthur did not enter Stonyhurst immediately but was enrolled at Hodder, the preparatory school linked to the senior college a short distance away and named after a little river than ran beside it, a tributary of the River Ribble which flowed just south of the main school. He travelled alone by train from Edinburgh to Preston, to be collected with other pupils from the station there for the drive to the school, twenty kilometres away. He admitted to crying from loneliness during the journey.

The preparatory school, in which Arthur was to be a pupil for two years, must have seemed a wonderful if alien world even if his first fortnight was marred by the news of the death of his grandfather, John Doyle: yet he is hardly likely to have grieved much, for the old man was a comparatively distant figure whom he had only occasionally met. The environment to which Arthur was used was urban, polluted and often violent, the streets busy, crowded and filthy with domestic garbage, effluent and horse dung. Hodder, on the other hand, was situated in open countryside close to the edge of Longridge Fell, itself on the rim of the Lancashire moors. To the north the land, which rose to six hundred metres, was bleak and rugged, intersected by clear, fast-flowing rivers and streams, sparsely populated by subsistence sheep farmers and, where there were still remnants of the great Forest of Bowland, woodsmen. The wind blew straight in from the Atlantic, bracing in the summer and cutting in the winter.

Whilst the topographical environment of Stonyhurst might have appeared strange, the school was somewhat more familiar and Arthur fitted in. There were no Eddie Tullochs here. The pupils were a cosmopolitan mix of nationalities bound by a common religion and purpose. As a Catholic élite, they had a dual *raison d'être* – to worship God in the manner of Rome and to strive for academic or sporting achievement. Or both. Along with Europeans, Americans and the children of Catholic parents who resided overseas, there was a substantial corpus of Irish Catholics in the school in addition to the children of some of the richest and most influential Anglo-Catholic families in Britain who gave Arthur his first encounters with the higher echelons of the upper class. The Jesuit brothers made no concessions to their wealthy pupils and were stringent in ensuring there was no favouritism, but Arthur, coming from a humble background, must have felt his lowly station keenly and perhaps suffered at the hands of boys who were both older and better off than he was himself. In his later writings, he was often critical of the aristocracy.

In general, Arthur's time at Hodder was happy. His masters were mostly younger Jesuit brothers who were kind and tolerant towards their pupils: his form master, Francis Cassidy, was only in his mid-twenties. A gentle, saintly and affectionate figure whom the boys greatly respected, and whom Arthur regarded as being 'more human than Jesuits usually are', he tempered the strict religious criteria of a Catholic education with a sense of humour verging upon fun. For Cassidy, boys were not implements of the Catholic faith nor frail willows to be bent to the religious wind but creatures of great human potential which he saw it his responsibility to nurture, encourage and, where possible, develop to its utmost. Ahead of his time, he was also a man who believed in the importance of intellectual creativity beyond the bounds of academic discipline. In particular, he encouraged the writing of poetry and stories and was himself a very effective storyteller. For Arthur, this latter skill was more than welcome: Cassidy took over where his mother had left off. In later years, Conan Doyle was to write to his former teacher, 'How well I remember the stories which you used to read to us and which I used to suck in like a sponge absorbs water until I was so saturated with them that I could still repeat them.'

Cassidy prompted Arthur to write poetry but his influence was to be far greater than this, for he was a brilliant exponent of the Jesuit concept that thoughts are more valuable than the printed word. The key to the doctrine was the development of memory. For most young boys, the learning of facts by rote was a chore but Cassidy made it enjoyable, teaching the use of mnemonics, rhymes and linked-image training. Having already learnt to memorise during his heraldry lessons with his mother, who frequently tested him on the intricacies of a crest or shield, Arthur took to Cassidy's lessons with gusto, acquiring the highly organised and developed, exacting and prodigious ability to recall facts and details almost at whim.

During the winter of 1869, Stonyhurst was hit by an epidemic of diphtheria. In the days before antibiotics, this was a much-feared disease from which the chances of survival were less than good: one in three sufferers died of it and survivors could be brain-damaged. Starting with the common symptom of a sore throat, within twenty-four hours a film of mucus covers the back of the throat. Breathing becomes difficult. Within ninety-six hours, the heart muscles and nervous system are hit, leading to paralysis or heart failure. A number of boys succumbed but Arthur escaped the epidemic: possibly, his life in the hugger-mugger, filthy streets of Edinburgh, where such diseases as diphtheria and tuberculosis were endemic, had given him a natural immunity.

When he was eleven and a half, Arthur went up from the preparatory to the main school in which there were about 275 pupils enrolled. It was, as such a transference always is for children, a shock. He was a pupil there from 1870 to 1875.

Established on its site in 1794, the college had moved from Belgium (Liège)

FRANCE

FROM where it was founded at St Omer in 1593, taking over a near-derelict Elizabethan country mansion, the gift of Thomas Weld of Lulworth. The Jesuits converted this into a school, adding new buildings, a church, an ambulacrum, a library, an infirmary and a mill which pumped water from a small lake. They also renovated and extended the gardens and grounds. Life in the school was, however, harsh. Hot water was a scarce luxury, heating by radiators or open fires just as rare. The wind coming off the moors hissed through cracks in the walls which common rumour had it the Jesuits had installed deliberately. The new buildings were magnificent but also cold: the dining hall had a marble floor. Conan Doyle's contention that the school had been built with vision rather than comfort in mind is borne out by the fact that there had been no ablutions constructed until 1851.

The spartan atmosphere in the school, no doubt engendered by the Jesuitical belief that the body must suffer for the soul to be saved, did not unduly upset Arthur. His home life was austere so he was, in effect, prepared for the stringent life of Stonyhurst.

Housed in cheerless dormitories, the pupils' day began at five o'clock to the sound of a wooden rattle. They washed in ice-cold water at troughs in bare, flagstoned bathrooms and got dressed in uniforms that were said to bear a marked resemblance to prison issue. Their diet was basic. Breakfast consisted of dry bread and milk diluted with water in summer, with oat porridge in winter, after which the boys had to walk through the school corridors deep in prayer. Midday dinner was usually a meat stew, most frequently mutton from the surrounding moors, with fish on Fridays and a pudding twice a week. At around four in the afternoon 'bread and beer' was served but the only common denominator the beer shared with real ale was its colour. Supper was usually hot diluted milk, bread lightly smeared with butter and, on occasion, boiled or baked potatoes. The only way a pupil could improve upon his diet was either by academic achievement – better food was offered as a reward for top grades – or by purchasing food in the nearby village of Hurst Green or the small town of Whalley, five kilometres' walk away. As Arthur's finances were as spartan as his accommodation, he must have lived upon what the school provided, unless classmates took pity upon him, sharing their tuck with him.

Just as the menu left much to be desired, so did the education. It was very traditional, lacking the flexibility to deal with an individual's abilities and weaknesses which was starting to appear in some of the more forward-looking public schools of the time. Teaching methods were old-fashioned, even outmoded, and lessons were dogmatically based upon the classics with a bias towards Latin, Greek and German. The school published its own Latin grammar textbook whilst English was taught by the rote learning of spelling, reading, dictation, composition and grammatical sentence analysis. In common with most public schools, Stonyhurst had its fair share of strange traditions. The various class years were called, descending in order from what would today be the sixth form, Rhetoric, Poetry, Syntax or Upper Grammar, Middle Grammar, Rudiments or Great Figures, and Figures or Little Figures. Various rooms in the school went by such names as Washington Place, Study Place, Shoe Place and Strangers Place. New boys were subject to initiation rites although what these were, and what rite Arthur was subjected to, are now lost in the school's mythology.

Despite its inadequacies, what Stonyhurst provided was a thorough education, with exacting tuition, yet it was founded not upon the precepts of intellectual curiosity or academic achievement but on fear and intimidation. Study was an obstacle to be overcome, like mortal sin, rather than a body of knowledge to be acquired for enjoyment or personal development. Punishment for failure was more prevalent than praise for success. As was inevitable in a public school, not to mention one based upon religious ideals, discipline was paramount and the responsibility, during Arthur's time, of Father Thomas Kay, Prefect of Discipline, for whom corporal punishment was a useful instrument of spiritual and academic advancement.

The pupils were constantly under supervision. Jesuit brothers participated with the boys in sports, took them for country walks, accompanied them to Hurst Green or Whalley, took every opportunity to converse with them and, when they were asleep, nightly stalked the dormitories. The pupils had little privacy, their continual organisation producing in them physical and psychological terror: the brothers were, by and large, not so much admired or respected but feared. The unwritten motto of the school might have been 'Eternal Vigilance Is the Price We Pay for a Healthy Community' and, certainly, this strict surveillance had its benefits. Homosexuality and masturbation, common in most public schools, were rare. However, the rules were still broken, for, boys being boys, they found ways around them. There was even an irregularly published unofficial school newspaper which must have been prepared without the brothers' knowledge.

Punishments were severe. Minor transgressions were punished with the 'penance-walk', the miscreant being made to walk in silence around the playground for up to an hour, meditating upon his misdemeanour and asking God's forgiveness. More serious crimes were dealt with by corporal punishment. Whereas some schools predominantly used a bamboo cane, Stonyhurst relied upon a 'ferula' (which the boys referred to as a 'tolley'). It was a flat piece of rubber or gutta-percha (a form of latex derived from rubber trees) about the size and shape of the sole of a very large shoe. The least one could expect was nine lashes on the palm of one hand: the maximum (called 'twice-nine' in the school vernacular) was nine on each hand. Arthur, who suffered this punishment, wrote, 'One blow of this instrument, delivered with intent, would cause the palm of the hand to swell up and change colour', and added that 'to take twice-nine upon a cold day was about the extremity of human endurance'. The blows, which badly bruised and swelled the flesh, could take up to a month to heal. The birch, a number of stout twigs bound together in a bundle, was also applied and Arthur was not infrequently beaten with it.

He seems never to have reported his beatings in letters home, possibly so as not to worry his mother or give her cause to wonder at his progress, accepting them with a certain pride: he was one of those boys who revelled in displaying to his peers how he could take physical punishment, not letting it break or get the better of him.

The rules Arthur most often broke were the run-of-the-mill schoolboy infractions. Smoking, which was condoned in some public schools, was forbidden at Stonyhurst. Arthur purchased a pipe with an amber mouthpiece – cigarettes were not yet in widespread usage – and joined the other outlaws in Yew Alley, a part of the grounds frequented by smokers. It was here he was apprehended, from time to time, puffing on his pipe: at other times, he was caught out of bounds in the village, buying tobacco.

The Jesuits' belief that a rod was a better teacher than a reward worked with some pupils but, with Arthur, it did not. His nature, shaped by his family background, responded to kisses not cuffs, and he rebelled against the brutality of the school disciplinary system. By his own admission, he went out of his way to be mischievous, to show that he would not be cowed by it. Fifteen years after leaving Stonyhurst, he wrote to the family of James Ryan, the only one of his school-friends with whom he stayed in contact, that the Jesuits had tried 'to rule too much by fear – too little by love or reason'. He ventured that the only reason he was not adversely affected by the punishments he had received was because he had been 'such an obstinate little mule'.

His obstinacy was not merely a character trait. Arthur had been brought up in a family where his mother had been forced to lay down carefully devised rules to meet the circumstances of her predicament and Arthur, being presented with rules that appeared arbitrary, defied them on a matter of principle. The Jesuits, like any religious order, demanded conformity, but Arthur, the street-toughened lad from Edinburgh, believed more in individualism and the conviction that authority for authority's sake was wrong. The Jesuits were dedicated, zealous, earnest and fearless, but they were also narrow-minded and intolerant to such an extent that Conan Doyle was to write in retrospect that nothing could exceed the 'uncompromising bigotry of the Jesuit theology'.

The most influential Jesuit in the school during Arthur's years there was George Renerden Kingdon SJ, although the Rector (or principal) was Edmund Ignatius Purbrick SJ. Kingdon was a medical doctor but he had refuted all scientific advance upon his entering the order, including seeking medical attention in times of sickness. Even in the distinctly passé confines of Stonyhurst, he was considered by many of his fellow Jesuits as old-fashioned. In his position as Prefect of Studies, he held a greater sway over the pupils than the Rector himself, both physically and mentally.

Kingdon's attitude, that religion triumphed over and was more important than scientific progress or understanding, was only a part of the overall devotional indoctrination into Catholicism that pupils underwent in both the preparatory and senior schools and which, at first, Arthur fervently embraced. When he took his first communion, in the spring of 1870, he wrote to his mother of the exquisite joy he felt on welcoming God into his life. By the time he left Stonyhurst, however, he was markedly less enthusiastic about the Christian faith.

According to James Ryan's daughter, who had heard the details from her father, Arthur had confessed his doubts about the validity of transubstantiation and it is certain that, the longer he remained at Stonyhurst, the less he felt an affinity for Catholicism. At first, with Cassidy's humanity, he may well have accepted the faith without too much intellectual criticism. However, as time passed and he grew older and more questioning, and he came under Kingdon's sphere of thinking and teaching, he reacted against it, distrusting the displays of public devotion and, in response to the Prefect of Studies' bigotry, he started to take an interest in science.

Yet it was not all rebellion which fired Arthur: he was less negatively influenced by some of the Jesuits' tenets. Being fond of inculcating a strong sense of military commitment in the service of God and good, they regaled him with the romantic, patriotic tales of former Stonyhurst pupils who had died in battle. It was even claimed by the brothers that the school had produced a higher-than-average number of decorated heroes although, compared to many other public schools, they had not. Stonyhurst, and the Jesuits in general, were fairly suspicious of the non-Catholic world and were inward-looking. It was not in their remit to produce heroes but rather to create in their pupils a sense of moral élitism which had them take on a superior air. If they fought at all, it would be in a crusade, not a political conflict. The vast majority of Stonyhurst's pupils went not into the armed forces but the professions, or themselves became Jesuits.

With rebellion in his heart, it is hardly surprising to discover that Arthur was not particularly popular with his teachers. He was noted for his personal untidiness, his individuality (of which his untidiness might well have been an exhibition), his determination verging (in the eyes of his masters) on stubborn pig-headedness, his not infrequent disobedience and his vocal opposition to the use of the tolley and the manner in which the Jesuits spied on the boys, preventing them from having any privacy.

Conversely, with his peers, he was popular. Abjuring a prominent part in class activities, he nevertheless had an agile mind and was known for his impromptu poetical parodies of college personalities and events. With Herbert Thurston, who, in later life, became a prominent Jesuit priest and well-known collector of heraldic crests, he wrote a comical – some would say vulgar – guide to the school. Understandably, this made him another thorn in the sides of the Jesuits.

Another reason for his popularity, and something that alleviated his feelings of rebellion, thus making the school somewhat tolerable, was the fact that Arthur was good at sports. Sturdily built, he was a natural athlete, larger than many of his contemporaries over some of whom he towered. It seems that, despite the meagre fare the boys were fed, Arthur thrived on it, developing quickly and rapidly outgrowing his clothes.

Games, as sports were traditionally called in public schools, were a source of great enjoyment for Arthur and he much preferred them to his studies. Being an integral part of the public school ethos, which generally demanded that its inmates both worked and played hard, where a pupil might fail in the classroom, he could become a success on the field or track.

Like many public schools, Stonyhurst had several sports uniquely peculiar to it. Two such games were called 'trap' and 'cat'. The former was a type of tag game whilst the latter vaguely resembled rounders or softball and was common in Jesuit schools on the Continent. The usual sports of cricket and football were also played but, at Stonyhurst, these had particular variations. Stonyhurst cricket utilised home-made balls and specifically shaped bats made of alder rather than willow. The balls were bowled underarm, the game played in March and April on gravel, not grass. More ordinary cricket, called London cricket to differentiate it from the school version, was played through the summer but only a single wicket was set up, the bat was club-shaped and the hard ball was made from tightly wound sheepskin. Football teams contained a varying number of players. The game, which could be very violent, allowed for the punching of the ball with a bunched fist.

With such a divergence from the accepted norms of the sports, it is not surprising to discover that Stonyhurst rarely played against other schools. This did not, of course, worry the Jesuits, who were reluctant to have their Catholic boys mix with Protestants although, towards the end of Arthur's years at Stonyhurst, there were inter-school cricket matches. Arthur excelled at cricket and was a school team captain. Indeed, so taken was he by the sport that he wrote to his mother, in June 1874, that when he returned to Edinburgh, he planned to join a cricket club, declaring that sports were more conducive to health than any amount of doctors' prescriptions.

Being of muscular build, he also did well at swimming, football, hockey and ice-skating. He additionally played rugby (to unique Stonyhurst rules), was fond of fishing in the nearby rivers Ribble and Hodder and, towards the end of his school life, took to billiards. Rugby he later considered the best of all team sports because it required stamina, agility, bravery and ingenuity simultaneously and, in later life, he denounced public schools that played the game according to individual sets of rules because this lessened the ability for boys to play universally.

Stonyhurst became Arthur's home for more than the duration of the academic terms. In the holidays, many of the pupils departed for their parental homes but a number remained in the school. Mary Doyle came to an accommodation with the Jesuits to keep her son through the short Christmas and Easter vacations in order to ensure that he did not come into contact with his father. Only for the six weeks of the summer holidays did he regularly return to Edinburgh. It must have pained her deeply to surrender her son not only to boarding school but also to a ten-month continuous stretch away in it, but that was the price she felt she had to pay to safeguard him from the contamination of her dipsomaniac, melancholic failure of a husband.

That being said, it seems that as Arthur got older he did return to Edinburgh other than in the summer.

His visits home can hardly have been easy for him. The lodgings in which his family lived were crowded, noisy and lacked privacy just as much as the Stonyhurst dormitory did. To the other children, he must have seemed at times almost a stranger on account of his long absences. The family had continued to grow. Another sister, Constance, known as Connie, had been born in 1867. Yet another child was born but it died. Arthur enjoyed his sisters' company, spending time trying to teach the younger ones: in a letter home in 1873, he wrote how he looked forward to taking up his duties as their personal schoolmaster when he returned to Edinburgh.

In addition, however, Arthur now had a brother as well, John Francis Innes Hay, born in 1873. He was primarily named after his grandfather and uncle who had died but was given his penultimate name out of deference to his godmother, Katherine Burton, John Hill Burton's wife, whose father was the famous Scottish antiquarian, Cosmo Innes. At first called Frank, he was known for the rest of his life as Innes although, in the family, he was sometimes nicknamed Duffy.

Life at school during the holidays was somewhat more bearable than during the term. The boys were still closely supervised but they were given some freedoms. Amateur dramatics were staged, in which Arthur took a keen part. They could go for walks on their own, could visit Hurst Green, could fish in the rivers. Their food seems to have improved in the holidays, too. One Christmas, Arthur reportedly claimed consuming, in the company of three other boys, 'Two turkeys, one very large goose, two chickens, one large ham and two pieces of ham, two large sausages, seven boxes of sardines, one of lobster, a plate full of tarts and seven pots of jam. In the way of drink we had five bottles of sherry, five of port, one of claret and two of raspberry vinegar; we had also two bottles of pickles.' It must be assumed they did not buy these items, nor have them provided by the Jesuits, but obtained them from food parcels sent from home. It is highly unlikely that Mary Doyle contributed much to this repast.

When he was not eating himself sick or stepping out on the boards in the school hall, Arthur availed himself of the school library.

Throughout his life, Arthur was to read exceedingly widely. His mother had introduced him to books, Francis Cassidy had further encouraged him and now, in the senior school, he was well into the habit. He read for information and for enjoyment but he also used

books as a means of escape from the asperities of Stonyhurst, just as
he had from the distresses of home life.

The subject matter of his reading was not out of the ordinary. Britain
being at the height of her imperial powers he was, like most boys,
fascinated with the Empire, gripped by ripping yarns set in foreign lands
filled with impenetrable jungles, distant mountain ranges and lost cities
inhabited by strange natives with stranger customs. In his early years,
Arthur recalled his favourite writer being Mayne Reid, a man who had
abandoned a career as a teacher to become a fur trapper and trader in
the wilds of America. He proclaimed that his favourite book was Reid's
The Scalp Hunter, from which he received not only a good narrative
but also a knowledge of botany and a burning puerile desire to see
the forests and prairies for himself which started a lifelong fascination
with America. Filled with the true ideals of Victorian morality – honour,
justice, fair play, a respect for women, uncomplaining suffering – the
story was narrative-led and written in a style that was to form the
bedrock of Conan Doyle's own writing in the coming years. By way
of Reid, he discovered other American authors such as Nathaniel
Hawthorne, James Fenimore Cooper and Bret Harte. *The Last of the
Mohicans* was one of his favourite stories and, twenty years after leaving
school, he declared Hawthorne's *The Scarlet Letter* the greatest novel
written to date in America, which does not say much for his opinion
of Mark Twain or Herman Melville.

Arthur might well have known, as he later put it, 'the Rockies like
my own back garden', but he did not restrict himself to American
novelists. He revelled in Sir Walter Scott's *Ivanhoe* and *Rob Roy* which
appealed to him for their medieval and Scottish backdrops. He had
owned a set of Scott's complete works from childhood and, by his
own admission, was much influenced by them in his thinking and his
later writing, considering Scott to be the foremost historical novelist in
the English language. With his fascination for history, he also enjoyed
Samuel Pepys, Charles Reade, the American writer Washington Irving
and Daniel Defoe. He did not restrict himself to writers in English, for,
by the age of fourteen, he was sufficiently fluent in French to be able
to read Jules Verne in the original.

Reading was for Arthur more than the satisfaction of a voracious
intellectual appetite, an entertainment or a means of escape. It was
also a part of his anti-authoritarian rebellion. He read books not only
in the library but also, by his own account, by 'surreptitious candle
ends in the dead of night, when the sense of crime added a new zest
to the story'. It is alleged he filched candle stubs, inserted them in a

bottle and, with his knees bent up to form a tent, read under the cover of his bed-sheets. Quite how he avoided setting light to his bedding is not recorded. Some of the authors whom he read were also to be enlisted as fellow rebels: it is not known if he obtained a copy of Defoe's *Moll Flanders* but it would not have been out of character, for the novel was listed on the Index Librorum Prohibitorum and reading it would have been an act of defiance against his Jesuit masters.

His source of books was not restricted to the school library. Michael Conan, who took a deep interest in his godson's education, mailed books to him and was keen to hear of his progress. This was not necessarily just Conan fulfilling his godfatherly role: if he was also, as might have been the case, financially assisting with the school fees, he would have wanted assurance that his money was not being squandered.

When, in 1873, Conan sent Arthur a copy of Thomas Babington Macaulay's *The Lays of Ancient Rome*, Arthur devoured it, placing him second in his list of favourite authors after Scott: Macaulay's five-volume *History of England from the Accession of James II*, which captured the seventeenth century in intimate detail, was one of the works to which Arthur returned again and again. His love affair with the historian's work began. Yet there was more to it than that. The teaching of history in Stonyhurst was at best banal. The lessons were little more than a recitation of dates and facts. Arthur's abiding interest in the subject took a hammering. Yet, with the arrival of Macaulay, not only was he rebelling against the Jesuits by reading a Protestant historian's work which was biased against Catholicism, but he was also reintroduced to history through Macaulay's brilliant ability to bring the past to life. Once again, as it had been with his mother, history was real.

It must be said that Michael Conan might have had an ulterior motive in sending the book. He was himself out of sympathy with the Jesuits and, as a learned man, he would have known Macaulay would not have been popular with the Stonyhurst masters.

One of Arthur's traits of character made him susceptible to the adventure novelists. He was without the streak of hidden guile that his Scottish upbringing might have inserted into him: he was intelligent and knowing but he lacked canniness, that ability to be secretively knowledgeable to the point of smugness. Owing to his mother's influence, he did have hidden sides but he was, at heart, a simple innocent at this stage in his life, who viewed the world in primary colours, without too many shades of grey. He was, therefore, deeply impressed by knowledge and those who gave or used it. Writers such as Macaulay seemed to him to be founts of wisdom and, as an impressionable youth, he no doubt dreamed of emulating them one day.

The first inklings that he might be following in their footsteps came about 1873 when Arthur started to realise that he had a modicum of literary and oratory skill. His elocution being excellent, he was frequently picked by the Jesuits to read aloud in the refectory: during meals, conversation was not always permitted and the boys ate to the sound of a reading from the scriptures or some other enlightening tome. In addition, Arthur discovered he had a feeling for the dramatic in a story whilst his imagination was fired by his book-reading and his standard of composition improved. He also continued to write poetry.

It was not long before Arthur came to appreciate the fact that he was far better at composition than the average Stonyhurst boy. This ability did not only manifest itself in his grades: he gained a reputation as a storyteller. He recounted hours sitting on a desk surrounded by junior boys, talking himself hoarse as he entertained them with heroic tales in foreign climes. As payment, or by means of bribery, he was given fruit, cakes or pastries and was known not to start a story, or move on to the next instalment, before receiving his due. At other times, he would stop at a seminal point in the plot to demand further payment before continuing.

His literary skill was not lost on the Jesuit brothers, either. He gained distinction in the school for a poem entitled 'The Passage of the Red Sea', the recognition of which was, by his own admission, to be a significant moment in his life: it is his earliest surviving writing. In his last year at Stonyhurst, he was also editor of a school yearbook which was produced and published in manuscript.

Being away from his family for long periods, and being close to his mother, Arthur wrote an inordinate number of letters home to her, something he started in school and continued until her death: at one stage, there were over fifteen hundred extant in the family archives. He might have been far away but he was never out of reach of his mother.

His letters were often very long and candid, going into the tiniest detail of his school life. When she mildly cavilled at him for his bad handwriting, he was apologetic but gave his excuses, which were often allied to sport-related injuries: he lost a fingernail playing hockey, his hand had been trodden on or, in one instance, he had suffered what he termed a slight strain in falling from the gymnasium roof. That his handwriting was poor on occasion as a result of the application of the tolley was not mentioned.

The tone of the letters was always loving and often familiar in a way one would not expect of a son writing to his mother. In his schooldays, Arthur addressed his mother as 'My dear Mamma' but their relationship was such that they could be far more informal: in 1879, he calls her 'old lady' although she was only forty-one at the time. When older, he sometimes started his letters simply with 'Dearest', such was the very close informality of their love, but most often he wrote to her as 'Dearest of Mams' or 'Dearest Mammie'. When speaking of her, he was said to refer to her usually as 'Ma'am' or 'The Ma'am', which term was apparently used by all her children. There is, however, some doubt about this, for Adrian, one of Conan Doyle's sons, was wont to give his grandmother a somewhat more imposing image than she perhaps merited. He insisted that his father's early biographers mention the term as it had a more noble ring to it than the familiar – and colloquially Irish – 'Mam'. After all, Queen Victoria had chosen to be addressed as 'Ma'am' and he wanted to give the impression of his family as having had noble, if no longer tenable, roots.

For the Christmas holiday of 1874, Arthur left Preston by train, but he was not bound for Edinburgh. He was on his way to London to accept an invitation to stay with his Uncle Richard and Aunt Annette. Setting off in the last week of November, the journey itself was an adventure as the train travelled at a snail's pace through thick fog for most of the way and was twice delayed by railway accidents.

Travel in poor weather in Victorian times had its drawbacks and dangers. Trains were the only viable and comparatively reliable long-distance means of transport but they were prone to crashes: the roads were little better than cross-country mud tracks and still used by inter-city coaches little changed since the days of the stage and highwayman. The journey from Preston to London by road took the better part of sixty hours, assuming two overnight stops in coaching inns. By rail, it took fourteen hours in good weather with a number of changes of train. Arthur was not to be deterred. He responded to the invitation by saying that he would get to London regardless of the weather and, so that they might recognise him at the station, described himself as '5 feet 9 inches high, pretty stout, clad in dark garments, and above all, with a flaring red muffler round my neck'.

The Doyle house at Cambridge Terrace being renovated at the time, he stayed at his uncle's studio at 7 Finborough Road in West Brompton where Aunt Annette, who had remained a spinster, kept house for her brother.

Uncle Richard was fifty years old, a lively and amusing character with a wide reputation as an artist, illustrator and cartoonist. His studio was filled with depictions of goblins, fairies and elves painted directly on to the plaster of the walls, but his eccentricity went beyond interior decoration. When he laughed, he was inclined to pull his head down inside his high, wing collar like a tortoise then thrust it out, twisting it and loudly guffawing. Aunt Annette, it seems, was a less extrovert person who lived very much in her famous artist brother's shadow.

Arthur was utterly enthralled by London. It was filled with hustle, bustle and history.

In 1874, London was a metropolis of four million people, one of the largest and most populous cities on earth. It was not, however, as it might be imagined today through the romantic eye of novels or television period dramas. The streets were covered in a thick mulch of horse manure, for there were estimated to be over 200,000 horses in the Greater London area. The air was polluted with sulphur, soot and smoke from over two million domestic chimneys, factory smokestacks and railway locomotive funnels, almost all of them burning coal. When it rained, or when winter snow thawed into slush, the poorly drained streets became ankle deep in what was euphemistically termed 'London mud'. This was a noxious, soot-blackened mixture of horse dung, earth, effluent and garbage. The air was just as foul: the word 'smog' was not coined until 1905 but the filthy mixture of smoke and fog that typified London winters was widespread. Every thoroughfare was crowded with hansom cabs, horse-drawn carriages and omnibuses, carts and wagons of every description. Beggars lingered on corners, street urchins pestered pedestrians, tinkers called out their wares, pick-pockets operated in the more fashionable streets and footpads hung around alleys or back streets ready to pounce on unsuspecting mugs and chumps. Traffic accidents were commonplace, many of them fatal. Kidnapping of wealthy ladies for ransom was rife as was murder, most instances of the latter being committed in the furtherance of theft. Garrotting and stabbing were the most frequent causes of violent death. It was officially estimated by the government that well over 150,000 Londoners made their living exclusively from criminal activity: official figures invariably played down the real truth lying behind statistics.

From the minute he arrived, Arthur immersed himself in the city. At the Tower of London, he saw the Crown Jewels, the suits of armour and instruments of torture, walking upon the very stones that had borne Richard II to his prison cell and Anne Boleyn to her execution. He was taken to St Paul's Cathedral, gazing upon the half-completed monument to the Duke of Wellington and Nelson's black marble tomb, in which the hero lay in a coffin carved out of the mainmast of the French flagship *L'Orient* taken at Trafalgar, before climbing to the Whispering Gallery in the dome. In Regent's Park, he toured the Zoological Gardens with a friend from Stonyhurst. He was also to meet his Uncle Henry and his wife, Jane, who were visiting from Ireland and staying with Uncle James in Clifton Gardens, near Lord's cricket ground. Accompanied by Uncle Henry, Arthur went to Madame Tussaud's waxworks at which he visited the current Napoleonic exhibition that purportedly included the covers of the bed in which Napoleon had died, discoloured with his blood. What impressed him most, however, was the Chamber of Horrors with its catalogue of murderers. Whether or not this aroused in him the first stirrings of the intense curiosity with the macabre and strangely terrible that he displayed in later life cannot be said. Uncle Richard took him to Hengler's Circus, Uncle James took him to the Lyceum Theatre where, from a private box, he saw Henry Irving in *Hamlet*. At the Haymarket Theatre, he attended a performance of *Our American Cousin*.

Yet there was one place in London Arthur wanted to visit above all others. It was Westminster Abbey. Whether or not he made his visit during this Christmas vacation or the following year when he next visited London is not clear but, bearing in mind his reason for going to the abbey, it seems likely he went there at the first opportunity. The object of his determination to visit the abbey was not the tombs of the monarchs of England but the grave of Thomas Babington Macaulay, who had died in 1859, the year Arthur was born.

Not surprisingly, Arthur's stay in London made a lasting impression on him. It was not just that he had, finally, visited the centre of the British Empire. He had also mixed with people, friends of his uncles or just passers-by in the street, who had previously never entered his sphere. The contrast between his sojourn in London and his family's life in Edinburgh must have been marked. His uncles were outward-going men, Richard almost a man-about-town, with wide circles of acquaintances and a broad sweep of interests. Arthur must have considered how little they were like his father, and how much Charles Doyle had failed in life compared to their successes.

After Christmas, Arthur returned to Stonyhurst to face the final months of study leading to his matriculation examinations after which he could leave school or go on to higher education. Sitting for the University of London matriculation examination board in the summer of 1875, he gained an overall mark of 70 per cent, which was considered high. Only eleven other Stonyhurst boys passed.

All in all, Arthur seems to have succeeded despite Stonyhurst rather than because of it: he survived the school, having avoided succumbing to its physical punishments or being unduly damaged by the psychological pressures of the Jesuits. Yet he admitted to never being happy once he had gone up from Hodder to the senior school. When he wrote many years later to the Ryans, he declared, 'I am bound to say, that I don't, looking back, consider the Stonyhurst system a good one, nor would I send a son there if I had one.' Later still, when writing his autobiography, *Memories and Adventures*, in the early 1920s, he referred to his seven years in the school as 'seven weary steps' yet he conceded that 'on the whole it was justified by results, for I think it turned out as decent a set of young fellows as any other school would do'.

The staff of Stonyhurst must have been glad to see the back of him. Arthur had been a rather troublesome pupil. Once, on being asked by a master what he hoped to be when he grew up, he had replied a civil engineer. The master had replied that he might one day become an engineer but that he would never be a civil one. Another anecdote, in a similar vein, was told by Conan Doyle himself. On his last day at Stonyhurst, one of the Jesuits masters told him that he had known him intimately for seven years and, without hesitation, declared he would never come to any good. Admittedly, Conan Doyle recounted this tale twenty years after leaving but such a memory does not fade with time. It must have both hurt and galled him at the time and prompted his probably justified assumption that the Stonyhurst Jesuits placed little store by the goodness of human nature.

The one Jesuit who had broken the mould was Francis Cassidy, who encouraged his pupils, understood their emotional needs and adjusted to or catered for them. The other Jesuits did not. They repressed their own emotions and stamped on any the boys might have shown. Had Cassidy been available to Arthur after he moved up to the senior school, matters might have been different, but he was not. Cassidy quit the preparatory school to become ordained not long after Arthur left, not returning until 1884, when he became the principal. The result of his departure was that, from the age of eleven and a half, Arthur had been no longer happy at school.

He might not have wanted to accept it but the Jesuits, perhaps despite both themselves and their pupil, had given much to Arthur. Their unemotional approach to life had by default driven him to read and escape through books, thereby galvanising his imagination and broadening his horizons. The psychological and physical oppression that caused him to rebel against them strengthened his character and, albeit subconsciously, taught him the important lesson that liberty and freedom, individuality and the right of self-determination were highly prized commodities worth defending. In short, they gave him a tradition of personal rebellion that remained with him all his life, making him question petty bureaucracies and, in time, take up causes he felt were just. They also taught him discipline and put a sense of order into his life. He might have been untidy about his person but his brain was logical, reasoning and organised. In this, they unknowingly provided him with the most important attribute of a writer: he was possessed of a firm strand of self-discipline with which he controlled and directed his art.

Beyond this, they additionally gave him the concept of the existence of a Higher Power. He did not leave the grasp of the Jesuits as a devout Catholic with a good Catholic mind. He questioned the faith yet he still believed in, as he put it, 'the prompting of some beneficent force outside ourselves, which tries to help where it can'.

Arthur had given little consideration as to what he should do after matriculating so the school suggested he might like to attend another, larger Jesuit school at Feldkirch in the Austrian Alps, ten kilometres from the Swiss border and five from Liechtenstein. The idea was that the school would give him further academic advancement and allow him to improve his knowledge of German. At Stonyhurst, Arthur had been in the top class for German so sending him to Feldkirch might have been the intention all along. At sixteen, he was also still too young for university entrance, and something had to be done with him other than to send him home to Edinburgh. He could have stayed on at Stonyhurst for what was known as a final Philosophy year, but Arthur had had enough of the school and his masters had probably had enough of him. Feldkirch presented a way of still keeping him away from his home background and his father whilst at the same time offering him a chance to mature and travel.

Arthur arrived at Feldkirch in the autumn of 1875, for a stay of one academic year. Who paid his school fees is unknown. Possibly the same arrangement as had come into play at Stonyhurst continued. Once there, Arthur wasted no time in making the most of all the school had to offer. He tobogganed down the slopes, skated on ponds, walked in the mountains, played football on stilts and took lessons in playing the bombardon, a huge brass valved bass tuba, in the school band: the sound it produced, he said, was akin to 'a hippopotamus doing a step-dance'. It required a sturdy youth just to lift and wear it, never mind blow a tune through its convolutions of pipes. Arthur, bedecked in a scarlet-and-gold band uniform, fitted the bill perfectly.

The school might have been run by Jesuits but it was not like Stonyhurst. The walls weren't cracked (deliberately or otherwise), the dormitories were heated, the food was better and well prepared. Even the beer was genuine and not just ale-coloured liquid. Discipline was much more relaxed, the teachers were altogether more considerate and understanding and Arthur studied hard. He ceased to be quite so resentful but he still kicked against the traces by founding and editing the *Feldkirch Gazette*. Its masthead motto, 'Fear not, and put it in print', might just as well have read the same as the Duke of Wellington's 'Publish and be damned'. In a brazen editorial, Arthur condemned the Jesuit brothers' practice of reading and censoring pupils' letters. The magazine was promptly proscribed.

Most of the pupils came from German Catholic families, but there was a small contingent of about twenty English and Irish boys. Arthur's German improved quickly, despite his spending much of his time speaking English with his fellow expatriates, and he was quick to pounce upon and read any German books he could master, being particularly fond of the German romantic writers such as Goethe and Schiller. Aware of his developing fluency, his mother requested that he write to her in French so that he should not become too Teutonic. At the time, he also began reading all he could get his hands on concerning Napoleonic history: perhaps his visit to Madame Tussaud's had lingered in his mind and allied itself to the fact that Napoleon had crossed the Alps by way of a nearby pass.

It was not all history and study. Whilst he was at Feldkirch, Arthur discovered a new, exciting and influential writer. It was the American novelist Edgar Allan Poe.

Born in Boston in 1809, the son of touring actors, Poe was orphaned as an infant and raised by his godfather, John Allan, a successful businessman in Richmond, Virginia. In 1815, Allan took him to England where he lived until 1820 when he returned to Virginia, enrolling in 1826 at the University of Virginia in Charlottesville. Leading a dissolute student life, he quit the university, estranged himself from his godfather, worked as a clerk, started to write poetry and enlisted in the US Army. After two years, he made it up with Allan who bought him a position at the US Military Academy, from which, after a few months, Poe was dismissed for neglect of duty. His godfather disowned him. He moved to Baltimore, worked as a journalist and married his cousin. For ten years, he nursed his wife through a long illness and, when she died, fell ill himself. He died, an alcoholic and probably an opium addict, at the age of forty.

The first of Poe's stories Arthur read was 'The Gold Bug', a tale about a search for hidden treasure. It astounded him. The next story he encountered was 'The Murders in the Rue Morgue'. Arthur was staggered by Poe's inventiveness: he may also have drawn parallels between Poe's life, literary ingenuity and his own life and embryonic talents. Poe was also attracted to the macabre, as was Arthur. And Poe was a rebel, albeit of a different sort.

Yet it was Poe's stories which had the impact upon him and he acknowledged it, admitting that at the time he had first read Poe his mind had been 'plastic. [His stories] stimulated my imagination and set before me a supreme example of dignity and force in the methods of telling a story.' At the same time, he also realised how the stories stirred up darker thoughts in him, for he went on, 'It is not altogether a healthy influence, perhaps. It turns the thoughts too forcibly to the morbid and the strange.'

Whatever the psychological effects Poe's stories might have had upon this plastic – if not elastic – mind, it has to be accepted that Edgar Allan Poe gave Arthur Conan Doyle his first encounter with the short story. It was from these brief tales that the latter learnt to understand, appreciate and assimilate the mechanics of short fiction-writing on which he was not only to build his own considerable literary reputation, and his greatest professional achievements, but also to shape the course of modern English literature.

His year at Feldkirch was, therefore, a seminal time but it did not, however, suggest to Arthur what he might do after it was over and he returned from Austria.

It was Mary Doyle, back in Edinburgh, who started to turn the tiller of her son's life. She was beginning to think that it might be a good idea for Arthur to attend the University of Edinburgh to read medicine. She may not have decided upon this academic course alone, for she had living with her as a paid lodger a man called Dr Waller who, whilst Arthur was at Feldkirch, had started to mail to him chemistry and mathematics textbooks which he had annotated. It is also possible that it was Waller, who had published a volume of his own poetry in 1875, who sent Arthur his copy of Poe's Tales of Mystery and the Imagination. Waller and Arthur also started to correspond, parrying philosophical points in their letters.

In such straitened circumstances, many an ordinary mother would have wanted her son to start earning upon gaining his education, contributing to the upkeep of the family, but Mary Doyle was no ordinary mother. She was ambitious for her son and looked to the future.

In the summer of 1876, after a farewell supper in Strasbourg with several of his fellow Feldkirch students, Arthur set off back to Edinburgh, stopping *en route* to visit Michael Conan and his wife, Susan, in Paris. He had, over his school years, corresponded with Conan, but it appears they had never actually met. His travelling arrangements organised by Thomas Cook, the original international travel agency, he arrived at the Gare de l'Est in Paris with virtually no money and had to walk the six kilometres to the Conans' home at 65 Avenue de Wagram, stopping only to buy a glass of liquorice and water on the way.

Michael Conan was aware of his godson's literary ability: he had been following it through their correspondence, Arthur having, from time to time, sent poems and possibly fragments of a prose journal to his godfather from Stonyhurst. Most of the verses were comic pieces but Conan had recognised their promise, reporting to Mary Doyle over Christmas 1875 that there could be 'no doubt of his faculty for that accomplishment. In each one of his more serious inspirations I found passages of thoroughly original freshness and imaginative refinement.'

Conan, whom Arthur described as a 'dear old volcanic Irishman', got along well with his godson. An intellectual and a thinker, Conan could be profound at times and, being widely read, he and Arthur could discuss literary matters and men whilst Conan's recollections, of his extensive travels in Europe, set Arthur's imagination going. His godfather's unequivocal anti-clerical attitudes also impinged themselves upon Arthur and gave him an added perspective on the Jesuit education from which he was, finally, liberated.

They also discussed the possibility of Arthur studying medicine, Conan drawing his attention to the fact that the course could put a heavy financial burden on the family in Edinburgh. Arthur's response was that he hoped he might get a bursary or some other academic award to help with the fees: university education was, in those days, by and large the preserve of the wealthy.

Apart from his going to Ireland to see the Foleys, his Austrian stay, with its side track to Paris, was Arthur's first overseas journey. It was to be the first of many he was to take throughout his life and it gave him a taste for travel. He developed over the years into a persistent and tireless world traveller. As a restless, energetic man who was always on the move, he enjoyed travel, the thrill of landing in new countries and meeting new people, of facing the challenges a fresh environment posed. He was also an unwaveringly curious man who was eager to discover new cultures: later, as a writer, travel sometimes afforded him the raw material of his stories. And much more.

The year in Austria had been his happiest time to date and he came away from Feldkirch with pleasant memories of both the school and the Jesuits who ran it. He later claimed he had come away with 'little to show, either mental or spiritual, for my pleasant school year in Germany', yet this is not really true. His imagination had been primed, his intellect had been widened. With the help of Edgar Allan Poe, he had received some self-taught tuition in literary construction. Even his sense of humour, which had previously been more of the schoolboy nature, had been rounded off by coming in contact with petty German bureaucracy, which he was to lampoon in his later stories through the dialogue of pompous officials and civil servants.

By the time he departed from Feldkirch, Arthur had matured into a thoughtful, intelligent and lively young man with a wisdom in excess of his years. His friends regarded him as loyal and staunch. His world until now having been predominantly masculine-orientated, he was somewhat at a loss when confronted by the opposite sex, but he was always courteous, gentlemanly and polite: his mother's teachings were not forgotten.

His schooldays, whether happy or not, had been in some respects a dream. He had been released into them from the misery of his family background which he had only had to handle during occasional school holidays. As the train headed from Paris towards the English Channel, he must have felt a heavy shadow fall across his heart. He was returning to Edinburgh, the poverty he had escaped for so long, a crowded home, a hassled mother and an increasingly ill, drunk and morose father. As he himself was to write, he was returning home 'conscious that real life was about to begin'.

3

A Raw-boned Cartilaginous Youth

It was often said of well-to-do Victorian families that the first son inherited his birthright (and indulged himself in politics, the arts, business or whatever else might appeal to him), the second son joined the military and the third went into the Church. For Arthur Conan Doyle, things were different. His family was poor, there was little to inherit and there were only two sons: and yet, in time, he was to encompass all three stations – polymath, adventurer-at-war, if not actual serving soldier, and, in a way, priest, albeit of a particularly esoteric and nefarious religion.

He was, however, to start off as a doctor.

The choice of a career in medicine was based on a number of mostly practical criteria. It was regarded as a respectable profession, was more or less guaranteed to provide a living after one had set oneself up in a practice, offered opportunities for advancement, and had a certain social cachet about it. In short, it looked attractive, but this was a misconception.

The anonymous author of *Confessions of an English Doctor*, published in 1904, who also read for his degree at the University of Edinburgh, stated that he knew of no profession more delusive than medicine. It was not all it seemed nor, according to him, all it was cracked up to be. In his opinion, it was one of the most difficult professions to enter, requiring an extensive investment in terms of both hard cash and hard work. He did not deny that it was a most splendid and noble profession but it was also, in practice, one of the most demanding, and anyone embarking upon it had to be very dedicated and conscientious, ready to come to terms with the inordinate amount of reading of complex texts that the medical student had to do, not to mention the large number of lectures he had to attend and facts he had to assimilate with little room for error or misinterpretation. After such a course of study, he then had to buy himself into a practice, or set up one himself from scratch, had to follow a set code of dress and behaviour and, in general, appear to be of a solid and trustworthy nature. Few doctors, he pointed out, ever became rich.

His advice was to think twice before entering the profession and he pondered on why young men ever wanted to be doctors. 'Youths,' he wrote, 'who imagine they would like to be doctors only think of nice horses, carriages, and shining tall hats; they dream the sensation of having great powers over humanity and of being paid splendid fees for doing quite easily so much good. No doctor will disillusion them; no doctor can afford to give himself away.' Whatever the youths felt, their parents had a different misconception. For them, doctors were reputable, gentlemanly pillars of the community, small and honourable businessmen whose profession was smart, upper-class and discreetly ostentatious: they could want nothing better for their sons. And, as far as the study of medicine was concerned, there were considered few better medical schools then – as now – than that of the University of Edinburgh.

Indeed, the Faculty of Medicine was regarded as one of the best in the world with an international reputation. A medical school was officially opened at the university in 1726 with a teaching hospital built three years later. In 1746, the teaching of clinical medicine commenced in which students were introduced to patients as a part of their course, the combination of higher education and clinical learning on the job being unknown elsewhere in Britain at the time. In 1876, the university introduced a Bachelor of Medicine degree to replace the Doctor of Medicine qualification previously offered, which permitted graduates to practise both nationally and internationally. and quickly doubled student enrolment. The result was that the School of Medicine became the wealthiest and most prestigious faculty, containing nearly half the university's students. Arthur Conan Doyle could not have joined a better course.

There was, in the Doyle family, no tradition of medical men: it was a predominantly artistic family. However, Mary Doyle's father, William Foley, had been a doctor, so the profession had been one she may have had in mind for her eldest son for some time. It had distinct advantages, too, apart from misconceived generalisations. Her son could live at home during his student years, saving money on expensive lodgings: the university had no halls of residence or student accommodation. Although the Students' Club was founded in 1876, providing meals for them during the day, the students had to live in rented 'digs', whole streets being tenanted by them. A newly arrived student had to scan the advertisement columns of local newspapers to find apartments for rent or was obliged to tramp the streets, enquiring at lodging houses or watching out for boards displayed in windows or over doors. Landlords were often grasping, landladies varying from martinets to mother-surrogates.

Conan Doyle seems not to have been bothered by staying at home: certainly, he showed none of the eagerness young men display in wanting to get away from home and maternal apron-strings. His relationship with his mother was such that he may well not have considered leaving her even if he had wanted to. For her part, she was glad to have her beloved Arthur home again. In just as resigned a fashion, he seems to have accepted the idea of reading medicine and becoming a doctor despite not having studied much science at Stonyhurst and not being too keen on having to return to a regimen of scientific academic work. Almost certainly, when he enrolled on the course, Conan Doyle had no medical vocation whatsoever: it was a profession in which he could feed himself and be respectable and that was the sum total of it. By the end of his second undergraduate year, however, a feeling of vocation had arrived and Conan Doyle realised he had the basic attributes required for the job. He was patient, diligent in his studies, observant and sympathetic towards the sick. He was also able to understand the subject matter and accept the rigours of the course on which he was neither an outstanding nor a marginal student: in short, he was a good average undergraduate.

If life as a student was a new experience for him so, to some extent, was his home life. He had, once more, to face the circumstances of his background, recording that 'the family affairs were still as straitened as ever . . . My mother had adopted the device of sharing a large house, which may have eased her in some ways, but was disastrous in others.' Quite how it was disastrous and in what measure remains open to speculation.

Mary Doyle continued to struggle with her family's situation and an increasing brood: another daughter, Jane Adelaide Rose (nicknamed Ida), had been born in 1875. As for her husband, he was in a steep decline owing to his alcoholism and his resultant mental health.

Charles Doyle, however, was not the only man living with the family. There was also Bryan Charles Waller.

For many years, it was assumed that Waller was an elderly man who was, in some capacity, a long-standing friend of the family. He was not. The truth has only comparatively recently come to light as a result of some astonishing detective work, worthy of Sherlock Holmes himself, conducted by Owen Dudley Edwards and published in his seminal book, *The Quest for Sherlock Holmes*. Researching in Edinburgh into Conan Doyle's early life, Edwards has discovered the truth behind Waller and the not inconsiderable part he played in Conan Doyle's life.

Waller was born in 1853 at Masongill, a small village a short distance from Kirby Lonsdale in the Pennines, close to the point where the borders of Yorkshire, Lancashire and Westmorland met, where his family owned land. Six years older than Conan Doyle, the young Waller is a shadowy figure about whom little is known. When he became Mary Doyle's lodger is uncertain but he was in residence with the Doyles by 1875 when the family moved from Sciennes Hill Place to a better abode at 2 Argyle Park. The rent in this new location was nearly double that of the former and it is likely that they could only afford this increase because of the contribution Waller's presence made to the family finances: he was a medical student at the university at the time.

After graduating in 1876, Waller did not move out but remained with the Doyles, continuing to study at the university where, in 1878, he gained his doctorate in medicine with the Gold Medal for an advanced thesis. Even then, he left neither the university nor the Doyles: he stopped in Edinburgh as a lecturer in pathology at the School of Medicine, worked as a consultant and began to publish in medical journals. He did not finally quit the Doyles' home until 1882, and it is not unlikely that, during his time as a lodger, he shared a study room in the Doyle household with Conan Doyle and might even have offered consultations to patients there.

What Conan Doyle thought of this arrangement can only be guessed at, for Waller's presence would have had its pro and cons. His being in residence must have made the lodgings all the more crowded, but his rent contributed substantially to the family's well-being and it might have been very advantageous for the young medical student to have a qualified doctor close at hand, to help with his studies. What was more, Waller was a literary man as well as a doctor.

With a certain pride, he claimed descent from Edmund Waller, the seventeenth-century poet who had inherited the town of Beaconsfield in Buckinghamshire, was educated at Eton and Cambridge, became a lawyer and royalist politician, and was instigator of Waller's Plot in support of Charles I against Cromwell's Parliamentarians, after the collapse of which he betrayed his fellow conspirators to save his own neck. Consequently, he was imprisoned in the Tower of London and banished abroad to France. After seven years, he returned to England, was pardoned under Cromwell's protection, poetically praised Cromwell, then, on the Great Protector's death, published poems rejoicing in his passing. He then supported the restoration of the monarchy under Charles II, returned to Parliament and became the Member for Hastings for the last twenty-six years of his life. To be charitable, Edmund Waller was a pragmatist: to be blunt, he was a man of pliable morality. A more recent relative was Waller's uncle, Bryan Waller Proctor, whose given name he shared. Under the pseudonym of Barry Cornwall, Proctor was a celebrity in literary London to whom Thackeray dedicated *Vanity Fair* and Wilkie Collins *The Woman in White*. Waller, who had mixed with his uncle's circle of friends, dedicated his book of poems, *The Twilight Land*, to him in 1875.

For Conan Doyle, to have such a man – not much older than himself – as his mentor must have been exciting. Yet Waller was also of a forceful personality and whatever advantage his literary connections or medical knowledge could have provided might well have been outweighed by his assertive confidence and, one might speculate, power. After all, he was wealthy and the family were in part dependent upon him. If Waller possessed any of his ancestor's guile and personality, he would not have been all smiles and pleasantries.

How Waller came to be the Doyle lodger is unknown: he might have come upon Mary Doyle as landlady simply by walking the streets looking for vacancy notices, but he might also have been recommended to her. He had lived for a while in London with his author uncle, prior to his arrival in Edinburgh, and it might be that he had met Richard Doyle in the whirl of literary London and been given her address.

However Waller arrived at Argyle Park, his status as mere lodger was not permanent. Edwards' study of valuation rolls and the City Directory of Edinburgh shows Charles Doyle as the rent-payer on the property in the financial year 1876/7. At that time, however, Charles Doyle was far from being in a position to be responsible for paying the rent. Not only was his condition worse but he was also now unemployed. Mathieson, who had hired and, to no small degree, protected Charles Doyle, was no longer in charge of the Office of Works and his successor had substantially reorganised it. Charles, who was only in his mid-forties, was dismissed in June 1876 with a pension of £150 per annum.

Thereafter, he was listed in the City Directory as an artist and Waller was given as the rent-payer. He continued to be so listed until 1881, even after the family had moved to 23 George Square.

In March 1877, Waller's father died and he inherited the family estate at Masongill but he did not return there: his mother, Julia, administered it in his absence. The reason for this is open to several interpretations.

Waller had, by now, clearly befriended the Doyle family or inveigled himself well into it. It may simply be that he had taken a liking to them and felt sorry for them when Charles, the sick drunkard, was made redundant, yet this seems to be giving him unwarranted saintly qualities. He may, as Edwards has conjectured, have been in love with one of the daughters: Annette was, by now, about twenty and of a courtable age. In fact, Waller wrote a forlorn poem, 'Annette's Music', which could imply that she had spurned him, but to assume this is to stretch the credibility of literary interpretation. Another cause for his involvement with the Doyles might have been that he was professionally interested in Charles Doyle's clinical depression and general condition which provided him with a suitable subject for study. A final reason, however unlikely it may appear, could be that he had a relationship not with one of the daughters but with Mary Doyle herself.

Whatever the truth, when Mary's tenth and final child arrived in March 1877, it was a daughter named Bryan Mary Julia Josephine: in the family, she was nicknamed Dodo. The source of the first and third given names is obvious: just as Innes had been named through the Burton connection, so was the last daughter linked to the Wallers. It was not just a matter of naming a child after a friend. It also signified a debt of gratitude and how much the family now relied upon Waller.

Once the decision was reached for Conan Doyle to seek entry to the university, Waller, who was almost certainly instrumental in the decision, prepared him for an examination to gain a bursary: paying the fees was going to be a major concern. Conan Doyle sat the examination in the summer of 1876 and was awarded the Grierson bursary amounting to £40 for two years. This, however, was rescinded when it was realised he wanted to read medicine and the grant applied only to arts undergraduates. In lieu, and as a sop to his disappointment, the university awarded him £7. Money was consequently tight throughout his student years.

After sitting what amounted to an entrance examination, in which Conan Doyle's grades were at best average, with only a grade D in German, despite his year at Feldkirch which seems not to have paid many academic dividends, he enrolled in the university at the beginning of the academic year in October 1876. He graduated five years later in August 1881.

The interim undergraduate years were not on the whole an enjoyable time. Conan Doyle found the academic work boring and he seldom made more than a passing reference to his student years during later life. In his semi-autobiographical novel, *The Firm of Girdlestone*, he wrote, 'The University is a great unsympathetic machine, taking in a stream of raw-boned cartilaginous youths at one end, and turning them out at the other end as learned divines, astute lawyers, and skilful medical men', and, in the same book, remarked caustically, 'Edinburgh University may call herself, with grim jocoseness, the "alma mater" of her students, but if she be a mother at all, she is one of a very stoical and Spartan cast, who conceals her maternal affection with remarkable success. The only signs of interest she ever deigns to evince towards her alumni are upon those not infrequent occasions when guineas are to be demanded from them.'

University education in the 1870s was not what it is today. The teaching was impersonal, students paid their fees directly to the professors and attended their classes. It was not far removed from buying tickets to attend lectures. Although medical students accompanied their professors on rounds of the wards in the hospital, there were no tutorials, no seminars and no small-class tuition. Students gathered information, collated their notes and learnt them. Professors were largely unapproachable and rarely spoke with their students except to instruct them. An example of the teaching system is shown by Conan Doyle's paying four guineas in 1877 to attend classes on surgery whilst, in 1878, he paid a further sum for a sixteen-month clinical surgery course.

The teaching was predominantly theoretical. Conan Doyle later said it was 'one long weary grind at botany, chemistry, anatomy, physiology and a whole list of compulsory subjects, many of which have a very indirect bearing upon the art of curing. The whole system of teaching, as I look back upon it, seems far too oblique and not nearly practical enough for the purpose in view.' This was referring to a university regarded as much more practical in its educational methods than most.

The teaching of surgery was conducted with students observing operations in a lecture hall in the centre of which was an operating table. There was little or no hands-on surgery but at least actual procedures were watched, with additional practical work in other areas of clinical medicine which students encountered in the wards of the Royal Infirmary, the Royal Edinburgh Asylum and the Royal Maternity Hospital.

In many other respects, doctors educated in the 1880s were the first 'modern' doctors. They were the first to be trained in the use of simple diagnostic methods, were the first in their profession to wear stethoscopes round their necks, shake the mercury down in their thermometers and time their patients' pulse against a pocket watch with a sweep second hand. Basic laboratory techniques were taught, microscopes were in common usage in pathology classes, and medicine was moving ahead in leaps and bounds with the more obscure fundamental functions of the body being studied and understood for the first time. As never before, diagnoses were being made upon considered detail and interpretation of symptoms, not just on educated guesswork or quackery: observation was, however, still the key word.

Conan Doyle declared that 'there was no attempt at friendship, or even acquaintance, between professor and students at Edinburgh', and this may have been so, but he came across many people who impinged themselves upon him. He might have been learning medicine but he also spent much of his time studying his fellow man as closely as he did a cadaver or a clinical chart. He once told G.K. Chesterton that no novelist had to go beyond a classroom, police station or assembly hall in order to discover all the fictional characters he could ever need.

The professors who taught Conan Doyle impressed him with their erudition, learning and, on occasion, eccentricity. He was also, as many medical students are when they first enter upon their career, surprised by their apparent heartlessness. Where he felt pathos for a patient, they exhibited little more than professional curiosity.

The most important professor was Sir Robert Christison who had held the chair in medicine at the university for nigh on fifty-five years and who retired during Conan Doyle's first year, aged eighty. Although he never actually lectured to Conan Doyle, Christison was omnipresent in university and city alike where his austere figure, with its frame of bushy whiskers, was revered, admired and instantly recognised.

One who did teach Conan Doyle was William Rutherford. An idiosyncratic, larger-than-life man with a booming voice and trim beard, he was an eminent physiologist, was Fullerian Professor of Physiology at the Royal Institution in London and author of the *Text Book of Physiology*, the standard tome of its day. Conan Doyle was fascinated by and in awe of Rutherford, whom he described, because of the square cut of his beard, as looking like an Assyrian. A popular lecturer, he had a bizarre and often gruesome sense of humour which prompted Conan Doyle to regard him as 'a rather ruthless vivisector'. He was to appear in later years in Conan Doyle's fiction.

Conan Doyle also encountered botany professor John Hutton Balfour, whom he compared to John Knox in both looks and bearing. Nicknamed Woody Fibre by the students – it was a favourite phrase of his and rather adequately described his tedious teaching methods – he established the Botanical Society and was distantly descended from Sir Andrew Balfour, who founded the Edinburgh Botanical Gardens. There were, of course, a number of other professors Conan Doyle experienced. Alexander Crum Brown, Professor of Chemistry, was noted for experiments that failed to work. Another was Sir Charles Wyville Thomson, the naturalist and explorer who had headed several famous deep-sea expeditions including the remarkable three-and-a-half-year, 68,890-nautical-mile voyage of HMS *Challenger*, searching for new forms of marine life and taking nearly four hundred soundings around the world. Andrew Maclagan, Professor of Forensic Medicine, was an expert in the determination of the time of death of a corpse and taught alongside Henry Littlejohn, another forensic scientist eventually to step into Maclagan's professorial shoes and be knighted. Yet there was one professor who was to have the greatest and most profound and lasting impact upon Conan Doyle.

Born in Edinburgh on 2 December 1837, Joseph Bell graduated from the university in 1859 at the early age of twenty-one. An outstanding doctor and scientist, he was one of the foremost medical teachers in Edinburgh in the latter half of the century and was a major contributor to medical advance. He spent his entire career in the city, starting off as a dresser and assistant to Sir Patrick Heron Watson, consulting surgeon at the Royal Infirmary, Queen Victoria's personal surgeon when in Scotland and honorary surgeon to Edward VII. In 1869, Bell applied to be appointed to the chair of clinical surgery, but the post went to Joseph Lister, the eminent physician and father of antiseptics. Never a member of the faculty of the university, although he was eventually made a member of the University Court, Bell rose through the ranks of his profession as hospital surgeon at the Royal Infirmary then senior and finally consulting surgeon both there and at the Royal Hospital for Sick Children. He published extensively, wrote a number of seminal textbooks and was, for twenty-three years, editor of the *Edinburgh Medical Journal*. At the Royal Infirmary, he taught clinical surgery – with students paying to attend his classes which were very popular and frequently overcrowded.

Known to the students as Joe, he was a sparse and lean man with the long and sensitive fingers of a musician, sharp grey eyes twinkling with shrewdness, an angular nose with a chin to match, unkempt dark hair and a high-pitched voice. He walked, according to Conan Doyle, with a jerky step, his head carried high. Blessed with a wry sense of humour, he spoke precisely and clearly but, in the company of patients, could slip at the drop of a hat into the broadest brogue. More than a medical man, he was also a widely read amateur poet, a competent raconteur, a keen sportsman, a naturalist and a bird-watcher. He was a good shot and enjoyed grouse-shooting: Conan Doyle met him on the Isle of Arran in 1877 whilst shooting there but it is not known if they did more than pass the time of day. In all probability, Conan Doyle made no attempt to talk to Bell, who was, to his students, a charismatic and fascinating man well above their station.

This fascination was based upon more than Bell's medical expertise. As much as he taught medicine, so did he teach the study of humankind, and it was this which Conan Doyle, also a student of those around him, found astounding. Bell was, he wrote, 'a very remarkable man in body and mind . . . He was a very skilful surgeon, but his strong point was diagnosis, not only of disease, but of occupation and character.'

It was Bell's dictum that a doctor had to be not only learned but also immensely interpretative of all relevant features of a patient. Diagnosis, he taught, was not made just by visual observation but also by the employment of all the senses: do not just look at a patient, he advised, but feel him, probe him, listen to him, smell him. Only then could a diagnosis be attempted.

Every Friday, Bell held an open out-patient clinic at the Royal Infirmary which students attended. Patients were prepared in an anteroom, wheeled in before the doctor who studied and diagnosed them: they were then wheeled out for treatment. The students scribbled notes as fast as they could. Bell waited for no man.

In 1878, Bell appointed Conan Doyle his clerk for these clinics. Why he chose him is a mystery although it was a part of the course that students should take on junior responsibilities now and then as part of their training. Whatever the case, it afforded Conan Doyle valuable experience. The job involved listing patients, drawing up brief case notes and ensuring they were presented to Bell on time and in the correct sequence. When he began, the doctor cautioned him that he would need to be aware of the local vernacular. Many of the patients were poor, receiving treatment free or at considerable reduction in exchange for being clinical examples. It was not long before Conan Doyle came upon a patient with a 'bealin' in his otter' which meant nothing to him: Bell, with a certain dry wit, translated this as an abscess in the armpit.

Bell's clinics took place in a large bleak room, the doctor sitting behind a large desk with the students fanned out behind him on chairs. From this position, Bell surveyed the sick that came before him, occasionally stepping forward for close examination. He felt them, manipulated their joints, sniffed their breath, looked into their eyes and ears, peered down their throats and ran an astute eye up and down them. His examination over, he commented not only on the patient's medical condition but also upon their lives which he deduced by acute observation. This was not exhibitionism. The wealth of laboratory tests available today was absent then and powers of deductive observation were essential.

He was helped by the fact that people lived more sedentary existences in the nineteenth century, often staying in one locale and with one form of employment all their lives. With such a comparatively stable personal history behind them, Bell was readily able to detect a patient's personal circumstances as well as his illness. An example might be Bell's guessing correctly that a man with a callused ball to his thumb was a sail-maker because his address was close by the docks and sail-makers used this part of the hand to push needles through canvas. A woman with muscular forearms and yet soft hands might be a laundress. Conan Doyle gave an oft-quoted illustration of Bell's observational powers:

> In one of his best cases he said to a civilian patient: 'Well, my man, you've served in the army.'
> 'Aye, Sir.'
> 'Not long discharged?'
> 'Aye, Sir.'
> 'A Highland regiment?'
> 'Aye, Sir.'
> 'A non-com officer?'
> 'Aye, Sir.'
> 'Stationed at Barbados?'
> 'Aye, Sir.'
> 'You see, gentlemen,' he would explain, 'the man was a respectful man but did not remove his hat. They do not in the army, but he would have learned civilian ways had he been long discharged. He has an air of authority and he is obviously Scottish. As to Barbados, his complaint is Elephantiasis, which is West Indian, and not British.'

In another instance, Bell correctly surmised a woman patient's circumstance. He arrived at it by judging from her accent that she came from Fife, that she had come by a particular road because of the clay on her boots and that she had dropped off an older child on the way as the child's coat she carried was too big for the toddler accompanying her. The dermatitis on her right hand told him she was right-handed and worked in a linoleum factory.

The students, Conan Doyle amongst them, at first found such accurate assessments near to miraculous, but once Bell explained his reasoning, they came to appreciate his lesson. Observation was a vital part of diagnosis. On the other hand, in retrospect, Conan Doyle found Bell's clinics somewhat cold. The non-fee-paying patients were, he felt, little more than specimens, trundled before the great man, used as teaching aids, then shuffled out again. They were given no privacy, their affairs were openly debated and their bodies turned this way or that by way of exhibition of their symptoms with no more regard than a horse-trader showing off a mare at market. It might have been cold-hearted, condescending and patronising, but it was free and, for the poor, clinics such as Bell's offered much-needed and often inaccessible medical attention.

Conan Doyle may have described his university years as one long weary grind but his student life had another side to it. He involved himself in a variety of sports, playing rugby for the university team (he was a forward) and cricket. When the opportunity arose, he also took part in boxing bouts, a sport he thoroughly enjoyed and at which he excelled although he rated himself as nothing more than 'a fair, average amateur'. In every sport to which he took, he was close to a natural, requiring little instruction before becoming proficient. Off the sports field, he went dancing in Edinburgh, travelled around Scotland (such as his holiday on the Isle of Arran in 1877) and went to the theatre whenever he could. On one occasion, he narrowly avoided being beaten up whilst waiting in a jostling theatre queue. A soldier, shoving his way forward, crushed a young woman against the theatre door. She screamed and Conan Doyle went to her aid, giving the soldier a piece of his mind. The soldier jabbed him in the ribs. He slapped the soldier's face. The soldier's mates gathered round. Conan Doyle was outnumbered and matters looked nasty, but the day was saved by the theatre opening. Conan Doyle threw the soldier through the theatre door and wisely went home. When not trouncing truculent troopers, he took part in the ordinary social life of the students and even penned a mildly satirical ditty about the professors.

Little is known of his fellow students: James Ryan, his Stonyhurst friend, came up to the university, also to read medicine, but ill-health prevented him from seeing the course through and he later set sail for Ceylon where his family were tea-planters. He died there in 1920. As for other friendships, Conan Doyle seems not to have made many of a lasting nature amongst his peers.

Yet his most frequent pursuit was his reading. Despite having a vast number of texts to read and learn as part of his studies, he still read avidly and widely, from fiction to theology, from poetry to philosophy. He borrowed books from the university library, from the public library and from Waller. He also purchased books from second-hand bookshops, paying twopence a volume. This sounds a paltry sum today but, as Conan Doyle himself pointed out, a mutton pie cost twopence and made up his lunch. There were days, therefore, when he had to choose between feeding his stomach or his intellect.

Without the bookshops and the theatre beckoning, money was already tight. Conan Doyle might have been living at home but this did not alleviate his or his mother's financial problems. To supplement the family income, to help pay a share of his keep and university fees, he decided to seek part-time or temporary employment. This was permitted by the university so he determined to squeeze a year-long course into six months and work for the other half of the year. It meant more concentrated studying when he was attending classes but he felt he had no option. He would not be any more of a burden on Mary Doyle than he had to be.

He was not alone in helping to bring in money. Waller's rent paid for the roof over their heads. Annette went to work as a governess in Portugal in 1879, remitting part of her salary home. Over the next three years, Lottie and Connie followed in her footsteps, the latter possibly going to school in Portugal, at Annette's expense. Yet there were still the younger children to house, educate, clothe and feed.

For his employment, Conan Doyle chose to become a medical assistant. This was allowed as assistants did not need to be qualified, could gain valuable experience on the job, could offset some of their work against their degrees and could earn a small salary on the side.

In May 1878, Conan Doyle travelled to Sheffield to work as assistant to a general practitioner called Richardson, for whom he acted as medical assistant and dispenser of drugs, doctors issuing their own prescriptions at the time and more often than not making a lucrative living from the activity. He lasted three weeks before Richardson dismissed him, probably for being not up to the responsibilities, insufficiently trained and too inexperienced.

From Sheffield, Conan Doyle travelled south to London where he stayed in Clifton Gardens with Uncle James, Uncle Henry and Aunt Jane. His relationship with them was a little strained, for they were wealthy and childless, and he was a poor, socially unconventional student. He advertised for a medical assistant's post and spent every morning studying. After noon, he walked around London, going to the East End which was, at the time, one of the greatest seaports on earth. Here, he chatted and drank with stevedores and sailors on shore leave, listening to their yarns and no doubt dreaming of adventure. He even contemplated joining the army or navy but, wary of his mother's wishes for him to be a doctor, decided against it.

Clearly, this stay of some weeks in London came at a nadir in his student life. Conan Doyle was short of money, humbled by his poverty, had just been dismissed from a medical post and was no doubt feeling the burden of his university course.

At first, he had no response to his advertisements; then, finally, he was offered a post by Dr Henry Francis Elliot who ran a practice at Ruyton-XI-Towns in Shropshire, a village eighteen kilometres north-west of Shrewsbury. With Elliot, he was more of a success, fitting in well to the rural practice and even gaining confidence by handling a dangerous surgical case himself when he had to take a piece of shrapnel out of a man's skull, the result of an exploding cannon at a fairground. When he was not busy, he strolled in the countryside, read books and even entered a medical essay competition, writing on the iniquity of alcoholism and drug abuse, a subject for which his family background must have given him ample information. It did not win the prize.

He enjoyed his stay at Ruyton-XI-Towns although he did not appreciate Elliot's being at times bad-tempered and opinionated, and a man who gave no truck to Conan Doyle's ideas and thoughts. When he opined his objection to capital punishment, the doctor flew into a rage and demanded that such thoughts not be aired in his house.

In October 1878, Conan Doyle returned to Edinburgh and university after working in Ruyton-XI-Towns for the best part of four months. He was richer by experience but still penniless, for Elliot had not paid him, merely giving him his board and lodging but not so much as his train fare on top of it. At least, he must have considered, he had not been a drain on his mother's meagre resources.

The next year, 1879, matters were different. With the Shropshire experience to his credit, he was given a real assistant's position, at a salary of £2 per month, with Dr Reginald Ratcliffe Hoare of Clifton House, Aston Road, Birmingham. He was, according to Conan Doyle, 'a fine fellow, stout, square, red-faced, bushy-whiskered and dark-eyed'. A friendly man, he was also a taskmaster who expected value for his £2, operated a twelve-hour day and stood no nonsense. The practice was a large one, in a poor district, but Hoare still paid himself a salary of £3,000 per annum, much of it derived from his dispensing of medicines for which, whilst he was there, Conan Doyle was responsible. In addition, he made house calls for Hoare, discovering the poverty of the industrial city which contrasted with that of predominantly non-industrial Edinburgh.

During the course of his visiting, Conan Doyle met a Herr Gleiwitz. He had been a well-known Sanskrit and Arabic scholar of international repute but was now down on his luck, earning a crust for himself and three children by giving German language lessons. Conan Doyle took such pity on him that, when Gleiwitz found it hard to settle the bill, Conan Doyle, having little money himself, is said to have given him his watch and chain.

Dr Hoare and his wife, Amy, took a liking to Conan Doyle, regarding him as they would their own son, and he returned to work for the doctor on at least two other occasions, each time being given more complex tasks to perform and cases to deal with, including several instances of midwifery. Remaining in contact with the couple for many years, Conan Doyle thought highly of Dr Hoare, whom he described as Dr Horton in *The Stark Munro Letters*. 'His heart,' he wrote, 'is broad and kind and generous. There is nothing petty in the man. He loves to see those around him happy; and the sight of his sturdy figure and jolly red face goes far to make them so.' In letters, he even addressed Amy Hoare as 'Dear Mam', a phrase he frequently used to his own mother. It would seem the Hoares gave Conan Doyle more than a part-time job. At a time when his life was in turmoil, they gave him an albeit temporary respite from his misery, a safe harbour into which he could sail when the seas got rough.

Rough seas of another sort filled seven months of Conan Doyle's student years and were the cause of his taking five, instead of the usual four, years to graduate. In early 1880, still on the lookout for temporary employment, he was presented with what he later referred to as 'the first real outstanding adventure in my life'.

When, in London in 1878, he had given a moment's thought to joining the navy he had considered signing up as a surgeon, not a sailor *per se*. Later, he toyed with the idea of seeking a post as a ship's doctor with a South American steamship company. No doubt he still remembered the matelots' tales he had picked up around the East End docks and taverns. These had been fanciful dreams but now they came to reality. A fellow student, Claude Augustus Currie, had succeeded in getting taken on as ship's doctor on an Arctic whaler out of Peterhead. At the last minute, however, he was unable to go. The ship's owners and captain had to have a doctor on board. Currie asked Conan Doyle if he would go in his stead. That he was unqualified did not matter: ship's doctors, even as late as 1880, were not much more than sawbones.

Needless to say, Conan Doyle accepted the vacancy with alacrity, despite being warned of the dangers. The pay was meagre at £2 a month plus three shillings a ton 'oil money', a bonus paid to all crew members according to how much whale oil the voyage realised. Conan Doyle was heedless of the danger and the low pay. He wanted the adventure just as much as – even more than – the money.

The vessel was the *Hope*, a steam-powered whaler of about four hundred tons. She sailed from Peterhead in the last week of February 1880 with a crew of around fifty, half of them Scottish, the other half Shetland Islanders. Fortunately, there was little call for Conan Doyle's meagre surgical expertise: it is doubtful he could have coped with any major medical emergency. He spent the voyage keeping the company of Captain John Gray, with whom he got along well, and separating brawling drunken crew members, yet he did not mind. This was what he had craved for years. He was at last riding his own adventure, experiencing the tough masculine life before the mast or, in his case, the funnel.

The voyage had the makings of a ripping yarn from the start. Less than twelve hours out from Peterhead, Conan Doyle got into a boxing fight with the ship's steward, Jack Lamb, whose eye he blacked. The fight was not occasioned by animosity. Lamb had been helping Conan Doyle to unpack his belongings in his cabin and had come across one of two pairs of boxing gloves. At this discovery, the steward insisted on going a few rounds with the doctor. It was, according to Conan Doyle, an unequal fight, for Lamb was short in both stature and reach. During the seven-month voyage, he gave Lamb boxing lessons and they became good friends, staying in touch for some years afterwards. Conan Doyle reported that Lamb, a baker by trade, had a 'beautiful and sympathetic tenor voice' and sang 'pathetic and sentimental songs', adding that 'it is only when you have not seen a woman's face for six months that you realise what sentiment means . . . he filled us all with a vague, sweet discontent, which comes back to me now as I think of it'. Besides the pugilistically inclined steward, the ship's cook was a soak who ruined the food on more than one occasion and was belted by a crew member with a saucepan. The assailant was a tall, handsome man who kept apart from the others and was said to be on the run from the law.

The first fishing area to which the Hope sailed lay between Spitsbergen and Greenland. By April, the seals had finished breeding and hunting for them, for oil and pelts, commenced. It was brutal work, for the seals were clubbed to death to protect their leather, but Conan Doyle did not find the killing any more distasteful than the ordinary butchering of domestic livestock for meat. It was, for him, merely a trade that kept many others in employment, although he recalled later that 'those glaring crimson pools upon the dazzling white of the ice-fields, under the peaceful silence of a blue Arctic sky, did seem a horrible intrusion'.

On one seal hunt on the icepack, Conan Doyle nearly lost his life, falling off a shelf of ice into the freezing sea and only saving himself by grabbing hold of the flipper of a dead seal. On another day, he slid into the sea on three occasions, having to take to his bunk whilst his clothes were dried on the ship's boiler. He was fortunate to have survived. At that time of year, although the water is not ice, the sea temperature can be below freezing and survival time is counted in minutes.

Two months later, the ship veered north to hunt for whales. Whaling was exhausting, violent and dangerous. The crew was frequently soaked to the skin with blood and a whale, hauled up on the deck for butchering, might well not be dead. One strike of a whale's fin could snap a man's limb like a twig or even kill. Conan Doyle joined in the hunting of whales with so much zeal that Captain Gray offered to take him on the next trip as a harpooner doubling up as doctor, paying twice the wage. For the medical student-cum-ship's doctor, whaling was an exquisitely risky sport and a whale, which was not as obviously mammalian as a seal, appeared 'to have but little sensibility to pain for it never winces when the long lances are passed through its body'.

The voyage was not all carnage. Conan Doyle spent some time studying his medical textbooks or recognising the seabirds following the Hope, on the watch for offal. He saw narwhals, polar bears, Arctic foxes and a grampus which he regarded as 'the most formidable of all monsters of the deep'. Quite what he was referring to is hard to tell: the word can mean a killer whale but it also refers to the comparatively harmless cetacean known as a cowfish.

The Hope seems not to have called at any ports during her voyage so Conan Doyle was without news from home for seven months and suffered from occasional homesickness, recording that a 'sense of loneliness also heightens the effect of the Arctic Seas'. He considered his months at sea were a time of mental idleness, for his shipmates were 'fine brave fellows, but naturally rough and wild'. He had with him, however, a small collection of what he thought essential reading, including works by Sir Walter Scott and essays by Macaulay which, if what he wrote in *Through the Magic Door*, a study of his favourite books and authors published in 1907, is true, he foisted off on the crew. 'Honest Scotch harpooners,' he wrote, 'have addled their brains over it; and you may still see the grease stains where the second engineer grappled with Frederick the Great.' Conan Doyle's shipboard popularity might be measured by the fact that he tried to interest the crew in Macaulay and they did not ostracise him or heave him over the side.

The voyage of the *Hope* gave Conan Doyle more than a taste for adventure. When he arrived back in Edinburgh in September 1880, he carried with him fifty gold sovereigns, the majority of which he gave to Mary Doyle, hiding them about his person and making a game of her having to find them. One can only imagine his pride. He was in possession of more money than he had ever had before and was, for the first time, able to contribute substantially to his family's well-being. For a short time, in his mind, they were not dependent upon Waller but upon him, the eldest son.

The trip had not only earned him a good sum in wages and bonuses but it had matured him, given him an experience he was never to forget. In an interview twelve years later, he said he had never 'had such a jolly time' and, in an article entitled 'Life on a Greenland Whaler', which he wrote for the *Strand Magazine*, he stated, 'The peculiar other-world feeling of the Arctic regions – a feeling so singular that if you have once been there the thought of it haunts you all your life . . . The perpetual light, the glare of the white ice, the deep blue of the water, these are the things which one remembers most clearly, with the dry, crisp, exhilarating air.' The atmosphere had particularly impressed him and to such an extent that he thought the Arctic could be used as a vast sanatorium in much the same way as the sick, especially those suffering from tuberculosis, were sent up mountains so the clean air might purify their systems.

Much as his character had matured, turning him into an independent adult, so had his body. Having joined in with the crew, sharing in the hardship and enduring the vicissitudes of their arduous labour, his muscles were firmed up and he was now physically very strong. 'I went on board the whaler a big, straggling youth,' he wrote, '[and] I came off it a powerful well-grown man.' He had celebrated his twenty-first birthday on board the *Hope* and was known to remark that he had come of age not in 1880, but at 80 degrees north.

Another aspect of Conan Doyle's character formed around this time. He became an agnostic.

For some time, he had been questioning his beliefs, probably as far back as his schooldays. In his autobiography, he recalled, 'I remember that when, as a grown lad, I heard Father Murphy, a great fierce Irish priest, declare that there was sure damnation for everyone outside the Church, I looked upon him with horror, and to that moment I trace the first rift which has grown into such a chasm between me and those who were my guides', whilst many years later he wrote of being made to read a text called *Hell Open to Christians*, graphically illustrated with pictures of the torments to which sinners could look forward: he was repulsed by the cruelty of the faith. His justified perception of the Jesuits as intolerant protectors of a narrow-minded theology made him further consider the doctrines of the Catholic faith which he regarded as Rhadamanthine and spiritually niggardly.

Yet Conan Doyle was not alone in his challenging. In the university, an intellectual debate had been going on for some years, the students being ardent followers of Huxley. The most important scientific thinker of the nineteenth century after Charles Darwin, Professor T.H. Huxley, known as 'Darwin's bulldog' because of his obdurate support of Darwin's theories of evolution, was the man who had coined the term 'agnosticism'. Where Darwin was the principal, Huxley was the promoter and, being an eminent doctor as well as a renowned scientist, he carried many in the medical profession with him. The reason and appeal of Darwin's theories, which had been propounded in his *Origin of Species*, published the year Conan Doyle was born, and in *The Descent of Man*, published in 1871, were such that thinking men found they had no alternative but to accept the premises of science and reject religious belief. Being around doubting and cynical students, undergoing a scientific education, reading widely, joining in the debate of science versus God, watching every day the misery and poverty of the sick to whom God seemed to have turned a blind eye – not to mention the circumstances of his own family – must all have helped to sway Conan Doyle's opinion.

He summed up his thoughts with the words, 'Judging it thus by all the new knowledge which came to me both from my reading and from my studies, I found that the foundations not only of Roman Catholicism, but of the whole Christian faith, as presented to me in nineteenth century theology, were so weak that my mind could not build upon them.'

Had she wanted to, Mary Doyle might have been able to use her influence to keep her son on the path of righteousness, yet she did not. She, too, was a doubter, her change of heart echoed in *The Stark Munro Letters* in an episode where Munro's mother's parting words to her son are 'Wear flannel next to your skin, my dear boy, and never believe in eternal punishment'. It is not hard to think that Mary might have said just those words to her son as he set off for Peterhead and the gangplank of the *Hope*. It was not long after this, a few years at most, that Mary Doyle became an Anglican.

Conan Doyle was not prevented from abandoning Catholicism. Waller was already either an agnostic or was unconcerned. He had actively prompted Conan Doyle to read Carlyle and Emerson and may well have given him his copy of Winwood Reade's *The Martyrdom of Man* which outlined the manner in which religion enslaved mankind. In his correspondence with Conan Doyle in Feldkirch he had advised, ' "Do" is a far finer word than "Believe" and "Action" is a far surer watchword than "Faith".' Michael Conan was not devout and had been wary of the Jesuits for years. Charles Doyle, on the other hand, was a zealously pious Catholic, but he appears not to have tried to influence his son. He was probably, by this time, too ill and drunk to care. Once more in *The Stark Munro Letters*, Conan Doyle outlined his relationship with and attitude towards his father at about this time, although the character of the father in the story is not like Charles Doyle: 'I admire him, yet I feel there is little intellectual sympathy between us. He appears to think that these opinions of mine upon religion and politics which come from my inmost soul have been assumed either out of indifference or bravado. So I have ceased to talk on vital subjects with him, and though we affect to ignore it, we both know that there is a barrier there.'

Conan Doyle's own account of his conversion to agnosticism appears in his autobiography. 'It was, then,' he wrote, 'all Christianity, and not Roman Catholicism alone, which had alienated my mind and driven me to an agnosticism which never for an instance degenerated into atheism, for I had a very keen perception of the wonderful poise of the universe and the tremendous power of conception and sustenance which it implied. I was reverent in all my doubts and never ceased to think upon the matter, but the more I thought the more confirmed became my non-conformity.'

Not surprisingly considering his upbringing, even though Conan Doyle rejected Christianity, he still felt a need to believe in something, tempering this with a logical Huxleian desire to have it proven. Never an atheist, he wanted to believe there was a force, a presence behind creation, but he refused to have this associated with an organised system of worship. As a result, he still read and thought about religion, hoping, perhaps, to discover a demonstrable truth.

Having escaped the clutches of Rome, Conan Doyle started to formulate the opinion that human life was merely a stage in some vast universal existence, death only a transition from one part to the next. Whilst sailing on the *Hope*, several of his crew-mates had recounted their spiritual experiences to him, these adding to the corpus of doubts or alternatives mingling in his mind. Indeed, the whole voyage had been something of a spiritual revelation for Conan Doyle. In the Arctic, he had seen nature unsullied by Man and he had seen it despoiled by the blood of clubbed seals.

For Conan Doyle, science could not exist without there being some spiritual quality to it. Existentiality was not enough. There had to be a purpose to creation, some design to it which implied it had a designer whom he could not bring himself to think was feckless, amoral and indifferent. He believed not so much in God in the Christian sense as in some overall powerful theistic entity, admitting to being, in the broadest sense, a nonconformist Unitarian, more critical of Christian teaching than the average adherent of that sect.

Throughout his medical studies, assistantships and voyage to the Arctic, Conan Doyle was writing poetry and short stories, most probably with Waller's encouragement. At first the stories, predominantly adventure tales or historical fiction, were written for self-indulgent reasons, but it was not long before Conan Doyle started submitting them to magazine editors. It is likely he saw them as a potential source of income: his father had earned a bit on the side from painting so why should the son not do likewise from his pen?

His first submission to an editor, in late 1877 or early 1878, was a short piece entitled 'The Haunted Grange at Goresthorpe – a True Ghost Story' and smacks of the kind of yarns he was telling in the Stonyhurst dormitories. Like his attempt at the medical essay on drink and dope, it was unsuccessful and was at first rejected although, five years later, a story with a very similar title, 'The Ghosts of Goresthorpe Grange', appeared in an issue of *London Society*.

It was in *Chambers' Journal*, a weekly Edinburgh publication, that Conan Doyle first made it into print with a story entitled 'The Mystery of Sasassa Valley'. Published on 6 September 1879, it was most probably written either early in the spring of that year or during the summer whilst its author was working for Dr Hoare.

The basis of the story is an African superstition concerning three young white adventurers in South Africa who uncover a native legend of a devil the eyes of which glow in the dark and terrorise the local tribesmen. The glowing eyes turn out to be diamonds for which the intrepid heroes are prospecting. With its mixture of adventure and the supernatural, it is not hard to see the influence behind the story. Conan Doyle's hero discovers than the devil's eyes are the treasure whilst Poe's hero in 'The Gold Bug' drops the gold bug through the orbits of a skull.

Chambers' Journal paid three guineas but the greater reward was Conan Doyle's realisation that be could earn money from his writing. That 'The Mystery of Sasassa Valley' might be a flash in the pan did not occur to him. He was on his way and his only regret was that the copy editor of the story had trimmed his manly dialogue and the characters' realistic oaths.

He wrote more short stories in a similar vein, filled with youthful exuberance and optimism, and sent them off to editors. None were accepted. They were much of a muchness, lost in the thrilling adventure genre writing of the time which was very popular but had a large body of writers churning out stories virtually identical to each other. Competition for publication was fierce. Editors were inundated with what was later termed pulp fiction. Rejection did not discourage Conan Doyle but short story publication had a drawback. It was the policy of most magazines to publish short fiction anonymously. It was going to be difficult for him to make his name from short stories.

The next story he sold was 'The American's Tale', accepted by *London Society*. This was followed by 'That Little Square Box' which was also taken by *London Society*, the editor sending him a letter suggesting he might abandon medicine for literature. Whatever such advice did for his ego, it proved once and for all that Conan Doyle was right in assuming he could write to supplement his earnings.

Conan Doyle's voyage on the *Hope* helped develop his ability as a writer. His horizons had been opened up with and by an assortment of men, whom he could never otherwise have encountered, entering his life. They were not educated men yet they had a basic, uninhibited and coarse appeal he could not ignore, and he appreciated their commonality. The crew also taught him a lot about human nature and character which he added to his fund of learning and observation of people. The lecture halls and wards of the Royal Infirmary taught him medicine but the *Hope* was his first classroom in the university of life. For a long time afterwards, many of Conan Doyle's stories relied upon the voyage of the *Hope* for raw material. Together with an intimate working knowledge of the sea and ships, the crew of the vessel reappeared as the basis for characters in many short stories and, later, in the Sherlock Holmes tales.

Story-writing was not the only literary skill and direction Conan Doyle embarked upon in his student years. He also commenced a lifelong career writing to the press, the freedom of which he unreservedly supported and the institution of which he believed to be one of the most valuable in society. Apart from anything else, he learnt that one could manipulate it.

The quantity of his journalistic correspondence over the years was to be staggering and it covers a vast range of subject matter upon which, at times, he wrote at considerable and time-consuming length. It was through the press he really showed to the public the polymath he was, with interests in all quarters and an often detailed knowledge of subjects ranging from the enfranchisement of women to the iniquities of motor car speeding laws. Yet he was no old fogey, sounding off in the broadsheets and tabloids. His arguments were always reasoned, his thoughts and comments original and individualistic, his conclusions circumspect and sapient.

His first known published correspondence was not to a newspaper but to the *British Medical Journal*. It appeared in the issue of 20 September 1879 and carried the address of Clifton House, Aston Road, Birmingham, Dr Hoare's practice. The subject concerned the contraindications of a drug he called gelseminum. Derived from the root of the Carolina jasmine, *Gelsemium nitidum*, the chief constituent was the poisonous, amorphous alkaloid named gelseminine. The drug, tasting very bitter as most alkaloids do, was prepared as a tincture and taken internally as a pain depressant. At the time, Conan Doyle was suffering from neuralgia and took the drug, which was not yet fully tested and did not enter the British *Pharmacopoeia* until 1898. It was, therefore, a 'new' drug. He took it not only to kill his pain but also as a means of experimentation, stating that he had 'determined to ascertain how far one might go in taking the drug, and what the primary symptoms of an overdose might be'. This was a risky thing to do. He was stepping beyond the bounds of medical knowledge and it was a brave man who experimented on himself although, no doubt, he enjoyed the buzz of excitement as he swallowed the next dose and sat about seeing what happened. Whilst this was a courageous action it was not out of the ordinary. Towards the end of the nineteenth century, there was a scramble to find new drugs, especially painkillers, to replace opiates, and it was not unusual for doctors personally to test potential concoctions. Vast riches lay in store for the discoverer of a new and non-addictive analgesic. What was unusual was that Conan Doyle, as a student, was doing his own research. If students became involved in testing, it was usually under the eye of a qualified doctor, and it might be that, whilst he was using his own body for private research, he might have had Dr Hoare standing by to assist if needed. Perhaps Conan Doyle, seeing others making money from research, decided to try yet another avenue of earning.

As if writing, medical studies and assistantships and drug research were not enough, it was whilst at university that Conan Doyle took up photography. Although photography had been invented as long ago as 1827, and Fox-Talbot's pioneer work was already over thirty years old, photography was still on a fast learning curve. It was, in other words, one of the new areas of scientific advance of the day, and this had an appeal for Conan Doyle. Not only was he at the barricades of medical advance in the university (and in his own room, with gelseminum), he was also up there with the new unfolding technology.

He came to it through William Kinnimond Burton, John Hill Burton's son, who was a keen photographer with his brother, Cosmo Innes: their grandfather, Professor Cosmo Innes, had been one of the first to experiment with photography and was a contemporary of Fox-Talbot. William and Cosmo had their own darkroom and photographic laboratory in a tower of their home, Morton House, and it was here Conan Doyle joined them at what was, despite their amateur status, the cutting edge of photographic progress.

The Burton brothers were members of the Edinburgh Photographic Society from 1880, at the end of which year William left to work in London. There, he befriended W.B. Bolton, editor of the *British Journal of Photography*, for which Burton wrote frequent articles. In 1881, he was elected a member of the Royal Photographic Society and was one of those who founded the Camera Club in 1885. Two years later, he went to Japan as Professor of Sanitary Engineering and Lecturer on Rivers, Docks and Harbours in the College of Engineering at the Imperial University of Tokyo, and died there from malaria in 1899.

It was not long before this new interest had Conan Doyle writing about it, and he published a number of articles in the *British Journal of Photography*, possibly at the instigation of Burton. In 1880, a series of articles was published under the covering title 'Where to Go with the Camera'. Latching on to the Victorian desire to travel, the articles described various places of natural beauty that might be of interest to photographers. Conan Doyle submitted a piece on the Isle of May, in the Firth of Forth, headed 'After Cormorants with a Camera'. The island was famous for its flocks of cormorants which were a tourist attraction. The article was in two parts, on 14 and 21 October 1881, and was reprinted by *Anthony's Photographic Bulletin* in New York. He was not to know it, but this was Conan Doyle's first appearance of many in the USA.

Conan Doyle had a firm ground knowledge of photography but, in his straitened circumstances, he could not afford expensive equipment. He owned only a small, inexpensive and very basic box camera, little more than a modern 'throw-away' camera. In his article, however, he claimed to have taken an expensive state-of-the-art, bellows-bodied, half-plate camera, which he may have borrowed from the Burtons, and a unipod of his own invention and design which, he wrote, 'simply consists of a stout walking-staff four feet long and shod with iron. This is fitted to the camera by means of an adjustable ball-and-socket joint. The advantages which I claim for this simple arrangement are not only its lightness (a consideration which will have weight with every practical worker in the open air) but also its cheapness, and the facility it affords for the focusing of a moving object. By it free movement is secured in every direction, both horizontal and vertical, while four inches of iron spike are sufficient to guarantee perfect steadiness.' The existence of this unipod, similar to monopod camera rests used today by sport and wildlife photographers, is dubious. Indeed, it has been conjectured that Conan Doyle did not actually take any photographs on the Isle of May and that his articles for the journal were, in fact, as much exercises in poetic description of place as they were about photography. He knew the technicalities of what he was writing about but there is no known proof that he actually took any of the pictures to which he referred.

In later years, Conan Doyle seldom referred to his photographic writings. They only came to light when John Michael Gibson and Richard Lancelyn Green researched their fascinating study of his photographic essays, published in 1982. Why Conan Doyle excised these pieces from his past is something of a puzzle. The Burton family, for all the help and friendship they had offered him and his family, was not to be mentioned in his autobiography. Once he was a famous writer, he kept dark information about his early years and any connections with people who might have known about his family circumstances. One can appreciate his secrecy up to a point yet this does not fully explain his attitude. Another reason might be a contribution to the *British Journal of Photography* in 1883, complaining about a piece concerning psychic photography and a psychic force known as Od', suggested by experiments conducted by Baron Carl von Reichenbach. With phrases such as 'no amount of concession would render tenable' and 'colossal practical joke' peppering Conan Doyle's riposte, he would also certainly have wanted to have had it forgotten when he later became a convinced spiritualist.

In August 1881, Conan Doyle was awarded his Bachelor of Medicine (MB) and Master of Surgery (CM) qualifications. He did not pass with flying colours, did not gain a first-class degree: but he passed and, when one considers how much he crammed into his student years, his level of pass is hardly surprising. He achieved average grades in all but two papers where his grades were higher. He spoke of himself as being a sixty per cent man, yet he can hardly have been an average or below-average student. Bell had chosen him as his clinical clerk and, years later, said in an interview that Conan Doyle had been one of his best students, observant and keen. However, as Bell was speaking with hindsight about a very famous author, his judgment may have been clouded. Furthermore, Bell could hardly have slated Conan Doyle after the latter had announced the link between the former and his famous detective, Sherlock Holmes.

Dr Arthur Conan Doyle, MB, CM, was now ready to embark upon his career as a general practitioner, yet his problems were far from over. For one, he was virtually penniless with insufficient capital to set up a practice. And there was still his family circumstance.

Charles Doyle's health and general demeanour had been steadily going downhill through Conan Doyle's university years. By 1879, it appears the situation with Charles remaining at home was no longer tenable and the solution was mooted that he might be placed in an institution. In short, Mary Doyle was at the end of her tether. It was probably also around this time that Mary started to turn against Catholicism. Quite why she decided to break with her faith is open to conjecture and a number of reasons have been suggested over the years. The most tenable is that she was distressed that the Church had not helped her in her predicament and dismayed that her devout Catholic husband, who had played an important lay part in the local Catholic community, had not had the Christian charity to care for his family.

Charles Doyle was sent to an institution called Fordoun House, in the village of Fordoun, twenty kilometres north of Montrose. It was a nursing home specialising in the treatment of alcoholics.

With Charles out of the way, life may have been less stressful at home but it was otherwise little altered. Fordoun House was not a charity and Charles's bed had to be paid for. Waller was still living with the family, settling the rent, which he continued to do when they moved to Lonsdale Terrace in 1881.

Conan Doyle's relationship with Waller is somewhat mysterious. He made no reference at all to him in his autobiography or other writings. This is curious when one considers it was Waller who, in large part, had kept the family together and seen that their heads stayed above water. It is almost certain that, had Waller not intervened as he did, the family would have been carted off to the poorhouse.

It was only Conan Doyle who seemed to cut Waller from his life. The remainder of the family stayed on good terms with him. In 1966, Adrian Conan Doyle, the writer's son, wrote to William S. Baring-Gould, the author of the seminal study on the Sherlock Holmes stories, *The Annotated Sherlock Holmes*, that Waller's influence on the family was 'deep'. He went on to add that Waller's correspondence with Conan Doyle still existed but the letters are not available to biographers and the Conan Doyle/Waller relationship can only be guessed at until they are released and published.

There are a number of reasons why Conan Doyle would wish to hide the part Waller played in his life and that of his family. First, a connection with Waller would have made public knowledge of Charles Doyle's dipsomania, of which Conan Doyle was far from proud, and he cut him out of the record for the same reason as he removed the Burtons. Waller was intimate with the full story of Charles's condition and, from 1878, with Conan Doyle often absent and Annette in Portugal, it was Waller who had helped Mary deal with her husband.

Second, Conan Doyle may have been ashamed that his family was 'kept' by the lodger who eventually became their protector so far as being listed as responsible for the rent. He must have been upset, even galled, that he was not playing the part of the eldest son but had been forced, albeit by circumstances, to delegate this to Waller. As an adjunct to this, it may well be that he felt guilty at having, in effect, abandoned his family to Waller's care by not being the breadwinner.

Third, Conan Doyle may well have resented Waller's influence upon the family and in particular his mother, who was, inevitably, finding Waller indispensable. Despite being the head of the family, going out to earn what money he could as an assistant or writer or crew member of a whaler, Conan Doyle was still being subjugated by Waller whose presence somewhat denigrated him, lessening his self-respect. Whatever the facts of the situation, with Waller a continual presence in his life, inveigling himself into every nook and cranny of the family, it is no wonder that Conan Doyle seems to have grown to resent him and to describe his sharing of their home as disastrous. He may well have been jealous of Waller's relationship with his mother, however this may be construed. Waller had arrived in his life out of the blue. Conan Doyle had returned from years at boarding school and his time at Feldkirch suddenly to find this forceful personality ensconced in his home. It was as if he was suddenly presented with an elder brother. The question might also be asked whether Waller had not become a surrogate son for Mary, a replacement *in absentia* for her real son.

Another possibility, although unproven, is that Mary Doyle and Waller, living crammed together under one roof, had formed a different type of relationship. Her life was miserable, testing her fortitude daily, and her marriage was far from perfect, so one could hardly have blamed her for falling in love with a man upon whose charisma, strength and support she heavily relied. Although she was around fifteen years older than Waller, a romantic attachment would not have been out of the question, and Mary must have yearned for love and support.

No matter how much one speculates upon the situation, Waller's presence meant one thing. With him looking after the family in Edinburgh, Conan Doyle was released to go out into the world.

4

Savages, Fever and George Turnavine Budd

At the time Conan Doyle graduated, there were only two routes into the medical profession as a general practitioner: one was to buy oneself into an existing practice, the other to set up in practice on one's own. Both required a substantial capital outlay. The alternative, such as joining a family practice, was not open to him. He could take up employment as an assistant, remaining as such until he was eventually made a junior partner in a practice, but this was not easy, for assistants could be found cheaply and students often filled the vacancies, creating fierce competition. Another possibility was to become a locum, an impermanent substitute for another doctor temporarily absent from his practice owing to ill-health or holiday. This was a tried and tested way of gaining experience and reputation, frequently turned to by young doctors, but it was hardly going to pay much of a wage and the work was peripatetic. The options and their disadvantages were not lost on Conan Doyle, who wrote, 'I knew from my Birmingham experience how long and rough a path it was for those who had no influence and could not afford to buy.'

Despite being aware of the pitfalls, he had high hopes which he had entertained for some years. In 1879, in a letter to his mother, he had written, 'I am beginning to see that I have certain advantages which, if properly directed and given a fair chance might lead to great success, but which it would be a thousand pities to nullify aboard ship or in a country practice. Let me once get my footing in a good hospital and my game is clear. Observe cases minutely, improve in my profession, write to the Lancet, supplement my income by literature, make friends and conciliate everyone I meet, wait ten years if need be, and then when my chance comes be prompt and decisive in stepping into an honorary surgeonship.' He went on, 'We'll aim high, old lady, and consider the success of a lifetime.' Clearly, he was aiming high but his self-assurance was unjustified for a nineteen-year-old, his confidence certainly misplaced. His ambitions were fired up not only to be a doctor but, in all probability, to earn sufficient by medicine and literature to alleviate his family's reliance upon Waller and accept more of his filial responsibilities.

Where most medical students entered their course intending simply to graduate and practise, regardless of how much money they might make once qualified, Conan Doyle's family situation dictated his future to some extent. Although he enjoyed writing, and was submitting stories to editors, he was also out to make as much money as possible, not because he was discontented with his chosen profession but because he wanted to maximise his potential for his family's sake. He had, because of his personal circumstances, been unable to plot his future but now, qualified, he started to map out where he was going both as a doctor and a writer.

In the summer of 1881, as soon as his final examinations were over, he began to make plans to jump-start his career. He applied for a number of hospital vacancies but was unsuccessful in securing any. For a short time, he returned to work with Dr Hoare and travelled to Lismore in July, staying with his Foley relatives. Quite how he managed to pay for this trip is unknown: he was not earning and the family finances were as tight as ever. Perhaps the Foleys or Waller paid for his ticket.

Whilst in Lismore, Conan Doyle fell in love with several young ladies introduced to him by his relatives. One, a Miss Jeffers, he described as a 'little darling with an eye like a gimlet'. Another, Miss Elmore Welden, was by all accounts a well-built, pretty Irish girl with dark hair and eyes to match whom Conan Doyle nicknamed Elmo. Their relationship was to last some while although mostly by letter.

Another direction in which his medical career might be advanced was by his taking another doctor's position aboard ship. Now with his degree in hand, Conan Doyle could sign on as a ship's surgeon with a larger salary than he had received on the *Hope*. A seaboard existence had a number of added attractions other than the income: he could save money by going on a voyage, for whilst his salary was paid, so was his keep, and such a job would give him adventure and travel. He toyed, as he had in London in 1878, with signing on with the army or navy or, failing that, going out to India as a government doctor. Any of these would have provided a steady and not ungenerous salary, but Conan Doyle finally decided against them. Military, colonial or imperial service would have taken him away from home for lengthy periods and he was loath to be out of touch for too long with his mother and the responsibility he felt he had for her and the other children.

Following the first course, of being a ship's surgeon, he applied for a vacancy on a passenger vessel but nothing immediately came of it. In all probability, he did not apply for one specific ship but registered his name with a shipping line or two for any position that might come up.

Then, suddenly, he received a cable from the African Steam Navigation Company offering him the post of medical officer aboard the *Mayumba*, with Captain Gordon Wallace as master. He quickly accepted, putting aside his anxieties over his future for a while and, according to some accounts, calling off a planned engagement to Elmo Welden to whom he was considering proposing. The salary was £12 a month, guaranteed. If he could work like this for a year or two, he might be able to save up enough to start or buy into a practice.

The *Mayumba* was a 1,500-ton stream-powered barque launched in 1859 which carried passengers and general cargo on a regular scheduled service to West Africa. She sailed from Liverpool on 22 October 1881 with a cargo of general goods, salt, Royal Mail sacks and about thirty passengers, most of whom were heading for Madeira although there were some (as Conan Doyle was to term them) 'pleasant ladies' holding tickets through to the African coast. They were, bearing in mind the times, most likely missionaries. In addition, the passenger list included a number of Africans of whom Conan Doyle wrote that their 'manners and bearing were objectionable' and one of them had 'a choice selection of the demi-monde of Liverpool to see him off'. They were, in fact, native chieftains with their wealth based in the lucrative palm oil trade and, as frequent passengers on the line, had to be shown due respect.

The voyage was not a pleasant one although, in 1907, Conan Doyle recounted to an interviewer with hindsight that it was delightful and, in his autobiography, he described the *Mayumba* as being a trim little steamer when she was, in fact, over twenty years old and the worse for wear. As they steamed down the Irish Sea, the weather was stormy and there was a near-collision with another ship in the seasonal October sea mist. Crossing the Bay of Biscay, notorious for its rough seas, many of the passengers (and Conan Doyle himself) suffered from seasickness.

Unlike during his trip on the *Hope*, the ship's doctor was kept fully occupied. He also came to the realisation that, no matter how sick a doctor might be, he still had to tend his patients.

Once they were past Cape Finisterre, the weather calmed and Conan Doyle started to enjoy the journey to Madeira and the Canaries. From the Canaries, the *Mayumba* sailed on down the African coast *en route* for Sierra Leone. With fewer passengers on board and the seas comparatively calm, Conan Doyle had a pleasant time, lazing on deck under the canvas sun awnings in the cool evening and 'watching the flying fish as they flickered, like bars of silver, over the crests of the waves. When the moon came out, too, our ladies used to be enticed upon deck, the music and songs would while away the time.'

As with most coastal trading vessels of the time, the *Mayumba* did not only call into major harbours but hove to off or alongside many minor ports, some little more than an agglomeration of huts on the beach or, less often, by a jetty. Conan Doyle saw little of charm in the coast. It was dreary, flat and uneventful, a thin green line that slid inexorably by over the port rail. The sun beat down with a tropical ferocity. When the ship turned in towards the coast, Conan Doyle must have smelled the unmistakable odour of West Africa, of dense foliage and hot mud. Closer to shore, the heat became almost unendurable: he recorded the climate as 'hot enough to render the weight of a napkin upon your knee at dinner time utterly unbearable'.

The main ports of call the *Mayumba* put into were Freetown in Sierra Leone, Monrovia in Liberia and Lagos and Port Harcourt in Nigeria. Conan Doyle described Freetown as 'a place of death', having little that was praiseworthy to say about the Europeans living there who were, in his eyes, a desultory lot who drowned their sorrows in the time-honoured colonial fashion, with alcohol. Looking at the expatriate traders and administrators whom he came across, Conan Doyle observed, 'One wondered whether the colonies were really worth the price we had to pay.' As the *Mayumba* sailed east under the bulge of West Africa, Conan Doyle felt 'the death-like impression of Africa [grow] upon me. One felt the white man with his present diet and habits was an intruder who was never meant to be there.' He also disliked some of the cruel things he saw. When the ship entered the Bonny River to make her way up to Port Harcourt, he was disgusted with the natives he saw along the shore, 'all absolute savages, offering up human sacrifices to sharks and crocodiles'. In fact, whilst he may have observed human sacrifice, it is more likely that what he was looking at was the conducting of funeral rites: a number of the tribes in the area used to cast their dead into the sea where, inevitably, they were consumed.

The Africans ashore were his least concern, however. On board, he had to minister alike to patients and crew who came down with both malaria and blackwater fever. In Lagos, Conan Doyle succumbed to fever himself along with another of the ship's complement. For some days, he was delirious. It is uncertain what he came down with but the most likely disease is malaria, for Conan Doyle recorded how he administered a lot of quinine to his patients and this was the best available cure at the time.

The other person died but the ship's doctor pulled through to go ashore and, hiring a native canoe, he was paddled through the mangrove swamps. On another occasion, he went crocodile hunting with a rifle and, as the *Mayumba* lay off Cape Coast (in what is today Ghana), he dived overboard and swam around the hull: it was as he climbed out of the water and started up the ladder that a shark arrived. His swimming in such waters was imprudent in the extreme and it is surprising that he was permitted to take the plunge. One has to presume that Captain Wallace, with whom Conan Doyle struck up a friendship that was to last some years by correspondence, was ashore on ship's business at the time and the swim was another example of Conan Doyle's zest for risky adventure.

Despite the hardships of the voyage, the fever-ridden coast and the heat, Conan Doyle nevertheless benefited considerably, for he saw, for the first time in his life, truly strange lands, native peoples, bizarre fish, colourful snakes, massive butterflies and an environment he had, until now, only read about in fiction. It was all grist for his own literary mill. In addition, he seems to have brought a fair amount of photographic equipment with him. The camera he used was the bellows-body half-plate camera he purportedly took to the Isle of May, made by Meagher: it was an expensive camera and is not likely to have belonged to him. In addition to the camera, he had a range of lenses, a tripod, developing and printing chemicals and twelve dozen photographic plates. For a darkroom, he adapted a bathroom by hanging a towel over the porthole and covered a ship's lantern with red cloth. His photography was, however, a cause of some discomfort to the passengers not long after they sailed into the tropics. A bottle of ammonia overheated, partly vaporising the contents. The bung blew, filling the cabins with what amounted to tear gas.

The subjects of his photography ranged from general views of the various ports into which the *Mayumba* called to a slave barracoon on the island of Fernando Pó (today known as Bioko), a shark off the side of the ship, natives (including one holding an umbrella and dressed in nothing more than a plug hat), a native prince and a chieftain called Wawirra, whom Conan Doyle referred to as an African Duke of Cambridge. As well as taking pictures, Conan Doyle wrote about his photographic experiences for the *British Journal of Photography*. 'On the Slave Coast with a Camera' appeared in April 1882 with 'Up an African River with the Camera' published three months later; 'With a Camera on an African River' was printed three years on in the autumn of 1885. Conan Doyle's opinion of West Africa is summed up by his advice to any reader of his first article who might hanker after following in his footsteps – 'Don't.'

Sharks, fever and crocodiles were only the most obvious of dangers Conan Doyle faced on his voyage. A more insidious danger was drink. At first, he liberally consumed alcohol but, after a while, consciously avoided it. 'I swore off alcohol,' he wrote, 'for the rest of the voyage. I drank quite freely at this period of my life, having a head and a constitution which made me fairly immune, but my reason told me that the unbounded cocktails of West Africa were a danger, and with an effort I cut them out.' What event if any might have caused him to take such a positive decision is unclear but it could well have been linked to his seeing the alcoholic consumption of Europeans on shore and being reminded, all too painfully, of Charles Doyle.

Once the *Mayumba* started sailing between ports along the coast, she began to take on a variety of passengers who were port-hopping, using the ship as one might today an airline shuttle flight. Most of these were deck passengers who did not book cabins but slept in the open, protected from the sun by canvas awnings. One who took a cabin, for three days, was the American consul to Liberia.

Liberia was a country founded in 1822 by American slaves, returning to Africa after escaping or being given their freedom. The consul, Henry Highland Garnet, was a former slave born into slavery in the USA in 1815. Lacking a leg, which had been severed in an accident, he had become a leading exponent of abolition in the 1840s. Where Conan Doyle had disliked the palm oil barons, he immediately took to Garnet, who was exceedingly intelligent and widely read. He had lived through slavery and emancipation and had, in his own way, contributed to the history of modern times. They spent their time together discussing literature and putting the world to rights. For Conan Doyle, Garnet was yet more of the raw material for his own intellectual and literary store. 'This negro gentleman did me good,' he declared, 'for a man's brain is an organ for the formation of his own thoughts, and also for the digestion of other people's, and it needs fresh fodder.'

What drew them together is not known but Garnet was in his mid-sixties by the time he boarded the ship, a fair age for Africans whose lifespan rarely reached sixty in those days. He was to die only three months later, so it might be assumed he had requested medical attention and Conan Doyle had given it. It was for only three days that they were together and yet, in that short while, Conan Doyle was to have his mind much expanded by Garnet, who pointed out to him the terrible human waste slavery caused. This had a lasting impact upon Conan Doyle who, as a man of honour and humanity, must have been appalled by an insider's story of slavery.

Garnet's conversations did more than provide fresh fodder for Conan Doyle's mind. They gave him much-needed intellectual stimulation in the middle of what was otherwise a sterile period. Furthermore, Garnet swayed his earlier opinion of black people who, until now, Conan Doyle had tended to dislike and regard as inferior. This is not to say Conan Doyle was a racist: he was merely echoing the thoughts of the time by which white men regarded black men as their brothers but with less evolutionary or civilised development. After meeting Garnet, Conan Doyle's attitudes changed. This was a man who had been born into and lived through the worst iniquity one race had, until then, ever inflicted upon another. The result was a conflict of emotion that Conan Doyle was to express in the *British Journal of Photography*. On the one hand, he wrote that he took photographs because he 'had a great desire to "astonish the natives" by representations of their own hideous faces', but, on the other, he mentioned seeing a canoe in which he saw the 'crew of red-capped copper-faced Kroomen clamber like monkeys down the falls, and then sit like swarthy Apollos with the long oars in their dark sinewy hands'. He elaborated on the ambiguity of his racial feelings by stating in his first article that 'a great deal has been said about the regeneration of our black brothers and the latent virtues of the swarthy races. My own experience is that you abhor them on first meeting them, and gradually learn to dislike them a very great deal more as you become better acquainted with them.' However, in the second article, he moderated and changed his opinion: 'With the exception of the natives, who have been demoralised by contact with the traders and by the brutality of the slave trade, the inhabitants of the dark continent are really a quiet and inoffensive race of men, whose whole ambition is to be allowed to lead an agricultural life, unmolested and in peace.' He had come to terms with racial issues a long time before they became a major social issue and was well ahead of his age in his humanist feelings.

The *Mayumba* seems not to have gone any further down the African coast than Bioko, at which point she turned about. The voyage was one on which the ship herself traded, Captain Wallace operating as sea captains had of old, in the days before ship's agents established themselves. On the outward-bound leg, Wallace went ashore and traded for his cargo with beads and dry goods such as axes, knives and umbrellas (regarded as status symbols by the natives), the purchased cargo to be collected on the homeward journey. Bit by bit, as the vessel steamed laboriously back to Liverpool, she took on palm kernels and oil, ivory, bales of cotton, mail and, of course, passengers.

According to a story he told some while later at a public meeting, Conan Doyle had gone to sea with a trading venture of his own. He claimed to have taken with him a number of firearms and boxes of ammunition which he hoped to sell for gold. He was unsuccessful. The local chiefs were, he maintained, already supplied with the latest Remington and Winchester rifles. In all likelihood, this was the result of a fiction writer entertaining an audience. Local tribes near the coasts, especially under colonial control in and around ports, were mostly unarmed for security reasons and, whilst it was not out of the ordinary for ship's officers to seek to trade a bit on the side, one has to question Wallace allowing weapons on his vessel. At sea, all guns were (and still are) kept under lock and key to avoid mutinous uprising. In addition, one wonders where Conan Doyle found sufficient capital to buy guns with which to trade when he could not afford to buy himself into a practice. The final nail in the coffin of truth comes with Conan Doyle's remark that, in the end, all he managed to do was barter one gun for a toothbrush.

Into the final stretch of the voyage home, north of Madeira, the *Mayumba* caught fire. One of the coal storage bunkers ignited, probably owing to a combination of heat and the pressure of the weight of coal in the bunker pressing down on coal dust at the bottom. Extinguishing such a blaze was difficult and time-consuming. The coal could not be easily removed from the bunker, which could not be flooded because this would unbalance the ship. Water touching the burning coal could also turn to steam and cause a build-up of pressure in the bunker. An additional problem was the *Mayumba*'s cargo: cotton and palm oil were highly flammable.

For two days, the ship sailed north still ablaze. It seems the captain decided to try to contain the fire and let it burn itself out, a wise decision if the cargo could be kept from igniting. So fierce was the blaze that the hull plates glowed at night and the passengers and crew were in constant alert to abandon ship if the plates buckled, warped or split. Conan Doyle was put in charge of keeping the passengers calm. Eventually, the fire subsided and the danger passed, although the *Mayumba* was so badly damaged that her owners sold her soon after her return to Britain. They were fortunate the bunker did not explode: coal dust can be as explosive, unstable and volatile as gunpowder.

Conan Doyle arrived back in the port of Liverpool on 14 January 1882. His original plan had been to remain on the *Mayumba* for a while, saving his money, but during the voyage he had decided against it. He had hated the Africa run, had frequently been bored, had missed intellectual stimulation (Garnet excepted) and found the job undemanding. On his arrival back in Britain, he wrote to his mother, 'I don't intend to go to Africa again. The pay is less than I could make by my pen in the same time, and the climate is atrocious.' He may have had a miserable time but the voyage paid dividends in giving him more material for his imagination.

After four months at sea Conan Doyle was, in many respects, back where he had started but with slightly more money in hand. His life was in crisis. No hospital posts were coming his way, he still had insufficient funds to buy into a practice and he was loath to return to sea. For a while, he seems to have festered until he received an invitation to London to visit his uncles and aunt. He accepted the invitation but added a polite warning that he had become an agnostic. This did not deter them so he took the train south for what amounted to a family conference on his future.

His relatives wanted to assist him. He was, after all, heir to the family and they could not let him sink although being a doctor did not, in their eyes, demonstrate the flair usually associated with a Doyle. What was on offer was not financial assistance. The relatives suggested instead using their influence to help him get started. If Conan Doyle were to set up a practice, they would see to it that his name got around their not inconsiderable social circle of predominantly Catholic friends and acquaintances. In short, he would become a doctor to the Catholic community. This was quite an opportunity, for he would be able to build a substantial patient list quickly, something most doctors found to be the most daunting aspect of their early careers. Conan Doyle turned the offer down: he was, he admitted, no longer a Catholic and to take up the offer would amount to hypocrisy.

Such honesty was commendable but it deeply shocked and hurt his uncles and aunt. His rebuttal of Catholicism, the religion that had been central to the devout Doyle family for generations, and their kindness was beyond their comprehension. Where Conan Doyle believed he was being sincere, his relatives considered him perverse in the extreme. Richard Doyle invited him to luncheon at his club – the Athenaeum – in an attempt to heal the rift, but to no avail. When they parted, the breach was wide, for he felt bitter towards them for their denial of his moral stand and his belief in the validity of his own conscience. As far as the Doyles were concerned, Charles's crown, as family pariah, had been passed on to his son.

The crisis deepened. Conan Doyle was now unemployed and had bitten the one hand likely to have fed him.

It appears he returned to work for Dr Hoare for a while. In an edition of the *Lancet*, published on 25 March 1882, there appears a letter from him dealing with a case of leucocythaemia (today called leukaemia): it carries the Hoares' address. In characteristic Conan Doyle style, the letter was cogent and direct, suggesting a leukaemia sufferer's blood should be examined microscopically, which was not common practice at the time. He might have been sitting at the bottom of the medical barrel but Conan Doyle was still in touch with the latest advances, contributing his own thoughts to current affairs and debates.

Matters came to a climax in the late spring of 1882 in the form of a cable from Plymouth, offering him a job. It was sent by Dr George Turnavine Budd, who was, to say the least, an eccentric and instrumental in setting Conan Doyle upon his life's course.

In *The Stark Munro Letters* and his autobiography, Conan Doyle refers to Budd under a different name, calling him Cullingworth, although, in fact, when the latter was published as a serialisation in the *Strand Magazine* in 1923, the hidden identity was revealed, although he reverted to the pseudonym in the book. Conan Doyle's secrecy was not out of fear of libel, for Budd had died in 1889, but in order to protect those of Budd's relatives, including his widow, who were still alive. Those who knew Conan Doyle well were long aware of who Cullingworth was: Budd was mentioned in letters to his mother and Dr Hoare.

In his autobiography, Conan Doyle described Budd as 'half genius and half quack'. Assembling a description of Budd from both the autobiography and *The Stark Munro Letters*, one arrives at a man who was five feet nine inches tall with an arched chest, broad shoulders, well-built torso and ugly face set in a square head with a bulldog's jaw-line, overhanging brows, small bloodshot eyes, a red nose and yellow teeth from between which bellowed a stentorian voice. He was also 'as strong mentally as physically' and a 'man born for trouble and adventure, unconventional in his designs and formidable in his powers of execution'.

Budd, who was also an Edinburgh graduate, came from a medical background, his family being well-known and respected doctors in the south-west of England. He and Conan Doyle had met at university where Budd was a renowned rugby player except, according to Conan Doyle, he was 'rather handicapped by the Berserk fury with which he would play'. It is more than likely that they met through the sport. He had a labile mind, never holding on to a subject for long before abandoning it for the next, forever dreaming up inventions or money-making schemes and not infrequently going from laughter to anger in seconds. As a student, he had never worked assiduously, unable to keep his attention on anything for long enough, although he was awarded an anatomy prize.

Whilst still a student, Budd had married a girl who was both under age and a ward of court, eloping with her and dyeing his blond hair black to escape detection. The outcome, according to Conan Doyle, was a brindled effect which he stated they might have got away with unnoticed in London but which made them stick out in the small village to which they had fled. Mrs Budd was a timid, quiet, pretty young thing held fast by Budd's dominant personality. As students, their married life started off in an unfurnished apartment where guests had to sit on piles of medical journals for chairs.

The reason for Budd offering Conan Doyle a post is unknown. It might be, as has often been suggested, that Conan Doyle's forthright character was a welcome foil to Budd's mercurial nature, but even Conan Doyle himself was puzzled by the offer: 'For some reason,' he wrote in his autobiography, 'he took a fancy to me, and appeared to attach an undue importance to my advice.' Whatever the reason, Mary Doyle was antagonistic towards Budd, whom she considered an ill-chosen acquaintance.

In the spring of 1882, Conan Doyle had not heard from Budd for some time. He had gone down from the university before Conan Doyle and was not a good correspondent. However, the year before writing his offer of employment, Budd had cabled from Bristol to Conan Doyle at Dr Hoare's to ask for his advice. Conan Doyle may well have been flattered, for Budd's background was somewhat exalted.

Budd's choice of Bristol as a place at which to establish his first practice was not merely fortuitous, for his late father, William Budd, who had died in 1880, had once owned a substantial practice there, taught at the University of Bristol, was physician to the Royal Infirmary and was regarded as one of the city's heroes. A famous medical figure, he was considered by some to be one of the founders of modern preventative medicine, the first doctor to study typhoid in depth, discovering the means of contagion and advocating the decontamination of drinking water with the need for sewage disposal. In Bristol in 1866, he virtually stamped out an epidemic of cholera.

It was, therefore, an astute decision on Budd's part to try to follow in his illustrious father's footsteps. He went about it, however, in quite the wrong way, renting his father's former house, taking on servants and surrounding himself with all the trappings of a gentleman doctor in the hope that this might attract hordes of well-to-do patients. It did not. In a matter of months, he was bust. The advice he requested of Conan Doyle was what he should do; it is also possible he asked him if he would lend him some money. Conan Doyle's counsel was for Budd to convene a creditors' meeting, admit his failings, leave Bristol and try his luck elsewhere. Budd accepted the advice. Conan Doyle wrote that Budd gave his creditors 'a long and emotional speech, reduced them almost to tears with his picture of the struggles of a deserving young man', with which he won them over and had his debts deferred. He then travelled south to Plymouth which had also seen a Dr Budd in the past: his uncle John had prospered there. He started his second practice in June 1881.

In his next cable, offering Conan Doyle a job, Budd declared his practice a great success. Conan Doyle should come posthaste, by the next train. Conan Doyle was immediately cautious and, rather than head for the nearest railway station, cabled back that he would only come for a permanent position. If the account in *The Stark Munro Letters* is accurate, Budd replied that he had treated thirty thousand patients in the last year, earning more than £4,000, and going on, 'All patients come to me. Would not cross the street to see Queen Victoria. You can have all visiting, all surgery, all midwifery. Make what you like of it. Will guarantee three hundred pounds the first year.'

Dr Hoare, Mary Doyle and Waller all did their best to discourage Conan Doyle from accepting Budd's offer but he felt he could not refuse it. Spurning all the warnings, he headed south to Plymouth.

One could argue that Conan Doyle should have exercised more caution. He knew what Budd was like but he wanted to believe in him. However, although he was a qualified doctor with solid assistantship experience and two sea voyages to his credit, Conan Doyle was still very young and idealistic with at this stage a simplistic view of the world, and he may well have been blind to Budd's deficiencies, under the spell of his charisma. On top of that, an assurance of £300 per annum was too much to turn down. That it was possible Budd was grossly exaggerating his success, or that there was something suspicious about his practice, seems not to have occurred to Conan Doyle who, being honest and honourable, did not consider others capable of wilful mendacity. For all his experiences and adventures and early maturity, he still viewed the world through somewhat tinted lenses which left him still innocent, naïve and, consequently, gullible: and Budd was of a breed he had not encountered before. Where Conan Doyle trusted Budd his mother, suspicious of him, did not. She was right.

Budd and his wife lived in a grand house at 6 Elliott Terrace, The Hoe, Plymouth, but the surgery was at 1 Durnford Street, Stonehouse, a working-class area of the city. Conan Doyle moved into a room in the house on Elliott Terrace. Judging by the description of Cullingworth's home and practice in *The Stark Munro Letters*, the house was expensively furnished and the surgery was situated in a large, square, whitewashed building at which patients waited on the staircase and in the coach house as well as in a waiting room.

Whatever doubts Conan Doyle might have harboured about the viability of the practice, they must have been dispelled on his first day when, arriving for surgery, he discovered about 140 patients waiting for them. Relying upon passages about Dr Cullingworth, one can draw up a pretty accurate picture of Budd's business, which was a slick operation preying upon the poor. Examinations were free between ten in the morning and four in the afternoon, but this was what, in modern commercial terms, might be described as a loss-leader. In other words, it was a come-on, but it worked, drawing large crowds. The consultation might have been free but the prescribed medicines arising from it were not: and Budd was a generous prescriber of drugs, some of which were little more than placebos, some effective and appropriate, some downright risky.

Budd was, in short, ethically dubious. Advising his new colleague not to be too polite to the customers, he bullied his patients, yelled at them and shoved them about with all the common insolence of a brutish schoolmaster. In this way, he was the talk of the area and this, in turn, brought him more work. His arrogance was, therefore, his advertisement, and he was clearly of the opinion that any criticism was good, regardless of what it said. If he had any, his genius lay in self-promotion. As for his quackery, that was just as easily recognised by the trained eye. Budd 'invented' his own wonder cures. One of these, 'Dr Budd's blood-tonic', was advertised for sale in the *British Medical Journal* where it was claimed it renovated the blood, cleaning it of 'impurities'. A bottle contained twenty doses and retailed at three shillings and sixpence, direct from the doctor himself. The extravagant claims Budd made of his tonic were utterly fraudulent. Supporting recommendations and reports of cures were concocted by Budd himself, who showed as scant a regard for medical ethics as he did for the sick who came to him. His wife dispensed the prescriptions and Budd banked the cash, admitting that he bent the rules which, he declared, were there to stop younger, go-ahead doctors from wresting the profession from the cartel of the elderly.

For all this, Budd was nevertheless a skilled doctor who applied Bell's criteria of diagnosis. Conan Doyle had 'no doubt he did a great deal of good, for there was reason and knowledge behind all that he did, but his manner of doing it was unorthodox in the extreme'. When he was not puffing up preposterous claims for his tonic, Budd was involving himself in proper medical matters. In 1880 alone, he published articles in the *British Medical Journal* on amyloidosis, gout, lung disorders, incontinence and the use of Esmarch's bandage, a sort of rubber tourniquet used in operations. Or so it seemed. His articles were largely theoretical and lacked the backing of research such as that done for Conan Doyle's article on gelseminum. Budd was really trading on his father's reputation in order to bolster his own. Interestingly, in December 1880, one of his articles was sharply criticised by a Dr Hoare of Birmingham.

Budd's scientific interests went beyond medicine. His over-active mind was always delving into something new, usually in the pursuit of extra sources of income. In a laboratory room at Elliott Terrace, he carried out assorted experiments, some of which were of a distinctly crackpot nature. When Conan Doyle arrived in Plymouth, Budd's latest project was a means of increasing the strength of an electromagnet to such an extent that it would deflect cannonballs. The experiments involved setting up a magnet in the room and firing a pistol at it. Another of his schemes was to start a local newspaper in which he would write pithy news pieces and articles with Conan Doyle providing fiction and poems: the paper was also to be used as a vehicle to fire off a barrage of invective and libel against anyone who sniped at Budd and his medical practice. Other plans were to specialise in ophthalmology (people paid a lot to preserve their eyesight) and emigrate to South America where eye specialists were few and far between, the profit to be made out of glasses promising to be astronomical.

Budd also had a suggestion for Conan Doyle, to tide him over until he had built up a patient list. It was that he should write a novel.

At first, Conan Doyle had few patients but, ensconced in a room in the surgery, he gradually built up a list, most of them surgical patients Budd passed on to him. His newfound status as a general practitioner also excited him. At last, he was a real doctor, albeit working in an unorthodox practice with a colleague who was not only charismatic but also fascinating. Conan Doyle liked Budd, for all his faults and eccentricities, and 'admired his strong qualities and enjoyed his company and the extraordinary situations which arose from any association with him'.

Yet, as time passed, Conan Doyle started to feel uneasy. Doctoring was, for him, founded on a sense of philanthropic altruism. Budd saw it as a way to get rich quick. It was not long before Conan Doyle's concern grew. Budd was living on the edge. His ethics were pliable and, although he was turning a good income, he was not paying off his Bristol debts. When Conan Doyle reported this in a letter to his mother, her response was predictable: leave Budd and get out of Plymouth.

Mary Doyle's fears were based on more than distrust. She believed, quite justifiably, that association with Budd would harm her son's future and reputation. At some stage, she was sure Budd was going to get involved in an ethical or malpractice scandal – or worse – and whoever was with him at the time would pay the price. Conan Doyle defended his partner quite vigorously against his mother's outspoken attacks and they came close to a major confrontation over the matter.

Yet, at the same time as he was defending Budd, Conan Doyle felt that their relationship was changing. Budd was cooling towards him, his attitude coloured by his having read one of Mary Doyle's critical letters. Conan Doyle, not considering his friend capable of such calumny, took no steps to hide his correspondence, which the Budds searched out and read behind his back.

For several weeks, Budd sulked. Then, in June (as *The Stark Munro Letters* portrays it), he announced that their partnership was not the success he had hoped it might be. Patient numbers, he claimed, were dropping off because patients were confused by seeing two brass name-plates on the door. He added, in a characteristically arrogant fashion, that patients were put in a quandary because they wanted to see him but were worried they might get foisted off on to Conan Doyle. Conan Doyle's response was to wrench his name-plate off the door, but Budd reiterated that their partnership was not working and was to cease. Somewhat magnanimously, he offered Conan Doyle a pound a week to help him start up his own practice, but it was a loan, not a gift or redundancy payment.

The relationship with Budd soured, Conan Doyle went to Tavistock, a market town on the edge of Dartmoor fifteen kilometres north of Plymouth, to see if there was a shortage of doctors in the town. There was not. His departure now inevitable, he left Plymouth for Portsmouth, travelling on an Irish coaster rather than taking the train. At the end of June, he landed at Clarence Pies in Southsea, which was the area of the town facing the sea and a resort, with his clothes, his photographic equipment, his diagnostic instruments, his top hat in its shaped metal box, his name-plate and less than £10.

One can readily imagine his intense disappointment. He had gone to Plymouth with high hopes and in high spirits. Now, in next to no time, he was unemployed again and homeless.

Why Conan Doyle chose Portsmouth has never been fully understood. He claimed it was because Portsmouth was similar to Plymouth, in that it was a thriving seaport with a large, middle-class, well-heeled population in which he could readily set up his stall and, in all probability, it was as simple as that. There was also a fair population of professional, wealthy people attached to the extensive dockyards, the home of the Royal Navy. Portsmouth being an historic city and the birthplace of both Charles Dickens and George Meredith, two of Conan Doyle's literary heroes, might have given the place an added romantic appeal.

In all, Conan Doyle probably only stayed with Budd for six to eight weeks, but the swindling doctor's influence was to last much longer. Echoes of Budd's personality were to sound for years down the corridors of his stories. When Conan Doyle had a villain or an eccentric, a bizarre or macabre character, a gifted madman or a devious schemer in mind, Budd must have stood up somewhere in his subconscious, shouting for attention. Through Budd, Conan Doyle had had yet another window opened for him on the human world and, for a would-be writer, nothing can be more valuable.

It is no hyperbole to claim that Budd could have ruined Conan Doyle's medical career. He may well have almost done so: such a blunt and acrimonious dismissal must have struck hard. Yet, at the same time, the events of the first six months of 1882 toughened Conan Doyle up and, by force of circumstance, he was made to step out on his own. His pride prevented him from returning to Edinburgh or going back to Birmingham to work for Dr Hoare, so he was left with only one choice – to face the future with gritted teeth and a determination to succeed as a doctor and, if he had any time left over and needed additional income, to try and cut it as an author.

5

The Doctor and the Detective

Conan Doyle could not afford to buy into a practice so he had to start one from scratch. Although the risks were considerable, the prospect exhilarated him. He had to find a house, rent it, equip it and advertise his presence. What he lacked in material possessions he made up for with self-reliant determination. Like Munro in *The Stark Munro Letters*, Conan Doyle was young and keen. He 'had been brought up hard and was quite prepared to rough it. I was well up in my work, and believed I could get patients.'

Setting up in one's own practice could be costly and difficult and, once under way, there was no guarantee of patients joining it. They had to be attracted and the practice gradually expanded by word of mouth and reputation. The author of *Confessions of an English Doctor* emphasised that a knowledge of more than medicine was required. A doctor had to know how to manage his practice, understanding the business side of a practioner's life. Whatever people thought of a doctor's life, it was often one of very hard work, full of worries and anxieties. The hours were long and virtually continuous. If they could not find someone to cover for them when sleeping or absent, even for a short time, they had to be on call constantly. If they were not there when patients called, they would lose them to a competitor. The average doctor was not as well off as he appeared to be. A doctor might have an imposing house, a smart carriage and subscribe to local institutions, yet these did not indicate a great deal of money but more an appreciation of the advantages of appearing to be flourishing. This subterfuge could drain profits to the dregs. It had done so for Budd in

Bristol. A doctor's house might have only a few rooms furnished, those the patients entered. The house itself was important: after studying the name-plate by the door, would-be patients surveyed the house, curtains, front garden. A tidy, well-kept house meant a successful doctor whose cures and treatments worked. A rich doctor was, moreover, more likely than a poor one to give treatment for free if he felt the case merited it, and a doctor's bill was often either ignored or paid very late. It was thought that if the doctor could afford a good house then he was sure not to be short of cash. The result was that, in the late nineteenth century, more than half the doctors in Britain had difficulty making ends meet.

Immediately upon landing in Portsmouth, Conan Doyle moved into temporary accommodation for 10s 6d a week, then set out to walk about town only to become involved in a street brawl with a man who was beating his wife. The area of his lodgings was not very salubrious and was most probably in the old town with its narrow, medieval streets clustered around the naval dockyards. Portsmouth was a seafaring town and consequently rough. Knifings, muggings, prostitution and the rolling of drunk sailors were common.

The next day, Conan Doyle strolled around Portsmouth and Southsea, noting possible houses for rent and the location of other doctors' surgeries. Finally, he decided on setting up at 1 Bush Villas, Elm Grove in Southsea.

Elm Grove was a good choice. The road was a main thoroughfare and constantly busy with pedestrians and vehicular traffic. What was not so good was the fact that Portsmouth, more especially the area around and including Southsea, was already well endowed with doctors and in Southsea itself, being a somewhat up-market district, the incidence of disease and illness was in any case not as high as in some other parts of the town.

1 Bush Villas was one of a pair of houses in Elm Grove, at the time a pleasant, elm tree-lined avenue in what was a seaside resort. It was built of red brick, had three storeys and was about fifty years old. Having been empty for a while, it was not in good repair or decoration. Next door but one was a hotel whilst on the other side was St Paul's Baptist Church for which the building had been used as a chapterhouse and to which it belonged. The rent was £40 per annum. None of the buildings remain, having been bombed in 1941. To secure the property, Conan Doyle gave his Uncle Henry and Budd as referees. For the first time ever, Conan Doyle was on his own, responsible only to and for himself.

Having rented the house, Conan Doyle bought £12 worth of drugs on credit, three chairs, two small tables, curtains, a fender for the grate, a washstand and bowl, an umbrella stand, a bed, a carpet and three pictures. These came from an auction in Portsea for a total of £4. As many doctors did at first, Conan Doyle put the furniture and carpet into the public rooms with medical textbooks, his doctor's case and the usual trappings of a surgery. The rest of the house, out of sight of the patients, was nothing more than a hovel in which Conan Doyle used his trunk as a larder and table, at which he sat on a small stool. A curtain hung across the hallway prevented patients from seeing the bare interior of the house, whilst more curtaining was arranged with the furniture in the consulting room to give the impression of space. The brass name-plate was mounted on the iron railings outside the house and a red lamp which was the sign of a general practitioner was purchased (also on credit): in a seaport such as Portsmouth, it might well have been misconstrued by sailors, but the surgery was just outside the disreputable area of the town so presumably no one mistook the house for a brothel. For his first few nights in his new home and business, Conan Doyle slept in his coat upon a mattress made of the straw the drug bottles had been packed in, having written to ask his mother to send him some bedclothes, which she did with a few other niceties such as a tea cosy and some ornaments.

All that remained was to wait for patients to arrive. Conan Doyle sat at his window on his first day and watched people read the name-plate, but no one came in. It was not permitted by law for a doctor to advertise, but Conan Doyle got round this with a cunning ruse that was discovered by Geoffrey Stavert when researching his intriguing book *A Study in Southsea: The Unrevealed Life of Doctor Arthur Conan Doyle*. He placed a notice in the *Portsmouth Evening News* of Saturday, 1 July 1882, running it on the next week, stating, 'Dr Doyle begs to notify that he has removed to 1, Bush Villas, Elm Grove, next to the Bush Hotel.'

At first, all seemed well, but a problem soon arose. Budd's promised pound a week failed to arrive. Instead, he wrote to say that he had found a scurrilous letter written by Mary Doyle to her son torn up in the fireplace in Elliot Terrace which libelled him and he was, therefore, having nothing more to do with him. It was true that Mary Doyle had written such a letter but her son had brought it away with him and now must have realized than the Budds had been spying on him. What was more, Budd had delayed writing and withdrawing his financial help until after Conan Doyle had signed his rental agreement. Clearly, Budd's bile was equal in quantity to his penchant for dubious medical practice.

He wanted to see Conan Doyle fail, which was something Conan Doyle himself could not understand. His honest nature told him that, once the pound was offered, it would be paid regardless, and he could not envisage someone breaking their word so easily and without any consideration for the result, for this was not the manner in which he would have behaved. In reply, he curtly told Budd he had now seen the true nature of his erstwhile partner and was of the same opinion as his mother, that Budd was a bounder. However, Budd's plans fell apart – as they so often did – and whilst Conan Doyle managed to keep going, Budd was in due course subject to official investigation that criticised his dispensing methods and left him paranoid with the fear that someone was out to poison him, chemically testing all his food before he ate it. He died in 1889, cut off by his family and leaving a wife and four daughters in penury. The cause of death was given as a cerebral abnormality, probably a brain tumour. Conan Doyle sent Budd's widow some money to help tide her over and, in later years, sent her occasional sums to help her raise her children.

When Budd's pound did not materialise, Mary Doyle sent her son the sum to make it up, dipping into her meagre savings for the payments. This must have caused her hardship but, ever supportive of her son, if critical of his choice of partners, she sent it all the same. The money did not come without strings, for Mary decided she wanted her other son, Innes, now ten years old, to go and stay with his older brother who, in any case, welcomed the move as he was feeling lonely in his new home. The weekly pound, plus an advance of £10 from the editor of London Society against future writing, settled the first quarterly rent and put Conan Doyle on a steady keel.

Innes's being sent south to Portsmouth at this juncture may have had another purpose, for his mother was moving. In 1882, Mary Doyle finally left Edinburgh to live on Waller's estate at Masongill. She was permitted to take Masongill Cottage, on the estate, rent-free for herself and her daughters, Ida and Dodo. After the squalor and misery of so many years in Edinburgh, the move must have been quite fabulous for the three of them. Gone were the polluted, sooty air of the city, the crowded streets and ever-present stink of effluent. In their place was a little village on the western edge of the beautiful Yorkshire Dales, not twenty-five kilometres from the sea at Carnforth and only five from the little town of Kirby Lonsdale. The wind was clean, the streams coming off the hills sparkling and potable. They had not known anything like it.

According to Edwards, Waller also returned to Masongill in 1882, living there until he died in 1932, surrendering his career in Scotland and no longer publishing medical papers. Quite what his motives were in returning can only be guessed at: he had inherited the estate from his father in 1877 but had no apparent reason to return. His mother was running the property and she may have been unwell (for she died, bedridden, in 1887) so that might have called him home. The owner of the estate also having to reside there as a stipulation in the terms of ownership might have been another reason. As for giving up his medical career, Waller may have decided to call it a day after failing to be appointed Examiner in Pathology in January 1881 and, later, to the chair of pathology at the university in Edinburgh. Or was it because of the Doyles that he went? There is some evidence to suggest that Waller may have taken Charles Doyle out of Fordoun House and moved him to Masongill by way of experiment, for it is said that he established what he referred to as a surgery on the estate. It is Edwards' opinion, and it seems more than feasible, that Charles may have been taken to Masongill but, when his health did not improve, he had to be returned to confinement. In a short story, 'The Surgeon of Gaster Fell', published in 1890, Conan Doyle wrote of a brother and sister looking after their father in a place described very much like Masongill, the father eventually being incarcerated in Kirby lunatic asylum. The similarity between the fictional father and Charles Doyle is striking: 'My poor father's disease [wrote the brother to the tale's narrator] rapidly assumed both a religious and a homicidal run, the attacks coming on without warning after months of sanity. It would weary you were I to describe the terrible experiences which his family have undergone.' The story was published in *Chambers' Journal* in 1890 but, even twenty-five years later, was cut by Conan Doyle before its book publication, presumably to avoid embarrassment to either himself or his mother. One has to wonder, however, if this really did happen and, if Charles Doyle was taken to Masongill, why he was not interned in a local asylum (as the character in the story was) rather than sent all the way back to Scotland where he lived for the remainder of his years.

The locals in Masongill thought of Waller as a cold fish. Although he would give medical advice and treat the sick in the absence of the local doctor, he was disliked as a snob and he controlled his tenants with petty rules. Conan Doyle's character Reverend Pinfold, in his novel *Micah Clarke*, is a cruel but accurate description of Waller, with his pompous manner, hooked nose and bandy legs: indeed, Waller was so bandy-legged that, when he died, it is reported his lower limbs had to be bound together so the undertaker could fit him in his coffin. He lived the life of a recluse at Masongill, conducting experiments in his surgery and marrying in 1896, at the age of forty-three, Ada, a local governess. They had no children and the estate was sold after their deaths.

What Conan Doyle thought of his mother living at Masongill, and accepting even more support from Waller, is not fully known, but he did resent Waller's continual presence in the family circle and he must have felt uncomfortable visiting his mother there. He must surely have been, even begrudgingly, grateful to Waller for his unstinting support of the family, and it has been said that he even had a portrait of him hanging in his home. Yet the fact remains he did not mention Waller at all in his autobiography.

If there was more to the relationship between Waller and Mary Doyle than is at first apparent, Conan Doyle's discomfort must have been considerable. It did not, however, prevent him from going to see his mother, and he was a regular visitor, often spending Christmas at Masongill throughout the 1880s. He even used the place in stories, for, in addition to 'The Surgeon of Gaster Fell', Conan Doyle wrote about Masongill as Dunklethwaite in a tale called 'Uncle Jeremy's Household', published in the Boy's Own Paper in 1886.

Mary Doyle lived at Masongill until 1917 despite, it is said, Ada Waller's dislike of her husband's friendship with her, which was so manifest that Waller was often to be found at Mary Doyle's cottage: he even frequently ate his meals there. Clearly, they meant a lot to each other because there was a real affection between them of which the latecomer, Waller's wife, was justly jealous.

She was not the only one to wonder what had gone – or was going – on between her husband and his former landlady. The Waller servants were also suspicious. According to an article published in the Yorkshire county magazine, the Dalesman, in 1975, written by W.R. Mitchell, who had spoken to some of the Wallers' servants, rumours were rife beneath stairs. It was implied that Waller and Mary Doyle had a stronger than platonic friendship and that Dodo was Waller's, not Charles Doyle's, child. When Waller died, the servants were ordered to take all his papers and notebooks from the attic and burn them. They did, but one of them read a few pages of a notebook before casting them into the flames. They contained an account by Ada of her insufferable life as her husband's wife.

The chances of there being an amorous relationship between Waller and Mary Doyle are, it must be said, not at all unfeasible if they are perhaps slim. However much she may have yearned for masculine love and companionship in her life over the years, an affair does not seem to fit into her nature as we know it, or comply with her belief in family honour. That Waller was not much older than her eldest son would also militate against such an alliance, especially in the mores of the times. Having said that, such an alliance would certainly account for Conan Doyle's excision of Waller from his writings. Even the servants' tittle-tattle might have been enough to secure the omission. He would have wanted to keep the facts, even the rumours, hidden to spare his mother and sisters any pain or embarrassment.

His mother might have been settled in Masongill, but Conan Doyle was not so secure in Southsea. Once more, the perennial problems that beset a young medical practitioner crowded in on him. A doctor of a mature age inspired confidence in his patients: youth was a handicap. He had to dress smartly in a frock-coat and top hat, and it was advantageous, so the author of *Confessions of an English Doctor* suggested, to grow a beard to look older. At all times, he had to be courteous, gentlemanly and seem wholesome, avoid drink and not be seen to smoke in public. Manners made the man in medical practice.

Initially, things were very hard indeed and filled with disappointment: when Conan Doyle thought he had his first patient it transpired it was a gas meter reader. It appears that the first *bona fide* patient was fairly prompt in coming forward, within the first five or six days, but, for some months, only a few a week turned up. This forced him to live exceedingly frugally, on no more than one shilling a day, drinking tea and eating only bread and bacon with a saveloy as a rare treat. In six months, he lost a stone in weight. Other luxuries were cut. He stopped smoking. He hired no servants, which must have caused people to talk. He went out in the late evening to buy his food in cheap stores in Portsea which usually catered to the poor and sailors and he did his own housework after dark so as not to be seen: the brass name-plate was always polished at night. It was also at night that he took his exercise, walking down to Clarence Parade, crossing Southsea Common and walking along the seafront or on the pebbled foreshore. He dared not go out by day for fear of missing a patient. Some nights, he would walk miles, out through Portsmouth to Portsdown Hill or right along the shore from Clarence Pier in the west to the spit at Eastney and the entrance to Langstone Harbour.

Those patients who did come to him were not of the well-heeled Southsea middle class but mostly poor, often only just able to pay his fee. In his autobiography, Conan Doyle told the story of being called out to see to a sick patient. Bending over the bed, he expected to see a child but what he actually saw 'was a pair of brown sullen eyes, full of loathing and pain, which looked up in resentment to mine. I could not tell how old the creature was. Long thin limbs were twisted and coiled in the tiny couch. The face was sane but malignant. "What is it?" I asked in dismay when we were out of hearing. "It's a girl," sobbed the mother. "She's nineteen." Oh! if God would only take her! What a life for both! And how hard to face such facts and accept any of the commonplace explanations of existence!' On another occasion, he treated a gypsy child with measles, which was a common killer in those days, and not only waived his charge but gave the child's family all the change in his pocket. Conan Doyle was greatly touched by such experiences and he never took advantage of the poor. He had lived like this and, in truth, was not so far off poverty himself. At times, he could not afford a stamp for a letter to his mother and he pawned his watch three times. For a while, he obtained his food by barter, exchanging it for treatment with an epileptic grocer; but the grocer died.

He might have despised Budd, but Conan Doyle did pick up one acceptable and necessary trait from him – the need for self-promotion – and, on 2 November 1882, an accident in the street outside the surgery gave him a fine opportunity. He attended the scene, then had the perspicacity to contact the local *Evening News* with a report about how a Mr Robinson had fallen from his horse in Elm Grove, owing to a stirrup breaking, the horse falling on him, whereupon he was 'conveyed to the house of Dr Conan Doyle, of Bush Villas, and that gentleman was able to pronounce that, though considerably shaken and bruised, there was no injury of any consequence'.

Although relations with his uncles were strained, Conan Doyle did receive an offer of help from Richard Doyle, who sent him a letter of introduction to the Catholic Bishop of Portsmouth. There being no Catholic doctor in Portsmouth, this letter could have been a godsend, but Conan Doyle burnt it. He would not compromise his ideals, although he did meet his Uncle Richard from time to time and even saved his life when on a visit to London by rushing him into hospital when he suffered a heart attack. Richard eventually died of apoplexy at the Athenaeum Club on 11 December 1883, having had a premonition of his demise which induced him to paint a watercolour of a hay wain piled up with corpses.

With young Innes residing in Elm Grove, the brothers got along famously, the lad glad to be away from an all-female household, Conan Doyle acting the surrogate father. Innes earned his keep by doing simple housework chores, going shopping or running errands and answering the door to patients in lieu of a maid. After the surgery was closed, Innes accompanied his brother on his long walks, providing a light relief for Conan Doyle's worries. In *The Stark Munro Letters*, he wrote of Innes, 'He shares the discomforts of my little menage in the cheeriest spirit, talks me out of my blacker humours, goes on long walks with me, is interested in all that interests me . . . I always talk to him exactly as if he were of my own age.' They were more than brothers but friends, despite their age difference. Conan Doyle had hardly ever been a brother in any case, being away at school, at university or at sea for most of Innes's life.

During the day, Innes attended a local preparatory school, Conan Doyle taking responsibility for seeing he was educated and, in effect, taking over full charge of his brother's upbringing. When not in school, Innes took an active interest in his big brother's life as a letter from him to Mary Doyle shows: 'We have made three bob this week. We have vaxenated a baby and got hold of a man with consumtion . . .' He also kept a daily log which gives some idea of life in Dr Doyle's surgery: 'This morning after breakfast Arthur went downstairs and began to write a story about a man with three eyes, while I was upstairs enventing a new water-works that will send rokets over the moon in two minutes and they will send small shot at the same distance then it was a quarter past one, so, I had to go and put on the last potatoes the only six we had in the world.'

Bit by bit, the practice grew and money started to come in so that, after six months, Conan Doyle was able to breathe more easily and allow for a few luxuries. He took up smoking a pipe again and, in December 1882, hired a housekeeper. She was also a good front, telling patients he was very busy but that he would squeeze them into his packed schedule. A motherly woman, she was to be reincarnated in due course as Mrs Hudson, Sherlock Holmes's housekeeper at 221B Baker Street.

With increased income, the house started to gain a bit of comfort. More furniture was purchased, the trunk no longer served as a table and the walls were painted or papered. Mary Doyle and Aunt Annette sent books, oddments of domestic possessions, a musical clock that chimed an Irish jig and a bust of Conan Doyle's grandfather, John Doyle, which stood on a table in the hallway, ready to impress patients. Some of his father's morbidly brooding paintings were hung on the walls although they were hardly appropriate for a surgery. His professional notepaper, paid for by Mary Doyle, bore the family heraldic crest.

In the first year, Conan Doyle earned £154. The following year he took £250, whereafter his earnings as a doctor stayed on a plateau of around £300 per annum for the remainder of his time in Southsea. When his first income tax return was sent back to him, Conan Doyle found that the revenue inspector had written 'Not satisfactory' across the document. Conan Doyle sent it back, marked 'I entirely agree', which produced a visit from the taxman and a call for Conan Doyle to appear before the inspectors, where he successfully justified his accounts as genuine. His brush with the revenue bureaucracy must have rankled for some while, for, eight years on, he published a letter in the local paper criticising the assessment methods.

Conan Doyle's practice was always small but not because of any failing on his part. He was respected, considered a good, kind man and a competent general practitioner, and an income of £300 a year was acceptable for a successful professional. His problem was that the town was well endowed with already established doctors, some of whom actually assisted him in gaining business. Dr William Royston Pike, Honorary Surgeon to the Royal Portsmouth Hospital, a medical referee for the General Assurance Company and former Medical Officer of Health for Southsea, referred patients to him, whilst a dentist practising across the road, William Henry Kirton, did likewise. Conan Doyle was also successful in being appointed consultant to the Gresham Life Insurance Company, for which he examined patients seeking cover. The local manager of the Gresham Insurance Company was George Barnden, a member of the Southsea Bowling Club of which Conan Doyle was also a member: whether he met Barnden through the club and was offered the post, or was put up for membership by Barnden, is unknown.

His joining of the bowling club, about ten minutes' walk from the surgery, must have been one of his first social moves. After games, the members decamped to the Bush Hotel which had an excellent billiards rooms, so Conan Doyle was able to kill two sporting birds with one stone, as well as meet local businessmen and hopefully gain a few patients along the way. During his time in Southsea, he rose to become president of the bowling club, winning a silver cigar case in a tournament. Indeed, it being the done thing for doctors to join every activity going, to enhance their social status as much as their patient register, Conan Doyle signed up with a number of sporting clubs.

Sport was important to Conan Doyle throughout his life. Proud of his sporting abilities, he considered the ability to play well and fairly the sign of a man and a gentleman. Energetic at everything he did, he wrote in his autobiography that sport 'gives health and strength, but above all it gives a certain balance of mind. To give and to take, to accept success modestly and defeat bravely, to fight against odds, to stick to one's point, to give credit to your enemy and value your friend – these are some of the lessons which true sport should impart.' He never played by halves and suffered for it. A blow from a cricket ball left a lasting weakness in his left leg, and he badly injured two ribs and broke three fingers playing cricket or soccer.

Football was one sport of which he was particularly fond and he was a founding member of the Portsmouth Football Club when it was inaugurated in the autumn of 1884. He often played in goal but, as Geoffrey Stavert has discovered, he also played as a back under the pseudonym of A.C. Smith. The local paper hailed him as 'one of the safest Association backs in Hampshire'. Smith played, by all accounts, a vigorous and tactical game, possessing a strong and accurate kicking ability. In the football off-season, Conan Doyle was a playing member of Portsmouth Cricket Club, which he successfully captained for several years, scoring over a century against the Royal Artillery at the beginning of the 1889 season. He was an all-rounder, a careful batsman and an adequate bowler, and declared that cricket gave him more pleasure during his life than any other branch of sport. Broken fingers apart, it seems he not infrequently suffered for it. He told Dr Hoare in 1890 he had strained his back so severely playing the game that he could hardly stand up.

It was not all hale and hearty sport, however. Conan Doyle also exercised his mind as much as his muscles by becoming a member of the Portsmouth Literary and Scientific Society, which met every other Tuesday through the winter months to debate current affairs or issues, or hear presentations by members or guest speakers. His joining had not only an intellectual advantage but a social and professional one as well. The society had many of Portsmouth's upper-class élite and upwardly mobile middle class amongst its number and, with the membership fee standing at one guinea, it was a select assembly, exclusively male until 1888, although women could attend meetings as guests. Conan Doyle was put up for election in November 1883 and, on 4 December, he gave his first address, entitled 'The Arctic Seas'. The lecture, accompanied by specimens loaned by a taxidermist, was very well received. Spurred on by his success, Conan Doyle played an active role in the society, being voted joint secretary for the 1886/7 season of events. He was a regular attender at meetings, actively participated in debates and presented talks on Edward Gibbon, Thomas Carlyle and George Meredith. He also devised his own ending to Dickens's enigmatic unfinished novel,

The Mystery of Edwin Drood, with which he entertained a meeting of the society.

The society had a lasting effect upon Conan Doyle. It brought him short-term benefits in the form of patients, but it also taught him to speak in public, widened his intellect and brought into his life people who were to greatly impinge upon it. With his prodigious memory – it was said that in later life he could recall minute details of a book he had not read for two decades – he squirrelled away information for later use in stories. Stavert has compiled a few examples. In 1884, General Alfred Wilks Drayson addressed the society on 'The Earth and Its Movement', talking at length about the ecliptic, the annual path traced by the sun in twelve months, which he called the Obliquity of the Ecliptic: in the Sherlock Holmes tale 'The Adventure of the Greek Interpreter', published in 1893, Holmes talks to Dr Watson about everything from 'golf clubs to the causes of the change in the obliquity of the ecliptic'. Later, in 1887, Reverend H. Shaen Solly spoke on the history of medieval miracle plays: in *The Sign of Four*, published in 1890, Holmes discusses the subject as if he were an authority on it.

Through the society and his sporting activities, Conan Doyle became widely known and liked. He was settled in his career, enjoying Portsmouth for its naval and literary history, and he continued with his hobby of photography, allied to which he carried on writing photographic articles. One, in May 1884, was entitled 'Easter Monday with the Camera', and contained the lines 'Portsmouth is never at any time a dull place. The coming and going of men-of-war and transports, the large garrison, the crowds of "blue jackets", and the fashionable influx into Southsea – all prevent its ever becoming so.' It went on to describe a huge parade by volunteers on Portsdown Hill on Easter Monday, which appealed not only to his photographic eye but also to his patriotism. Even Innes enjoyed the military atmosphere of the city, and Conan Doyle wrote that 'his future career was marked out by his natural tastes, for he was a born leader and administrator'. Innes was to grow up to become an adjutant-general.

As a young doctor, Conan Doyle was a handsome man with greyish blue eyes, a receded brow, brown hair slicked down with hair oil, sideburns and a thick moustache. Over six feet tall, he weighed at least fifteen stone but it was all trim, lean muscle. He carried himself erect, proud but not haughty and, although he was by no means wealthy, he was a beacon to pretty girls and their bridegroom-hunting mothers. He lived a full social life, receiving visits from relatives and friends, attending dances and generally behaving himself save for one slip when he got, as he put it, drunk as an owl at a dance and proposed to a number of young women, one of whom contacted him the next day to say she had accepted his proposal but had meant not to. He was let off lightly. Such conduct could have done for his practice.

Young ladies seem not to have held a significant place on his agenda in Southsea. He was still in touch with Elmo Welden and, although their relationship had cooled, they did meet when she was on holiday on the Isle of Wight during which they made at least one trip to the theatre in London, meeting Aunt Annette at the same time. After a quarrel, Elmo went to Switzerland and Conan Doyle had little to do with the fair sex. That was to change in 1885.

Conan Doyle took in a young man as his patient. He had been under Dr Pike's care but Pike had called Conan Doyle in for a second medical opinion. The patient, Jack Hawkins, was suffering from cerebral meningitis, having come to Portsmouth in October 1884 with his widowed mother and elder sister from Minsterworth in Gloucestershire. Their lodgings were unsuitable for an invalid so Conan Doyle took Jack in as a resident at Bush Villas. There was no cure for meningitis and he survived only a few days. As a result of tending for Jack and consoling the family on his death, he met Louise, Jack's sister.

The circumstance of their coming together had much to do with their developing relationship. A withdrawn, sweet-natured girl, Louise was grief-stricken. Conan Doyle was strong and protective. He called her Touie and later declared that 'no man could have had a more gentle or amiable life's companion'.

Twenty-seven years old, she was not a beauty but her round face and full mouth held a certain innocence. Her hair was light brown and slightly frizzy, her eyes large, doe-like and blue-green whilst her nose was broad yet appealing. Her body was well rounded and petite in a plumpish sort of fashion. Her character was gentle, quiet and stoical, yet she had a subtle sense of fun.

The relationship burgeoning, Mary Doyle travelled from Masongill to meet Louise and approved of her. The engagement was announced in late April 1885. The next month, Louise and her mother went to stay at Masongill and the wedding took place on 6 August, at St Oswald's Church in Thornton-in-Lonsdale, three kilometres from Masongill. For some unfathomable reason, Waller was best man. After visiting Stonyhurst, where Conan Doyle played a game of cricket, they honeymooned in Dublin. Across the Irish Sea, he had another – and final – contact with his old school: he abandoned his bride for yet another cricket match in which he played for a Stonyhurst team on tour in Ireland. This was to set a pattern throughout their marriage: whatever the diversion, if Conan Doyle wanted to pursue it, Conan Doyle did. His wife was obliged to tag along.

The school seems to have made little of the fact that Conan Doyle was a former pupil, more or less ignoring him even after he became famous. The history of the school, published in 1901, made no mention of him. The most illustrious old boy was given as Charles Waterton, the naturalist-cum-explorer of South America who died in 1865. No doubt part of the reason Conan Doyle was no longer actively remembered by the school lies in the fact that he had renounced Roman Catholicism and, later in life, became a devout spiritualist who concertedly attacked his former faith.

The honeymoon over, the couple returned to Bush Villas. Mrs Hawkins moved in with her daughter and son-in-law, and Innes went off to board at Richmond Public School in Yorkshire, of which Waller was a former pupil. The fees were most likely paid by Conan Doyle's sister, Annette.

Of his marriage, Conan Doyle wrote, 'there was no single occasion when our affection was disturbed by any serious breach or division, the credit of which lies entirely with her own quiet philosophy'. In short, they were very close but there was little passion between them. He doted upon her with the respectful adoration of a Victorian husband, his powerful character counteracting her simplicity and meekness. While he attended surgery, his sport and other gentlemanly pursuits, she, admiring her husband's cleverness, ran the house, sewed and played the piano. She was the perfect doctor's wife and a good professional attribute, for married doctors were preferred by female patients and the right wife could encourage patronage or popularity. In addition, Louise also received an annual income of £100 from her late father's estate, meaning they could enjoy, as Conan Doyle put it, 'the decencies, if not the luxuries, of life'.

Whatever good Louise brought to the practice, Conan Doyle was simultaneously busy bettering himself to raise his local profile. He became a member of the British Medical Association and, over the winter of 1884, had written an original research thesis on *tabes dorsalis*, a wasting of the spinal cord, thought to be a syphilitic condition but which Conan Doyle believed due to the constriction of the blood supply. He also experimented on himself again, to determine the effects of amyl nitrate inhalation. Submitting his thesis to the University of Edinburgh in the spring, he was called to Edinburgh in July, orally examined and awarded a doctorate in medicine, allowing him to add the letters MD after his name.

Conan Doyle was now reasonably comfortably off. He was better qualified and could have looked to a future as a specialist, was happily married, organised literary soirées in his house and was a respected local figure: the Southsea Bowling Club gave Dr and Mrs Doyle a dinner service as a wedding present and token of their regard for their president. Yet this was not all. Marriage had brought something else.

'After my marriage,' he wrote in his autobiography, 'my brain seems to have quickened and both my imagination and my range of expression were greatly improved.' He kept an intricate diary of his everyday life and read as widely as ever, from the latest medical journals to reference tomes and the newest fiction, gleaning facts, listing books read and developing ideas in a number of card-bound exercise books. Methodical all his life, these notebooks were the database of his creation, containing research notes, plans for stories, recorded conversations of interest – anything of use to a thinking man or a writer.

His letters to the press and journalism continued, too. He denounced the suspension of the Contagious Diseases Acts in the *Medical Times and Gazette*, wrote about gout in the *Lancet*, advocated the building of a local recreation ground, commented upon the value of American medical diplomas, supported plans for a memorial for Queen Victoria's jubilee and championed vaccination by criticising those who condemned it as risky.

Much of Conan Doyle's medical background came to light with the 1984 publication of *The Medical Casebook of Doctor Arthur Conan Doyle* by Alvin E. Rodin and Jack D. Key. In a closely researched study, they showed how imaginative and advanced Conan Doyle was in his medical thinking, particularly concerning bacterial infectious diseases and methods of immunisation. Amongst other details they discovered, they indicated the importance of an 1883 article he wrote for *Good Works* entitled 'Life and Death in the Blood'. Whilst a medical piece, it asked the reader to shrink himself to microscopic size for a tourist trip through the blood system, looking at the cells, seeing how toxins attack and antitoxins protect, watching the war between bacteria and blood. It was pure science faction, a precursor to his science fiction stories and the basis, eighty-three years on, of the Oscar-winning sci-fi movie *Fantastic Voyage*. Perhaps there was something about Elm Grove and King's Road that made them conducive to science fiction: it is appealing to think how often Conan Doyle, going to the shops, passed by the draper's store less than a hundred metres from his surgery where, from 1881 to '83, one of the shop assistants was a young man called H.G. Wells. They must even have met, for the proprietor of the shop was one of Conan Doyle's patients.

All the while, Conan Doyle ploughed on with his fiction-writing, squeezing this in between patients, working on it in the evenings. The fallacy that he wrote because he lacked patients is untrue: the more his practice grew, the more he wrote. A very fast writer, though his copperplate handwriting rarely suffered from speed, he had the enviable knack of being able to drop a story in mid-sentence when the doorbell sounded, then pick it up again the minute the interruption was past. Additionally, the original material set down was largely unchanged, for his manuscripts show few corrections or alterations. He could also switch himself off from his surroundings and write regardless. Jerome K. Jerome recorded how Conan Doyle 'would sit at a small desk in a corner of his own drawing-room, writing a story, while a dozen people round him were talking and laughing. He preferred it to being alone in his study. Sometimes, without looking up from his work, he would make a remark, showing he must have been listening to our conversation; but his pen had never ceased moving.'

His output of short stories was vast, covering a wide scope of subject matter from thriller to historical, medical to sporting. It may be argued, although Conan Doyle himself insistently refuted it, that he was the father of the modern short story, for he approached the genre with a taut control and disciplined structure that have been the basis for short fiction ever since.

Prolific he may have been, but he was still not always successful in placing his work. Most of his stories were adventure yarns for magazines such as *London Society*, *All the Year Round*, *Temple Bar* and the *Boy's Own Paper* and he earned between three and four guineas for each. One tale in the *Boy's Own Paper* in 1884, 'Crabbe's Practice', was about a young and unprincipled doctor not unlike Budd. In 1883, the *Cornhill Magazine* took 'J. Habakuk Jephson's Statement', based upon the finding of the *Marie Celeste* 'ghost' ship. The hero of the story is a consumptive American doctor sailing for his health who, in passing, delivers a strong condemnation of slavery. It was Conan Doyle's first break into real literature, for the magazine took only quality fiction. The fee was twenty-nine guineas. Conan Doyle was staggered.

Critical response to the story was excellent. The *Illustrated London News* compared it to Edgar Allan Poe and, the story being published anonymously as was editorial policy, both critics and readers ascribed it to Robert Louis Stevenson. The *Boston Herald* accepted the fiction as truth. So convincing was the story that Her Majesty's Advocate General in Gibraltar, where the ghost ship had been taken for examination, issued an official denial.

Such success pleased Conan Doyle but it did not go to his head. He still wrote for the pulp market because he needed the money, and other submissions to the *Cornhill Magazine* were gently but firmly rejected by the editor, James Payn, an experienced all-round jobbing writer who believed in encouraging young talent. His editorial judgment was good; his handwriting, however, was virtually illegible due owing to rheumatoid arthritis and Conan Doyle had a hard time deciphering his rejection slips.

Payn was, nevertheless, greatly to influence Conan Doyle's literary future by not only publishing the story but introducing him to literary circles. In 1884, Conan Doyle attended a dinner at the Ship Hotel in Greenwich, held for contributors to the magazine. There, he met Payn and a number of other literary or artistic figures of the day, including the artist and novelist George Du Maurier. It was the first occasion on which Conan Doyle mixed with those who were to become his peers.

Conan Doyle knew literary success on a grand scale would not come through short stories. He had to write a novel with his name on the cover. Unfortunately, the manuscript of one early novel, *The Narrative of John Smith*, was lost in the post. This might have been just as well. Conan Doyle wrote that it was 'of a personal-social-political complexion' and 'perilously near to the libellous'.

Undeterred by rejection or loss, he soldiered on, facing disappointment with stoicism. Or complaint. He entered a competition in the magazine *Tit-Bits*, but lost to what he considered was an inferior entry. So incensed was he that fair play had not been seen to be done, Conan Doyle offered to put up £25 to match a similar sum from the publishers if the entries were reassessed by an independent judge. Not surprisingly, he received no reply.

Early in 1884, Conan Doyle began a new novel, *The Firm of Girdlestone*, which he dedicated to William Burton. Nearly two years in the writing, the main character was Thomas Dimsdale, a medical student at the University of Edinburgh, and the story contained many autobiographical fragments. Thomas failed his course and was employed by John Girdlestone, an African trader: Conan Doyle, drawing upon his *Mayumba* voyage, had a field day criticising her owners. The novel was well written, the action convincing and the characters good if one-dimensional, but it was poorly paced with too much description padding out a predictable narrative. Publishers were unanimous in their rejection although the story was later serialised in the *People* and published as a book in 1890, much rewritten by Conan Doyle, who summed it up with the remark, 'Save for occasional patches it is a worthless book . . . too reminiscent of the work of others.' An attempted collection of short stories similarly found no fortune.

In a lecture he gave to the Authors' Club in 1896, Conan Doyle said the turning point in a writer's career comes not when he sends out or sells his first efforts but when he is first commissioned to write. His first commission, he claimed, was 'to translate an article about gas-pipes, from the German, for the "Gas and Water Gazette"' in November 1886. It was entitled 'Testing Gas Pipes for Leakage'.

This may well have seemed a turning point to Conan Doyle but a much greater one had already unwittingly occurred, for, in April 1886, he had finished a novella entitled *A Study in Scarlet*.

The main character was a detective called Sherlock Holmes.

In the December 1900 edition of the *Westminster Gazette*, Conan Doyle said the idea of writing about a detective came to him around 1886 when he had read some detective stories and thought they were nonsensical because the plots, often thin, unimaginative and imitative, either revolved about coincidence or relied for their denouement on the authors revealing vital clues that had previously been hidden from the readers. Furthermore, the detectives themselves were stereotypes who lacked depth and did not display their lines of deduction. He wanted to create, he said, 'a scientific detective, who solved cases on his own merits and not through the folly of the criminal'.

In short, Conan Doyle shrewdly spotted a gap in the market, yet he did not set out to write a series of detective stories but just one short novel.

The word 'detective' was conceived in 1843, the year Edgar Allan Poe's 'The Gold Bug' was published. Poe, influenced by the memoirs of Eugène Vidocq, head of the French Brigade de Sûreté, who was the first police officer to compile a criminal database, laid the foundation for detective fiction with five short stories written between 1841 and '44. 'The Murders in the Rue Morgue', 'The Purloined Letter' and 'The Mystery of Marie Rogêt' are the first-ever true detective stories, the former the first where the sleuth was the hero. His detective, Auguste Dupin, was an astute observer and analyser of facts, deducing the truth from clues as Sherlock Holmes was to do forty years on.

Conan Doyle admitted a great debt to Poe. In 1894, when he was in New York, he was asked if he had been influenced by Poe; he replied, 'Oh, immensely! His detective is the best detective in fiction.'

He expanded upon this, adding, 'I make no exception . . . Dupin is unrivalled. It was Poe who taught the possibility of making a detective story a work of literature.' Later, in *Through the Magic Door*, he wrote of Poe as 'the originator of the detective story; all treasure-hunting, cryptogram-solving yarns trace back to his Goldbug', which, of course, Conan Doyle had read as a student at Feldkirch. On 1 March 1909, when Conan Doyle presided at a centenary celebration of Poe's birth at the Authors' Club, he declared Poe's stories were 'one of the great landmarks and starting points in the literature of the past century . . . Where was the detective story until Poe breathed the breath of life into it?'

The debt is considerable, for distinct affinities exist between Poe's detective stories and the Sherlock Holmes tales. Both Sherlock Holmes and Dupin have admiring sidekicks who narrate the stories, both are composed, self-centred eccentrics with private incomes freeing them from workaday labours and cares, and both live almost hermit-like solitary lives. They each have the ability to divine the thoughts of others and solve crimes by applying their not inconsiderable intellects and powers of logical deduction and observation. Both are aristocratic and hubristic, but here the dissimilarities begin, for Sherlock Holmes is of common stock whilst Dupin is actually titled and, as a literary character, Dupin does not evolve but Sherlock Holmes does. Fictional he may be, but Sherlock Holmes is a living, almost tangible, character with real failings and definable traits with well-developed self-assurance and a mien of infallibility that is not only captivating but also realistically likeable. Poe had no awareness of his audience whilst Conan Doyle, ever conscious of it, never forgot who he was writing for or, as it were, speaking to. The result is obvious. Dupin is a paper character; Sherlock Holmes, with his dry wit, confident air and acerbic tongue, is flesh and blood.

The similarities do not end with Sherlock Holmes. Conan Doyle's stories owe an allegiance to Poe, too. In 'The Murders in the Rue Morgue', the murderer is an orang-utan whilst in Conan Doyle's *The Sign of Four* the culprit is a simian pygmy; in 'The Gold Bug', a code is deciphered on the basis of the letter *E* being the most commonly used in the English language and, in the Sherlock Holmes story 'The Adventure of the Dancing Men', published in the *Strand Magazine* in 1903, Sherlock Holmes likewise breaks a code. The comparisons are so obvious as to verge upon authorial reverence. Even Poe's fascination with the macabre and supernatural, induced by his alcoholism and opium addiction, rubbed off on Conan Doyle who, although he avoided directly writing about it in relation to Sherlock Holmes, did hint at the supernatural in such stories as *The Hound of the Baskervilles*.

Initially, Conan Doyle was a little reluctant to admit the influence of Poe. He even had Sherlock Holmes dismiss Poe in *A Study in Scarlet*, in which Watson remarks to Holmes, 'You remind me of Edgar Allan Poe's Dupin', to which Sherlock Holmes curtly responds that Dupin was 'a very inferior fellow'.

For all his influence, however, Poe was not the only writer to impinge upon Conan Doyle. Émile Gaboriau also left his mark. In his autobiography, Conan Doyle states, 'Gaboriau had rather attracted me by the neat dovetailing of his plots.' Gaboriau's detective was called Lecoq and, like Sherlock Holmes, he was a keen observer and deducer; he was also a skilled master of disguise, a technique Sherlock Holmes employed many times. Like Dupin, Lecoq also had a foil, a character called Father Absinthe who was in many respects a forerunner of Sherlock Holmes's Dr Watson. He was a bit of a dullard, slow on the uptake and always in need of having the latest twist in the investigation explained to him, Lecoq displaying his cool logic through his expositions. Gaboriau provided another original of which Conan Doyle was to take heed: Gevrol of the Sûreté is the mould for Conan Doyle's Inspector Lestrade of Scotland Yard. To a lesser extent, Conan Doyle was also influenced by Charles Dickens's Inspector Bucket in *Bleak House* and Wilkie Collins's hook-nosed Sergeant Cuff in *The Moonstone*. Conan Doyle was familiar with Collins's stories and once contrasted him with Émile Gaboriau. The central feature of the plot of *The Moonstone*, a stolen gemstone of great value and beauty, was borrowed by Conan Doyle for *The Sign of Four*, although he expanded the single gem into a whole treasure. Add to these sources of inspiration the vast number of murders and crimes reported in the national daily press, which Conan Doyle read avidly, the common availability of gory stories in the form of penny-dreadful novelettes and the popularity of blood-and-guts playlets staged at every fair and carnival, one of which was frequently held on Southsea Common, not far from his surgery, and one can see that Conan Doyle was flooded with images and ideas upon which he could draw.

Having settled on writing a detective story, Conan Doyle was presented with the need for a memorable and original name for his hero. The name was important, for upon it hung the character and personality of his invention.

His first choice was Sherrinford Holmes, which metamorphosed briefly into Sherrington Hope. Conan Doyle's first notes for *A Study in Scarlet* read, 'Ormond Sacker – from Afghanistan. Lived at 221B Upper Baker Street with Sherrinford Holmes – The Laws of Evidence. Reserved, sleepy-eyed young man – Philosopher – collector of rare Violins. An Amati ... chemical laboratory ... "I have four hundred a year – I am a Consulting detective ..."' Then the name became Sherlock Holmes.

The origination of the name has puzzled, confounded and confused biographers, literary historians, critics and Sherlock Holmes aficionados for over a century. One possible source is a village in County Kildare called Sherlockstown. Sherlock, as a surname, was common in those parts of Ireland invaded by the Vikings: it is Old Norse for 'fair-haired'. A cricketer of the day might have been the source, as Conan Doyle once claimed it was, for there were other characters in the Sherlock Holmes stories who were lifted from the sport. Mycroft (Sherlock Holmes's brother) derived from Thomas and William Mycroft, who played for Derbyshire, whilst Roylott, the blackguard in 'The Speckled Band', came from Arnold Rylott, who played for Leicestershire. There was a well-known violinist called Alfred Sherlock. A number of Irish Catholic divines, whom Conan Doyle may have come across at Stonyhurst, bore the name, as did a contemporary at the school, Patrick Sherlock. Yet the most fascinating potential source has been discovered by Stavert who, searching contemporary Portsmouth newspapers, found a Chief Inspector Sherlock mentioned in connection with a criminal investigation reported in the *Evening News* on 4 January 1883. Conan Doyle read the paper every day.

As with Sherlock, so with Holmes: the source is uncertain but the most likely source is Oliver Wendell Holmes, the American essayist, novelist, poet, physician and professor of anatomy, of whom Conan Doyle wrote in *Through the Magic Door*, 'Never have I so known and loved a man whom I had never seen.' He had first read Holmes's work while in university and he greatly admired it and its creator, who was, like himself, a man of many talents. At the time Conan Doyle was embarking upon his first Sherlock Holmes story, Oliver Wendell Holmes was setting off on a much-publicised European tour of which Conan Doyle would have been more than aware.

Other possibilities exist, of course: the myth-makers have been as busy over the years looking for sources for the surname as they have the given one. Conan Doyle had previously used the name Holmes for a character in his photographic essay 'After Cormorants with a Camera'. As a medical student, he must have come across Timothy Holmes, author of *A System of Surgery*, a textbook often referred to by Joseph Bell. In 1921, Conan Doyle remarked in a speech that he could not remember how he had arrived at the name: he had simply come upon it, he said, in a search for something ordinary.

Dr John Watson, now almost as famous as his detective friend, started life as Ormond Sacker. Once again, the literary sleuths have been at work. One likely source is Dr James Watson, a fellow physician in Southsea and a member of the Portsmouth Literary and Scientific Society, a fellow Scot who had served as doctor to a British diplomatic mission in Manchuria. Another possibility is Dr John Watson, a noted writer on India where he had served in the army, to be wounded in the First Afghan War. Sherlock Holmes's companion, readers were told, had served in the Second Afghan War. Conan Doyle, the prodigious reader, may well have been aware of the real Watson and his books. Then there is Sir Patrick Heron Watson to whom Bell was assistant and whom Conan Doyle would certainly have known of and seen in his student days. It is Edwards' contention that both Holmes and Watson may have their roots in Conan Doyle's medical student years. Bell's *A Manual of the Operations of Surgery* has references to a Mr Holmes in respect of the excision of hip joints whilst Sir Patrick Heron Watson was an expert on knee joints. The truth of the matter is that no one knows for sure.

On 8 March 1886, Conan Doyle began writing, finishing his novella about three weeks later. At first, he called it *A Tangled Skein*, but changed this to *A Study in Scarlet*, based upon Sherlock Holmes's comment, 'the scarlet thread of murder running through the colourless skein of life'. Of course, Conan Doyle was not to know it at the time but this was the most important book he ever wrote. It gave birth to Sherlock Holmes, outlined how he and Watson came to be together and set in motion one of the most astonishingly successful characters in English literature, a forerunner of everyone from Hercule Poirot to James Bond. In other words, Conan Doyle created the first major serial character.

The story is not skilfully crafted. It has a weak American flashback section and the basic plot is derivative of Robert Louis Stevenson's *The Dynamiter*, published the year before. Sherlock Holmes and Watson find a corpse in a house, the description of which is not unlike Bush Villas, to which Sherlock Holmes has been summoned. On the wall is written a single word, 'Rache', which Sherlock Holmes declares is German for 'revenge'. The dead man, Enoch Drebber, is an American whose secretary, Joseph Stangerson, is murdered later on, the deaths a retaliation connected with the Church of Jesus Christ of Latter-day Saints, otherwise known as the Mormons.

The fact that Conan Doyle chose to write about Mormons might seem fortuitous, but it was not. They were, at the time, much in the press, criticised for their polygamy and regarded with some degree of fear and loathing by upright Christians. He may also have attended a lecture at the Portsmouth Literary and Scientific Society in 1885, given by Mr J. Charlton, agent of the Chicago and Illinois Railroad, who had travelled through Utah and described the Mormons he had met and the life they lived in their new paradise. It is indicative of how prominent the sect was when, shortly after he finished working on the novella, *The Times* carried an article entitled 'The Last Struggles of the Mormons', outlining the American government's legislative and judicial persecution of the sect, seeking to drive them out of Utah, their leaders proclaiming they would make a final stand in Nevada for their right to be polygamous. Despite the high profile the Mormons had in the public consciousness, however, Conan Doyle still got some of his facts wrong, but he was cannily accurate in his choice of subject. What he was doing was, in the best fashion of the commercial novelist, writing for the market. Futhermore, the use of a religious cult as a king-pin in a plot was not untried. It had been successfully used by Wilkie Collins in *The Moonstone*.

The story is highly readable but has its defects. Yet it contains in embryonic form all the facets that would make the later Sherlock Holmes stories great. Watson is a doubter, Sherlock Holmes is shrewd and clever, the police are bumblingly over-confident. The basic structure of most of the Sherlock Holmes stories is cast with Holmes and Watson together in Holmes's rooms when a client arrives. They go to the scene of the crime or mystery, Holmes poses a series of idiosyncratic and seemingly obscure questions to a bewildered Watson, there are one or two sequences of action, the obvious solution is turned on its head by a sudden revelation then, back in Baker Street, Sherlock Holmes concludes the investigation. It was a winning formula.

Prompted by the success of 'J. Habakuk Jephson's Statement', Conan Doyle submitted the story for serialisation to James Payn at the *Cornhill Magazine*. Payn rejected it as being too short for serialisation but too long for a single issue. Clearly, he did not realise its potential and must have considered the market in such stories to be flooded.

The months went by. Conan Doyle mailed it to an assortment of publishers. Arrowsmith sent it back without reading it: it is said that Conan Doyle submitted his manuscript rolled into a cardboard tube and that, when the story was returned, it had not even been flattened out. Frederick Warne & Co. rejected it. He forwarded it to Ward, Lock & Co., which had a reputation, as Conan Doyle put it, of making 'a speciality of cheap and often sensational literature'. The editor-in-chief, Professor G.T. Bettany, gave it to his wife, who was a published novelist and short story writer. According to her, she instantly approved of it and, on 30 October 1886, Ward Lock offered £25 for the copyright. Conan Doyle replied requesting royalties but the publishers refused. They wanted an outright purchase not because they saw the potential in the story but simply because it was company policy.

Conan Doyle felt he had no alternative but to agree. At least, he must have thought, it would get the novella into print. The contract was drawn up three weeks later but the story, much to Conan Doyle's chagrin, was not published until November 1887, and then it was not an individual book but included in *Beeton's Christmas Annual*, a miscellany published every year since 1867 when it was founded by Samuel Orchart Beeton, husband of the ubiquitous Isabella Mary Beeton of cookery and household management fame.

A Study in Scarlet was the main item in the annual, which was priced at one shilling and bound in red-and-white softback covers on which the title was printed in scarlet. It was illustrated by D.H. Friston, who drew Sherlock Holmes as a tubby, decadent-looking figure and Watson as stocky. Along with the story were published two drawing-room plays entitled *Food for Powder* by R. André and *The Four-Leaved Shamrock* by C.J. Hamilton, in addition to a number of minor articles, puzzles and humorous pieces. The annual, being perennially popular, sold out in fourteen days.

Not being a book in its own right, the story was not widely reviewed in the national press, although it did gain a few mentions. Conan Doyle and the publishers were particularly pleased with a good review in *Longman's Magazine*, and the *Scotsman* declared that the author showed genius. In Portsmouth, the *Hampshire Post* reviewed it at length and with much praise, which pleased Conan Doyle and no doubt set his patients talking.

It did not die after inclusion in the annual but was published by Ward Lock as an individual volume in its own right in July 1888, the edition illustrated by Charles Doyle, who produced six pen-and-ink drawings which looked dated. Locked away in care, he was out of touch with modern tastes. Yet the pictures were very interesting, for Sherlock Holmes was a self-portrait of the young Charles, tall and thin with a beard and a mild, rounded face. Who suggested him as illustrator is unclear, and one must suppose Conan Doyle put his father forward for the commission, although what his motives were is just as uncertain. Perhaps he wanted to give his father something to do in his dark empty hours in his nursing home or, just as likely, he wanted somehow to share his good fortune with him, bring him into the fold of the artistic Doyle clan once more, for now Conan Doyle was, like his forebears, a man of the arts.

A Study in Scarlet was reprinted in 1889, and often thereafter, but Conan Doyle earned not a penny more from it. He had relinquished all rights in the story for a paltry £25.

Just as there has been much guesswork over where Sherlock Holmes's and Dr Watson's names came from, so there has been even more conjecture as to whom they were based upon. Most believe Sherlock Holmes to be based upon Joseph Bell and Conan Doyle himself. This is to over-simplify the situation. Writers rarely base a character upon one single, living person. Literary creations are not individuals but composites. The search for provenances and origins may well be a fascinating subject for speculative scholarship but it is ultimately little more than an academic exercise. The most important aspect of the matter is that the character is realistic enough to the reader as to take on flesh and blood, to become so real that suspended disbelief becomes convinced reality. This is exactly what Conan Doyle achieved with Sherlock Holmes, to such an extent that the Post Office still received letters for him as recently as the 1950s.

Conan Doyle consistently claimed that Sherlock Holmes was substantially based on Joseph Bell. He wrote, 'I thought of my old teacher, Joe Bell, of his eagle face, of his curious ways, of his eerie trick of spotting details. If he were a detective he would surely reduce this fascinating but unorganised business to something nearer to an exact science.' Near the end of his life, on a gramophone recording made for His Master's Voice, Conan Doyle spoke about how he came to write Sherlock Holmes. 'I thought I would try my hand at writing a story,' he says on the record, 'where the hero would treat crime as Dr Bell treated disease, and where science would take the place of chance.'

If, Conan Doyle surmised, Bell's powers of observation and deduction which he used on his patients could be relevant to a doctor, then why should they not also be relevant to a detective? It was only a matter of transferring the skills from one profession to another. What might lead to a real diagnosis could also lead to a fictional arrest.

In *A Study in Scarlet*, Sherlock Holmes shows Watson how he determined that his friend had been in Afghanistan: it was no different from Bell's assessment of the Scottish soldier with Barbados leg. Holmes's conclusion went: 'Here is a gentleman of a medical type, but with the air of a military man. Clearly an army doctor then. He has just come from the tropics, for his face is dark, and that is not the natural tint of his skin, for his wrists are fair. He has undergone hardship and sickness, as his haggard face says clearly. His left arm has been injured. He holds it in a stiff and unnatural manner. Where in the tropics could an English army doctor have seen much hardship and got his arm wounded. Clearly in Afghanistan.'

In his autobiography, Conan Doyle addressed a question he was often asked, as to how much of Sherlock Holmes there was in him. He admitted it was 'one thing to grapple with a practical problem and quite another thing when you are allowed to solve it under your own conditions. I have no delusions about that. At the same time a man cannot spin a character out of his own inner consciousness and make it really life-like unless he has some possibilities of that character within him.'

Sherlock Holmes most assuredly did have a lot of Conan Doyle in him or, if not possessing actual characteristics, then he did have some that the author would have considered a part of himself, facets of his own self-image. Amongst other similarities, Sherlock Holmes and Conan Doyle both boxed, both were tall and physically strong, both enjoyed a good joke. As a detective, Sherlock Holmes had 'a horror of destroying documents, especially those which were connected with his past cases', whilst Conan Doyle stockpiled notebooks, scrapbooks and boxes of ephemeral knowledge to such an extent that, when he died, it was sixteen years before it was all catalogued. Another of his creator's traits Sherlock Holmes shared was his untidiness. Both their minds were ordered but their studies were not: Louise frequently complained about the piles of documents her husband hoarded. Their interests were similar as well: both spoke French and German, both were interested in France and French culture. The Francophile in them led, in 1996, to a split in followers of Sherlock Holmes: at an exhibition in Paris, it was claimed that Sherlock Holmes was French on account of his grandmother, Emilie Vernet, the sister of the French artist Carle Vernet, whom Richard Doyle had much admired, and who was said to have been executed on the guillotine during the French Revolution. Such are the lengths to which Sherlock Holmes fanatics will go; such is the testament to Conan Doyle's remarkable character construction.

There is more: when Sherlock Holmes first arrived in London, he rented lodgings in Montague Street in Bloomsbury. When Conan Doyle and Louise moved to the capital they took rooms in Montague Place, just around the corner. In saying his grandmother was the sister of Vernet (and that 'Art in the blood is liable to take the strangest forms'),

Holmes was being compared to Conan Doyle's background of artists with an oblique reference, perhaps, to Charles Doyle. Both Conan Doyle and Sherlock Holmes had only one brother and both were gallant men of honour, always eager to see justice done and the underdog defended. And both were agnostics. The biggest dissimilarity lay in the fact that Sherlock Holmes was a man whose body was merely an adjunct to his brain and intellect, whilst Conan Doyle was far more physically a man of action.

Yet all this balancing of comparisons is, in many ways, just a game. Every writer puts something of himself into his favourite creations, and all Conan Doyle was doing was following the age-old dictum of the good novelist: write about what you know. In a pamphlet he published in 1943, Adrian Conan Doyle remembered an American journalist, Hayden Coffin, saying Conan Doyle privately told him that if anyone was Holmes, then he had to confess that it was him, yet he also admitted on a different occasion that Sherlock Holmes was a mixture of Poe's Dupin and Joseph Bell. According to his son, Conan Doyle often made Bell-like assessments in his everyday life, studying diners in a restaurant and guessing from their appearance or behaviour who or what they were. He was usually correct.

Dupin, Bell and Conan Doyle aside, there were other pieces to Sherlock Holmes's make-up. Like Charles Doyle, Sherlock Holmes was sometimes remote and almost manic in his activity, falling afterwards into lonely exhaustion. He had Oliver Wendell Holmes's sagacity and eloquent oratory, quick brain and expert knowledge of tobacco. As Edwards has pointed out, he was, in common with Professor Christison, not averse to experimenting upon himself. As a toxicologist, Christison once dosed himself on calabar bean and very nearly died as a result.

In *A Study in Scarlet*, Stamford, who is about to introduce Watson to Sherlock Holmes, warns him, 'Holmes is a little too scientific for my tastes – it approaches cold-bloodedness. I could imagine his giving a friend a little pinch of the latest vegetable alkaloid, not out of malevolence, you understand, but simply out of a spirit of inquiry in order to have an accurate idea of the effects. To do him justice, I think that he would take it himself with the same readiness. He appears to have a passion for definite and exact knowledge.' When Watson replies to this, saying, 'Very right too', Stamford goes on, 'Yes, but it may be pushed to excess. When it comes to beating the subjects in the dissecting-rooms with a stick [to ascertain how long bruising may occur post mortem] it is certainly taking rather a bizarre shape.' Christison had done just this when involved in studying the notorious Burke and Hare murders in

1828. It appears, therefore, that Conan Doyle was almost certainly thinking of Christison when he wrote at least this part of the story.

Without doubt, Sherlock Holmes was a fusion of a potentially wide number of sources. Dr Watson, on the other hand, was somewhat more compact and, inevitably, there is much of Conan Doyle in him. Both the creator and the created were middle-class Victorian general practitioners, educated and men of action who possessed courage and loyalty. They were each commonsensical, practical and genial, enjoyed stories about the sea and sport, playing rugby and billiards, and were, at times, a little naïve.

Adrian Conan Doyle believed Watson to be substantially based upon Alfred Herbert Wood, who was later to become Conan Doyle's private secretary. Born in 1866, educated at Portsmouth Grammar School, Wood won an open scholarship to Brasenose College, Oxford, then, having graduated, returned to join the teaching staff of his old school. He and Conan Doyle probably met through sport. This assumption, however, is unlikely. At the time Conan Doyle invented Watson, he hardly knew Wood. He was, in any case, too young to be the original model for Sherlock Holmes's companion. The Watson of the later stories, however, does bear a close resemblance to the older Alfred Wood, and was described in the story 'The Adventure of Charles Augustus Milverton' as being 'a middle-sized, strongly built man – square jaw, thick neck, moustache'. As the stories progressed, and Conan Doyle came to closer grips with his characters, so it follows his models for them could have changed.

Another candidate was a fellow doctor from Edinburgh, David George Thomson, whom Conan Doyle first met at university and with whom he was friendly throughout his life. Another keen photographer, Thomson worked for a while under Joseph Bell but was eventually made superintendent of the County Mental Hospital in Norwich, where Conan Doyle often called upon him. According to another asylum doctor, Conan Doyle once asked Thomson what he thought of Watson. When Thomson replied negatively, Conan Doyle is alleged to have said, 'I'm sorry you think that. I rather modelled him on you.' There is, however, no corroborative evidence so, as with Sherlock Holmes, we must conclude that Watson was a mixture.

The speculation does not end there. Ever since Conan Doyle's death, there have been long, detailed discourses about the bases for many of the other characters in the Sherlock Holmes stories as well as all his other fiction. As any writer does, Conan Doyle utilised people he met, 'borrowing' the names of real people sometimes simply to amuse himself or them. Two examples of many hundreds illustrate what he did. Gibson and Green have shown how he mentioned the Burton family: in an early short story, 'Our Derby Sweepstake', published in *London Society* in 1882, there is a company called Innes and Burton, and a quip of a letter being sent to Mr Burton complaining about the drainage system. Later, in the Sherlock Holmes story 'The Adventure of the Illustrious Client', Dr Watson uses a calling card in the name of Dr Hill Barton, a pun on John Hill Burton.

Entire books have been devoted to the subject of Conan Doyle's sources; but, at the final count, what does it matter? The important thing is that Conan Doyle was such a superbly skilled writer that he gave us one of the most enduring and realistic characters in popular world fiction.

6

Putting Out Cargo

At first, the arrival of Sherlock Holmes in Conan Doyle's life did little to alter it. There was no inkling of the meteoric success to come apart from a dribble of fan mail to which he assiduously responded. Life went on. Conan Doyle attended his surgery, his meetings and his sports fixtures. His marriage was happy, if perhaps unexciting, Louise playing her part as doctor's spouse and housewife, welcoming patients, entertaining visitors and not intruding upon either her husband's creative or his social existence.

On top of all his other activities, Conan Doyle also started to take a part in local politics, becoming vice-president of the Portsmouth Liberal-Unionist Association. It was an exciting time politically, for a general election was called for the summer of 1886 and party officials would be kept busy in the hustings. Although he was never a truly partisan political animal, Conan Doyle felt he had to contribute, for one of the main election issues was the Irish situation.

The two parties in English politics were the Conservatives under Lord Salisbury and the Liberals led by Gladstone. The Conservatives were made up predominantly of the upper classes, landowners and businessmen, whilst the Liberals represented the rest of the electorate. Hampshire was a Conservative stronghold but the city of Portsmouth was a Liberal enclave. The Liberals, however, were divided by Gladstone's Home Rule for Ireland policy which advocated an autonomous parliament for Ireland as the only viable solution to stopping what was then, as now, referred to as 'the troubles'. Many Liberal supporters believed Ireland should remain in the United

Kingdom, these calling themselves Liberal Unionists. Despite his Irish ancestry, Conan Doyle was one of them, for he fervently believed in the eventual unification of all English-speaking nations, especially Great Britain and the USA: that many of the Irish spoke Gaelic seems not to have altered his views. He not only backed the Liberal Unionist cause but actually spoke publicly for it just before the election in June 1886, in support of Sir William Crossman, the parliamentary candidate for Portsmouth. In actual fact, Conan Doyle had not been slated to give the speech. He was dumped with the responsibility as vice-president of the local party when Crossman was late arriving for a rally. Conan Doyle found himself in front of three thousand potential voters, which he described as one of the tight corners of his life. A few weeks later, perhaps spurred on by his oratorical success, he published a letter in the *Evening News* justifying his decision to vote for the Unionist candidate and, when Arthur Balfour, the future Prime Minister, visited Portsmouth to deliver a political speech eighteen months later, in support of Ireland remaining in the United Kingdom, Conan Doyle and several other supporters collared some hecklers who were shouting abuse. A fight broke out during which Conan Doyle was struck on the head with a stick and had his top hat stove in.

As if politics were not enough, in January 1887 he was enrolled into freemasonry, becoming a member of the Phoenix Lodge, No. 257, which met at 110 High Street. Quite why he joined the freemasons is open to speculation. Most men – predominantly from the middle classes – became masons in order to further their businesses. A masonic lodge was (and still is) a place where local men met as equals, where contacts were made and minor deals sealed between brothers 'on the square'. It is possible that Conan Doyle's practice could have gained a few patients through his membership, but not many: professional self-advancement could not have been his aim. The religious foundations of freemasonry were tenuous: a candidate for brotherhood had merely to admit to a belief in a higher being which was referred to in the rites as the Grand Architect of the Universe. Conan Doyle could certainly not have joined for spiritual reasons, although he would not have been apathetic towards the concept of a Grand Architect. He might have joined to kick at the traces of Catholicism, for membership of the order was an excommunicatory sin in the eyes of the Vatican, or he may have joined because he approved of the brotherhood's philanthropy. It seems, however, that he soon realised this was more self-interested than universal, for, in time, he became disillusioned with the brotherhood. The secret rituals and paraphernalia must have seemed petty to a man of action and intellect such as himself. He made no effort to further his rank in the masons and, within two years, he resigned although, fifteen years later, in 1901, he accepted honorary membership of St Mary's Chapel No. 1, Edinburgh.

In the Portsmouth Literary and Scientific Society, on the sports field, in the masonic lodge and on the platform of politics, Conan Doyle mixed with all the important locals, yet his practice did not grow and he continued to live modestly. His literary career might have been moving up a notch but he still had a comparatively low income. He employed a maid but he had no assistant and at no time did he own a horse or carriage. Most of the other local doctors maintained several servants and had the means to keep carriages either at home or in nearby stables in which they rented a loose box and the services of a groom. According to Conan Doyle, he maintained a bicycle on which to do his rounds.

To improve his earning capacity, Conan Doyle gave thought to specialising in the treatment of eye diseases and began studying ophthalmology. The idea might have been brewing in his mind for some time, planted there by Budd: in *The Stark Munro Letters*, Conan Doyle has Cullingworth declare, 'I've taken to the eye, my boy. There's a fortune in the eye. A man grudges a half-crown to cure his chest or his throat, but he'd spend his last dollar over his eye. There's money in ears, but the eye is a gold mine.'

He studied at the Portsmouth Eye Hospital under a friend and ophthalmic surgeon, Arthur Vernon Ford, son of a former Portsmouth Lord Mayor and the hospital's founder. Only three years old, the hospital was already treating two thousand cases a year, and Conan Doyle, who studied optics, took on non-surgical work such as eye testing. His career plans as an eye doctor were to do his initial studying in Portsmouth, go overseas to advance these, then return to Britain to set up in a specialist practice in London. His writing would not be abandoned: literature, he wrote to his sister Lottie, would be his 'milch-cow'. Working at the hospital also brought in a few patients to Bush Villas, for it became known that he was able to 'do eyes'. He prescribed and fitted spectacles, increasing his earnings without the expense or effort of gaining a new qualification. What was more, he could charge more for eyes: a receipt survives which reads, 'To testing child's eyes, etc. 5/. Nov. 26th/90'. Five shillings was double the normal half-crown fee for an ordinary medical consultation.

The Fords had a far greater impact upon Conan Doyle's life than merely steering him towards ophthalmology, for it was most likely through his friendship with them that he first attended a seance.

Conan Doyle had rejected Catholicism and organised religion but he still read widely on theological issues and the relationships between science, ethics and religion. He had a need to believe in something and his belief encompassed an intelligent force in nature which underlay all creation, which he was convinced was not a random occurrence. Freemasonry had offered him a Grand Architect but he had not been able to pin his flag to the masonic mast and he was still looking to fill the doubt within him.

It seems that Conan Doyle's first discovery of spiritualism was in January 1880 whilst staying with the Hoares in Birmingham, a few weeks prior to sailing for the Arctic, when he attended a lecture on the subject. On that first encounter, he had been curious but very sceptical. In Southsea, his curiosity expanded into a deep interest in what would today be termed alternative religion.

Like many others at the time, Conan Doyle wanted to obtain tangible, physical evidence that a man's soul could be proven to exist autarkically, separate from the flesh and blood. Conan Doyle's medical education told him this was not possible, but the doubt lingered and was the cause of his wide reading on spiritualism and related religious matters.

Spiritualism is based upon two seminal assumptions. One is that, upon death, the soul leaves what is termed the earth plane of living existence for a number of other spiritual or heavenly planes. The other is the premise that communication is possible between the earth plane, upon which the living preside, and one or more of the spiritual planes. The idea was not new but rooted in religions which, for the Victorians, gave it a certain historical credibility and provided a fundamental explanation for the concept of Christian resurrection. Christ, in other words, did not die but went to the next plane although the Christian Church made no effort to explain this marvel. Spiritualism did.

In doing so, it attempted to establish links between the physical and the metaphysical, leading to such famous spiritualist phenomena as rapping noises coming from beyond, movement by poltergeist, the emanation of auras, telepathy and clairvoyance, most often induced or conducted by or through a medium. The absence of scientific proof of the cause of paranormal phenomena resulted in a spiritualist philosophy the doctrines of which were known collectively as spiritualism.

The movement began in the USA in 1848 in the village of Hydesville, near Rochester in upstate New York, where a family called Fox claimed to have communicated with a spirit that made knocking sounds. By

1854, there were said to be three million spiritualists in North America served by ten thousand mediums. It was not long before the craze was worldwide. By 1865, Britain was awash with mediums jumping on the bandwagon, faking seances in darkened rooms but raking in the money. Chicanery was the name of the game, with hidden accomplices, spring-loaded tables, secret drawers, sleight of hand and hidden pockets producing everything from blocks of ice to everyday household objects. By 1880, those truly interested had had enough. The fakers and true spiritualists alike were hounded by the press and in January 1882 the Society for Psychical Research was inaugurated by Frederic W.H. Myers and Edmund Gurney, both fellows of Trinity College, Cambridge. Respected for their eminent scholarship and positions in the academic world, they set about debunking the fraudsters with a set of basic objectives which were to investigate telepathy, hypnotism and clairvoyance, study hauntings and ghostly appearances and look into the production of physical phenomena. In other words, they wanted scientifically and objectively to prove the existence of the spirit world.

Not long after settling down in Portsmouth, Conan Doyle had become professionally fascinated by hypnotism and mesmerism, so called after an eighteenth-century Austrian physician, Friedrich Anton Mesmer, who proposed that stroking a magnet over a diseased organ caused an invisible force field to affect and cure the tissue: he was two centuries ahead of his time and the discovery of microwave treatment. This led Conan Doyle into learning about Buddhism, reincarnation and karma. From Buddhism he came to Theosophy, an occidental reinterpretation of Tibetan Buddhism upon which Madame Blavatsky founded an entire movement. His belief faded when Blavatsky was exposed as a fraud, but his curiosity lingered.

The date of Conan Doyle's first psychic experience is unknown but, as researched by Stavert, it seems most likely to have occurred through his relationship with the Ford family. Arthur Vernon Ford had an elder brother, Douglas Morey Ford, a local solicitor with literary pretensions having published two novels, to whose daughter, Delia, Louise was godmother. Douglas's wife, Honor, was a medium of sorts who conducted 'table turning sessions' at her home on Grand Parade.

Whatever interest the Fords engendered, it was increased by Conan Doyle's friendship with one of his patients and a fellow Literary and Scientific Society member, Major-General Alfred Wilks Drayson, FRAS, who was conducting his own spiritualist experiments after having had several 'conversations' with a dead brother. In many ways, Drayson was a man after Conan Doyle's own heart. A retired mathematician and one-time professor at the Royal Military Academy in Woolwich, he was quite famous for his resolution of what he termed the second rotation of the earth by which he explained the procession of the equinoxes and the changes in polar distance. Initially scorned by the scientific community, his hypothesis was eventually accepted. A distinguished career soldier, he had travelled extensively in India, South Africa and Canada and was a well-published writer, having brought out several books of memoirs, some stories and, as an expert billiards player, *The Art of Practical Billiards for Amateurs*, in addition to a book on whist, *The Art of Practical Whist*, and a huge corpus of journalism. Conan Doyle was impressed by Drayson's scholarship and regarded him as little short of a genius.

Conan Doyle also started to hold seances of his own at Bush Villas at one of which a detailed message came through the ether from a commercial traveller killed in a theatre fire in Exeter, the spirit requesting that the sitters contact his family at a place called Slattenmere in Cumberland. In an astounding exhibition of gullibility hardly befitting a scientifically trained mind, not to mention one as active as Conan Doyle's, he wrote and mailed the letter as requested from beyond the grave. There is no such place as Slattenmere in Britain and it was returned by the Royal Mail dead letter office.

Perhaps as a result of this experience, Conan Doyle questioned Drayson about fraudulent mediums, to which Drayson's ambiguous reply was that both this world and the next were full of charlatans, and he advised Conan Doyle to choose his companions with more care. The onus of the truth was hidden in a plausible explanation, dupery being dismissed as just as commonplace in spiritualism as in the rest of the world. Conan Doyle based his conception of spiritualist chicanery upon this premise for the rest of his life.

Drayson held seances in his home, too. These were conducted both to contact the dead and as a means of experiment. Conan Doyle thought table-rapping and other manifestations required controlled experimentation but, despite his own doubts and the returned letter, he nevertheless attended an increasing number of sessions, being impressed by some of the events he witnessed. At one seance, he was particularly inspired by a spirit called Dorothy Poslethwaite who said she had died in Melbourne, five years before, at the age of sixteen. Claiming she had been to school with one of those present, she began tilting the table to spell out their headmistress's name. Dorothy got it right, which Conan Doyle considered undeniable evidence of the spirit's existence and her presence in a plane that circumferenced the world. Fictitious Slattenmere was one thing; Melbourne, Australia was another.

The mediums controlling many of the Southsea seances were said to be either a railway signalman's wife or Mrs Maggs, wife of the editor of several local newspapers. Both specialised in apports, the physical manifestation of items that appeared suddenly as if out of thin air, purportedly coming with the aid of spirits. Mrs Maggs was said to have been sent various foodstuffs from Brooklyn, New York by spirit mail in response to spirit gifts sent by Drayson to spiritualists in America.

For six months, from January to July 1887, Conan Doyle and a friend called Henry Ball started to experiment in telepathy, sometimes with a medium called Horstead. Conan Doyle recorded that he and Ball could on occasion picture the item of which the other was thinking. Seated one behind the other on chairs facing in opposite directions, one would draw a diagram and the other copy it telepathically.

Gradually, Conan Doyle came to be utterly convinced that psychic phenomena existed and that spiritualism was feasible. He was very impressed by the number of famous scientists who believed in spiritualism, yet one of his main weaknesses was that he could not believe such major scientists capable of slapdash interpretation of facts, even if they were emotionally involved in the outcome of their deductions. An example of Conan Doyle's fallibility may be found in his reading of *Researches into Modern Spiritualism* by Sir William Crookes, the discoverer of thallium and pioneer in the chemistry of 'rare earths'. Crookes had shown some scientific objectivity in his spiritualist investigations but this went by the board when he became emotionally entangled with Florrie Cook, a famous, very pretty young medium.

On 2 July 1887, Conan Doyle had a letter published in *Light*, the journal of the London Spiritualistic Alliance, the subject of which was a seance he had attended. During the seance, conducted through a medium who was 'an old gentleman . . . reputed to have considerable mediumistic power', a spirit cautioned him not to read Leigh Hunt's *Comic Dramatists of the Restoration*, which he had had it in mind to read for a few days. According to Conan Doyle, what actually happened was that the medium picked up a pencil and 'after a few convulsive movements, he wrote a message to each of us. Mine ran: "This gentleman is a healer. Tell him from me not to read Leigh Hunt's book."' He added, 'The message of one of my friends, referring to his own private affairs, was as startlingly correct as mine.' The warning, he later wrote, proved to him 'that it was absolutely certain that intelligence could exist apart from the body'.

The letter was, in effect, a public declaration of Conan Doyle's conviction and a brave thing to write, for although spiritualism was not publicly ridiculed, it was considered not far from dotty and certainly not the sort of thing with which a respectable doctor should associate himself. Conan Doyle seems not to have lost any patients as a result of the letter; instead, he was contacted by Myers who, with Gurney, had published a weighty two-volume edition of their investigative results entitled *Phantasms of the Living*. They asked him to assist with on-going research. The next month, Conan Doyle wrote to *Light* again concerning Richard Hodgson, a well-known investigator into and debunker of spiritualism, who was currently exposing all mediums. 'As a Spiritualist,' Conan Doyle declared staunchly, 'I for one should like to see every possible facility given to Mr Hodgson in his investigations. If spiritualism be true and the phenomena genuine why should the mediums be warned against Mr Hodgson or any other inquirer?'

Clearly, Conan Doyle was no doubter. He was convinced that whilst fake mediums could, and perhaps should, be unmasked for the good of spiritualism, the remainder had nothing to fear. He further showed his interest a year later when the Hampshire Psychical Society was founded with Conan Doyle one of the three vice-presidents.

In future years, Conan Doyle was to claim he had been objective and dubious of spiritualism in his Southsea years but the evidence goes against this contention. Moving in spiritualist circles, and under the influence of Drayson, at the time he seems to have been convinced. He even wrote in one of his notebooks, 'The end and aim of spiritual intercourse is to give man the strongest of all reasons to believe in spiritual immortality of the soul, to break down the barrier of death, to found the grand religion of the future.' What he had lost in turning his back on Roman Catholicism and organised religion he had replaced with a dubious alternative.

Understandably, some of Conan Doyle's literary work from the start of his Southsea days reflected his growing fascination with the paranormal, the supernatural and his grand religion, although it is unfair, as some critics have done, to say that these factors were central to his muse. Conan Doyle merely used his interest to spin a good tale, to refine his innate ability to disturb his readers, especially in his horror stories where several themes were dominant. Revenge, always a potent emotion in any writer's arsenal, features prominently in many of his stories, not to mention a fair number of the Sherlock Holmes tales.

Sexual guilt or obsession also appear. Yet the most prevalent theme is an abiding and deep-rooted curiosity about the unknown. This is a motif Conan Doyle returns to time and again, allying it to a Gothic terror of women as representatives of the unknown, as objects of desire yet fear, creatures in which are embodied the primeval dread of love and death. In such stories, one sees an inner Conan Doyle, a man fascinated by the macabre world beyond death where passion is quenched only by an horrific death and the dark swirling mist of supernatural eternity.

A number of these early stories were collected in an anthology, *Dreamland and Ghostland*, published in 1886 by George Redway of Covent Garden, which was advertised as 'An Original Collection of Tales and Warnings from the Borderland of Substance and Shadow, Embracing Remarkable Dreams, Presentiments, and Coincidences; Records of Singular Personal Experiences by Various Writers; Startling Stories from Individual and Family History; Mysterious Incidents from the Lips of Living Narrators; and some Psychological Studies, Grave and Gay'. Conan Doyle's contributions were written in the first person as if they purported to be true.

One of these early stories was entitled 'The Captain of the Polestar', and appeared in *Temple Bar* magazine in 1883. A ghost story, justifiably hailed by some as a literary *tour de force*, it is about a trip to the Arctic sailing under an obsessive and unstable ship's captain, Captain Craigie, living on the edge of insanity and haunted by his dead mistress whose spirit he follows on to the icecap where he dies. The atmosphere is tense with a subplot in which the crew are afraid their ship will become held fast by pack ice. A brilliant sea story as well as a horror story, it is told as through the diary of a medical student, John M'Alister Ray, acting as ship's doctor. As in other stories, Conan Doyle drew upon his own experiences aboard the *Hope*, adding to it signs of the captain's approaching madness which he might have based upon his knowledge of Charles Doyle's mental deterioration.

'John Barrington Cowles', a short story published in *Cassell's Saturday Journal* in 1884, displays Conan Doyle's extreme interest in the supernatural. The narrator is an Edinburgh medical student, Robert Armitage, who lodges with another student, John Cowles, who is fixated by a mysterious girl called Kate Northcott. On the eve of their wedding, Cowles discovers she is a werewolf and takes flight, but she follows him and they die by falling off a cliff as Cowles embraces her in one last surge of sexual passion. Another story, 'The Man from Archangel', which Conan Doyle often described as his finest piece of writing, published in *London Society* in 1885, also deals with sexual obsession. The main character, John M'Vittie, rescues the mistress of a Russian sea captain from a shipwreck but is at a loss when confronted by her beauty and sexuality. In the end, the Russian takes her away to her death.

Perhaps one of Conan Doyle's most daring stories of the time, touching upon the very taboo subject of necrophilia, was 'The Ring of Thoth', published in 1890 in the *Cornhill Magazine*. Cashing in on the intense public curiosity about Egyptology, in which, needless to say, Conan Doyle was not only interested but well read, the plot centres around an ancient Egyptian priest of Thuthmoses who has discovered the secret of eternal life. Possessing the knowledge, he unwraps the mummy of his lover so they might be reunited. Upon exposure to the air, the embalmed mummy rapidly disintegrates and the priest dies of *locomotor ataxia* whilst embracing his decomposing mistress. Presumably, the disease to which the priest succumbs, caused by syphilis, was contracted by his sexual depravity with the dead woman. The story combines Conan Doyle's medical knowledge, his interest in the supernatural, the influence of Edgar Allan Poe and his fascination with the bizarre and macabre, far removed from the general view of him as a cricketer, doctor and Liberal Unionist activist. Certainly, it seems as if the family doctor of Bush Villas had a darker, repressed side to his nature which only appeared in some of his writings.

Achieving publication for ghost, horror and detective stories was one thing but, whilst he was waiting through 1887 for *A Study in Scarlet* to appear, Conan Doyle was concerned with writing a book that would establish him as a serious literary novelist. 'To test my powers to the full,' he wrote in his autobiography, '. . . I chose a historical novel for this end, because it seemed to me the one way of combining a certain amount of literary dignity with those scenes of action and adventure which were natural to my young and ardent mind.'

The idea for his historical novel had been with him for nearly two years, during which time he had researched the background, but it was July 1887 before he embarked upon it. It was called *Micah Clarke* and was subtitled 'His Statement as Made to His Grandchildren Joseph, Gervas and Reuben During the Hard Winter of 1734'. It was completed by the end of January 1888. The longest of his historical novels, he got his inspiration from Macaulay, upon whose *History of England* he relied for much of his research.

Set in the late seventeenth century, it took the form of a first-person narrative related by an old man, Micah Clarke, about his adventures as a youth. Conan Doyle was at home with a first-person approach to a story: he had used it often enough before and even relied upon a local background, having Clarke hail from Havant, a small town nine kilometres to the east of Portsmouth. The novel relives the ill-fated 1685 Monmouth Rebellion, led by the pretender to the throne, James Scott, Duke of Monmouth, the illegitimate son of Charles II, who sought to take the crown after the succession of the Catholic James II but was defeated, captured and beheaded. Central to the story is a group of English Puritans for whose austere and devout lives Conan Doyle showed much sympathy, writing that for him they represented 'liberty and earnestness in religion'. He considered they were good, simple people, better by far than their monarch who was, after all, a papist from whom they had to protect their lands.

The tale reaches its climax with the Battle of Sedgemoor at which the Duke was defeated, a section of the book that is extraordinary for Conan Doyle's superb description of the battle as seen through the eyes of the foot-soldiers. In the aftermath, when the infamous Judge Jeffreys arrives to conduct his 'Bloody Assizes' to execute the rebels, Conan Doyle avoids the historical stereotype of the wicked hanging judge and deals with him as a handsome character fallen in human grace. The main characters come alive, the descriptions are vivid and the scenes accurate as a result of Conan Doyle's painstaking research. Historical veracity, however, is somewhat flexible, for Conan Doyle deliberately distorted fact to suit fiction. The Duke of Beaufort is portrayed as a double-crosser, playing each side against the other to back the winner, and the Duke of Monmouth's bastardy is questioned by his possession of a secret marriage contract between his mother, Lucy Walters, and Charles II. Conan Doyle wanted to have a dig at the validity of the Catholic claim to the throne.

The book served other purposes, however. It brought Conan Doyle to maturity as a writer, taught him how to sustain a long, involved narrative inhabited by realistic characters who interrelated and interacted like actual people. He also learnt the lessons of genuine research, which not only lent reality to stories but also gave them originality.

Restless as ever, Conan Doyle did not take time off after *Micah Clarke*. Within three months, he had started yet another novel, *The Mystery of Cloomber*, which he completed by June 1888. It was a blatant pro-spiritualist tale of revenge based upon the Theosophist concept of the *chela*, a person who can call up spirits and travel through the astral planes. After *Micah Clarke*, it was a shallow, almost ephemeral story not worthy of its author. Set in Edinburgh and parts of Scotland where Conan Doyle had gone on walking holidays, it is about an English officer serving in the East who murders a Buddhist sage to spend the remainder of his life escaping from vengeful monks who finally catch up with and kill him, the officer meekly succumbing to his death. The research, if Conan Doyle did any at all, was shoddy in the extreme: the Buddhist monks wear red Muslim fezes whilst Ram Singh, their leader, has a Sikh name and the narrator refers to them all as 'Hindoos', which is an entirely different religion. First appearing in serial form between August and November 1888, it was published as a novel by Ward and Downey in time for Christmas.

The ease with which this piece of spiritualist tosh found a publisher was not shared by *Micah Clarke*. Payn rejected it and told Conan Doyle he was wasting his time and wits by writing what is now termed faction: that Sir Walter Scott had already done so seems to have been overlooked. Blackwood's criticised the characters as being too modern and the direct speech as being inaccurate for the period setting. The publisher Bentley & Co. declared it was devoid of interest whilst Cassell opined that historical novels were commercially unsuccessful. The Globe Newspaper Syndicate, receiving it for possible serialisation, stated it was a failure because it lacked female reader appeal, a love interest and sensationalism. Their rejection letter was addressed to Dr A. Corran Boyle. Finally, the manuscript reached Longmans where Andrew Lang, an influential critic and historian, accepted it. Contracts were signed in October 1888 and the book published the following February. For the first time, Conan Doyle was assured a royalty of 10 per cent.

A few weeks before the novel appeared, Louise gave birth to their first child, Mary Louise, on 28 January 1889. It is not certain if Conan Doyle delivered his own baby but what is sure is that at first he refused to have her baptised. This was most unusual. With infant mortality being quite high, babies were usually taken to the font within days of birth. Mary Doyle, now an Anglican, was disturbed at discovering the baby had not been christened when visiting her grandchild a year later. At her insistence, Conan Doyle caved in and the little girl was finally baptised an Anglican in July 1890. The baptismal names were entered in the church records as Mary Louise Conan Doyle: all Conan Doyle's children were so named, as if the surname were a double one, although it was, in legal terms, plain Doyle.

Micah Clarke was extensively reviewed. Those who praised it compared it to Robert Louis Stevenson, as they had 'J. Habakuk Jephson's Statement', but those who took against it hammered it for playing fast and loose with historical facts. The public, however, took to it. It had been published as a single volume rather than what was commonly termed a 'three-decker', an edition split between three volumes because of its length, and, as a single book, it drew more attention. It was reprinted three times in ten months, a dozen times in four years, a school edition came out in 1894 and it sold well in America. Encouraged by such success, Conan Doyle decided to produce another historical novel and set about preparing to write *The White Company*.

Stavert's research shows that, in February 1889, the Portsmouth Literary and Scientific Society hosted a lecture by the Very Reverend Dr Kitchin, Dean of Winchester. It was entitled 'Some Notes on Mediaeval Commerce', and dealt with everyday life in the reign of Edward III. The talk was highly detailed, covering subjects ranging from peasants' diet to crime and craft guilds. Conan Doyle, in seconding the vote of thanks, regretted the fact that school history lessons were not as interesting. It seems as if Kitchin's talk set his mind concentrating on the fourteenth century, the grandeur of courtly tradition, knights in armour, the code of chivalry and his long-abiding interest in heraldry as well as a new awareness of the common man's lot.

Six weeks later, in the company of Drayson, Arthur Vernon Ford and H. Percy Boulnois, the Borough of Portsmouth Engineer, he travelled to the New Forest, staying at Emery Down near Lyndhurst. Conan Doyle immersed himself in the mood of the forest, walking the sylvan lanes, visiting the Rufus Stone at the site of the murder of William Rufus, the eleventh-century King of England, and the ruined Cistercian abbey at Beaulieu. He rented a hunting-box, a small woodland cottage containing the barest essentials, not far from Lyndhurst, returning for a few weeks in the late summer, surrounded by well over a hundred books as well as folders of documents either purchased or loaned from the public library in Portsmouth. His research was extensive, minutely detailed and perhaps required the peace and quiet of the forest: it seems Conan Doyle might have found domestic life rather tiresome with a young child in the house. Furthermore, he fell in love with the New Forest.

The research was, he considered, utterly vital. In short fiction, he felt, dramatic impact was paramount, but in sustained fiction, especially historical fiction, fine and accurate detail was imperative to success. He had to build in his mind an exact idea of the fourteenth century in its every aspect. In his autobiography, he summed up his feelings by writing, 'It is a great mistake to start putting out cargo when you have hardly stowed any on board.' He stowed away all he could lay his hands on, reading and sifting information which he entered in cross-referenced notebooks. One volume in particular provided Conan Doyle with a wealth of material and was central to his research. It was W. Longman's *Life and Times of Edward III*, an astonishing feat of historical reconstruction published in 1869.

By September, Conan Doyle was already writing the story, which was initially shaped into three rough but anomalous sections, perhaps anticipating a publisher's wish to cut it into a three-decker. Part one, starting in the Abbey of Beaulieu in the New Forest, concerns the formation and departure of the White Company, a group of bowmen commanded by Sir Nigel Loring which Alleyne Edricson joins, becoming Sir Nigel's squire. It went on to tell of their crossing to the Continent, their battles and adventures in France and Spain with Alleyne eventually winning his spurs, the hand of Maude, Sir Nigel's daughter, and his own knighthood. It is a boisterous tale about the bowmen and their love of sport and chivalry, both of them close to Conan Doyle's heart.

Nine months later, in July 1890, the novel was finished. It took much longer than Conan Doyle's other books partly because he wanted to get it just right and partly because he truly inhabited the narrative, which came alive for both him and his reader. The result, with which Conan Doyle was hugely pleased, was the best medieval novel in English literature apart from Sir Walter Scott's *Ivanhoe*. Conan Doyle claimed that, as he finished the manuscript, he declared aloud to himself, 'Well, I'll never beat that', and hurled his pen across the room where it stained the wallpaper. In 1921, when the journalist Herbert Ashley asked Conan Doyle which book he had most enjoyed writing, Conan Doyle was emphatic. It was *The White Company*, written, he said, when 'I was young and full of the first joy of life and action and I think I got some of it into my pages'. Payn accepted the story for serialisation in the *Cornhill Magazine* throughout 1891. He was thrilled by its vitality and came to regard it as one of his major publishing triumphs. In October, it was published as a three-decker novel.

Although confident of the book himself, Conan Doyle was worried about its critical reception. He had reason and summed up the reviews in a letter to his mother in mid-November. 'They are none of them hostile [he wrote] and yet I am disappointed. They treat it too much as a mere book of adventure – as if it were an ordinary boy's book – whereas I have striven to draw the exact types of character of the folk then living and have spent much work and pains over it, which seems so far to be quite unappreciated by the critics. They do not realise how conscientious my work has been.' In his eyes, *The White Company* was not a ripping yarn but a serious book about the bowman, whom he considered the most important soldier in English military history. One critic enraged him by condemning his mentioning a carriage as having existed in 1367: it had – he found the fact in his researches. Yet he also seems to have listened to the cavilling, for, in an interview in the *Bookman* in 1892, Conan Doyle admitted that 'as a rule, where historical novels fail is in the fact that there is too much history and too little novel.'

Conan Doyle could afford to ignore the critics. *The White Company* was a runaway success and set his reputation as a serious novelist. The three-decker edition soon sold out with over fifty one-volume editions following. It is the most widely published historical novel written in the English language, apart from *Ivanhoe*. Its standing may be judged by the fact that, when Britain was blockaded in the Second World War and paper was scarce, the government especially ensured that sufficient stocks were available to keep it in print. Being a stirring and patriotic tale, it was deemed a national morale booster. It is still in print to this day, a remarkable achievement.

Believing them to be his best work, Conan Doyle always thought highly of his historical novels. Any praise for them was gratefully received. Just after the First World War, at a luncheon given by the Dramatists Club, Edgar Wallace happened to say that Conan Doyle was primarily considered as the creator of Sherlock Holmes but that he amounted to much more as author of *The White Company*, which resulted in Wallace and Conan Doyle taking a long post-luncheon walk together in the nearby park despite their being at odds over spiritualism, of which Wallace strongly disapproved and over which he was publicly to attack Conan Doyle in the future.

Conan Doyle planned a sequel, which actually turned out to be an historical prequel: entitled *Sir Nigel*, it did not appear for fifteen years but, with *The White Company*, Conan Doyle considered it 'did thoroughly achieve my purpose, that [the two books] made an accurate picture of that great age, and that as a single piece of work they form the most complete, satisfying and ambitious thing I have ever done'.

The writing of *The White Company* had, however, been interrupted, which may have been the cause for it taking so long to be completed. The interruption was caused by a request from *Lippincott's Monthly Magazine* for another Sherlock Holmes story.

Lippincott's Monthly Magazine was an American publication. *A Study in Scarlet* had appeared in the USA. Conan Doyle received no payment for it, yet neither did the publishers. In effect, it came out as a pirated edition, for America was not a signatory of the Berne Convention of 1887 and, consequently, non-American authors had no copyright protection in the USA until the Chase Act of 1891 and Congress's approval of the International Copyright Act. Pirated it may have been, but it was also immensely successful and very well reviewed.

It was James Payn who was responsible. Payn had suggested to an agent acting for the American publishers, visiting Britain to commission books, that he approach Conan Doyle. In August 1889, Conan Doyle was invited to London to meet Joseph Marshall Stoddart, for many years editor of the *Encyclopaedia Americana* but now managing editor for *Lippincott's Monthly Magazine*. They dined together at the Langham Hotel in Portland Place. Conan Doyle was not Stoddart's only guest. As well as a Member of Parliament, Thomas Patrick Gill, there was present Oscar Wilde.

Both writers, having been wined and dined, agreed to write for the magazine. Conan Doyle recollected the evening in his autobiography: 'It was a golden evening for me . . . [Wilde's conversation] left an indelible impression upon my mind. He towered above us all, and yet had the art of seeming to be interested in all that we could say. He had delicacy of feeling and tact . . . He took as well as gave, but what he gave was unique. He had a curious precision of statement, a delicate flavour of humour, and a trick of small gestures to illustrate his meaning, which were peculiar to himself.' Wilde admitted enthusiasm for *Micah Clarke*, which endeared him to Conan Doyle. They even had a brief correspondence which, in later years, Conan Doyle was keen to point out was entirely impersonal and quite professional. What he thought of Wilde and the scandalous life he lived may be guessed, and he did not want to be associated with it.

Conan Doyle wrote to Stoddart a few days after their meeting that 'As far as I can see my way at present my story will either be called *The Sign of the Six* or *The Problem of the Sholto*. You said you wanted a spicy title.' It ended up as *The Sign of Four*. Wilde's contribution was arguably his most famous story, *The Picture of Dorian Gray*.

It was Conan Doyle's first commission, gas piping apart, and he must have been thrilled. The fee must have thrilled him, too. He was paid £100 for not less than forty thousand words for the magazine serial rights only: he retained the book rights. His confidence soared and Stavert has found the proof of it. On 12 October 1889, a share prospectus was issued for the Portsmouth and South Hampshire Electricity Supply Company which was raising capital to erect a generating station to supply Portsmouth and the surrounding villages with power. According to the list of founder subscribers, Conan Doyle applied for fifty ordinary £5 shares and one £5 founder's share. As it is known the medical practice income had levelled off at around £300 per annum, such an expenditure on speculative stock indicates Conan Doyle's conviction about his future.

The story was written and mailed by early October. Conan Doyle must have dashed it off in order to return to *The White Company*. His unprofessional haste showed, for *The Sign of Four* contained clumsy errors. In it a letter is quoted which was written on 7 July but it becomes September before nightfall, whilst Watson has a leg wound that was previously a shoulder injury. Conan Doyle picked up the chronological mistake himself and had it corrected when the book was typeset.

Despite this carelessness, the story succeeds in achieving Conan Doyle's intended dramatic tension, mixing together aspects of Wilkie Collins's *The Moonstone* and borrowing from Poe's 'The Murders in the Rue Morgue'. Revenge is, once more, the motive for murder and the story goes up to but not over the boundary with the supernatural. In outline, Miss Mary Morstan comes to ask Sherlock Holmes to go to a rendezvous with her. Sherlock Holmes and Watson comply. They meet Thaddeus Sholto, the son of a friend of Mary's father who had vanished a decade before, returning from India. Sholto explains that their fathers had obtained a treasure whilst running a penal colony in the Andaman Islands, Sholto senior dying before revealing the treasure's hiding place. A group of men known as 'The Four' was involved. Now Sholto's brother, Bartholomew, has discovered the treasure, but has been murdered by a poisoned thorn which Sherlock Holmes deduces is an Andaman Island blow-dart. A chase ensues and the original thief of the treasure tips it into the Thames whilst the simian-like native with the blowpipe is shot.

The story is famous for more than its action. It is here that Conan Doyle first shows Sherlock Holmes injecting himself with cocaine whilst a shocked Watson looks on. The scene is enthralling, a famous moment in the annals of English literature. Also expanded here is the relationship between Sherlock Holmes and Watson with the former shown, along with his eccentricities, in the cocoon of his rooms in Baker Street, living the bachelor life. In addition, and perhaps heeding the Globe Newspaper Syndicate criticism of *Micah Clarke*, Conan Doyle added a love interest. Watson proposes to and marries Mary Morstan whom he describes: 'Her face had neither regularity of feature nor beauty of complexion, but her expression was sweet and amiable, and her large blue eyes were singularly spiritual and sympathetic. In an experience of women which extends over many nations and three separate continents, I have never looked upon a face which gave a clearer promise of a refined and sensitive nature.' The portrayal comes close to describing Louise.

The response the story received when published in magazine form in the USA and Britain, in February 1890, as well as when it came out as a book published by Spencer Blackett in October, was very favourable, but Conan Doyle did not rest on his laurels. He managed to sell the second serial rights to have the story reprinted in the *Bristol Observer*, the *Glasgow Citizen*, the *Hampshire Telegraph* and the *Birmingham Weekly Magazine*.

In summary, 1890 was a good year for Conan Doyle. Stoddart published *The Sign of Four* in February. A collection of ten short stories, *The Captain of the Polestar*, appeared the next month, dedicated 'To my friend Major-General A.W. Drayson as a slight token of my admiration of his great and as yet unrecognised services to astronomy', to be followed by another collection of stories, *Mysteries and Adventures*, which brought together material published in *London Society* to which Conan Doyle had sold the entire rights. This publication infuriated him: the contents were early stories, inept by comparison with his recent work and better suppressed. As he observed years later, harking back to this collection, 'Have a care, young authors, have a care, or your worst enemy will be your early self!' *The Firm of Girdlestone* was finally published in April and, in July, *The White Company* was completed. Conan Doyle's life looked settled, yet there was change in the air.

That November, on what seems to have been the very spur of the moment, Conan Doyle reached a decision that was to radically change the course of his future. It began with a sudden decision to go to Berlin to visit Robert Koch, the eminent bacteriologist, who was advocating his new lymph inoculation cure for tuberculosis, first announced at the International Medical Congress of Berlin in August. Doctors from all over Europe and the USA were converging on Berlin to learn more. Conan Doyle determined to join the rush. Although he had few consumptive patients on his books, he had long been interested in immunisation and had followed developments in bacteriology. There may have been other reasons for his journey. Just as he had escaped to the New Forest for a short while, so this gave him another excuse to flee temporarily domesticity and the daily routine of his practice. It was also some while since he had last been abroad and, after a year of considerable creative output, he might have felt an urge to test pastures new. Whatever his reasons, his sudden departure, at what he described as a few hours' notice, was somewhat out of character for a man who usually planned his life although, *en route*, he paused in London long enough to pick up a commission to write an article about Koch for the *Review of Reviews*.

Conan Doyle arrived in Berlin in the middle of the month to discover it bulging with medical journalists, doctors and academics all come to attend Koch's daily demonstrations held in a variety of locations around the city. He tried to obtain tickets for one of these events in the Berlin University Medical School but there was not a seat to be had and, try as he might, he could not get to Koch who was, in any case, regarded somewhat as a medical parvenu. In lieu of meeting the great man, Conan Doyle obtained a set of lecture notes from an American doctor from Michigan called Hartz and succeeded instead in examining some of Koch's patients who had received his treatment.

It took him no time at all to decide that Koch's treatment was still experimental and untested and its publication premature. He saw that it was not the certain cure it was purported to be and, angry that sufferers' hopes might be raised, returned to the Central Hotel where he was staying and wrote to the *Daily Telegraph* in London, stating, 'Great as is Koch's discovery, there can be no question that our knowledge of it is still very incomplete, and that it leaves issues open to question. The sooner that this is recognised the less chance will there be of serious disappointment among those who are looking to Berlin for a panacea for their own or their friends' ill-health.' For his piece in the *Review of Reviews*, he went so far as to spell out his concern: 'It would be an encouraging of false hopes to pretend that the result is in any way assured.'

The moment that was to alter his life, however, did not happen in Berlin but on the train going there, when Conan Doyle fell into conversation with Malcolm Morris, a Harley Street dermatologist. He told Conan Doyle that a general practice in a provincial town was not the path to fame and fortune: he should go to London and specialise. When Conan Doyle replied than he had been taking an interest in ophthalmology, Morris advised him to go to Vienna to study the subject – for which Vienna had a world-class reputation – then set up in practice in London. Morris's comments also lent gravitas to Conan Doyle's own considerations of two years before.

What Morris was saying was, to some extent, what Conan Doyle wanted to hear. He was stuck in a rut in Southsea, his practice having reached its potential. If he was to remain in medicine, he would have to advance, whether or not he had a calling for it. Ophthalmology was, for him, not really a vocation but simply a means of bettering his lot which, if he was lucky, would not only bring him patients but afford him time to write.

He returned to Portsmouth, on 22 November, a changed man. He had, he wrote, 'spread my wings and had felt something of the powers within me'. Two days later, in a local newspaper interview, he stated he would soon be winding up his practice and quitting Southsea. His mind was made up and, as ever, once it was set there was no turning. When he asked her advice, his mother agreed. It was time for a change. Louise, it appears, was informed that they were leaving for Vienna, information she received with her usual equanimity. That she was suddenly being uprooted from her home and was to be parted from her young child, her mother and her friends appears to have been of no concern to her husband. His course was logged, his sail was set and she just had to meekly follow on, the dinghy behind his galleon.

The practice being too small to sell, it was closed. Conan Doyle passed his patients over to the care of Dr Claude Claremont, who ran a surgery further down Elm Grove and who had substituted for Conan Doyle on his various absences: it is likely they covered for each other from time to time. The Portsmouth Literary and Scientific Society threw him a farewell dinner at the Grosvenor Hotel on 13 December, presided over by Dr James Watson. Drayson proposed a toast to Conan Doyle who recounted his first evening in Portsmouth and the fight in which he had got embroiled. Clearly, Conan Doyle was a popular fellow and he was forever to have a soft spot in his heart for Portsmouth and Southsea.

Mary Louise, now nearly two years old, was sent across the Solent by paddle steamer to stay with her maternal grandmother, Mrs Hawkins, who was now living on the Isle of Wight. Conan Doyle paid up his lease on Bush Villas, packed his furniture into store and travelled north with Louise to spend Christmas at Masongill, stopping on the way to visit the Hoares in Birmingham. After Christmas, the couple set off for Vienna. Years later, Conan Doyle wrote in memory of the time, 'Now it was with a sense of wonderful freedom and exhilarating adventure that we set forth upon the next phase of our lives.'

7

Characters, Crime and Cocaine

The Conan Doyles arrived in Vienna on 5 January 1891, and rented rooms in a small *pension*. The following day, Conan Doyle started writing a story under commission to a penny rag called *Answers*. The story was *The Doings of Raffles Haw*, the idea coming to him whilst they were travelling across Europe. A novella of thirty thousand words, it was completed in just over three weeks.

Although it was not published until 1892, Conan Doyle hoped the commission advance would go some way towards paying for his projected six-month stay in Vienna. Certainly, attempting to recoup some of the costs in this way was a good idea but, if he had not fully sorted out how he was going to pay for the trip before he set off, it suggests he embarked on this venture without too much preparation. The story itself is very weak, about a chemist who discovers the secret of alchemy, becomes a multimillionaire and turns into a philanthropist but who then, far from helping the working class, turns it into a society of idle, discontented layabouts. Only Conan Doyle's knowledge of chemistry carries any authenticity in what is otherwise a banal tale, but the ease with which he obtained the commission shows how his literary career was advancing.

Conan Doyle studied at the Krankenhaus, but no sooner did he start attending lectures than another sign of his ill-preparedness raised its head. His command of German was insufficient for him to understand the specialised terminology of the lectures, a problem he had not anticipated and which nullified his being in Vienna. He admitted he would have learned more by remaining in London. The result was that he and Louise did not stay as long as they had planned and Conan Doyle turned the trip into an extended vacation during which he attended more to his literary fiction than to his medical future.

Once he had decided to give the lectures a miss, Conan Doyle started to enjoy himself. Vienna was cultured, exciting and romantic. He visited cafés, skated with Louise at the Prater and was introduced to the fringes of Viennese society by Brinsley Richards, the *Times* resident correspondent. In his autobiography, Conan Doyle reckons he spent four months in Vienna but, according to his diary, he left for Semmering on 9 March, so his sojourn was not much above two months. Travelling back to Britain by way of Venice, Milan and Paris, he did actually gain a little ophthalmic knowledge by visiting Edmund Landolt, one of the first ophthalmologists to publish extensively on diseases of the eye in Paris.

On 24 March, he and Louise arrived back in London and immediately rented rooms at 23, Montague Place in Bloomsbury, right behind the British Museum and facing its rear entrance: the building was demolished a few years later to make way for the University of London Senate House complex. In addition, he signed to pay £120 per annum for a front room and a share of a waiting room at 2 Upper Wimpole Street, fifteen minutes' walk away and just around the corner from Harley Street, famous then as now for its medical surgeries. Here, he set up as a consulting oculist, starting his practice on 6 April: that he had not a single relevant qualification and only his experience in Portsmouth to back him up did not deter him. He even became a registered member of the Ophthalmologic Society of the United Kingdom and, according to some sources, gained himself a brief affiliation with the Royal Westminster Eye Infirmary, today the world-famous Moorfields Eye Hospital, situated near Covent Garden. Hopes of establishing even a modest practice, however, were optimistic in the extreme. His consulting room was on the very periphery of the medical sphere of Harley Street and Wimpole Street, he was unknown and he had no contacts who would refer patients. He was later to record that he walked to his consulting rooms at ten o'clock in the morning and sat there until late afternoon without so much as a knock on the door: indeed, it seems he did not acquire one patient all the time he was there, which does not seem to have been much more than a month.

Although, in later years, Conan Doyle looked with wry amusement on his brief ophthalmologist's practice, joking that he was the one waiting in the waiting room, an interview he gave in August 1892 had him declaring that he was, for months, actually rushed off his feet with a morning surgery followed after lunch by work in the afternoon at the infirmary. Being left no time to write, he had decided to 'throw physic to the dogs' and turn to a literary career. The whole of this seems to be Conan Doyle covering up for his failure as an ophthalmologist. Perhaps he realised that his practice was built on shifting sands. It may be said, therefore, that his failure as an ophthalmologist was due to his inadequate planning, which had started from the moment he set off for Vienna, his lack of any real desire to continue in the competitive world of medicine, and his inner longing to become a writer.

The dearth of patients was, of course, a godsend to Conan Doyle's literary aspirations. He used the time to write, which he did in longhand, spurning the typewriter he had bought when in Southsea but which he never used. His daily output was, he reckoned, about three thousand words. This may seem an exaggeration, but it must be true when considering the speed with which he satisfied commissions. It means he could produce with pen and ink at the speed modern writers do with a word processor. What is more, this figure includes creative thinking time, and his handwriting did not suffer as a result. How he failed to suffer from cramp or repetitive strain injury is a wonder in itself. Quite possibly, his enjoyment of sport had toughened up the sinews in his wrist.

Whatever his daily output rate may have been, by April 1891 the Sherlock Holmes short stories were under way, the medium for them ready and waiting.

Newspapers, journals and magazines were in their heyday. The cost of wood pulp was low because the Scandinavian and Canadian forests were coming on line. Printing machines were becoming more sophisticated and operated at higher speeds. Type was still hand-set by armies of compositors but half-tone photographs were now possible instead of line drawings and steel or copper engravings. Advertising revenues rocketed to meet the cost. The result was that, in ten years from 1875, print circulation in Britain more than trebled.

The public themselves also craved the printed word. The Education Act of 1870 had made elementary schooling compulsory across the nation, considerably lowering the illiteracy rate. On top of that, increased mechanisation in factories allowed workers more leisure time in which many turned to the pleasures of reading. To meet this demand, publishers increased production manyfold, especially where catering for the semi-literate who were, from their elementary education, able to read but not to a very high intellectual standard. For them, penny weeklies such as *Answers* (founded in 1888) and *Tit-bits* were created. Fortunes were being made, but not just out of the working class. The middle class also wanted entertaining in print, their taste being for informed articles on politics, the theatre, the arts, science, travel and sharp critical journalism questioning, often controversially, the politics and arts of the day. With the advent of mass railway travel and the rise of the urban commuter, there was also a need to provide reading material for travellers. News-stands sprang up on every corner and news stalls appeared on railway platforms. Magazines such as the *Illustrated London News* and the *Review of Reviews* appeared, richly illustrated, well printed and expertly edited. Britain was awash with the printed word as never before.

One of the barons of this new press empire was George Newnes, who had started *Tit-bits* in 1881, the title coming from the contents which consisted of titbits of information, short and punchy informative articles, facts and figures, humour, readers' correspondence and short, sometimes serialised, stories. So successful was this publication that Newnes went on to develop niche market publications – he was amongst the first to publish women's magazines – and, in January 1891, a monthly called the *Strand Magazine*, which was funded more or less entirely from the profits of *Tit-bits*.

The editor Newnes appointed to run it was Herbert Greenhough Smith, an erudite, well-read and strongly built man with a receding hairline, a bushy Victorian moustache, iron-framed spectacles and a somewhat square head. Four years older than Conan Doyle, Greenhough Smith was educated at St John's College, Cambridge and edited the magazine from its first issue until his retirement in 1930. Following the style and content of the American magazine *Harper's New Monthly Magazine*, the *Strand Magazine* consisted of high-quality illustrations, fiction, interviews with the famous or the interesting, and factual articles that appealed to the readership. An example of a typical early issue is that of July 1892 which contained some fiction (including a story by Jules Verne, a serial by Alexandre Dumas and an on-going saga which must have been in opposition to Conan Doyle entitled 'A Romance from a Detective's Casebook' by Dick Donovan), a children's story for parents to read to their offspring, a humorous article about animals called 'Zig-Zags at the Zoo', factual articles (the evolution of the cycle, the raising of a sunken ship, the story of Mont Blanc), biographical portraits of celebrities (including Lord Herschell, several cricketers and Alexandre Dumas) and popular composers, a long illustrated interview with the veteran journalist George Sala, and some pages of humorous cartoons. Published from offices in Southampton Street, just off The Strand from which it took its name, editorial policy dictated that the magazine should be illustrated on every page to give it a modern and appealing look, and that it should be aimed at the middle classes rather than the readership of *Tit-bits*. It was an instant success, the first issue selling over 300,000 copies.

Such an active and competitive popular press was perfect for the development of writers' careers. All the publications were permanently hungry for copy and editors were forever scouting round for new talent to snap up or poach from an opponent. It was, in short, a writers' market.

Around the time the *Strand Magazine* started up, Conan Doyle seems to have realised he was possibly on to a good thing with Sherlock Holmes who might, given luck, be a valuable second string to his literary, not to mention financial, bow. He also realised that if he were to concentrate on writing about one serial character and publish in just one periodical, he could perhaps gain a dedicated readership and build up a reputation for himself and the periodical. Sherlock Holmes seemed a likely candidate for such a plan. Some argument exists as to whether this scheme of things was devised by Conan Doyle who then took it to the *Strand Magazine* or whether Newnes or Greenhough Smith thought it up and approached Conan Doyle to get hold of Sherlock Holmes. In all probability, it was a mixture of the two. Established characters were already beginning to prove popular with those buying the new magazine, and it took no major leap of authorial or editorial imagination to see where the future might lead. A serial, however, could be disadvantageous because a reader missing an episode would lose the thread of the narrative. 'Clearly [Conan Doyle wrote] the ideal compromise was a character which carried through, and yet instalments which were each complete in themselves, so that the purchaser was always sure that he could relish the whole contents of the magazine.'

Where Sherlock Holmes was concerned, Conan Doyle was very shrewd. He had his finger on the readers' pulse. All he needed to do was diagnose their needs and meet them, which is what he did with Sherlock Holmes but not with all his fiction: Sherlock Holmes was tailored to the market whilst much of his other work was not so specifically targeted.

Possibly before he went to Vienna, but certainly by early 1891, Conan Doyle acquired a literary agent, A.P. Watt, to represent him. Literary agents were a new phenomenon on the scene, encouraged into business by the thriving world of publishing. Watt was the first who set up his business in 1875 and coined the phrase 'literary agent' to describe himself. By 1890, he was successfully handling a number of authors and building a strong client list.

The decision to seek an agent was another astute move on Conan Doyle's part. If he was going to Vienna for six months, as he had planned, he would have needed someone to keep his work on the boil and his name in front of editors.

In January, Watt submitted a Conan Doyle story entitled 'The Voice of Science' to Greenhough Smith, requesting £4 per thousand words. The fee was agreed, the story appearing in the March issue. On 3 April, Conan Doyle sent Watt a new Sherlock Holmes short story called 'A Scandal in Bohemia'. In his diary, he recorded that he finished 'A Case of Identity' on 10 April and, ten days later, sent off 'The Red-Headed League' followed a week after by 'The Boscombe Valley Mystery' and, next, 'The Five Orange Pips', although he did not part with this until 18 May. Watt forwarded 'A Scandal in Bohemia' and 'The Red-Headed League' to Greenhough Smith who, around about the time he retired from his editorship, remembered the stories as being 'a god-send to an editor jaded with wading through reams of impossible stuff! The ingenuity of plot, the limpid clearness of style, the perfect art of telling a story! The very handwriting, full of character, and clear as print.' He went on, 'I at once realised that here was the greatest short story writer since Edgar Allan Poe.'

After reading the first stories from Watt, Greenhough Smith contracted Conan Doyle to a series of six Sherlock Holmes stories, the first, 'A Scandal in Bohemia', appearing in the July 1891 edition of the magazine. Conan Doyle received on average £35 for each of the first six tales. Thus began the rise of Sherlock Holmes and Conan Doyle's association with the *Strand Magazine* which brought him fame and fortune, simultaneously boosting the magazine to the heights of considerable success and reputation. Conan Doyle even purchased shares in the company in due time, such was his close affiliation with it.

The first six stories, those mentioned above plus 'The Man with the Twisted Lip', appeared between July and December 1891. With those written, Conan Doyle had no thoughts of writing more but, by October, when it was clear how popular Sherlock Holmes had become, Greenhough Smith requested six more. Conan Doyle, whose agile mind was, by now, moving on to other ideas, decided to demand a higher price. Partly, he did this politely to discourage the editor from asking for more Sherlock Holmes stories, yet it is just as likely that A.P. Watt encouraged him in order to test the waters and judge how far Greenhough Smith might go and, thereby, reach an estimate of the current value of Conan Doyle and his work. When Watt went to

Greenhough Smith, he requested £50 a story. The editor agreed without demur by return of post, adding that he should like to have copy as soon as possible. How Conan Doyle and Watt responded to this reply is unknown but can be imagined. They both must have realised that, with Sherlock Holmes, they had a very viable commercial property.

Conan Doyle knuckled down. His method of working out a plot was simple and the same as that employed by any other detective writer before or since. He invented the crime and its solution, plotted the outline and course of detection, then, constructing the characters within it, sat down and wrote it, concealing the solution until the climax. The methodology seems obvious to the sophisticated reader of today but Conan Doyle was frequently asked, throughout his life, how he constructed the stories and if he knew how they would end. 'People have often asked me [he wrote in his autobiography] whether I knew the end of a Holmes story before I started it. Of course I do. One could not possibly steer a course if one did not know one's destination.'

The second six Sherlock Holmes stories to appear were 'The Adventure of the Blue Carbuncle' (January 1892), 'The Adventure of the Speckled Band' (February), 'The Adventure of the Engineer's Thumb' (March), 'The Adventure of the Noble Bachelor' (April), 'The Adventure of the Beryl Coronet' (May) and 'The Adventure of the Copper Beeches' (June). The first dozen were then collected into a book under the title *The Adventures of Sherlock Holmes*, published later in 1892 and dedicated to Joseph Bell. The first edition sold over seven thousand copies inside a month.

By the end of a year of stories, Sherlock Holmes had become a well-known, established character. Conan Doyle, his creator, was hugely famous, but this had not even been a gradual process. It was with the very first short story, 'A Scandal in Bohemia', that his fame took off.

The origins of the story were founded in Conan Doyle's visit to Vienna. The tale centred upon Irene Adler who, in Sherlock Holmes's eyes, 'eclipses and predominates the whole of her sex' and was always 'the' woman. An opera singer, she had recently had an affair with the King of Bohemia whom she intended to blackmail with an incriminating photograph. In trying to outsmart her, Sherlock Holmes disguised himself as a clergyman and a groom but she got the better of him, becoming the only woman in Holmes's life who ever interested him and whom he was always to regard with high esteem. In other words, she was the only woman ever to triumph over the great detective, which action captivated him. When the case was solved, he accepted a photo of her in lieu of a fee. Who Conan Doyle based Irene upon has long been a subject of speculation. Some believe his model was Lola Montez, a famous adventuress who, after an acting career in London, became the mistress of Louis of Bavaria in the late 1840s. Others assert that it was Ludmilla Hubel, a singer and actress who became emotionally entangled with Archduke John Salvator of Tuscany, Emperor Franz Joseph's nephew. The affair had been the talk of the town when Conan Doyle was in Vienna, photographs of them appearing in the Viennese press in an attempt to besmirch her reputation. Their subsequent story is the stuff of a Conan Doyle mystery: the Archduke defied both his father and uncle and married Hubel, renouncing his inheritance. The couple sailed for South America on the Archduke's yacht. Neither they, nor their vessel, were ever heard of again. The name Irene, it has been suggested, was drawn from Irene Vanburgh, a contemporary star of the London stage, whilst Adler may have been taken from Viktor Adler, the leader of the Social Democrats in Vienna who had been the centre of attention during Conan Doyle's visit because he was deemed a threat to the throne.

Conan Doyle's timing of the story was immaculate if, perhaps, fortuitous. Royal scandals were all the rage at the time and, as now, drew much public interest. When 'A Scandal in Bohemia' was published in July, it made Conan Doyle famous almost overnight. Readers, enjoying not only the outrage of a scandal but also the intrigue, searched for the true identity of the fictional King of Bohemia and Irene Adler. Many believed the tale to be some kind of *roman à clef*. Whilst Sherlock Holmes sought to solve a crime, the readers hunted for the hidden key in the story.

Two more of the first dozen tales were important in Conan Doyle's development of Sherlock Holmes and the stories. In 'The Boscombe Valley Mystery', Holmes shows characteristics that were to recur in future stories and proved very popular. As well as solving a crime, Holmes passes moral judgment upon the perpetrators, placing himself above the law of the land but firmly within the structure of natural justice. In the story, Holmes resists having the murderer, John Turner, apprehended because he is suffering from a fatal illness. This decision is but one of many throughout the stories which has Holmes putting his own spin on the law. 'The Speckled Band', perhaps Conan Doyle's most famous Sherlock Holmes story after *The Hound of the Baskervilles*, became so popular partly because it revolved around the classic detective fiction problem of a crime committed in a locked room. The villain,

Dr Grimesby Roylott, is killed by an Indian swamp adder which wraps itself around his head. However, it was not the mystery that made the story seminal. It was the fact that Conan Doyle, realising that he could not sustain the timeline, abandoned the chronological sequence of the stories. From here on, Watson recounted different cases that occurred throughout his friendship with Sherlock Holmes. This allowed Conan Doyle to write as many stories as his imagination could foster, but it also gave rise to a major concern amongst what are now referred to as Sherlockians. These are a band of utterly dedicated Sherlock Holmes devotees who have studied – and continue to study – the stories with an infinitely fine-toothed literary comb. Since 'The Speckled Band' was published, they have puzzled or argued long and hard over the dating and 'true chronology' of the tales. This obsession with discovering the minutest detail of Sherlock Holmes's life was something Conan Doyle never anticipated. Had he realised his readers down the ages would be so pernickety, he might have been more precise – or mischievously devious – with his creations.

The public response to the Sherlock Holmes stories was massive and took Newnes by surprise. Each issue of the *Strand Magazine* was ardently awaited at the news-stands. Queues formed on publication day. Arthur Conan Doyle was soon a household name and a noteworthy literary figure. In December 1891, he was the subject of one of the *Strand Magazine*'s 'Portraits of Celebrities at Different Times' articles, the piece promising that the 'extraordinary adventures of Sherlock Holmes, which have proved so popular with our readers during the past six months, will be continued in the new year'. No fictional character had ever become so universally known in such a short space of time. In a matter of months, Sherlock Holmes was as well known as Queen Victoria and better known than many of the leading political figures of the time. He remains almost as well known to this day.

The question must have been one Conan Doyle asked himself in the early days – what was it that made the corpus of Sherlock Holmes stories so very successful and enduring? The factors are numerous.

The concept of a series of stories based upon two individual characters was central to the success. Readers could develop a relationship with them, identify with them and feel they knew them: and, as with any friendship, they were always wanting to know more. Sherlock Holmes's attitudes and Watson's reactions were also frequently those of any discerning reader and, therefore, the reader/character bond was strengthened through common beliefs and realisations. Additionally, the formula Conan Doyle had devised, and to which he adhered quite rigidly, gave the stories an instant accessibility.

Sherlock Holmes's character was, of course, crucial. Conan Doyle constructed a highly complex person who was so brilliantly portrayed as to be almost real. He was, from the start, a true heroic figure in command of an agile and logically cool analytical mind which he used to fight evil and injustice. His physical appearance was described in *A Study in Scarlet*. He was over six feet tall and very lean with an evident incisiveness brought about by his acute senses: his hearing was highly tuned, his eyes piercingly sharp although they could, at times, be distant when he was in one of his 'intervals of torpor'. He had a thin, aquiline nose which enhanced his air of alertness and decision. His chin was square and determined and his frame, though sparse, physically powerful.

No matter what horrors he beheld or what tight spots he found himself in, he was invariably cool and collected although, when hot on the trail, he could become electrified with suppressed excitement. Untouched by sentimentality or emotion he had, as Watson put it in 'A Scandal in Bohemia', a 'cold, precise, but admirably balanced mind . . . the most perfect reasoning and observing machine that the world has seen'. Not only was he unmoved by emotion, but he spurned it in case it affected his logic. In *The Sign of Four*, Holmes says, 'Love is an emotional thing, and whatever is emotional is opposed to that true, cold reason which I place above all things. I could never marry myself, lest I bias my judgement.' It follows that no women entered into his life: romance was not a part of Sherlock Holmes's scheme of things, a factor that increased the reader's belief in his powers. In Conan Doyle's time, celibacy was considered beneficial to intellectual prowess, sexuality numbing the senses. That being said, Sherlock Holmes did consider female intuition to be important and admitted as much in 'The Man with the Twisted Lip'.

As all heroes should be, Sherlock Holmes was almost always right but never patronising about it, although he carried many of the aloof aspects of an upper-class upbringing. A man of authority, he was always respected, even held in awe by everyone except the most debauched or evil of his adversaries and the odd choleric member of the aristocracy whom he invariably – but politely – put in his place. He frequently disdained others in authority whom he considered somehow lacking. In other words, as was the case with Conan Doyle himself, Sherlock Holmes did not suffer fools gladly. Despite his almost superhuman intellect, Holmes is a man like others. He has expensive tastes, enjoys fine food and superior wines, appreciates fine art, enjoys the opera and plays the violin.

Conan Doyle was far too masterly a writer, whether by design or intuitiveness, to make Sherlock Holmes too perfect. He had his faults, a haughty arrogance being the most apparent, but he possessed many enviable qualities that gave him an added realism and endeared him to readers. He was independent and had a private income which allowed him the freedom to pursue his detective work. In the mould of the true Victorian gentleman, he was a patriot, respectful of women (as was his creator), gallant and well mannered without being foppish. He was also, on the somewhat negative side, often inordinately proud, occasionally intractably stubborn and not averse (once again, like Conan Doyle) to letting his fists do the talking. His strong-willed obstinacy also supported his famous vices of smoking tobacco and taking dope. Being a confirmed bachelor made him identifiable to male readers and enticingly available to female readers, this enhanced by the hint of a long-lost love affair which Sherlock Holmes had to sacrifice for the sake of Victorian propriety.

The most important thing about Sherlock Holmes was that he was seen to be extraordinary, not just in his detective life but as a character. Conan Doyle achieved this by giving him specific and highly memorable eccentricities, a technique many writers have since emulated and imitated: one has only to think of Ian Fleming's James Bond with his shaken-not-stirred dry martinis, his love of Bentley cars and his preference for a Walther PPK automatic. Sherlock Holmes's foibles included keeping his cigars in a coal scuttle, his tobacco in the toe-end of a Persian slipper and his unanswered mail stapled to the mantelpiece with a jackknife.

Conan Doyle's readers soon came to understand that Sherlock Holmes was, his eccentricities apart, a remarkable man who was an analytical chemist, an authority on tobacco and capable of identifying individual newspaper typefaces at a glance. He could do without sleep for days on end or slumber for just as long without rousing. When he chose, he could move from near-coma to action in minutes, could disappear without explanation and was a master of disguise. Whilst on the track of a crime, he could do without food for long periods, then, when he did eat, he had the palate of a discerning gourmet. He continuously smoked cigars, cigarettes or a pipe, his heavy black shag, one of the most tar-rich tobaccos known and often associated with rough, industrial manual workers, adding to the enigma of the man.

Sherlock Holmes's pipe-smoking was more than an affectation or addiction. As a doctor as well as a smoker, Conan Doyle was aware of nicotine stimulation and put this knowledge into Sherlock Holmes's possession: he would categorise a case by the amount of tobacco he needed to get his brain working. The case of 'The Red-Headed League', for example, was considered a 'three-pipe problem'.

Perhaps the most famous of all Sherlock Holmes's eccentricities was his drug habit, which has raised intense debate for over a century. Why, it has been wondered, did Conan Doyle make Sherlock Holmes a cocaine user, begging the question as to whether Conan Doyle himself was an addict?

From early in his literary existence, Sherlock Holmes took drugs. Morphine was mentioned but the main drug he used was cocaine. As a doctor, Conan Doyle was aware of the specific symptoms of cocaine usage and he gave them to Sherlock Holmes, who typically exhibited periods of prolonged sleep, general tiredness, occasional lassitude and mental depression. His nervous restlessness, his ability to do without sleep for long periods, his mood swings and his ability to drop into a deep somnolence all point to an addiction of some sort.

In *A Study in Scarlet*, Watson, not yet familiar with his friend's personal habits, records, 'for days on end he would lie upon the sofa in the sitting-room, hardly uttering a word or moving a muscle from morning to night. On these occasions I have noticed such a dreamy, vacant expression in his eyes, that I might have suspected him of being addicted to the use of some narcotic, had not the temperance and cleanliness of his whole life forbidden such a notion.' Such symptoms are more relevant to opium or morphine use than cocaine. However, in *The Sign of Four*, it is obvious that Sherlock Holmes has a cocaine addiction. Watson reports, 'Sherlock Holmes took his bottle from the corner of the mantelpiece, and his hypodermic syringe from its neat morocco case. With his long, white, nervous fingers he adjusted the delicate needle, and rolled back his left shirt-cuff. For some little time his eyes rested thoughtfully upon the sinewy forearm and wrist, all dotted and scarred with innumerable puncture-marks. Finally, he thrust the sharp point home, pressed down the tiny piston, and sank back into the velvet-lined arm-chair with a long sigh of satisfaction. Three times a day for many months I had witnessed this performance . . .'

When Watson summons up the courage to confront his friend about his drug use, the result is a ready admission: '"Which is it today," I asked, "morphine or cocaine?" He raised his eyes languidly from the old black-leather volume which he had opened. "It is cocaine," he said, "a seven-per-cent solution. Would you care to try it?" . . . "I suppose that

Left: Arthur Conan Doyle, aged 5, a pencil drawing by his uncle, Richard Doyle.

Right: John Doyle, Conan Doyle's grandfather, the famous political cartoonist known as 'HB'.

Left: Michael Conan.

Conan Doyle, aged six, with his father, Charles.

Mary Doyle, Conan Doyle's mother, aged about 30.

Joseph Bell. (Royal College of Surgeons, Edinburgh)

The *Hope*, a steam-powered whaler of about 400 tons.

The ship's doctor – Conan Doyle (third from left) on board the *Hope*, 1880.

Dr. Arthur Conan Doyle M.B. C.M.,
graduate of the University of Edinburgh.

Dr. George Turnavine Budd.

6, Elliott Terrace, Plymouth, where Conan Doyle lodged with Budd: formerly a
gentlemen's club, it was well beyond Budd's means. (Martin Booth)

A picnic outing of inmates of Sunnyside asylum, June 6, 1889: Charles Doyle (top row, first left) holds his diary. (Angus Health Trust)

Left: Louise Hawkins, Conan Doyle's first wife.

Louise and Conan Doyle on their tricycle, by the front door of the house in Tennison Road, South Norwood.

Conan Doyle on skis in Switzerland. (*Strand Magazine*)

Undershaw, the house Conan Doyle built in the 'Surrey Highlands' at Hindhead. (The Mansell Collection)

Right: George Gissing,
E. W. Hornung, Conan Doyle
and H. G. Wells in Italy,
1898.

Left: Conan Doyle, motor
fanatic, with his motorbike at
Undershaw in February,
1905.

Right: William Gillette.

W. G. Grace bowls out Conan Doyle: an illustration from the *Strand Magazine*.
(*Strand Magazine*)

its influence is physically a bad one. I find it, however, so transcendingly stimulating and clarifying to the mind that its secondary action is a matter of small moment."'

Watson implores Sherlock Holmes to give up drugs, warning him of the dangers, but the detective considers them worth the price. When struggling with a difficult case he can, he says, dispense with his drugs but, once he is back to his everyday existence, he needs them to combat 'the dull routine of existence', his mind desperate for 'mental exaltation'.

In 'The Man with the Twisted Lip', Sherlock Holmes jokes with Watson about his cocaine injections, denying that he has included opium smoking in his list of depravities. In the course of the investigation, they go to an opium den in the East End of London, the interior of which Conan Doyle describes in considerable detail although he clearly knew little about opium smoking, for he assumes it was smoked like tobacco. How Conan Doyle got his information is unknown. He could well have gone to a den, for such establishments, of which there were a number in the dockland area of London where they catered predominantly to the small Chinese community and oriental seamen, were not infrequently visited by curious tourists or those out to look for the exciting, seamier side to the metropolis. Charles Dickens certainly visited one. He went to the rough end of London with the police, in order to research *The Mystery of Edwin Drood*, and saw an old crone smoking opium. It is, in fact, unlikely than Conan Doyle went to such lengths to research his story. He was not in the habit of looking so deeply into the factual bases of the Sherlock Holmes tales and he more than likely drew his information from newspaper and magazine accounts such as the anonymous article published in the *Strand Magazine* in the summer of 1891, about a visit to the same opium den as Dickens had gone to on Ratcliffe Highway.

The real reason why Conan Doyle made Sherlock Holmes an addict was not to give him a flawed character (addiction was not censured in Victorian times, as it was subsequently to become) or a peculiar foible. It was because he wanted his readers to view Holmes as an aesthete. Drug addiction had a romantic, artistic ring to it. Poets and writers, artists and musicians were, as the parlance had it, *habitués*, their habits a sign of their uniqueness and intellectual or even spiritual superiority. Drug-taking was an acceptable vice and few readers would have condemned Sherlock Holmes for his addiction. Only the grand curmudgeon, George Bernard Shaw, criticised Holmes as 'a drug addict without a single amiable trait'. Cocaine, the drug of preference of the upper classes or well-to-do, of which Conan Doyle accurately wrote, squarely outlining its stimulation of the mind, was exotic. Opiates were common, frequently found in many medicines and, apart from that, they had connotations of association with low-class Chinese. Such a drug as opium would never do for such a high-class man as Sherlock Holmes.

Conan Doyle's choice of cocaine was also based upon his knowledge of it gained as a result of his being a doctor. A stimulant that acts on the higher levels of the mind, it induces restless activity, promoting a euphoric sense of physical and mental potency through which weariness and hunger are eradicated. Its after-effects, however, are severe headaches and a deep depression. Derived from coca leaves which are used by South American Indians who masticate them, it had been known of in Europe since the sixteenth century, although it was not until 1860 that the alkaloid was purified and named cocaine. It is almost certain that Conan Doyle would have come across it in use during his Southsea years, for it was commonly used as an anaesthetic in eye surgery and, later, in dentistry, but his knowledge may have predated his graduation from Edinburgh.

There was intense scientific and medical interest in the potential of coca in the 1870s. Dr Alexander Hughes Bennett of the University of Edinburgh investigated coca leaves and cocaine in some depth, publishing his results in both the *British Medical Journal* and the *Edinburgh Medical Journal*. Experimentation into coca was also conducted by Professor Robert Christison in 1870, when he believed he was more than likely the first man in Europe to conduct such experiments, repeating his work in 1875 and publishing the results in a paper entitled 'Observations on the effects of the leaves of Erythroxylon coca' in the *British Medical Journal* in 1876. For the second series of experiments, he had obtained his supply of leaves from Professor Charles Wyville Thomson, who gathered them for him during the HMS *Challenger* expedition. Prior to Thomson's return, his supply had been small and erratic. Christison's work consisted of taking sustained physical exercise as a control, chewing coca leaves and then repeating the exercise, usually in the form of a long walk, observing the effects of the drug in terms of preventing tiredness and appetite. Not only did he self-experiment but he also recruited students into his research programme. Christison's experiments were conducted before Conan Doyle joined the university, but the outcome of them was probably still a discussion point amongst undergraduates, and Christison was still a leading light in the university. In *A Study in Scarlet*, Sherlock Holmes's experimenting on himself could well be based not upon Christison's trial of such things as the calabar bean but, more pertinently, upon his chewing of coca leaves, which was well known amongst the medical faculty students, some of whom had, in any case, been guinea-pigs.

Once it was discovered that cocaine was an excellent local anaesthetic, it quickly became an important part of a doctor's cabinet and, throughout the 1880s, a vast number of papers were published about it. Conan Doyle would therefore have known all about the uses of cocaine and how it was possible to administer it. In addition, whilst he was starting to plot out *A Study in Scarlet*, an article on the subject of cocaine appeared in *Chambers' Journal*, condensing all the recent data, so this may have helped to stimulate his imagination. If not, coca products were plentiful enough. Coca lozenges, wine, sherry and port were available commercially. Many patent medicines contained it. Coca-Cola, first sold as a syrup in the USA in 1886, and advertised as the 'intellectual beverage', contained coca as its active ingredient until 1903.

Another source of Conan Doyle's knowledge may have come to him through his awareness of his father's medical condition. Charles Doyle was by now suffering from epileptic fits, for the treatment of which various drugs including morphine were prescribed. There were behavioural similarities between Sherlock Holmes and Charles Doyle, for both exhibited the symptoms of sudden explosions of creative energy followed by periods of exhaustion and insularity. It may have been the case that cocaine, the new 'wonder drug', was also tried out on Charles Doyle to see if it had any effect upon his seizures.

As time passed, the disadvantages of cocaine started to reach the journals. Its side effects were studied and the problems of addiction were recognised. By the 1890s, cocaine was being considered dangerous, and Conan Doyle, who kept abreast of scientific advancement, started to play down Sherlock Holmes's drug usage, Dr Watson's attitude towards it becoming increasingly hardened and disapproving. In 'The Adventure of the Missing Three-Quarter', Holmes himself remarked in retrospect that his hypodermic syringe was an 'instrument of evil' and Watson spoke of his friend's 'drug mania' threatening his career. 'For years,' Watson declared, 'I gradually weaned him from that drug mania which had threatened once to check his remarkable career. Now I knew that under ordinary conditions he no longer craved for this artificial stimulus; but I was well aware that the fiend was not dead, but sleeping.' Conan Doyle was ahead of his time, aware that drug addiction was rarely overcome and could only be suppressed, not extinguished.

Sherlock Holmes was at least right up to date in his addiction, and he must be the earliest fictional recreational abuser of cocaine. The use of cocaine as a leisure drug did not reach Europe from the USA until well into the 1890s and, even then, it was restricted to a very small coterie indeed.

Certainly, Holmes was addicted, but this does not address the perennial question of whether or not Conan Doyle ever tried the drug himself. He did experiment with gelseminum and it is logical to think that he might have similarly tested cocaine upon himself to see what effects it might induce. On the other hand, he could have read a paper published in the *Transactions of the Medical Society of Virginia* in November 1887 by William A. Hammond, a retired Surgeon General of the US Army. Hammond had conducted experiments on himself, injecting cocaine and recording the effects of increasing doses which he found expanded mental activity, inspiring a sense of exhilaration and a burning desire to write which he did with a lucidity that amazed him. Hammond's work was known in Britain and reported in the medical press. Conan Doyle would almost certainly have come across it.

If he tried cocaine, or chewed coca leaves, Conan Doyle was certainly never addicted to them. There are no signs of his having a dependency. His fertile mind and energetic lifestyle were the result of his own impetuosity and verve rather than an artificially stimulated state. The only dangerous drug he is likely to have taken, but was never addicted to, was opium. It was in common medical use and there was hardly a member of the British population who did not take it at some time to cure fever or diarrhoea. This may account for the content of some of his more fantastic stories, but there is no way of proving the fact.

Conan Doyle may never have come across a cocaine addict upon whom he could base his description of Sherlock Holmes's habituation but there is one highly possible candidate for cocaine usage whom he may have used as a model. It is Dr George Turnavine Budd.

Budd was in the year above Conan Doyle at the University of Edinburgh and so he must have begun his studies there in 1875 when Christison was in the closing stages of his testing programme. Such an eccentric character as Budd, had he had the opportunity, would have jumped at the chance to sample coca leaves, which rumour would have suggested were a powerful mental and physical stimulant. If he did join Christison's team, did he then, as a doctor with access to it, progress to cocaine? He was certainly very free in the heavy doses of drugs he prescribed to his Plymouth patients and he seems to have had a casual attitude towards drugs in general.

This may well be wishful thinking, but it is certainly not out of the question. Cocaine had already been in existence for twenty years. Although it did not come into general use until after 1884, and Conan Doyle was with Budd in 1882, it was assuredly available and a known quantity. A letter entitled 'The Use of Coca' by J. Alexander Bell, published in the *British Medical Journal* as early as 1874, covered the use not only of coca but also of cocaine, which was to enter the United States pharmacopoeia in 1880.

Budd exhibited great mood swings, bouts of considerable frenetic energy, and he seemed hardly ever to flag. As a stimulant, cocaine counteracts depression, filling its user with high spirits and optimism, one effect being to make otherwise improbable enterprises take on aspects of feasibility. Budd's endless schemes to make money would qualify him for addiction in this respect.

In *The Stark Munro Letters*, there is a description of Budd falling ill, his symptoms including a high temperature, headaches, renal pains and loss of appetite: Conan Doyle put this down to rheumatic fever, which may well have been the correct diagnosis, but there is one other interesting and perhaps relevant symptom. Budd felt as if there was, as he put it, 'a mouse nibbling inside my left elbow'. Adverse reactions following a cocaine overdose are fairly frequent and do not depend upon the amount taken but upon the individual: anxiety, cold sweats, insomnia, impotence, undue aggressiveness, paranoia and hallucinations are all signs of a high dosage. The hallucinations are commonly tactile and the sensation of insects or tiny animals crawling on or under the skin is the most frequent.

By the time Budd died in 1889, his mental condition had severely deteriorated, and it must be remembered that he was very aggressive and became paranoid, convinced that someone was trying to poison him. His obituary in the *Plymouth Western Morning News* stated that 'Overwork brought on congestion of the brain'. Perhaps Budd gave more to Conan Doyle's writing than has hitherto been thought.

The character of Watson was another reason for the success of the Sherlock Holmes stories. Chronicler, friend and observer, he was the complete antithesis of Holmes. Where the great detective was arrogant, corybantic and self-absorbed, Watson was indulgent, patient, generous and loyal. He was the commonsensical mortal to Holmes's immortal, the human to his eccentric superhuman. Readers trusted him as a doctor and a comparatively stable individual, and he was the perfect literary device to take them into the convolutions of the plots.

Watson's reactions to events were normal and echoed those of the readers. When he was surprised or shocked, so were they. His morality, sense of common decency, honesty and integrity were traits to which they themselves aspired. A representative of the readers, Watson was a stereotypical Victorian, middle-class gentleman. Indeed, in 'The Adventure of the Abbey Grange', Holmes tells him, 'Watson, you are a British jury, and I never met a man who was more eminently fitted to represent one.'

Acting as an intermediary, Watson fulfils a vital narrative role. He is the eyes and ears of the reader, their advocate when it comes to questioning motives and deductions, their representative at the scene of the crime. He was, in many respects, a camera. A lingering judgment of Watson portrays him as dense, a man whose wit is not quite quick enough to keep up with Sherlock Holmes. This is wrong, and possibly brought about by theatrical and cinematic interpretations of his character rather than literary ones engendered by the page. Conan Doyle, aware of this opinion of his character, defended him by saying that those who considered Watson to be a fool were simply admitting that they had not read the stories with sufficient attention.

The universal appeal of these two remarkable inventions relies upon their being archetypal. Holmes is a mysterious and even threatening genius, an eccentric and obsessive addict who runs roughshod over the law when it suits him, albeit in the cause of justice. Watson, on the other hand, is a loyal, brave and considerate henchman. They complemented each other and set the mould for a century of detective fiction: Sherlock Holmes had Watson, Poirot had Captain Hastings, Lord Peter Wimsey had his valet Bunter and now, 120 years later, Inspector Morse has Lewis.

Sherlock Holmes appealed to male readers but his gallant attitudes towards women, even though he actively suspected and disliked them in the stories, prevented him from being alienated by female readers. Although he respected women, Holmes was never comfortable with them. One always had the feeling he felt out of his depth in their company and had to stand off from them. He was not a misogynist, but a confirmed bachelor who was set in his ways. The women whom he met were usually all of a type, damsels in distress coming to the knight for salvation from their woes. They lacked any real literary depth and were quiet, delicate creatures who needed protection. Conan Doyle's weakness in writing about women – and, therefore, his character's reticence in dealing with them – stemmed from his own inward desire to be the man, the protector, the saviour of women in peril. Conan Doyle found himself at a loss at times when dealing with what today would be termed women with balls. Both Conan Doyle and Sherlock Holmes would be horrified, even terrified, of the power-dressing career woman of the modern day. They would be at a loss in her company.

The timing of the stories, 'A Scandal in Bohemia' aside, could not have been better. Violent murder was, in the public consciousness, rampant across the land. The utterly gruesome Jack the Ripper murders of prostitutes in London had occurred in 1888, the perpetrator was never caught and speculation was rife as to his identity, candidates ranging from the artist Walter Sickert to Sir William Gull and the Duke of Clarence. The press was full of murder and crime coverage and Conan Doyle's Sherlock Holmes tales catered to the public taste. There may, in the face of the low detection rate of real crimes, have even been an underlying psychological yearning for a figure like Sherlock Holmes, who always got his man and who jeered at police inefficiency.

Conan Doyle's mastery of the short story form was supreme. He had a vivid use of language, an ear for reported speech, could compress a plot down to its essence without losing its power, had an innate sense of pace and never padded his tales out for effect. When *The Adventures of Sherlock Holmes* appeared, Dr Joseph Bell himself reviewed it for the *Bookman*, complimenting Conan Doyle for his skilful plots and the fascinating twists and turns they took, which criticism must have greatly pleased the author. He must have felt as if Sherlock Holmes himself were congratulating him.

Good though the stories are, they do contain a lot of slapdash writing. In the first two stories, one can perhaps forgive Conan Doyle his carelessness. He was writing at speed, in longhand and tying down a full-time job as a general practitioner at the same time, but, later on, there can be no real excuse for his many errors. This careless attitude towards the stories came about because Conan Doyle regarded them as little more than light fiction, good little money-earners. The effort of painstaking research that he applied to his historical novels was, he felt, wasted here. The stories did not require close research and the audience was not demanding. They, Conan Doyle thought, just wanted an easy read. The possibility never dawned on him that Sherlock Holmes would become what he did, an object of intense literary scrutiny.

A few examples of Conan Doyle's many mistakes show just how imprecise and negligent he was. As already mentioned, Watson's wound caused problems. He was said to have been wounded in the shoulder by a bullet from a *jezail*, a native Afghan musket, but, in *The Sign of Four*, the injury has moved to his leg. Sherlockians, trying to defend this error, have propounded theories as to how a single bullet could strike both limbs. In the later stories, the wound is still in Watson's leg but, by the time he tramps across Dartmoor in *The Hound of the Baskervilles*, it no longer causes him pain and he can run at speed. The bumbling Inspector Lestrade of Scotland Yard also undergoes a transformation by inconsistency. In *A Study in Scarlet*, he is a 'little sallow, rat-faced, dark-eyed fellow', but in *The Hound of the Baskervilles* he has become a 'small, wiry bulldog of a man' with a limp, which would have precluded him from police service. Was it simply that Conan Doyle had momentary lapses of concentration? Possibly, but some of his errors were elementary. For example, in 'The Man with the Twisted Lip', Dr Watson's wife called her husband James when his name was John: perhaps Conan Doyle was remembering Dr James Watson of Portsmouth.

The lack of research showed badly at times. In *A Study in Scarlet*, Sherlock Holmes reasoned that the villain was killed by ingesting what he called 'South American arrow poison'. This was curare, which was occasionally used in surgery as a muscle relaxant, a fact Conan Doyle must have known. He must also have been aware that, taken internally, it is comparatively harmless and has to be injected into the bloodstream to become deadly. Later, in 'The Adventure of the Silver Blaze', Conan Doyle placed a horse-racing stables on Dartmoor where the landscape is totally unsuitable for racehorse rearing, and his ignorance of the business of racing and training was so great as to draw a withering critical response from a racing newspaper. It stung Conan Doyle but he did not seem to learn from it.

One of the inconsistencies in the stories, which has resulted in a bizarrely amusing consequence, concerns Watson's dog, which was a bull pup, either a bulldog or a bull terrier. It appears in *A Study in Scarlet* but is never mentioned again. This has set the Sherlockians thinking. According to Baring-Gould, the reasons for the dog's disappearance are as follows: Holmes was once bitten by a bull terrier in his student days and, assuming Watson's pup had made a lunge for him, he demanded that Watson get rid of it; Mrs Hudson objected to it on the grounds that she owned an ancient terrier and did not want them to fight; the pup was accidentally killed when Watson stumbled and dropped it whilst carrying it up the stairs to Holmes's first-floor sitting room; the pup was a victim of Holmes's chemical experiments; it ran away. Others have speculated as to why Watson had a dog in the first place. Until he moved into 221B Baker Street, he had been living in a private hotel in The Strand which would have forbidden the keeping of pets and, besides, his income was too insecure to afford a dog. The truth of the matter is that Conan Doyle simply forgot the creature, but this has not prevented bizarre interpretations as to the fate of the temporary canine.

Some of the stories exhibited factual inaccuracies or flawed logic. Whilst private detectives did exist in London in the 1880s, they were never afforded police co-operation as Sherlock Holmes was and they did not become involved in criminal work, primarily restricting their business to divorce, missing person or debt-collecting cases. The vast majority were not self-employed but in the pay of solicitors or barristers. Where logic breaks down it does so quite obviously. In *A Study in Scarlet*, an old woman visits Sherlock Holmes, but is in reality a young man in disguise through which, incredibly, Holmes fails to see. Disguises are often important aspects of a story, requiring on occasion a very quick change of clothing and identity. At various times, Holmes disguises himself as a plumber, a labourer, a groom, an old sailor, an opium addict, a crippled bookseller, a priest, a tramp and an old crone. For some of these, he had to alter his appearance far too quickly for the effect to be practical. A considerable suspension of disbelief on the part of a Conan Doyle reader was – and is still – vital.

Other glaring mistakes include errors in chronology and, in some instances, descriptions of certain aspects of London. Conan Doyle drew most of his early information from street maps, never visiting the places where he set the action. The result is that a site in London is often actually given the description of streets he had known in the Edinburgh of his student days, the Birmingham he had visited when working for Dr Hoare, and the less salubrious areas of Portsmouth.

None of this bothered Conan Doyle. For him, the plot and characters were all. He once declared, 'accuracy of detail [in short stories] matters little. I have never striven for it and have made some bad mistakes in consequence. What matter if I hold my readers?' Up to a point, he was right. He gave his readers a new and engrossing hero and they, in return, were forgiving.

These faults were missed or overlooked by readers because they were often camouflaged by the skill of the storytelling and by Sherlock Holmes's methods of deduction, many of which included actual detective methodology. This separated the stories from other detective fiction of the time. Although Conan Doyle did not, as is often supposed, invent any major crime-solving techniques, he wrote about them in such a convincing way as to make it appear as if he – or rather Holmes – had done so. The reliance upon clues was paramount. When Holmes noted, in *A Study in Scarlet*, that the *A* in *RACHE* was written in the German style, when he assessed a man's occupation and immediate history just by observing him, the readers were captivated. This was, for them, a unique experience. Sherlock Holmes seemed to have almost magical powers and yet they were always readily understood when the explanation came.

When clues were not so evident, Holmes relied upon scientific investigative techniques. This was utterly new in both fiction and fact. No other fictional Victorian detective had Holmes's scientific bent, which was another example of Conan Doyle writing not just of but for the time. Science and technology were making great strides in the closing decades of the nineteenth century, their progress impinging upon everyday life. Scientific advancement was a part of common existence, so it naturally followed that Sherlock Holmes would be up to date in his thinking. Both Edgar Allan Poe and Gaboriau had used specific lines of investigation, but Conan Doyle took these much further, developing them, embellishing them, adding to them from his medical knowledge and his imagination. He wanted Holmes to be involved in, as he put it, an exact science and, whilst he might not have invented criminal investigative procedures, he certainly promoted them and made them well known. The study of dust, tracks in the earth, calligraphy, poisons, marks and stains, the shape or position and angle of wounds were all to play a part in Holmes's case studies. All of them are now intrinsically important aspects of forensic science.

Conan Doyle had his medical books to help him devise and hone some of Holmes's skills. His knowledge of diseases, poisons and drugs, as well as some forensic medicine picked up at Edinburgh, all enhanced the stories, but he had no other single source of information at the start of Holmes's career. However, just before he embarked upon the short stories, a book was published which could have been a boon. In 1891, Hans Gross published the first major study of criminality, *Criminal Investigation*, although much of its content had already been published in academic articles, and Conan Doyle may well have been aware of it.

Other techniques Conan Doyle placed at Sherlock Holmes's disposal included the microscopic study of small particles, the study of handwriting and the breaking of secret codes and ciphers, such as that worked out by Holmes in 'The Adventure of the Dancing Men'. The code Holmes broke, in which letters are substituted by drawings of stick men, was a well-established cipher known as the Pig Pen Code or the Julius Caesar cipher. It was used by spies in the American Civil War and frequently relied upon by the Italian Carbonari secret society.

Whether or not Conan Doyle introduced new scientific methods to criminology, many people believed at the time that he did, and this conception has survived to the present day. The Sherlock Holmes stories certainly have had an influence on crime detection world-wide. The complex computerised relational database used by the British police today is called 'Holmes'.

If Sherlock Holmes is identified with anything other than detection and his quirky habits, it is with London and the late Victorian era. As T.S. Eliot wrote, 'in the Sherlock Holmes stories the nineteenth century is always romantic, always nostalgic, and never silly'. It was a safe, ordered and cosy world where hansom cabs arrived on time, telegrams always got through, the mail was efficient, the trains kept to their schedules and, when Holmes placed an advertisement or a letter in a newspaper, it always elicited a reply. In the country as a whole, there existed a sense of the social order starting to disintegrate but, in the stories, it prevailed. Many of the villains Holmes came up against were not working-class rabble but middle- and upper-class individuals who, for all their criminality, did not worry the readers. They might be mugged by a thug on the streets of their neighbourhood but, through Sherlock Holmes, they saw the real criminals not as lurking down-and-outs in alleys but privileged professionals in wing collars who were nothing like as threatening. The crimes in the stories were rarely gratuitously violent, unlike in reality. Neither the victims who came to seek Holmes's help nor the criminals he brought to justice questioned the established order. They were, by their quiescence, almost romantic figures symbolising a social stability that did not exist in fact.

The setting of the stories has held readers from the very beginning with its amalgam of the familiar and the malefic. Vice and criminality thrived in the underbelly of Victorian England. Official estimates claimed that between a quarter and a third of all Londoners were actively engaged in some form of criminal activity. The police and the victims of crime could use some help. Then along came Sherlock Holmes, efficient, romantic, eccentric. He fitted the bill and he reassured people. He was on their side and, with his skills based (it seemed) on the infallible tenets of science, was successful. That he was fictional was not always considered. There was always the hope that if he was not real, there would be someone like him who was. He even lived at a genuine London address. Or so people thought.

Why Conan Doyle decided on settling Sherlock Holmes in Baker Street is not known for sure. Sir Harold Morris, one-time Member of Parliament for Bristol, claimed in 1960 that his father, Malcolm Morris, had suggested it, the house having been his grandfather's when he retired from the Bombay Civil Service, yet the chances of this being the case are slim. When Conan Doyle encountered Malcolm Morris on the train going to Berlin in 1890, establishing a friendship with him, he had already placed Sherlock Holmes in residence at 221B Baker Street in *A Study in Scarlet* in 1886. Furthermore, in the previous year, in 'Uncle Jeremy's Household', Conan Doyle had the main character, Hugh Lawrence, in some respects a forerunner of Sherlock Holmes, also living in Baker Street.

Conan Doyle's descriptions of especially the seedier parts of the urban landscape of London are one of the memorable aspects of the Sherlock Holmes tales even if, on occasion, the origins of the author's vision lay in other cities. He may have had to rely at first for his knowledge on a post office map of the city, but his depiction of Victorian urban life was accurate, sharp and vivid, and his readers, even those who were Londoners, could readily recognise their world. Nineties London was a vibrant place. Staid Victorian attitudes were slipping and people with more money in their pockets and time to spend it went out looking for entertainment. Theatres flourished, restaurants and public houses did a roaring trade, and the music hall was in full flow. The London Conan Doyle described was what he now saw around him, a throbbing metropolis with busy streets, thriving trade, chaotic traffic, crowded railway stations, an underground train system the envy of the world, teeming docks, barrow-boys and tinkers, classy hotels and gin shops, emporia to suit all tastes and purses. Every street assailed the senses with the hubbub of voices, the chime of horse tackle, the scent of horse dung and the tang of coal smoke. London was the redolent, jostling, resonant hub of the British Empire, the greatest ever known.

This was the world in which Sherlock Holmes moved. Not for him the salons of the rich but the cockle stalls and roast chestnut barrows, the public bar and the bustling streets of the common man: and this world was to become synonymous with him. The London of the 1880s and '90s was and still is the London of Sherlock Holmes. When he took Holmes out of town on a case, Conan Doyle's descriptions of rural England were just as captivating, just as accurate and just as emotive. A train journey with Holmes and Watson is a nostalgic trip into the past, into a landscape unsullied by the internal combustion engine and inflatable tyre. To this day, Dartmoor conjures up an image in many minds not of bright summer uplands but gloomy, sodden, mist-wreathed heathland roamed by a blood-curdling hound.

It was not only places Conan Doyle recreated so well. He also captured the mood of a landscape through its weather, especially its bad weather. One of his most memorable passages is a description of a winter's morning in 'The Adventure of the Beryl Coronet'. It reads, 'It was a bright, crisp February morning and the snow of the day before still lay deep upon the ground, shimmering brightly in the wintry sun. Down the centre of Baker Street it had been ploughed into a brown crumbly band by the traffic but at either side and on the heaped-up edges of the footpaths it still lay as white as when it fell. The grey pavement had been cleaned and scraped, but was still dangerously slippery, so that there were fewer passengers than usual. Indeed, from the direction of the Metropolitan station no one was coming save the single gentleman whose eccentric conduct had drawn my attention.' There is little literary fabrication here. This is a description of a scene with which Conan Doyle was intimately familiar.

Over the years, readers have tended to associate Sherlock Holmes with London fog but, in fact, Conan Doyle did not use fog all that much. 'The Adventure of the Copper Beeches' is one instance of a foggy day in London: 'It was a cold morning of the early spring, and we sat after breakfast on either side of a cheery fire in the old room in Baker Street. A thick fog rolled down between the lines of dun-coloured houses, and the opposing windows loomed like dark, shapeless blurs, through the heavy yellow wreaths. Our gas was lit, and shone on the white cloth, and glimmer of china and metal, for the table had not been cleared yet.' Where it does appear it is used to create feelings of either comfortable security, as in the quotation given, or terror or sadness. The reason why the image of fog has become so ingrained in the public psyche is probably the poetic licence exercised by the many film directors who have tackled the stories.

It was not long before the Sherlock Holmes stories became popular in the USA, where there was a similar explosion of the printed word, especially in the eastern seaboard states. Readers there enjoyed the stories, found Sherlock Holmes quaintly European and yet still fascinating, considering than the tales gave an accurate if stylised picture of England and English life. For many who had emigrated within a generation or so of the stories being published, they provided not only a good yarn but a sentimental journey back home to lost roots.

Whatever their faults or strengths, the Sherlock Holmes stories succeeded and have endured because they were told with such mastery, such panache, such excitement. They also work on so many levels, as evocations of their period, as adventure stories, as intellectual conundrums, as allegories of good and evil and, more recently, as ideal material for adaptation for the stage or screen. The characterisations of Holmes and Watson are unsurpassed in English literature. What started off as a means of making some ready money has turned into a truly memorable and universal fictional character known around the world like no other.

The success was not all Conan Doyle's, however. Part of the achievement has to be put down to Newnes's decision that every page of the *Strand Magazine* had to carry an illustration. The Sherlock Holmes stories, therefore, had to have an artist seconded to them who would illustrate all the stories consistently. The artist chosen by Greenhough Smith and the art editor, W.H.J. Boot, was Sidney Paget, born in 1860 and a student of the Royal Academy School. He was, in fact, appointed in error. Boot had wanted Walter Paget, Sidney's brother, who was an illustrator for the *Illustrated London News* and had already done the drawings for Sir H. Rider Haggard's *King Solomon's Mines* and *She* as well as Robert Louis Stevenson's *Treasure Island*. However, the invitation was sent by mistake to Sidney Paget at his studio at 11 Holland Park Road, Kensington.

In all, Sidney Paget provided 357 drawings for the Sherlock Holmes stories, having his brother, Walter, sit for the character. A tall, elegant man, Walter Paget was to regret accepting the task, for he was not infrequently accosted in the street as Sherlock Holmes. Such was the effect of Sidney Paget's authoritative style and the vast readership the stories received that one anecdote has Walter Paget attending Covent Garden opera house when a woman pointed him out and yelled, 'There goes Sherlock Holmes!' which caused him to spend the entire performance hunched in his seat. Watson was most likely modelled upon an old art school acquaintance of Paget's called Alfred Morris Butler, who became an eminent architect.

Conan Doyle approved of Sidney Paget's strong line drawings which so appropriately complemented the stories. His appreciation was shown in June 1893, when he sent Paget a silver cigarette case as a wedding present. It was engraved 'from Sherlock Holmes'. In actual fact, Paget drew a character which was not that much like Conan Doyle's original visual idea. Paget's Holmes was more handsome. Conan Doyle had envisaged an ugly man with a thin, angular face, a hooked nose and two small eyes set close together. In stature, he was tall but also cadaverous. Paget's beautification of Holmes paid dividends. Women were attracted to his austere looks whilst men sought to emulate his style of tailoring. Paget was also responsible for one of Holmes's most famous attributes. In 'The Boscombe Valley Mystery', Conan Doyle dressed Holmes in a 'long grey travelling cloak and close-fitting cloth cap', but Paget changed this into a hooded coat and deerstalker hat such as he wore himself when in the country. The image stuck, to be reinforced ever since by every actor who had ever played the part.

Until his death in January 1908, Paget drew every Sherlock Holmes illustration to appear in the *Strand Magazine*. After his death, Conan Doyle chose Arthur Twiddle as his replacement. He had already illustrated one of the Holmes books and Conan Doyle's novel *Sir Nigel*. One story, however, entitled 'The Adventure of the Dying Detective', was illustrated by Walter Paget, in the December 1913 issue of the magazine. In 1914, Frank Wiles illustrated all nine instalments of *The Valley of Fear* in addition to three of the last Sherlock Holmes stories. In America, Frederick Dorr Steele was commissioned to illustrate the Holmes books, giving a different interpretation of how the great detective looked. Yet the illustration that has stuck in the public consciousness is Paget's picture of an elegant aesthete, the true and lasting figure of Sherlock Holmes on the page.

8

A Suburban Gentleman of Letters

On 4 May 1891, Conan Doyle collapsed at home in Montague Place, suffering a severe bout of influenza which was, before the invention of antibiotics, a potential killer. For the first week, he was seriously ill and his death was considered a possibility. During the crisis, lying in his sickbed, he gave much thought to his future and decided he would quit medicine, at which profession he was not having much success, and make his living as an author. 'I determined [he wrote] with a wild rush of joy to cut the painter and to trust for ever to my power of writing. I remember in my delight taking the handkerchief which lay upon the coverlet in my enfeebled hand, and tossing it up to the ceiling in my exultation. I should at last be my own master. No longer would I have to conform to professional dress or try to please anyone else. I would be free to live how I liked and where I liked.'

As a doctor, Conan Doyle had had to dress soberly, be at all times courteous and deferential, kind and helpful, considerate and punctilious. Now he could discard the silk top hat, put on a tweed jacket instead of a frock-coat and wear brown shoes in place of black if he so desired. And he did. Yet the other, gentlemanly attributes remained with him.

Conan Doyle did not dislike being a doctor but he must have felt frustrated and depressed at not being able to further his career, although its stagnation was, in effect, of his own making. As a doctor, he was competent and sympathetic, well read and conscientious. He made several valuable contributions to medicine in articles he published in professional journals.

Changing career horses was not as risky as it might seem. Conan Doyle had made no money from doctoring for six months and he was better employed actively writing than passively waiting for patients in Upper Wimpole Street. In addition to his Sherlock Holmes income, he had received £57 8s 9d in April for a short story called 'Lot No. 249', £40 and £50 respectively for the American serial rights to *The Doings of Raffles Haw* and *A Scandal in Bohemia*. The international copyright laws were now ratified in the USA, so he could now demand overseas earnings.

As soon as he was well enough, Conan Doyle set about moving house. He no longer needed to live in central London so, on 25 June, the family left Montague Place for 12 Tennison Road, South Norwood. The suburb, which was on the fringes of Greater London, abutted on to the open Surrey countryside and consisted of streets of comfortable middle-class homes. It suited Conan Doyle perfectly, affording him the peace and quiet to write but easy access to London by train. It was also, much to his delight, close to a recreation ground that included a cricket pitch. The house was large, with sixteen rooms on three floors, and built in red brick with a balcony over the entrance porch, a central gable and dormer windows set in the roof. One of a row, it stood back from the road with trees growing in a front garden and was approached by a short drive. The gardens were walled and, at the rear, there was a tennis lawn shared with neighbouring houses.

Conan Doyle established himself in a study on the ground floor to the left of the front door. Upon the wall he hung paintings by his father and a sketch said to have been drawn by John Doyle, showing Queen Victoria as a child riding in Hyde Park. On the shelves were souvenirs of his voyages on the *Hope* and the *Mayumba*, including the skull of a seal.

With a list of tasks to be done pinned over the mantelpiece, although not transfixed by a jackknife, he began life as a full-time author. His working day began after breakfast and paused at lunch, to recommence at five o'clock and finally end at eight. As well as writing, he set up a photographic darkroom and busied himself with his old hobby, selling his ophthalmologic equipment to finance it. Photography became one of his passions again and he took his camera with him whenever he went on trips, although most of his surviving photographs are of the family rather than far-flung countries. In the afternoons he walked, played tennis or rode his tandem tricycle, often going for long rides with Louise, who did her best to show an interest in everything concerning her husband's new life. She did not, it seems, at any time question his decision to become a professional writer. As she always had, she trusted his judgment and allowed herself to be under his protection. When not cycling or playing tennis, Conan Doyle played bowls and joined local football and cricket clubs. In the summer of 1891, he even toured abroad to Holland where his team played a United Holland side at The Hague, Conan Doyle saving the team from an ignominious defeat by bowling out the last four members of the Dutch team with hardly a run added to the score. The British team tried to carry him shoulder high from the field of triumph but could not support his weight.

His income increased. When *The White Company* was published in October 1891, he received £250 on top of the £200 he had been paid for the serial rights. The next month, he was paid £125 from Balestier for the American rights, bringing his earnings for the year to just over £1,500, three times what he could optimistically have earned from family doctoring. Living comfortably and with money to spare, he bought 250 shares in Newnes's publishing company and, in November, paid £260 for two hundred shares in *Tit-Bits*; the next month, he bought a few more. It was ironic that he was now a shareholder in a magazine the editor of which he had castigated eight years or so previously.

With his increased wealth, Conan Doyle saw himself in a position, for the first time, to help his family. When his sister Connie returned to England from Portugal late in 1891, she came to live at South Norwood. Some time later, Lottie was also to move in. Both sisters were no longer obliged to work the long and arduous hours of a governess.

For Annette, however, it was too late, for she had died in Portugal of influenza, early in 1890. In his autobiography, Conan Doyle describes her as his 'noble sister', and so he might, for she had been remitting the bulk of her salary as a governess home to her mother. Writing to Mrs Hoare at the time of her death, Conan Doyle said Annette's life had been one of total self-sacrifice for which he, as the eldest son, might well have felt guilty, for she had, in some ways, taken over his responsibilities. The spiritualist in him could not believe that such a perfect and selfless person could die and leave nothing behind.

Around this time, Conan Doyle appears to have started sending his mother a regular allowance, although he had almost certainly been sending her smaller sums from time to time throughout his Southsea years. Innes, who was now in his late teens and a student at the Woolwich Academy, where he was preparing for a career in the army, also benefited. Conan Doyle kept in touch with his younger sisters as well, offering a prize of a guinea to Dodo if she could pre-guess the outcome of Sherlock Holmes's latest adventure. She won the prize more than once.

Whilst busy with Sherlock Holmes, Conan Doyle was also engaged in other work which was, as he put it, 'less remunerative but . . . more ambitious from a literary point of view'. The Sherlock Holmes tales were coming at a rate of about one a month, but he also spent much time researching a new historical novel. It was not unusual for him to be working on several projects simultaneously, as well as journalism, and he estimated he wrote 210,000 words in 1891.

One of his projects that year was a novel, Beyond the City, a sort of soap novel about suburban life in South Norwood. Originally entitled Good Cheer, it was commissioned and contracted in June by the magazine Good Words, which paid £150 for it, the length being around 42,000 words. It was due for delivery in September but Conan Doyle produced it within six weeks. Two of the characters, Clara and Ida Walker, were modelled on Connie and Lottie, whilst many of the others were neighbours and acquaintances. It gently sent up the rising feminist movement, the main character, Mrs Westmacott, being a tall, masculine woman familiar with weight-training, equipped with muscles to match her bustles, a loud and sharp tongue, a chain-smoking habit (women were 'not seen' to be cigarette smokers), and a propensity for wearing double-breasted jackets. A short medical story he published in 1894, 'The Doctors of Hoyland', was also a sideswipe at the New Woman. In the tale, the resident doctor in a small town, James Ripley, is stunned when a new doctor arrives and turns out to be a woman, Verrinder Smith, who has studied and conducted original research under a scholarship in Edinburgh, Paris, Berlin and Vienna, and is far more up to date than Ripley. Conan Doyle may have mocked feminism and been in awe at the prospect of a female doctor, yet he defended women's rights to be professionals even though, in later years, he vehemently took against suffrage. Beyond the City was published in the Christmas number of Good Words in 1891, in book form in 1892, but was not a raging success.

By the end of the year, having completed the next half-dozen Sherlock Holmes stories, he wrote a third long historical novel, The Refugees: A Tale of Two Continents. It was completed in February 1892 but not published until the May of the following year. Originally, it was to be a sequel to Micah Clarke, but Conan Doyle gave up on that plan and changed it to a story about the religious wars of the seventeenth century, centring on the tribulations of the Huguenots who escaped to America. Whereas Micah Clarke took the part of the English Puritans, so this tale sided with the French equivalent. The Catholics, once again, got a bad press, although he was to praise the individual courageous zeal of the Jesuits. It was set partly in France and partly in America, Conan Doyle collecting his research for the latter from the writing of the American historian Francis Parkman, whom he much admired, hoping the American section of the story would appeal to American readers. It appeared as a three-decker from Longman, Green & Co., with simultaneous serial publication in *Harper's New Monthly Magazine* in the USA. He had written it at the rate of fifty manuscript pages a week with, he recorded, an output of ten thousand words in one twenty-four-hour period. The critics were not unkind but also not enthusiastic, and the book did little to enhance Conan Doyle's reputation. He vowed never to write another three-decker.

The story did have one beneficial effect. Conan Doyle received a letter from Robert Louis Stevenson in August 1893, posted from Samoa. Stevenson praised *The Refugees*, especially its descriptions of the France of Louis XIV's court. The two men corresponded throughout 1893. Conan Doyle had never met Stevenson but he had admired his writing for years, even taking a few ideas from it. Stevenson, for his part, read Sherlock Holmes tales to his household in Samoa, reporting that 'The Adventure of the Engineer's Thumb' had been well liked but, as the natives did not know how to make up stories themselves, he had told them as if they were fact. Having also studied at Edinburgh University, Stevenson spotted Sherlock Holmes's source. After reading one of the stories, he wrote, 'Only the one thing troubles me: can this be my old friend "Joe" Bell?' They had more in common than their alma mater. In one letter, Stevenson addressed Conan Doyle as 'O frolic fellow Spookist', for they were both interested in spiritualism. At some time during that year, Conan Doyle even thought of going to Samoa, but the trip never came off.

Two months after finishing *The Refugees*, Conan Doyle embarked upon yet another historical novel which he wrote between April and June 1892. Entitled *The Great Shadow*, it was published that October by Arrowsmith, who had commissioned it. Set in Napoleonic times, the Great Shadow of the title was Napoleon Bonaparte himself, who had 'cast that great shadow over Europe, which darkened the nations for five-and-twenty years'. Conan Doyle was fascinated by Napoleon but the book dwells too much upon the Battle of Waterloo which is, admittedly, both gripping and realistic: a cannonball 'knocked five men into a bloody mash, and I saw it lying on the ground afterwards like a crimson football. Another went through the adjutant's horse with a plop like a stone in the mud, broke its back and left it lying like a burst gooseberry.'

Since coming to live in London, Conan Doyle had started mixing in literary circles. His output was so extensive, especially after he gave up medicine, that he was producing far more than the *Strand Magazine* could accept. He submitted to a wide range of other publications, one of which was the *Idler* Magazine edited by Jerome K. Jerome. Jerome was one of Conan Doyle's first literary friends, whom he described as 'an adventurous soul', but, although he praised his *Three Men in a Boat*, he criticised Jerome as having a serious side to his humorist character by virtue of which he was frequently hot-headed and politically intolerant. Through Jerome, he also became friends with Robert Barr who, with Jerome and George Brown Burgin, co-edited the magazine. A large, shambling man, Barr was, according to Conan Doyle, 'a volcanic Anglo- or rather Scot-American with a violent manner, a wealth of strong adjectives, and one of the kindest natures underneath it all. He was one of the best raconteurs I have ever known, and as a writer I have always felt that he did not quite come into his own.' Burgin, according to Conan Doyle, was 'like some quaint gentle character from Dickens'.

The *Idler* held literary afternoon tea parties at its offices in Arundel Street, running down between The Strand and the River Thames close to the beginning of Fleet Street. These teas often extended themselves into riotous dinner parties accompanied by substantial quaffings of alcohol brought in from one of the many small drinking establishments in the area which catered for lawyers from the nearby Temple. At these gatherings, Conan Doyle met J.M. Barrie, Israel Zangwill, Eden Phillpotts, Anthony Hope, Barry Pain and Gilbert Parker. It was not long before Conan Doyle was accepted into this circle. With his quick wit and fund of anecdotes, he was soon very popular, the measure of his popularity being seen in the dedication to a collection of Jerome's essays. It reads, 'To Big-Hearted, Big-Souled, Big-Bodied Friend Conan Doyle'.

Popular and famous as he was, Conan Doyle did not let this go to his head. He remained an approachable, likeable man, larger than life in many respects, courteous, polite, considerate and generous. He never spoke maliciously of anyone nor did he gossip. He was best summed up by Eden Phillpotts, the novelist, playwright and assistant editor of a popular magazine called *Black & White*, who wrote of him as 'a big man in mind and body'.

In some ways, Conan Doyle was very un-writer-like. He was not in the least bookish and was not precious about his art. Anthony Hope, the author of the 1894 bestseller *The Prisoner of Zenda*, said Conan Doyle looked as if he had never heard of a book; someone else described him as looking more like a farmer than a writer, a police officer than an author. Now in his mid-thirties, he had the vague appearance of a more muscular version of the German Kaiser Wilhelm. Though not fat, his figure was larger than it had been. With the upright stance of a guardsman, he wore his light brown hair trimmed short and moved with precision. His head was large, he sported a thick, somewhat blond moustache, his large eyes were usually either very active, sparkling with eagerness or fun, or, on occasion, fixed with a faraway stare.

He might now move in literary circles but he also kept up his sporting activities, these sometimes combining. He played cricket for J.M. Barrie's team, which included A.E.W. Mason, the novelist, and an old Stonyhurst acquaintance, Bernard Partridge, who worked for *Punch* but wrote for the *Idler* as well. The team was called the Allah-Akbarries, which was a play upon Barrie's name and the Arabic phrase meaning 'May the Lord help us': today, it would be termed a celebrity team, for the players were all writers or in the theatre. The others regarded cricket as light entertainment but Conan Doyle took it seriously. He only played to win, although, in his autobiography, he remembered they 'played in the old style, caring little about the game and a good deal about a jolly time and pleasant scenery'. It has been said that he also sometimes avoided the post-match eating and drinking sessions. This was not snobbery on his part. Despite his fame as a writer and his reputation as a jolly companion, Conan Doyle still sometimes found himself ill at ease in the company of literati. He felt he was not a complete part of this world and preferred at times to be on his own.

It was inevitable that he should become a member of a number of literary clubs and societies. He was elected into the Vagabonds and the Authors' Club, founded in 1884 by Sir Walter Besant to champion the rights of authors. Conan Doyle was a prominent member of this club, became in time a long-standing chairman and, with Anthony Hope, one of its most prominent members. He was also voted in as a member of the Reform Club, where he not only extended his list of acquaintances but also started to mix with those in positions of power in the literary world, such as Sir John Robinson, editor of the *Daily News*, and Wemyss Reid, who ran the *Speaker* and published a number of Conan Doyle articles and poems. Later, in 1901, he joined the prestigious Athenaeum Club, remaining a member to his death.

As Conan Doyle's fame grew, interviews and articles about him began to appear in magazines. Harry How, who was one of George Newnes's top celebrity interview journalists, wrote an article, 'A Day with Dr Conan

Doyle', for the *Strand Magazine* issue of August 1892. How describes
Conan Doyle as tanned and bronzed, a 'happy, genial, homely man;
tall, broad-shouldered, with a hand that grips you heartily, and, in
its sincerity of welcome, hurts'. With the article were photographs,
including some of the South Norwood house, Conan Doyle and Louise
sitting on their tandem tricycle in front of the porch, a specimen of
a manuscript page and a portrait of Joseph Bell. For the literary
magazines, he gave interviews of an artistic nature. In a piece by
Robert Barr, published in both the *Idler* and *McClure's Magazine* in
the USA, he stated that art was primarily meant to entertain, to 'help
the sick and the dull and the weary'. He did not believe that fiction
had to be realistic but he put great store in a personal belief that a
golden age of fiction was about to dawn in which novelists would
greatly affect and change society.

One of Conan Doyle's closest friends was James Barrie, the playwright
and author of *Peter Pan* who, like Conan Doyle, had a fascination with
the supernatural, ghosts and spirits, fairies and pixies and elves. Conan
Doyle admired Barrie's writing and Barrie returned the compliment: they
were also both, like Stevenson, graduates of Edinburgh University and
followers of cricket. They did not meet only in literary London and at
cricket matches. In March 1892, Conan Doyle visited Barrie, his family
and his parents at Glen Cova, twenty-five kilometres from Kirriemuir on
the banks of the River Esk. They fished for salmon together and, when
Barrie grew weak from his bronchial attacks, Conan Doyle attended
him in his sickbed.

Several months later, Conan Doyle was away from home again, taking
a holiday in Norway in the company of Louise, Connie and Jerome K.
Jerome, who left his wife at home, something he did quite often when
going away for a break from writing and editing. Over the years, there
has been some speculation about this trip: it has been proposed that
Jerome was wooing Connie, but this is not true. Jerome was already
married and faithful. His attitude, as he put it, was that 'love is like the
measles; we all have to go through it. Also like the measles, we take
it only once.' In his autobiography, *My Life and Times*, Jerome wrote
of the Doyles as 'a vigorous family . . . both mentally and physically.
I remember a trip to Norway with Doyle and his sister, Connie: a
handsome girl, she might have posed as Brunhilda.' This is hardly
the description of a man paying court; besides, Conan Doyle would
not have allowed any form of impropriety to occur. It was simply not
his way.

The holiday was taken partly at Louise's insistence. She was pregnant, in poor health and wanted to get away for a rest. The trip consisted of a cruise to the Norwegian fjords, but the crossing of the North Sea was rough, which made Louise even more ill. Connie, on the other hand, seemed to revel in the inclement seas. Jerome recorded how she 'enjoyed it: she was that sort of girl: it added to her colour and gave a delightful curl to her hair. She has a sympathetic nature, and was awfully sorry for the poor women who were ill. She would burst in upon them every now and then to see if she could be of any help to them. You would have thought her mere presence would have cheered them up. As a matter of fact, it made them just mad. "Oh, do go away, Connie," I heard one of her friends murmur, while passing the open door, "it makes me ill to look at you."' As for Conan Doyle himself, Jerome recounted that he 'was always full of superfluous energy. He started to learn Norwegian on the boat. He got on so well that he became conceited and one day, at a little rest house up among the mountains, he lost his head.' His recollection continues with an account of what happened on a trip ashore to a mountain rest-house, travelling by *stolja*, a one-man pony trap. Conan Doyle got into conversation with a young Norwegian officer, in Norwegian. He believed they were discussing the weather and the state of the roads, but some hours later, it was discovered that Conan Doyle's pony was missing. What had actually happened was that the officer's pony had gone lame and Conan Doyle had unwittingly permitted the officer to take his animal. A waiter in the rest-house assured Conan Doyle that he had said 'Certainly, with pleasure' and 'Don't mention it' several times. Thereafter, Jerome remembered, Conan Doyle spoke markedly less Norwegian.

In the manner of the true writer, Conan Doyle also arranged for them to visit a leper colony – leprosy was widespread in Norway – in case he found material for a story. He used his medical credentials to get them in. He also discovered the existence of what might prove to be a new sport at which he could try his hand. It was skiing.

Not everything, however, to which Conan Doyle turned his hand was a success. On his return from Norway, a telegram awaited him from Barrie, inviting him to visit Aldeburgh in Suffolk. Barrie's bronchitis was now very bad, he was slipping towards a nervous breakdown and badly needed Conan Doyle's help with a libretto commissioned by D'Oyly Carte who, having fallen out with Gilbert and Sullivan, was looking for new material. Barrie had accepted the commission only to find it was beyond him, both artistically and, now, physically. He was, however, under a contractual obligation. Conan Doyle was utterly ignorant of operetta but agreed to help his friend. Barrie had sketched out the plot and written Act I. He then passed the manuscript over to Conan Doyle whose heart sank. It was trite and weak. Conan Doyle rewrote and reshaped some of the lyrics for Act I, then wrote Act II, working alongside the composer of the score, Ernest Ford. Based upon the exploits of two young men who invade a girls' school to be chased out by the provost, the operetta was entitled *Jane Annie; or The Good Conduct Prize: A New and Original English Comic Opera*. The plot was shallow, the lyrics barely adequate and the music competent but not extraordinary: it was certainly no Gilbert and Sullivan look-alike. First performed on 13 May 1893 at the Savoy Theatre, it ran for seven weeks and was a resounding failure. The critics hated it. George Bernard Shaw panned it in the *World*, writing that it was 'the most unblushing outburst of tomfoolery that two respectable citizens could conceivably indulge in publicly'. He was right.

After the operetta bombed, Barrie wrote a spoof Sherlock Holmes story which he sent to Conan Doyle. It was called 'The Adventure of Two Collaborators', Conan Doyle describing it as 'a rollicking parody'. In the story, Sherlock Holmes was amusing himself with a little revolver practice in 221B Baker Street – 'It was his custom of a summer evening to fire round my head,' wrote 'Watson', 'just shaving my face, until he had made a photograph of me on the opposite wall, and it is a slight proof of his skill that many of these portraits in pistol shots are considered admirable likenesses' – when two literary visitors arrived demanding to know why the public were not queuing up to see their operetta. Holmes was not very keen to see them, explaining, 'I am not particular about the people I mix among for business purposes but at literary characters I draw the line.' Holmes refuses to comment or go to the theatre and see the operetta for himself, despite the larger of the two visitors warning him menacingly that his 'continued existence depends on it'. Holmes is adamant and that's the end of him. His last words are, 'Fool, fool! I have kept you in luxury for years. By my help you have ridden extensively in cabs, where no author was ever seen before. Henceforth you will ride in buses!'

Another literary figure to enter Conan Doyle's life around this time was George Meredith. Regarded as a grand old man of English literature, he was lionised by younger writers. Conan Doyle considered him the most important writer in the land, although, writing later in his autobiography, he said, 'I have the greatest possible admiration for him at his best, while his worst is such a handicap that I think it will drag four-fifths of his work to oblivion. If his own generation finds him hard to understand, what will our descendants make of him? He will be a cult among a few – a precious few in every sense. And yet I fully recognise that his was the most active original brain and the most clever pen of any man, novelist or otherwise, of my time.' He thought Meredith was limited because of the three vital requisites any author had to possess – intelligibility, interest and cleverness. Meredith, he deemed, really only commanded the last.

On several occasions in 1892, Conan Doyle visited Meredith at his home at Box Hill in Surrey, either on his own or in the company of J.M. Barrie and Arthur Quiller-Couch. He also lectured on Meredith at the Upper Norwood Literary and Scientific Society, of which he was a member. His visits, which amounted to a form of literary pilgrimage, were not necessarily joyous affairs. Meredith, who had been a well-known bon viveur in his youth, was no longer able to drink and he drew sad delight from seeing Conan Doyle down a whole bottle of burgundy on his own. Like his father, he enjoyed burgundy above other wines but was careful to moderate his intake. Meredith was also fiercely independent despite his poor health. He was unable to keep his balance and kept falling over but refused help in getting up. He was, at times, crotchety and irritable but Conan Doyle accepted this as a part of the great writer's temperament and dismissed it.

By February 1892, Greenhough Smith was demanding more of Sherlock Holmes. Writing to his mother, Conan Doyle said, 'Under pressure I offered to do a dozen for a thousand pounds, but I sincerely hope that they won't accept it now.' They did. It was an unheard-of sum for the time but Newnes was a shrewd businessman and knew he would recoup the outlay. Conan Doyle, however, cautioned that he could not deliver the stories quickly as he was working on other books. He was also considering the unthinkable.

During the previous November, in a letter to his mother, he wrote, 'I think of slaying Holmes . . . and winding him up for good and all. He takes my mind from better things.' His mother, who was a keen Sherlock Holmes reader, proud of her son's success and no doubt as shrewd as Newnes, replied, 'You won't! You can't! You mustn't!' Conan Doyle heeded this advice, trusting his mother's judgment, yet only for the time being. In truth, he was in two minds about killing Holmes off. Six months later, he told an interviewer that he was temporarily holding back from writing more Holmes stories because he did not want to spoil a character of which he was fond, assuring him he had enough plot material in hand to continue with another series. It must also be said that, despite his assassinatory thoughts, Conan Doyle had most certainly grown to prefer cabs to omnibuses.

The next twelve Sherlock Holmes stories started to appear in the *Strand Magazine* in the December 1892 issue and ran until December the following year. They were, consecutively, 'The Adventure of the Silver Blaze', 'The Adventure of the Cardboard Box', 'The Adventure of the Yellow Face', 'The Adventure of the Stock-broker's Clerk', 'The Adventure of the "Gloria Scott"', 'The Adventure of the Musgrave Ritual', 'The Adventure of the Reigate Squires', 'The Adventure of the Crooked Man', 'The Adventure of the Resident Patient', 'The Adventure of the Greek Interpreter', 'The Adventure of the Naval Treaty', and 'The Adventure of the Final Problem'. These were collected together in volume form as *The Memoirs of Sherlock Holmes*, published for Christmas 1893. One of the stories, however, 'The Adventure of the Cardboard Box', was excised from the book. The reason for this decision is unclear, but it may have been because the story involved adultery, which was socially risqué at the time, and alcoholism, which touched a raw family nerve.

Just as there has been much speculation as to whom Conan Doyle based his characters upon, so has there been much searching done to discover the source of his plots. Conan Doyle read very widely indeed. Fiction, historical books, the daily press, general magazines and professional journals, religious tracts, memoirs, current affairs, travel, politics – everything he could lay his hands on. With his highly retentive memory in addition to his copious note- and scrapbooks, he possessed, in modern terminology, a substantial database of knowledge upon which he could draw at will.

In many cases, he did use an idea he had gleaned from somewhere. Some originated from magazine or newspaper reports. One of his biographers, Charles Higham, who seems to have set himself the task of finding out where every one of Conan Doyle's plots originated, suggested that an article in the *International Review* of March 1882, which gave a detailed and horrific insight into the Andaman Islands natives, could have been used by Conan Doyle in writing *The Sign of Four*. In the January 1890 edition of the *Cornhill Magazine*, to which Conan Doyle subscribed, there were several accounts of recent cases heard before the provincial assizes, one concerning a young man caught in a potential scandal, the other about a scarred and filthy beggar: Conan Doyle might have joined these together for the plot of 'The Man with the Twisted Lip'. Such assumptions are somewhat speculative, but not without justification. Of course, he also relied upon personal experience. The harpooners in the later Sherlock Holmes story, 'The Adventure of

Black Peter', came from his trip on the *Hope*, whilst the snake in 'The Speckled Band' may have come to him from a clockwork snake he is said to have kept in a basket, with which he allegedly enjoyed alarming gullible visitors.

Some plots were given or suggested to him by friends or relatives. Others he drew by extrapolating them from novels he had read. The plot of 'The Adventure of the Copper Beeches' was given to him by his mother. The young woman who hires Sherlock Holmes, Violet Hunter, is a governess who, on taking up her position, has to cut her hair and wear what dresses her employer dictates. Three of Conan Doyle's sisters had been governesses and, through them and his mother, he would have known all about the vicissitudes of the job and the often unfair demands made of young women in such employ. On top of that, Conan Doyle enjoyed gothic fiction and had read Charlotte Brontë's *Jane Eyre* to which the story bears more than a passing resemblance. A few stories had their conception in current or recent affairs. 'The Adventure of the Naval Treaty' was similar in some respects to the case of Charles Marvin, a civil servant in the Foreign Office, who sold the text of a secret treaty signed between England and Russia to the *Globe* newspaper.

As his fame grew, Conan Doyle started to receive ideas from his readers. In his interview with him, Harry How states that, on the day he visited South Norwood, Conan Doyle had been sent the details of a poisoning case in New Zealand and, the day before, documents concerning a disputed will, mailed from Bristol. Greenhough Smith, aware that he was under pressure to produce stories, also suggested plot material which he came upon either through his own interest in criminal cases or in submissions to the magazine. Conan Doyle was grateful for this help but how much he relied upon it is not known. What is important is his relationship with Greenhough Smith, which was based upon more than the latter's editorial abilities and occasional collaborative assistance. They were also friends and Conan Doyle, valuing friendship and loyalty, remained faithful to his editor and the magazine, resisting offers from other magazines, the editors of which would have greatly improved upon Newnes's price for the rights to a new Sherlock Holmes story, breaking the *Strand Magazine*'s monopoly. When, in February 1916, Conan Doyle handed Greenhough Smith the manuscript of 'The Adventure of the Golden Pince-Nez', he inscribed on the front, 'A Souvenir of 20 years of collaboration'. As for the basis of the stories, they are, in any case, immaterial. Authors get their ideas from a wide variety of sources, the important thing being that they use them with originality.

Sherlock Holmes and the *Strand Magazine* were, in the eyes of the public, virtually synonymous. The appearance of Conan Doyle's name on the cover of an issue automatically boosted circulation by 100,000 copies. By 1896, it had a monthly circulation exceeding half a million and was found everywhere. Conan Doyle, returning from France on a cross-Channel ferry, reported, 'Foreigners used to recognise the English by their check suits. I think they will soon learn to do it by their Strand magazines. Everyone on the Channel boat, except the man at the wheel, was clutching one.' Such was the awareness of Sherlock Holmes that other journals started to mention him: the October issue of *Tit-bits* in 1893, for example, featured a Sherlock Holmes Examination Paper consisting of twelve questions about Holmes's methods. Three prizes were offered for correct answers plus a tie-breaker, Conan Doyle supplying autographed copies of *The Memoirs of Sherlock Holmes* to the runners-up.

The most bizarre twist to the Sherlock Holmes saga was already under way by this time. Some people were beginning to think that Holmes was a real person.

As early as *The Sign of Four*, Conan Doyle had begun to receive mail as if Sherlock Holmes were flesh and blood. A tobacconist in Philadelphia wrote to ask if Conan Doyle could send him a copy of the monograph in which Holmes described the differences in the ash of various varieties of tobacco. Conan Doyle was highly amused by the letter. People then started to look for 221B Baker Street, which was a fictional address. At one stage, a group of French schoolboys on a trip to London, when purportedly asked what they would first like to visit, said they wished to begin their tour at Sherlock Holmes's lodgings. By the autumn of 1892, Conan Doyle was being sent mail for Sherlock Holmes, something that continued for the rest of his life. This correspondence came from all over the world and some reached him either through the magazine or by way of Scotland Yard, which also received post for the detective. Most of it, however, was forwarded by the General Post Office from Baker Street. One letter in later years was received addressed to 'Konan Doille auteur de Cherloc Cholms Angleterre'. Many of the letters asked for Conan Doyle's autograph but a good many more asked for Holmes's autograph, requesting that Conan Doyle forward the letter to Sherlock Holmes for his reply. Some of the letters even enclosed gifts for Holmes in the form of pipe-cleaners, violin strings and shag tobacco. No one, it seems, sent him cocaine. Letters not addressed to Conan Doyle or Sherlock Holmes were sometimes addressed to Dr Watson, a press cutting agency actually enquiring of

Watson if Sherlock Holmes might want to subscribe to it, no doubt so that he might learn more of his own exploits. Others not seeking an autograph offered their help. When Holmes later announced that he was retiring to the country to keep bees, one woman enquired as to whether he might want a housekeeper (presumably she wanted to oust Mrs Hudson, if she were still in his employ) whilst an apiarist offered his advice on setting up and maintaining beehives.

Sherlock Holmes's popularity and the belief that he was real caused problems for Conan Doyle, not the least of which was his confusion at the success of the stories. Whilst he was pleased to be rich and famous, it irked him. He wanted fame, but as a serious historical novelist. Instead, what he thought of as little more than pulp fiction, which he rated rather caustically as 'police romances', was what he was known for. The success of the stories not only surprised but worried him. It is more than likely he was disturbed by the fact that his literary historical novels were not only interrupted by Sherlock Holmes but were not up to par, whilst his commercial pot-boilers – inexplicably – were. He was galled to be famous because of what he considered his secondary output which, he believed, got in the way of the appreciation of his best, historical, writing. In his own words, he was 'in danger of having my hand forced, and of being entirely identified with what I regarded as a lower stratum of literary achievement'. That the success of Sherlock Holmes might have promoted the sales of his other books did not occur to Conan Doyle, and it is certainly a fact that his career would not have taken off as spectacularly as it did without the detective. In a later letter to Vincent Starrett, who was to be Holmes's first 'biographer', Conan Doyle wrote, 'It was really very kind of you to write so heartily about Holmes. My own feelings towards him are rather mixed, for I feel that he has obscured a good deal of my more serious work, but that no doubt will right itself in time – or if not, it does not really matter.'

The stages through which Conan Doyle's relationship with Sherlock Holmes passed can be imagined. At first, he would have been pleased that so much attention was being paid to his character, and he would have revelled in the attention. When the first letters came, he would have been wryly entertained by them, but this would have become tedious as the volume of mail increased until, eventually, he would have been utterly fed up with it. He was an author, but the mail came for his character, asking him to solve problems and crimes.

On occasion, large fees were offered if he could persuade Holmes to take a case on. At other times, Conan Doyle was offered Holmes's fees because the correspondent assumed that he – being the detective's creator – possessed his fictional skills. Sometimes, Conan Doyle was fascinated by a problem and did try to help, sequestering himself in his study and trying to guess himself into Sherlock Holmes's shoes. Usually, however, he replied by pointing out that he was not Sherlock Holmes and was annoyed that people drew such a thin line between him and his imaginary character. His feelings towards the matter are summed up in a piece of doggerel he penned in response to a piece of criticism, written as a long poem, which suggested that he had borrowed from Edgar Allan Poe and that Sherlock Holmes had then contemptuously dismissed Dupin. The critic, Arthur Guiterman, wrote in 1912,

> Sherlock your sleuthhound, with motives ulterior,
> Sneers at Poe's 'Dupin' as 'very inferior'!
> Labels Gaboriau's clever 'Lecoq', indeed,
> Merely 'a bungler', a creature to mock, indeed!
>
> This, when your plots and your methods in story owe
> Clearly a trifle to Poe and Gaboriau,
> Sets all the Muses of Helicon sorrowing.
> Borrow, Sir Knight, but be candid in borrowing!

Conan Doyle's riposte ended,

> But is it not on the verge of inanity
> To put down to me my creation's crude vanity?
> He the created, the puppet of fiction,
> Would not brook rivals nor stand contradiction.
> He, the created, would scoff and would sneer,
> Where I, the creator, would bow and revere.
> So please grip this fact with your cerebral tentacle,
> The doll and its maker are never identical.

It must be said that, at times, Conan Doyle's attitude was ambivalent. He hated the attention Sherlock Holmes received and yet he was not averse to encouraging the myth. When he received letters addressed to the great detective, he took to replying to some of them by postcard, often signing them 'Dr John Watson' out of devilment.

Joseph Bell was dragged into the Sherlock Holmes maelstrom, too. His name had been mentioned in Harry How's article in the *Strand Magazine*, and although Bell was flattered to have been chosen as the model for Sherlock Holmes, he modestly dismissed his own observational skills.

In a letter published with the article, he wrote, 'Dr Conan Doyle has, by his imaginative genius, made a great deal out of very little . . .' and claimed Conan Doyle owed to him 'much less than he thinks'. Some years later, he was to add, 'Dr Conan Doyle's education as a student of medicine taught him to observe, and his practise, both as a general practitioner and a specialist, has been a splendid training for a man such as he is, gifted with eyes, memory and imagination.' To Conan Doyle himself, Bell wrote, 'You are yourself Sherlock Holmes!'

Yet the word was out. Bell and Sherlock Holmes became synonymous and Bell started to get requests to help solve mysteries. Eventually, he actually took an interest in forensic science, assessing medical evidence and, on more than one occasion, actually assisting the Edinburgh police with criminal investigations, his keen observations causing him to take the stand as an expert prosecution witness. With a colleague, he even tried to investigate the Jack the Ripper murders. Both he and the colleague came to the same conclusion but what it was has never been released, nor have the many Ripperologists been aware of his involvement.

The Conan Doyle family in South Norwood continued to grow. The child Louise had been carrying on the trip to Norway was born in November 1892. It was a son whom they called Alleyne Kingsley, although he was always known in the family by his second name. The month before, Lottie had moved in and must have been a great help to Louise with the new baby.

A regular visitor to the house was E.W. Hornung, working as a lowly journalist at the time, who was courting Connie. They had met as a result of her having been introduced socially to members of the Hornung family whilst she was governessing in Portugal. The Hornungs, who were of Slav origin and traced their family back to Transylvania, were involved in pig-iron and iron ore shipping between the Continent and Middlesbrough. Connie was, by all accounts, not the Brunhilda of Jerome's memory but a very pretty young woman. Hornung was not her first suitor but she had dismissed the rest. Conan Doyle reported to his mother, 'I like young Willie Hornung very much. He is one of the sweetest natured and most delicate-minded men I ever knew.' He and Connie married in the summer of 1893. At the time, Hornung's income was so low Conan Doyle kept on paying Connie's allowance to help the couple.

Hornung went on to become a famous author himself. He published fifteen novels but is best known now for his creation of another famous literary character, A.J. Raffles, the gentleman criminal and burglar who always got away with it. He structured his main characters, Raffles and his narrator sidekick, Bunny, on Sherlock Holmes and Watson. The difference was that, with Conan Doyle, the hero was a crime-buster whilst Raffles was quite the opposite – he was a master thief. The moral skeleton of the stories was therefore reversed. It is also possible that Hornung took his hero's name from Conan Doyle's character, Raffles Haw. He first hit it big with *Raffles, the Amateur Cracksman*, which was published in 1899 and dedicated to Conan Doyle, who praised it but later summed up the Raffles stories as 'rather dangerous in their suggestion. I told [Hornung] so before he put a pen to paper, and the result has, I fear, borne me out. You must not make the criminal a hero.' He was, in part, correct. Much as Sherlock Holmes was thought able to solve real crimes, so Hornung was to be accused of providing real criminals with inspiration. Conan Doyle also declared that, just as Sherlock Holmes had harmed his serious work, so Raffles detracted from Hornung's other writing. There were a number of attempts to make Conan Doyle and Hornung collaborate on a Sherlock Holmes-meets-Raffles story, but both writers rejected the idea.

Despite his doubts over the morality of the Raffles stories, Conan Doyle continued to both like and admire his brother-in-law. In his autobiography, he described him as 'a Dr Johnson without the learning but with a finer wit. No one could say a neater thing, and his writings, good as they are, never adequately represented the powers of the man, nor the quickness of his brain.' Conan Doyle's examples of Hornung's humour show him to have had some of Samuel Johnson's dry and quick turn of phrase. When shown a newspaper cutting in which the subject was said to have run a hundred yards in less than ten seconds, Hornung declared, 'It's a sprinter's error', and, when Conan Doyle enquired of him why he never played golf, he replied it was 'unsportsmanlike to hit a sitting ball'. Of Sherlock Holmes he wittily remarked that 'though he might be more humble, there is no police like Holmes'.

Whatever his developing attitude towards Sherlock Holmes, Conan Doyle was becoming tired of writing the stories. The publisher's deadlines were tight and he was feeling the pressure on top of his other literary work. 'The difficulty of the Holmes work,' he wrote in his autobiography, 'was that every story really needed as clear-cut and original a plot as a longish book would do. One cannot without effort spin plots at such a rate. They are apt to become thin or to break.' The time was drawing nigh to do him in before, as Conan Doyle put it, Holmes did *him* in.

The timing of the death of Sherlock Holmes has about it an air of genuine mystery. The solution hinges on how many times Conan

Doyle visited Switzerland in 1893. He most definitely went in August, accompanied by Louise, but one of his biographers, John Dickson Carr, the famous crime novelist, claims he also took his wife to Switzerland early in the year, and it has been assumed that Carr was right because he had access to Conan Doyle's personal papers. There are, however, doubts. First, Louise had only just given birth and must have been breast-feeding baby Kingsley, whom she is hardly likely to have taken with her on such a trip. Second, she was not very strong and, whilst Switzerland was considered good for the constitution, it would not have been an easy journey, being in the depths of winter. If this trip occurred, it would seem most probable that Conan Doyle took it alone.

What is not disputed is that, at some time in 1893, Conan Doyle visited the spectacular Reichenbach Falls at Meiringen, twenty-five kilometres east of Interlaken. A famous sight, they were on every Victorian tourist's itinerary and noted in Thomas Cook tourist brochures as one of the sights of the northern Swiss Alps. A bridge spanned a deep water-cut abyss which was surrounded by awesome cliffs. It was here, in a setting of plunging water and sheer rock faces, Conan Doyle decided Sherlock Holmes would die. It was, he wrote in his autobiography, 'a terrible place, and one that I thought would make a worthy tomb for poor Sherlock, even if I buried my banking account along with him'.

Yet when did Conan Doyle see the falls, in January or August? The doubt exists because of a letter he wrote to his mother on 6 April saying, 'I am in the middle of the last Holmes story, after which the gentleman vanishes, never to return! I am weary of his name.' There is some doubt that the story he refers to was 'The Adventure of the Final Problem', in which Holmes dies: it may be he was working upon another story which he subsequently adapted or altered. There is firm evidence that 'The Adventure of the Final Problem' was not written until later in the year, after Conan Doyle returned from Switzerland at the end of August, having been to the falls in the summer.

There are several reasons to suppose he did not see the falls in January. One is a practical problem. The bridge over the falls was usually closed in the depths of winter so tourists could not approach close to the cataract. Conan Doyle could still have seen the falls from below, but they would not have so impressed him, for not only would he fail to view them from a spectacular vantage point but they were also not as spectacular in winter, with less than a third of their summer flow rushing over them.

Richard Lancelyn Green discovered correspondence between Watt, Conan Doyle and his publishers which suggests 'The Adventure of the

Final Problem' was only included in the second volume of Sherlock Holmes stories, *The Memoirs of Sherlock Holmes*, published at Christmas 1893, as an afterthought. The American serial rights purchased by *Harper's New Monthly Magazine* for the set of stories that included 'The Adventure of the Final Problem' did not, in fact, include the rights to this fatal story. Furthermore, an entry in Conan Doyle's accounts for 20 October 1893 records him being paid separately for 'Sherlock Holmes' last story', which suggests the story was written late in the summer, after August.

There is yet another clue as to when Conan Doyle finally decided upon where and how to kill Sherlock Holmes, provided by a Methodist minister, Silas B. Hocking. Hocking met Conan Doyle at the Rifel Alp Hotel at Zermatt. In his memoirs, Hocking goes into the meeting in detail, describing how he, Conan Doyle and a priest called Benson visited the Findelen glacier, three kilometres east of Zermatt. 'It was a pleasant walk for the most part,' he wrote, 'mainly through pinewoods. Then we descended into a narrow valley and found ourselves at the foot of the glacier which rose above us steep as a house roof, and in parts much steeper. Our guide went in front and with his axe cut steps in the ice and we ascended in single file. Once on the top walking about was comparatively easy.' This would indicate a summer visit.

Hocking goes on to outline a conversation he had with Conan Doyle whilst strolling on the glacier and 'making detours to avoid crevasses'. Conan Doyle said he was going to kill off Sherlock Holmes. Benson argued for his continuing to live but Conan Doyle seemed adamant. They reached a deep crevasse where Hocking claims he suggested that Holmes might die falling down such a one. Conan Doyle agreed with a laugh that it was not a bad suggestion. Hocking finishes, 'Anyhow, Doyle did bring him out a few months later, and caused him to disappear over the Reichenbach Falls.' The crucial phrase is 'a few months later'.

By the end of August, Conan Doyle was back in England, due to set off on a lecture tour, but within a few weeks, Louise developed a severe cough and a sharp pain in her side. She had not been well for over a year and had been frequently weakened by her pregnancy. A Dr Dalton, who lived nearby, examined her. A Harley Street specialist, Sir Douglas Powell, confirmed Dalton's fears. Louise had tuberculosis of the lungs. There was no cure for TB and the strain Louise had contracted, known as galloping consumption, was considered the worst form. Powell's prognosis gave her not more than a few months. Conan Doyle, it appears, had not noticed the onset of the disease.

At more or less the same time as Louise was diagnosed terminally ill, more bad news arrived. On 10 October, Charles Doyle died, a patient of the Crighton Royal Institution, Dumfries.

For decades, the detailed truth about what had happened to Charles Doyle was unknown, suppressed by the Doyle family. Then, in 1977, a book of Charles's unknown drawings and watercolours surfaced. They had been purchased in the 1950s in a job lot at a house sale in Hampshire. The book is now known as *The Doyle Diary*. The owner, having possessed it for over twenty years, finally approached a gallery, which recognised the works' provenance. Edited by Michael Baker, a television documentary producer, the diary was published in 1978 and resulted in Baker conducting some remarkable original research into the last dark, sad years of Charles Doyle's life.

Charles had been institutionalised at Fordoun House because of his alcoholism, but he later became epileptic, which condemned him for the rest of his life to an asylum. Before epilepsy was fully understood, sufferers were almost invariably locked away in the madhouse for their own safety and that of others. However, Charles Doyle does not seem to have been dangerously insane.

In May 1885, Charles Doyle attempted to escape from Fordoun House. He managed to get hold of some drink, became violent, smashed a window and tried to make a break for it. He was, of course, apprehended and soon committed under a detention order to Montrose Royal Lunatic Asylum where he was held in a fee-paying patients' wing called Sunnyside until January 1892, at which juncture he was transferred for three months to the Edinburgh Royal Infirmary. Records there state that he was emaciated, suffered memory loss and whiled away his time drawing and reading religious texts. Mary Doyle was kept informed of her husband's whereabouts but it appears she was not aware of his condition and she did not visit him. From Edinburgh, he was sent on to the Crighton Royal Institution, a large mental hospital near Dumfries. He was by now very ill. When he died, the cause of death was stated to be epilepsy, but was possibly cardiac failure brought on by a fit. Charles was a private patient at the institution and, according to Baker's researches, was held there on an almost informal basis: it seems as if the detention order had been relaxed, possibly because of his failing health.

Two independent doctors signed the papers that first committed Charles Doyle to an asylum, Waller and Conan Doyle having nothing to do with the act, although Waller, as a qualified doctor, knew the family and its circumstances intimately, had seen Charles's deterioration over the years and could vouch for the need to incarcerate him for the sake of the safety of Mary Doyle and her daughters. He was committed because he was hearing voices in his head.

How Conan Doyle felt about his father being locked away is a subject of speculation. He must have been saddened but he might also have felt guilty. And scared. If his father were truly insane, he had the worry that the insanity might be hereditary and, if it did not visit him, might skip a generation and affect his children. Whatever the case, Annette certainly felt sorrowful at her father's plight. When she died, she bequeathed her entire estate of £420 for the sole purpose of Charles's care.

Baker's publication of *The Doyle Diary* brought into doubt the true nature of Charles's condition. At the beginning of the diary, which Charles started on 8 March 1889 and which is actually more sketchbook than text, are the words 'keep steadily in view that this Book is ascribed wholly to the produce of a MADMAN Whereabouts would you say was the deficiency of intellect? or depraved taste If in the whole Book you can find a single Evidence of either, mark it and record it against me'.

It appears that Charles was keeping his mind busy designing a wide range of items, including sets of playing cards which he believed might have commercial potential. He wrote in the diary, 'I asked them to be all sent to Mrs Doyle and submitted to Publishers, but as I have never had a single Book or Drawing acknowledged by her or other relatives I can only conclude that they see no profit in them. In these circumstances I think it would be better that these Books should be entrusted to the Lunacy Commissioners to show them the sort of Intellect they think it right to Imprison as Mad & let them judge if there is any question for publication.'

The misery these words convey is considerable. One can imagine the warders of the asylum patronisingly taking his designs and throwing them away; or, perhaps, they did send them to the family but Waller intercepted them or advised Mary against any course of action.

What is clear from the diary is that Charles believed his family had abandoned him. Yet he still loved Mary and his children. 'This being Easter Monday [he wrote] – and time to go to bed I wish to record my respectful gratitude to the Authorities here, having a Strong impression I will have no opportunity of doing so personally – and to request that my two little Sketch Books might be sent to my poor dear wife Mary – not on account of their worth but just to show who I was thinking of, and besides there are lots of ideas in them which under professionable advise might be utilized – that's all I've got to say – except God Bless her & the rest of them – who I dare say all forget me now – I don't – them—' The most poignant picture in the book is a pen sketch on page twenty-seven. It depicts the elderly, bearded and steel-rim-bespectacled Charles sitting beside a pretty young woman who is busy sewing, a cat curled at her feet. He is gazing up at her in wistful adoration. The caption reads, 'Mary, my ideal home ruler. No repeal of the union proposed in this case.' This prompts the further thought that a man able to play with such a pun on the current Home Rule for Ireland political situation was nothing like as insane as his guardians might have supposed. Charles also followed his son's literary career with pride, noting the critical response *Micah Clarke* and *The Mystery of Cloomber* received.

The sketches and watercolours in the diary, although indicative of a distinct and original artistic talent, are often macabre. The imagery may well have been one of the factors keeping him in an asylum. Young frail girls – who might be fairies – come face to face with huge birds and massive polecats; a squirrel carries a human infant like a nut; pixies try to steal a dead bird from the mouth of a dog; the royal coat of arms has its motto, 'Honi Soit Qui Mal Y Pens', twisted into 'Honey Swore It By Eighteen Pence'. Many of the sketches show life in the asylum but others are self-portraits of Charles meeting death or, in one instance, being carried off in the mouth of a living sphinx. Mortality is a recurring theme throughout the book which stylistically reminds one of a cross between William Blake and Edward Lear.

Although fantastical and often grotesque, the pictures do not suggest the work of a genuine madman. Charles was far more of a drunk than a deranged lunatic. He seems still to have been comparatively in command of his senses, and his fits were more than likely caused by alcoholic damage to his nervous system than true epilepsy. That he was of a depressive nature, neurotic and the possessor of what Victorians termed 'morbid tendencies and humours' is true, but this is not to say he was insane. He even kept his sense of humour, for, on page fifty-six of the diary, he noted, 'I believe I am branded as mad solely from the narrow Scotch Misconception of Jokes – If Charles Lamb or Tom Hood had been caught, they would have been treated as I am, and the latter would probably have never written "the Song of a Shirt"—'

An obituary appeared in the *Scotsman* on 23 October, nine days after the funeral. It outlined his famous antecedents, described his paintings as crude but containing a 'natural genius' and ended parsimoniously, 'he was a likeable man, genial, entertaining and amusing in conversation . . . He was a great reader, and was in consequence well informed. His abilities and gentlemanly manner ensured to him a cordial welcome wherever he went.'

Although his father caused much suffering to his family, Conan Doyle felt compassion for him, although he never openly admitted it. As a child, he had had little affection for, or indeed contact with, Charles but, as he reached adulthood, he came to understand and pity him, respecting his talent as an artist. It must be remembered that Conan Doyle had several of his father's pictures hanging in his study.

In an interview he gave in 1907, Conan Doyle said, 'My father, Charles Doyle, was in truth a great unrecognised genius. He drifted to Edinburgh from London in his early youth, and so he lost the chance of living before the public eye. His wild and strange fancies alarmed, I think, rather than pleased the stolid Scotchmen of the 50's and 60's. His mind was on strange moonlight effects, done with extraordinary skill in water colours; dancing witches, drowning seamen, death coaches on lonely moors at night, and goblins chasing children across churchyards.' In his autobiography, he went further by remarking, 'My father's life was full of the tragedy of unfulfilled powers and of undeveloped gifts. He had his weaknesses, as all of us have ours, but he had also some very remarkable and outstanding virtues.' He even went so far as to organise an exhibition of Charles Doyle's work in 1924, entitling it 'The Humorous and the Terrible'. The art critic for *The Times* did not like it. He declared there was no real artistic merit in the pictures and added, 'The terrible did not terrify us. The more deliberately humorous did not amuse us.' He did, however, conclude, 'But nearly everything charmed us.'

Whatever compassion Conan Doyle felt for his father in later years, he took the usual Victorian attitude towards drunkenness. It was morally indefensible. In the Sherlock Holmes story 'The Adventure of the Abbey Grange', a violent alcoholic husband is murdered, but Holmes excuses the murderer. Several other villains in the stories are drunks, whilst in *The Doings of Raffles Haw*, the character MacIntyre exemplifies the devious scheming drunkard hunting out his bottle.

Conan Doyle may have felt guilty about his father but he should have felt more so about Louise. As a doctor, he should have recognised her condition long before it developed advanced symptoms. With hindsight, he realised that he had not only ignored the symptoms but had possibly exacerbated them. He was keen to take Louise on long tricycle rides despite her general weakness, and although he did most of the pedalling, these outings still tired her. Taking her to Norway whilst she was pregnant and, if the trip occurred, to Switzerland in January, could not have helped matters. It was not that he deliberately neglected his wife, nor that he was being specifically selfish: it was more a case of his being overly busy, living the life of the writer, working away at his serious books, meeting deadlines for Sherlock Holmes stories and not paying her the attention she was due as his wife.

When Powell's prognosis was made, Conan Doyle was loath to accept it. He would not give in to fate and decided, as soon as possible, to take Louise to Davos in Switzerland. It was believed that TB could be cured by a prolonged stay in a clear high-altitude atmosphere.

By the end of November, Conan Doyle and Louise were in Davos. Who went with them is the subject of some controversy. Some commentators say the children accompanied their parents, with Lottie acting as governess and to assist with Louise. Others state only Conan Doyle and Louise went abroad, the children remaining in South Norwood with their grandmother, Mrs Hawkins. Leaving the children behind posed no problem. They had stayed in the grandmother's charge before and it was common practice in Victorian households for children to be placed with relatives, nannies or governesses for even quite long periods. Leaving them behind seems to have been the most practical of decisions.

Louise was to spend some years overseas, breathing in unpolluted air and keeping her illness in abeyance. Although she was henceforth an invalid, occasional relapses threatening her life, she lived for another thirteen years.

It was whilst Conan Doyle was in Davos in December 1893 that 'The Adventure of the Final Problem' was published in the *Strand Magazine*. The news of Sherlock Holmes's forthcoming demise had actually been leaked in *Tit-Bits* the month before, prompting J.M. Barrie to pen another parody, 'The Late Sherlock Holmes', which came out in the *St James's Gazette* shortly after the real story. Barrie's send-up dealt with Holmes's disappearance over the Reichenbach Falls, a doctor (thought to have been Watson's accomplice) pushing him over the drop after having been heard in recent months to mutter such statements as 'Holmes has been getting too uppish for anything', he was 'sick of the braggart's name', and that if the 'public kept shouting for more Holmes he would kill him in self-defence'.

'The Adventure of the Final Problem' is not the best Sherlock Holmes story but it is inevitably one of the most memorable. Professor Moriarty, the master criminal, nemesis and antithesis of Holmes, falls to his death over the Reichenbach Falls, Holmes locked in his grip. Paget's illustration shows the two figures in mortal combat on the brink of the chasm.

Who Moriarty, the 'Napoleon of crime . . . a genius, a philosopher, and abstract thinker', was based upon has never been ascertained, but there are those who would have him modelled on Christison. The name may have been sourced from either a pupil Conan Doyle knew at Stonyhurst, who was a clever mathematician, won the subject prize in 1873 and went on to become an eminent judge, or his brother, who won the same prize the following year. (The evil Professor Moriarty is a mathematician.) Other candidates are Major-General Drayson (Moriarty wrote a study of asteroids), James Payn (whom he physically resembled) and a famous criminal called Adam Worth who was nicknamed 'the Napoleon of crime' and one of whose exploits, tunnelling into a bank from a neighbouring property, had netted him $450,000 and given Conan Doyle the basis for the plot of 'The Red-Headed League'.

When Sherlock Holmes and Moriarty went over the falls, there was a massive public uproar which astonished Conan Doyle. More than twenty thousand people cancelled their subscriptions to the *Strand Magazine*. The shareholders grew jittery and both Newnes and Greenhough Smith, who had begged Conan Doyle not to kill Holmes, were very worried. Abusive mail arrived at the editorial offices by the sackload whilst hundreds more letters were sent direct to Conan Doyle beseeching him to reverse Holmes's death. One letter from a woman reader began, 'You brute!' People wore black armbands in public mourning. Newspapers around the world reported the death as a new items and there were obituaries by the score. *Tit-Bits*, perhaps in an attempt to regain some of the income lost by the *Strand Magazine*, announced the instigation of a Sherlock Holmes Memorial Prize. Sherlock Holmes clubs sprang up in America. And evil, it seemed, had triumphed over good.

9

A Widening of Horizons

Davos, in a valley five thousand feet up in the Swiss Alps, was a small town surrounded by pine forests and high peaks. Under snow for nearly half the year, it was famous as a health resort, especially for TB sufferers, with clear air and long hours of stark sunshine. The majority of the population consisted of English consumptives who led a busy social life. They might have been at Cannes or Monte Carlo were it not for the terrible mortality hanging over them. When someone died, they were discreetly spirited away to the not surprisingly large cemetery. Some visitors rented chalets, others stayed in one of three large hotels. Conan Doyle and Louise took rooms at the Kurhaus Hotel.

Fortunately, Louise was not in much pain. She bore her disease with fortitude, was optimistic (a common trait amongst tuberculosis sufferers) and enjoyed both the scenery and the resort atmosphere. Most of her time was spent lying on her back on the hotel verandah under cloudless skies, swaddled in rugs and blankets, sucking in the sharp air that was part of the treatment. By early 1894, she showed a marked improvement. Conan Doyle stayed with her as much as he could but business and writing commitments frequently took him away. Every time he left Davos, it was no doubt with mixed feelings. He would have wanted to stay with Louise but the atmosphere of the town was gloomy. Robert Louis Stevenson, who had taken the cure there a decade before, said Davos had 'a certain prison-like effect on the imagination', whilst Conan Doyle remarked that life in Davos was 'bounded by the snow and fir which girt us in'.

Despite the misery of the place, Conan Doyle was stimulated by the alpine air and got down to work. With Sherlock Holmes dead, he was able to explore other creative avenues. In addition to working, he lectured quite frequently to the Davos Literary Society, wrote letters, went on sleigh rides, walked in the pine forests, skated, tobogganed, read and took photographs. He also imported something he remembered having seen in Norway – skis.

Conan Doyle played an important part in the history of the sport of skiing in Switzerland. By the end of January 1894, he was writing that once his current work was finished, he would be out all day on his Norwegian skis. He had recently read an account by the explorer Nansen of his crossing of Greenland on skis, and felt Switzerland might provide good skiing terrain. Until now, although skis were known in Switzerland, the Swiss went about on snowshoes or with sledges.

He teamed up with two local carpenters and sledge-makers, Tobias and Johann Branger, who had already been experimenting with skis for about a year, teaching themselves the basic techniques, much to the derision of the locals: so embarrassed were they by the hoots of mockery they received that they took to practising after dark. In March 1893, they had crossed the Furka Pass to Arosa, dragging a pole as a brake and strapping their skis together to form a toboggan when the descent grew too steep. Now, with Conan Doyle, they set about improving on their knowledge. Eventually, the rudimentary techniques worked out, they set off to climb the Jacobshorn, a 7,700-foot mountain four kilometres south-west of the town. From the peak, they could just make out the crowds in Davos waving flags to celebrate their achievement. It was the first time an alpine mountain had been conquered on skis.

On 23 March 1894, they set off once more for the Furka Pass, crossing it at eight thousand feet. Conan Doyle went with them. They were equipped with eight-foot-long strips of elm, each four inches wide and tied on to their boots with twine. Conan Doyle wore Harris tweed knickerbockers. It was a thrilling and, at times, dangerous journey. At a near-sheer slope, the Brangers removed their skis and bound them together to make something akin to a modern snowboard. This done, they glided down the mountain. When Conan Doyle removed his skis, they slid away before he could bind them so he had no alternative but to follow on the seat of his knickerbockers. 'My tailor [he later wrote] tells me Harris tweed cannot wear out. This is a mere theory and will not stand a thorough scientific test. He will find samples of his wares on view from the Furka Pass to Arosa.' Arriving in Arosa, Tobias Branger signed the hotel register on behalf of them all: much to Conan Doyle's delight, he entered 'Sportesmann' under 'Profession' for him in the ledger.

Upon returning next day, he wrote to his mother, 'Yesterday I performed a small feat by crossing a chain of mountains on snowshoes (Norwegian skis) and coming down to Arosa. Two Swiss accompanied me. I am the first Englishman who has ever crossed an Alpine pass in winter on snowshoes – at least I think so. We left this at four in the morning and were in Arosa at 11.30.'

The following winter, Conan Doyle described his skiing adventures in the *Strand Magazine*. The article, 'An Alpine Pass on Ski', described how they had 'shot along over gently dipping curves skimming down into the valley without a motion of our feet. In that great untrodden waste with . . . no marks of life save that of chamois and of foxes, it was glorious to whizz along in this easy fashion.'

Conan Doyle declared in his autobiography, 'I can claim to have been the first to introduce skis into the Grisons division of Switzerland or at least to demonstrate their practical utility as a means of getting across in winter from one valley to another.' He did not, as many would have it, actually introduce skis into Switzerland, yet he did suggest and promote skiing as a sport, especially what is now called cross-country skiing, a form of long-distance hiking by ski. Contrary to what has often been suggested, he did not initiate downhill skiing, which was begun by Matthias Zdarsky at Lilienfeld in 1896, nor was he, indeed, the first Englishman to ski at Davos. That honour is attributed to a Colonel Napier. Whether he was the originator of skiing or not, Conan Doyle was sure in his mind of one thing. He was, he said, 'convinced that the time will come when hundreds of Englishmen will come to Switzerland for the "ski"-ing season, in March and April'. A plaque acknowledging his part in the history of Swiss skiing hangs in Davos to this day.

Early in 1894, Conan Doyle finished *The Stark Munro Letters*, which he openly conceded was autobiographical save for a chapter featuring Lord Saltire. Written as a sequence of letters from a young doctor at the start of his career to an American friend, Herbert Swanborough in Lowell, Massachusetts, it draws for much of its content upon Conan Doyle's time in Plymouth and Southsea, which he calls Bradfield and Birchespool respectively. The book had been a long time in the making, starting off possibly as early as 1885 with some preliminary jottings to which he returned in 1891 and tinkered with until the book was finally completed. It is a fascinating study of the professional and in places religious hopes, fears and doubts of a young doctor. It must be borne in mind that it was a novel and, therefore, contained elements of embellishment and imagination, but even Conan Doyle later stated that, at least where Budd was concerned, it was pretty near to the truth.

Also present in the story were Mary Doyle, Innes, Dr Hoare, his Doyle uncles and Louise, amongst others.

Other than as a fund of biographical information, the book is also valuable as an immensely amusing story, containing some outstandingly comical interludes, and a platform upon which Conan Doyle outlined his religious and philosophical thoughts as well as his struggle to come to terms with the past. Conan Doyle's break with Catholicism is echoed in Stark Munro's thoughts: 'Is religion the only domain of thought which is non-progressive, and to be referred forever to a standard set two thousand years ago? Can they not see as the human brain evolves it must take a wider outlook? A half-formed brain makes a half-formed God, and who shall say that our brains are even half-formed yet? . . . Catholicism is the more thorough; Protestantism is the more reasonable . . . Catholicism expects civilisation to adapt itself to it . . . When first I came out of the faith in which I had been reared, I certainly did feel for a time as if my life-belt had burst.' Stark Munro does not dismiss religion but rejects the rigid dogma as he does atheism, believing in some form of God.

For some while, Conan Doyle had been too preoccupied with his work to pay much attention to psychic phenomena, although he had not ceased being interested in the subject. The circles in which he moved were not of the sort to be bothered too much with spiritualism. In his own words, he said that his life was so busy he had little time for, as he put it, religious development. Domestic life and his engagement in sport, the hectic whirl of literary life, the birth of his son and the arrivals of Connie and Lottie had filled most of his time. Yet now, in Switzerland, surrounded by those waiting to die, Louise included in their number, he found his attention shifting again to the dilemma of what lay at the core of the human spirit.

In November 1893, Conan Doyle joined the British Society for Psychical Research and began to read the society's publications, received from Oliver Lodge, one of the founders with whom he was in correspondence. Lodge, a renowned physicist, pioneer of wireless and radio telegraphy and the first Principal of Birmingham University, was friendly with both Gurney and Myers. His opinions on psychical research and spiritualism coincided with Conan Doyle's, and their wide-ranging spiritualist correspondence continued for the rest of Conan Doyle's life. In addition, he remained in touch with Myers, with whom he shared the view that man's role in the grand scheme of things could only be justified by understanding the basis of personality. The issue of the society journal Conan Doyle was sent two months later included an address by Arthur Balfour, its newly elected president, dealing with mesmerism. Conan Doyle was fascinated and started work on a macabre novella, *The Parasite*, subtitled 'A Mesmeric and Hypnotic Mystery'.

Although not strictly about ghosts and the after-life, it was Conan Doyle's first book concerning psychic phenomena. In summary, the story centres on Professor Austin Gilroy, a psychically doubting neurasthenic physiologist who is converted to the truth by a crippled and somewhat plain female mesmerist. Through her hypnotic power, she gains control over people, forcing them to do her bidding. Although Gilroy views her seances as 'something between a religious ceremony and a conjuror's entertainment', he is nevertheless ensnared by her – 'I was her slave, body and soul, and for the moment I rejoiced in my slavery' – and finds she has used him unconsciously to help rob a bank and has set him up to murder his own fiancée whom he does not, at the last moment, kill. To free himself, he decides to do away with the mesmerist, but when he arrives to do the deed he finds her already dead.

It is a contrived yarn which Conan Doyle later disowned, possibly because of its portrayal of sexual domination, yet it is an intriguing insight into the relationship between sexual obsession and hypnotism with which he had long been fascinated: the theme is not unlike that of his short story 'John Barrington Cowles', written a decade before.

To what extent the plot and subject had anything to do with Conan Doyle's own sexuality is the subject of speculation. Much has been written about and hypothesised concerning Conan Doyle's repressed sexuality. Theories have ranged widely and drawn no conclusions. In many respects, Conan Doyle was no different from any other man of his time, constrained by the morality and hypocrisy of the Victorian era, governed by the codes of honour and loyalty his mother had instilled in him, obliged by the society in which he lived to suppress his deeper emotions. Whatever came out in his writing was no more than would have emanated from many writing within the confines of the age.

At the same time as he was working on *The Parasite*, Conan Doyle was also gathering together a collection of short stories entitled *Round the Red Lamp, Being Facts and Fancies of Medical Life*, which was to be published in autumn 1894. It comprised fifteen stories, most of them based upon a doctor's life, the title coming from the red lamp that hung outside a general practitioner's surgery. Many aspects of the stories were autobiographical and based upon Conan Doyle's experiences as a medical student or at Southsea. A number of them had been written specifically for Jerome K. Jerome's *Idler*. Jerome had requested some powerful and realistic stories but, when they came, they were considered a little too powerful and too realistic, and he only published three of them, although he owned the rights to eight.

'The Curse of Eve' was originally about a mother who dies in childbirth, the father attempting infanticide because he thinks the baby has murdered its mother. Conan Doyle, who, as a doctor, must have come across – or heard about – the event, did not consider the story objectionable or too strong. It was the sort of reality doctors faced in their everyday business. His opinion was altered, however, after he read the story aloud to an Authors' Club meeting, and, for the published version, the mother and child survived, which was, in effect, a weakening of the impact and message of the original, which sought to show the horrors of childbearing. Another of the stories had a similar theme. In 'A Medical Document', the wife demands her policeman husband be handcuffed to her during an eight-hour labour, her thrashing about wearing his wrists raw, of which she approves, as she believes he should share her pain. A second theme in the tales, and one Conan Doyle returned to a number of times, concerned the results of improper surgery. In 'The Case of Lady Sannox', a famous surgeon, Douglas Stone, has an affair with the opprobrious but beautiful ex-actress, Lady Sannox, whose husband, disguised as his own Turkish butler, orders Stone to operate on a mysterious, veiled and comatose patient. Stone, thinking the patient is Lord Sannox, who has cut his lip with a poisoned dagger, slices a disfiguring V of flesh from the lip to remove the site of the poison. He then improbably discovers that his veiled patient is Lady Sannox and loses his mind whilst she, no longer pretty, enters a convent. 'The Surgeon Talks' deals with a patient who needs an ear removing. As he is about to be chloroformed, he kicks over the candle in the operating theatre but, in the darkness, is grabbed, picked up, smothered with an anaesthetic mask and operated upon. Only when the mask is removed at the end of the procedure is it discovered that the ear of an assistant surgeon has been cut off in error. Despite the title of the book, it also contained two straight horror stories, as if there were not enough horror already.

By April 1894, Louise's health was much improved and her doctors gave her permission to make a short trip to England, to visit the children and her mother in South Norwood. Within eight weeks, however, she was back in Davos, accompanied by Lottie, who was to be her companion and help. Although he made two brief trips to Davos before September, Conan Doyle remained in London. He had a number of projects in the air and had been sent an invitation to lecture in America in the autumn. His reputation was by now truly international, thanks predominantly to Sherlock Holmes, and he had given lectures throughout the British Isles as well as in a few places in Europe, but to be asked to lecture in America gave him immense pleasure. With Louise's constitution improved, he accepted.

Before crossing the Atlantic, however, he had a number of other matters to deal with including, in the summer, rehearsals for a play based upon one of his short stories. *A Story of Waterloo* was a one-act play Conan Doyle had adapted himself from 'A Straggler of '15', which had been published in *Harper's New Monthly Magazine* three years before. The subject of the play was Corporal Gregory Brewster, aged ninety, who had served under Wellington in the Napoleonic War. Now almost deaf and distinctly crotchety, Brewster narrates his experiences.

The rights in the play had been bought by Henry Irving in 1892 for £100, but he had not had the opportunity or the time to stage it. That it was also so short militated against production. Now, Irving included it in a double bill with another short play, *The Bells*, a melodrama about a murderer who is haunted by the insidious sound of church bells which reminds him of his crime. The plays were first performed on 21 September 1894 at Prince's Theatre, Bristol. The novelty of a play by Conan Doyle, performed by Henry Irving, drew a massive press interest. The Great Western Railway had to lay on a special journalists' train. The performance gained a standing ovation. Bram Stoker, later to be world famous as the author of *Dracula*, who was Irving's private secretary and touring manager for twenty-seven years, noted in his diary, 'New play enormous success. HI fine and great. All laughed and wept. Marvellous study of senility. Eight calls at end.' Conan Doyle was absent from this triumphant first night, for he was already *en route* for the USA. It must be said the triumph was due more to Irving's acting than Conan Doyle's writing. Nevertheless, when it opened the following May in the West End, at the Lyceum Theatre, it was a critical success with everyone except George Bernard Shaw, the detractor of Sherlock Holmes and newly appointed theatre critic for the *Saturday Review*, who was trying hard to be controversial in order to establish a reputation. In 1897, Irving performed the play for Queen Victoria's diamond jubilee in front of an audience of two thousand soldiers from across the Empire. Conan Doyle's pride was limitless.

Once the play was well into rehearsal, Conan Doyle embarked upon another, *The House of Temperley*, also intended for Irving. It was at first thought he would co-write it with his brother-in-law, E.W. Hornung, but they decided against collaboration after less than a week. The play was only one act long by the time Conan Doyle sailed for the USA, and he set it aside for the time being.

With Louise back in Davos, Conan Doyle's life settled back into its former routine. He dined in London, attended literary gatherings, gave interviews and became, once more, one of London's most popular literary lions. When not living the life of letters, he researched in the Reading Room of the British Museum, in the London Institution Library, or at the library of the Society for Psychical Research, corresponded with Lodge and Myers, kept abreast of current affairs and added to his scrapbooks, plotted out stories and wrote notes for his American lectures on George Meredith, Robert Louis Stevenson, J.M. Barrie, Rudyard Kipling and others – and, of course, his own works. At first, he had been reluctant to include himself as a lecture topic but changed his mind. No doubt he realised his audience might want to know a little more about him.

When his studies lagged, he went to Lord's cricket ground to watch W.G. Grace, one of the most famous cricketers of all time, play in the county championships. Over the years, Conan Doyle himself played for the Marylebone Cricket Club (the famous MCC), sometimes as a team member for first-class matches against Warwickshire, Derbyshire and Kent. Against the former, he achieved a hat-trick and, on one occasion, he actually bowled out W.G. Grace. His achievement was recorded in verse, his lines about Grace going:

> Before me he stands like a vision,
>   Bearded and burly and brown,
> A smile of good-humoured derision
>   As he waits for the first to come down.
>
> A statue from Thebes or from Cnossus,
>   A Hercules shrouded in white,
> Assyrian Bull-like Colossus,
>   He stands in his might.
>
> With the beard of a Goth or a Vandal,
>   His bat hangs ready and free,
> His great hairy hands on the handle,
>   And his menacing eyes upon me.

Grace's menacing eyes forecast the future: he soon bowled Conan Doyle out.

Just before leaving for America, Conan Doyle took part in another sort of sport – ghost-hunting. With Dr Sydney Scott and Frank Podmore, leading members of the Society for Psychical Research, he went to Charmouth in Dorset where a number of spiritual disturbances were said to be occurring in the home of a Colonel Elmore. According to Jerome K. Jerome, these turned out to be the responsibility of the colonel's very-much-alive but neurotic middle-aged spinster daughter who agreed to stop her pranks so long as her father was not told. In his autobiography, Conan Doyle makes no mention of this but remarks that, several years later, a child's skeleton was unearthed in the garden, which was the root cause of the phenomena.

Conan Doyle sailed for New York in September aboard the North German Lloyd liner *Elbe*. With him went Innes, now twenty-one and a subaltern in the Royal Artillery Regiment. The crossing seems to have been uneventful save for a matter of flags. The German crew were not well disposed towards the British so, when the voyage gala was held, they decked out the saloon with the flags of many nations, but not Britain. The patriotic Doyles took umbrage and made a Union Jack which they hung with the others.

The lecture tour was organised by an impresario called Major James Burton Pond, a veteran of the US Civil War who ran a very successful agency handling lecture and music performance circuits across the USA: he had been responsible for Mark Twain's famous lecture trips. Conan Doyle's tour was to have him lecturing on himself and the work of other British authors as well as giving readings from his own books. The tour started in New York in the first week of October. Conan Doyle and Innes were put up in an annexe of the Aldine Club, a recently formed society for men engaged in the literary and publishing world. In all, he made over forty appearances across the north-eastern and mid-western USA, visiting amongst other cities New York, Boston, Washington DC, Chicago, Indianapolis, Cincinnati, Toledo, Detroit and Milwaukee.

The first lectures were hard. Although he was used to speaking publicly back home, here he knew he had to make a good impression. His reputation in the USA depended upon it. He faced the platform and was so nervous even Major Pond noticed the fact. At one New York venue, the Calvary Baptist Church, he slipped as he mounted the stage, dropping his lecture notes. Blushing, he carried on with his talk, his notes in disarray, but the audience did not seem to mind. They found him charming and unpretentious, no doubt owing to his own decision that his presentation should be as natural as possible and nothing like the theatrical shows many authors put on, in which they appeared on stage in costumes appropriate to their stories or wearing dandified 'literary' outfits. The critics liked him, too. One wrote that he spoke in a 'melodious, hearty, welcoming voice; a modest man, too, for he spoke deprecatingly of himself; modest, also, because of jewellery he showed only a tiny stud and the bar which held in place his watch-chain'. The *New York Recorder* went into more detail, stating that the audience liked not only his lecture but also his 'hearty, cheery, sympathetic voice'. Throughout his life, Conan Doyle spoke quietly with a marked, but not heavy, Edinburgh accent although, when the need arose, he could boom like a sergeant-major. He usually spoke quite slowly, enunciating clearly in a deep, resonant bass and, when he read or recited, his voice took on an attractive lilt, the cadences undulating and flowing.

The tour was frenzied, Major Pond making the most of Conan Doyle's time. The lectures were, in some respects, the easiest part. At least then Conan Doyle was in command. The rest of the time he was travelling by train from city to city, attending receptions and parties, giving interviews, staying for one-night stands in strange hotels and doing his best to see what he could of America. The constant journeying, pressing of the flesh and functions exhausted him. He was not keen to meet the sort of people who crowded in on him, attended his lectures and came to the parties. American society dames were not to his liking. Many who attended his lectures did not come to hear him speak but to see what the inventor of Sherlock Holmes looked like. Their expectations were often dashed: they expected to find a tall, thin, clean-shaven aesthete, not a powerful, muscular man with a bushy moustache and a Scots burr to his voice. It was a problem that dogged him all his life: the doll and its maker were certainly far from identical.

Regardless of the tight schedule, he still managed a few side trips. In Cambridge, he visited Mount Auburn Cemetery and the grave of Oliver Wendell Holmes who had died on 7 October. It was one of the disappointments of his life that Conan Doyle missed meeting Holmes, a doctor turned writer like himself. He wrote in *Through the Magic Door* that 'it was one of the ambitions of my lifetime to look upon his face, but by the irony of Fate I arrived in his native city just in time to lay a wreath upon his newly turned grave'. It being the fall, he was struck by the beauty of autumnal New England, visited places in Boston associated with Poe and met other authors including the poet Eugene Field, with whom he forged a long-lasting friendship, in Chicago.

Not all his contacts were Americans. He spent Thanksgiving with

Rudyard Kipling, whom he had not met before, at his home near Brattleboro in Vermont, staying for two days. They shared common interests and tastes in sport and literature but disagreed over Conan Doyle's ideas on Anglo-American relations: Kipling was not a little anti-American, despite his expatriate status and having an American wife. They played golf. At least, Conan Doyle did. 'I had brought up my golf clubs,' he later wrote, 'and gave him lessons in a field while the New England rustics watched us from afar, wondering what on earth we were at, for golf was unknown in America at that time.' The rustics must have been bemused: they already regarded the intensely private Kipling as something of an oddity. Despite his golf lesson – Kipling did not like the game – they parted good friends. This was a rarity, for Kipling was reserved and wary of friendship, yet he thereafter included Conan Doyle on his very short list of friends. Conan Doyle, when he returned to England, sent Kipling a pair of skis.

Towards the end of the tour, Conan Doyle met Sam McClure, the editor and publisher of *McClure's Magazine*, founded the summer before, which had published some Sherlock Holmes stories and bought the American serial rights to *The White Company*. When they met at the Aldine Club, McClure apologised for not having attended Conan Doyle's lectures but said he was preoccupied. The magazine was in financially dire straits, unable to pay its printers or authors, and McClure had reached the end of his credit. Conan Doyle, impressed by McClure's dogged enthusiasm, decided to invest in the magazine. He had made a clear profit on the tour of around £1,000, so he went to McClure's office and wrote out a cheque for $8,500 in return for a thousand shares which, McClure remembered, 'was exactly the sum we were owing to English authors. When that check was written, it put new life into the office staff. Everyone in the office felt a new vigour and a new hope.' Conan Doyle held the shares for twenty years.

A farewell dinner was thrown for him by the Aldine Club on 6 December. By now, his public speaking skills were much improved and he is said to have told what he later referred to as an apocryphal story. Arriving in Boston, a cabbie had refused his fare, asking to be paid with a ticket to the lecture. Conan Doyle demanded to know how the cabbie knew who he was. The cabbie's response was to point out that Conan Doyle's coat lapels were badly twisted downward where they had been grasped by the intransigent New York reporters, his overcoat showed the slovenly brushing of the porters on the through sleeper from Albany, his hair had the Quakerish trim of a Philadelphia barber, his right overshoe had Buffalo mud on it, his clothing smelt of a

Utica cigar, his bag had a scattering of Springfield doughnut crumbs on it and, finally, his walking cane was stencilled with his name. The anecdote ends with Conan Doyle declaring he now knew where Sherlock Holmes went when he died and that, if he was to write more stories about him, he knew to find him in Boston.

Conan Doyle and Innes left New York on 8 December aboard the Cunard liner *Etruria*, bound for Liverpool. Conan Doyle was exhausted, spending most of the voyage in his cabin. The tour, however, was deemed a great success. The Americans had taken to his modesty and plain speaking. An article published in America the following March summed him up: 'His personality is a peculiarly attractive one to Americans because it is so thoroughly wholesome. The first impression which he makes is one of entire health of body and mind . . . [He was] simple, sincere, unaffected and honest.' Awards had been showered on him and Pond, who had tried to persuade him to stay longer, said he would pay him more than any other English author if he agreed to return for a hundred-engagement tour. Conan Doyle declined to extend his stay: he had promised to be home for Christmas.

He had gone to America with preconceived ideas of what he would find. He had already written about the country in his fiction and felt an affinity for it. It exceeded his expectations. He found the people delightful, the wide open spaces and distances astonishing, and he was glad the romance of the pioneer was not dead. 'The race,' he wrote to his mother, 'as a whole is not only the most prosperous, but the most even-tempered, tolerant, and hopeful that I have ever known.' The only aspect he seems not to have liked was the same one that strikes Europeans to this day: he found the heat of hotel lobbies and railway carriages oppressive. He was himself hot-blooded and rarely wore an overcoat regardless of the weather. When giving his lectures, he found the atmosphere of the halls so stifling he removed his waistcoat and buttoned up his jacket to cover his shirt front.

Although he was grateful for his reception in the USA, in one respect he misunderstood it. He had seen himself as a sort of ambassador for international relations, believing that the people who flocked to see him were interested in forging links across the sea. His modesty did not let him realise that all they really wanted was to see the 'father' of Sherlock Holmes. His great hope, of Anglo-American unification, was hardly feasible, although he dedicated *The White Company*, in 1891, 'To the Hope of the Future, the Reunion of the English Speaking Races This little Chronicle of our common Ancestry is inscribed', and, just before his departure for New York, he had stated in an interview for the *Cincinnati*

Commercial Gazette, how he hoped 'to see a warmer friendship between the two great nations of the English speaking race. There is no subject on which I take so keen an interest . . . I believe the English speaking races must either coalesce, in which case the future of the world is theirs, or else they will eternally neutralize each other and be overshadowed by some more compact people, as the Russians and the Chinese.'

With the hindsight of modern history, his remarks show a considerable astuteness but, at the time, Anglo-American unification was far from possible, for relations between the USA and Britain were atrocious. A year later, he wrote to *The Times*, pointing out that the British were being intransigent and that many Americans viewed the British as the British did the French, with suspicion. His solution was simplistic. 'I should like to see,' he declared, 'an Anglo-American Society started in London with branches all over the Empire, for the purpose of promoting good feeling, smoothing over friction, laying literature before the public which will show them how strong are the arguments in favour of an Anglo-American alliance, and supplying the English Press with the American side of the question and vice versa.'

From Liverpool, Conan Doyle took the train to London and then, almost immediately, set off for Davos where the family was staying for Christmas in the Grand Hotel Belvedere. He remained in Davos with Louise for the rest of the winter but he was not idle. He was busy on a new set of stories with a new serial character.

He had invented Brigadier Gerard in the spring of 1894 and had completed several stories before going to America: he read one, 'The Medal of Brigadier Gerard', on the tour before it was published in the *Strand Magazine* in December. Now, in Davos, he wrote more tales for the magazine under the blanket heading of *The Exploits of Brigadier Gerard*: they were collected as a single volume and brought out in February 1896. With Sherlock Holmes dead, he saw the value of creating another recurring character.

The spark that set Brigadier Gerard alight was the English translation of *The Memoirs of Baron de Marbot*, a real-life French baron and soldier, which had first been published half a century before. De Marbot, a captain in Napoleon's army, was intelligent, honourable and brave but also vain. Inspired by the book, Conan Doyle determined to write about the life of a soldier in Napoleon's empire. Already immersed in the Napoleonic era, he continued to read everything he could on the subject. 'For three years,' he wrote, 'I lived among Napoleonic literature, with some hope that by soaking and resoaking myself in it I might at last write some worthy book which would reproduce some of the glamour of that extraordinary and fascinating epoch.' Napoleon had always fascinated him. 'He was,' he stated, 'a wonderful man – perhaps the most wonderful man who ever lived. What strikes me is the lack of finality in his character. When you make up your mind that he is a complete villain, you come on some noble trait, and then your admiration of this is lost in some act of incredible meanness.' It was not quite an opinion shared by the British man in the street but this did not deter Conan Doyle. He was on the trail of a good historical yarn and nothing was going to deter him once his heart was in it.

The stories were, as with so many of Conan Doyle's tales, presented in the first person, by an elderly Etienne Gerard, sitting in a café drinking wine and recounting his life between 1807 and 1815, during which time he was promoted from lieutenant to colonel. He is portrayed as courageous and boastful, laughing in the face of danger and revering his emperor. The stories speed along, punctuated by severed heads and a good washing of blood, glorifying warfare and manly derring-do. They are also cliché-ridden, the characters shallow, and the action sequences, though immediate, become tedious after a while. For all that, the stories are superbly told, the research is impeccable and the French attitude is exact. The research paid dividends. What is more, Conan Doyle enjoyed writing them – they took him little effort with the research already done – but he always considered them his 'little book of soldier stories' and not serious literature. He could not see anything that was light in style as having lasting value, but these stories, with their action and vitality, were far better than many of what he thought of as his serious historical novels.

As well as being historically accurate, the Brigadier Gerard stories also contained the humour that the longer historical stories often lacked, to their detriment, but which was one of the endearing traits of the Sherlock Holmes stories. The humour was not just a series of comical asides but went towards building up Gerard's character, so that he became almost as realistic as Sherlock Holmes. An example of this humour can be found in one of the best of the stories, 'How the Brigadier Slew the Fox'. Gerard loses his way behind British lines and becomes involved in a fox-hunt. Seeing it as a chance to escape, he steals a mount and joins the hunt but quickly falls for the thrill of the chase. Finally, he catches up with the fox and kills it with his cavalry sabre, much to the enraged yelling of the British huntsmen which he, being a self-professed authority on all things British, thinks is their shouted praise for his expertise.

Today, the stories are very dated and seem almost like children's fiction, but it might be argued that, had Gerard been as universal a character as a detective, he could have survived the test of time, for he was a realistic and breathing entity.

Although never as successful as the Sherlock Holmes tales, there was a demand for the Brigadier Gerard stories and Conan Doyle wrote sixteen of them in all, which made the soldier his most successful character after Sherlock Holmes and Watson. Once more, a character he had created as an amusing pot-boiler became a mainstay, although Conan Doyle was to admit in due course that the stories did earn their place in the genre of historical fiction.

During the winter in Davos, he increased his skill at skiing and, with the Brangers, mapped out trails that tourists might follow across country. As the snows thawed, he even designed and set out a golf course, but was annoyed when the cows ate the hole pennants. As the summer of 1895 swelled he, Louise and Lottie left Davos for Maloja near St Moritz and, later, Caux. Conan Doyle, ever restless to be writing, started yet another novel, *Rodney Stone*, which was completed by the end of September. It was another historical piece, set just before Regency times and about society life and prizefighting, the research carried out for the dormant play, *The House of Temperley*, serving as the background. As Conan Doyle knew only too well, every scrap of knowledge a writer accumulates will come to be of use in some way.

Conan Doyle was a fan of the fights. He not only boxed himself, and had done so since his student days, but he also went to tournaments and boxing matches. For him, boxing was the finest non-team sport of all, and he admired the courage it required for a man to take to the ring and stand his ground with nothing but his skill, bravery and fists with which to defend himself. He argued for the sport against its detractors, stating, 'Better that our sports should be a little too rough than that we should run the risk of effeminacy.' Clearly, the doctor in him was set aside where boxing was concerned, and he gave no thought to the brain damage the sport could inflict. As well as being keen on boxing, Conan Doyle was also fascinated by the history of the sport and was, through his reading, very knowledgeable. He believed bare-knuckle fighting, for all its brutality, was chivalrous and that boxing had been denigrated in recent times by the instigation of the Queensberry Rules, enforced in 1867, which had outlawed bare knuckles and heralded not only the use of boxing gloves but also the influence of gambling upon the outcome of bouts.

Rodney Stone, once more told by an elderly narrator reliving his youth, harked back to the bare-knuckle days. It captures the society of the age well and the action in the story is supremely handled but, as in so many of Conan Doyle's historical stories excepting the Brigadier Gerard tales, the inclusion of real historical characters such as Horatio Nelson and the Prince Regent was little more than a contrivance to capture the feel of the period. In actual fact, they either bogged the story down or gave it an unfortunate literary pretentiousness.

The novel did much to promote public interest in boxing, a fact often disputed by critics. Conan Doyle himself thought the book played an important part in the popularising of the sport, especially during the 1920s when the story was reprinted a number of times in the press, causing him to rate it highly. It was also financially very successful. Smith Elder & Co. paid £4,000 in advance royalties, the *Strand Magazine* put up £1,500 for the British serial rights and McClure went to £400 for the American serial rights. The sums paid were exceedingly high but they indicate Conan Doyle's status as a popular author: £4,000 in 1895 was the equivalent of £210,000 in 1995.

The novel was not his only boxing story. He also wrote a number of short stories and a novella-cum-long story, 'The Croxley Master', which he produced in 1899. It was not autobiographical but it contained much gleaned from Conan Doyle's time at Edinburgh University. The hero of the story is a medical student who, strapped for cash because his bursary application is mishandled by the academic administration, takes an assistant's post to a general practitioner in Sheffield. To earn some extra money, he agrees to fight the local champion, the Croxley master. The tale was included in *The Green Flag and Other Stories of War and Sport*, published in 1900.

Apart from boxing, sport did not often play an important role in Conan Doyle's writing, which is surprising when one considers the part it played in his life. Billiards, fishing and golf hardly appear despite, in the case of the former, Conan Doyle being an avid lifelong player of well above average ability. In 1913, he even entered the Billiard Amateur Championships, getting a bye in the first round, winning the second and being defeated in the third by one of the finalists. Football, even his beloved cricket, seldom feature, and he penned only one notable cricketing piece, 'The Story of Spedegue's Dropper', published in the *Strand Magazine* two years before his death and constructed around a true event when he was bowled out by A.P. Lucas with 'the most singular ball I have ever received'. Lucas bowled badly, the ball rose thirty feet in the air, then fell vertically on to the bails. The story is one of the gems of cricketing literature.

Whilst Louise and Lottie were staying at Caux in October, Conan Doyle returned briefly to Britain on business. It was not his first trip back that year – he had been over on at least one other occasion in May – but this time he was introduced to the novelist Grant Allen. Conan Doyle had heard of him and had read his strongly agnostic scientific writings. Allen had suffered from tuberculosis himself but had not been able to afford prolonged visits to the likes of Davos. Instead, he found that living at Hindhead in Surrey had cured him. The air there, he attested, was as good as any to be found overseas.

Hindhead was a hamlet on the main coach road to Portsmouth, eighty kilometres south-west of London. The area was being opened up for development, with gentlemen's country residences appearing in the woods along the high road and surrounding country lanes. Estate agents promoted the hills around it as the Surrey Highlands. Conan Doyle had reconciled himself to the fact that Louise would probably have to spend the rest of her life overseas but they both wanted to return. Her health had improved in Switzerland and she might be fit enough now to finish off her treatment in England.

He immediately visited Hindhead, reporting that 'its height, its dryness, its sandy soil, its fir trees, and its shelter from all bitter winds present the conditions which all agree to be best'. He purchased a plot of land near the crossroads in the centre of the village and commissioned his old Southsea spiritualist friend Henry Ball, who was an architect, to design and oversee the building of a house.

Grant Allen, who was born in Canada and lived near by in a house called The Croft, was to become a good friend. Not only did Conan Doyle share his agnostic views but Allen was also a humanist who had been Professor of Mental and Moral Philosophy at a college in Spanish Town, Jamaica, educating negroes, which he believed was a debt the white man owed to them for having enslaved their race. He published over thirty novels and, as he lay dying in 1899, he asked Conan Doyle, from his deathbed, if he would complete his detective novel *Hilda Wade*, currently being serialised in the *Strand Magazine*. Conan Doyle felt obligated to do so following Allen's outlines. It was not the first request he had had to assist a fellow writer posthumously: in 1895, Robert Louis Stevenson's executors asked him to finish his last novel, *St Ives*, but Conan Doyle had not felt he was equal to the task so Arthur Quiller-Couch completed it instead.

With the house under construction by a local builder from Guildford, Conan Doyle returned to Caux and then, in November, he travelled with Louise and Lottie via Rome to Brindisi where they boarded a ship for the port of Alexandria in Egypt, which country was considered beneficial to tuberculosis sufferers. They hoped a winter in Egypt would see

Louise finally cured. Egypt was the setting of another apocryphal Sherlock Holmes legend: it was said Conan Doyle discovered on landing at Alexandria that the Holmes stories were being used as a training text by the Egyptian police.

They remained in Egypt for six months, taking up residence at the Mena House Hotel, twelve kilometres outside Cairo and near the Pyramids. It was a grand establishment with all the trappings of Empire, frequented by British army officers and their ladies, the servants beturbaned and the rooms luxurious. Apart from the usual recreational facilities, it also boasted a golf course of sorts, of which Conan Doyle later wrote, 'if you sliced your ball, you might find it bunkered in the grave of some Rameses or Thothmes of old'. He also took to riding every morning, going for a dawn gallop on an Arab stallion which, on one occasion, threw him and then kicked him in the right eye. He nearly lost his sight and had to have five stitches in his eyelid which, for the rest of his life, drooped slightly. The desert impressed him but climbing the 137-metre-high Great Pyramid of Giza did not: the achievement, he claimed, realised little, for, as many other tourists have discovered, the climb was hot and unpleasant and the view not particularly exciting in the interminable Egyptian desert haze. He also attempted to speak Arabic and described how he tried to explain the principle of an eclipse of the moon. He pointed to the moon and the earth, then to a horse standing near by casting a shadow upon the ground. After a few minutes, his nonplussed Arab interlocutor got up and started to look at the creature's hind legs. Conan Doyle, it seems, had persuaded the Arab that his horse was sick. Clearly, the famous author and traveller had not learnt from the error of his ways in Norway.

Much of Conan Doyle's time was spent out of doors with Louise who had to take the air, but, like Lottie, he found the dry heat oppressive and tiring. It was difficult to work, but he did begin a novel entitled *Uncle Bernac* and started adapting one of James Payn's novels into a play called *Halves*. It had a hackneyed plot about two young brothers who promise to meet twenty-one years later and share whatever fortunes they have made. It was staged in 1899 and did moderately well.

Being a famous author, Conan Doyle mixed with Cairo society, occasionally staying overnight in the town at the Gezirah Palace Hotel. He became a member of the Turf Club, where he chatted with diplomats, military officers and, amongst others, Evelyn Baring, Baron Cromer, whose nickname was Over-Baring which summed up his character. He was notorious for once having halted an important diplomatic meeting because he had a lawn tennis engagement. Cromer, who had a penchant for meeting writers and was a close friend of Edward Lear, got on well with Conan Doyle, who was also introduced at the races to Lord Kitchener, the sirdar of the Egyptian Army.

To escape the heat and alleviate the boredom of hotel life, Conan Doyle took Louise and Lottie on a Nile cruise, setting off on 3 January 1896 aboard Thomas Cook's paddle steamer *Nitocris*. The journey had moments of intense beauty: 'Sunset left a long crimson glow over the Libyan desert,' Conan Doyle recorded. 'The river ran as smooth as quicksilver, with constant drifts of wild duck passing between ourselves and the crimson sky. On the Arabian side it was blue-black until the edge of the moon shone over low mountains.' They sailed as far as Wadi Halfa on the Sudanese border, visiting temples and archaeological sites *en route*.

The journey was long, 1,300 kilometres from Cairo to Wadi Halfa, and the further south they sailed, the more dangerous it became, for the Sudanese tribes were rebelling and often rode up to the banks of the Nile to shoot at passing ships. Wadi Halfa was, Conan Doyle wrote, a 'dreadful little suntrap' occupied by 2,500 Nubian and Egyptian soldiers commanded by two dozen British officers. Beyond the settlement stretched the vast wastes of the Sudan. In a journal Conan Doyle kept of the trip, which has never been published, he noted visiting a village that had recently been attacked by dervishes, seventeen of the villagers being massacred. It prompted the thought that a dervish leader could, with consummate ease, capture a Thomas Cook tour party. The result of this observation led to his writing a novel at the end of the year, *The Tragedy of the Korosko*, about a group of tourists caught by the Mahdi off their tour boat. It was, he later wrote, intended to show 'the effect upon the character of a varied group of people when they are suddenly plunged into frightful disaster'.

The novel is heavily laced with Conan Doyle's skilful evocation of the Nile, the characters of the passengers tightly drawn and the narrative well paced with a taut climax that shows, as with his awareness of the potential threat of the Russians and the Chinese in terms of world domination, Conan Doyle's consciousness of the latent power of Islam. One of the captured passengers, Colonel Cochrane Cochrane, indicates how astutely Conan Doyle had been studying the officers he met in Cairo and, to some extent, how ridiculous he viewed their strutting and posing. The fictional colonel dyes his hair and laces himself into corsets to maintain his gentlemanly appearance. He is one of Conan Doyle's most successful tragicomic characters. The story, one of his best since Sherlock Holmes was killed off, was a considerable success both as a serial in the *Strand Magazine* and as a book published in February 1898, dedicated to James Payn.

The Nile trip completed, Conan Doyle left Louise and Lottie and set out on a trip with an acquaintance, Colonel Henry Lewis, to visit an ancient Coptic monastery by the salt lakes, eighty kilometres out into the desert. It was an eventful outing. Thomas Cook provided them with a carriage which looked like a gilded coronation coach for an Eastern potentate: it had originally been made for Napoleon III when it was thought he was going to open the Suez Canal. They ran out of water, were then caught in a rainstorm, the carriage driver got them lost and they spent the night in a hut. When they finally reached the monastery, the monks were apathetic and unwelcoming, their library strewn on the floor. The abbot was ill, so Conan Doyle examined him. His assessment of the monastic community was summed up by the words 'it was said to be the fear of military service which caused many of the monks to discover that they had a vocation'.

On returning to Cairo, they found that war had been declared against the Sudanese dervishes. The Egyptian Army, staffed by British officers with the ranks being a mixture of British and native troops, was already marching on Dongola. Kitchener commanded the forces and was spoiling for a fight to regain face by revenging the murder of General Gordon in Khartoum in 1885. The Khalifa, Abdullah el Taashi, leader of the dervishes, needed a bloody nose, and popular opinion in London, with which Conan Doyle concurred, wanted Kitchener, who was already on the path to national hero status, to give him one.

Here was a chance Conan Doyle could not miss. It was, he wrote, 'impossible to be near great historical events and not to desire to take part in them, or at the least to observe them'. Press accreditation being the only way he could get to attend the fighting, he telegraphed the *Westminster Gazette* in London, offering to be its honorary war correspondent. The paper agreed so he purchased appropriate clothing, a revolver and ammunition and headed south to Aswan, where he was stuck for a week. The press corps gathered there had been instructed to join an Egyptian cavalry regiment, but the journalists saw no story in it so they set off across the desert on camels. Conan Doyle rode with them. It was an extremely foolhardy thing to do and they were extraordinarily fortunate not to be taken by the dervishes who were roaming the desert guerrilla-style. Thirty years later, Conan Doyle was 'still haunted by that purple velvet sky, by those enormous and innumerable stars, by the half-moon which moved slowly above us, while our camels with their noiseless tread seemed to bear us without effort through a wonderful dream world'.

He did not get on with his camel. When it suddenly knelt to eat, he was thrown off it. 'It is,' he wrote, 'the strangest and most deceptive animal in the world. Its appearance is so staid and respectable that you cannot give it credit for the black villainy that lurks within. It approaches you with a mildly interested and superior expression, like a patrician lady in a Sunday school. You feel that a pair of glasses at the end of a fan is the one thing lacking.' One dawn, they were approached by a black Nubian warrior who alarmed them. Conan Doyle said 'a more sinister barbaric figure one could not imagine', and stored the experience away to be transformed later into a short story, 'The Three Correspondents'.

Reaching the Nile again, they went by river to Wadi Halfa, where they discovered that the fighting was not due to start for some weeks. Disappointed, Conan Doyle observed some military exercises and dined with Kitchener. The other correspondents remained in Wadi Halfa, but he had to return to Louise in Cairo, travelling on an Arab cargo dhow, eating unleavened bread and tinned apricots, the only food available on board.

The heat of the approaching Egyptian summer was getting the better of Louise, so the decision was made to sail for England where, at a Royal Academy banquet on 1 May, Conan Doyle proudly displayed the ulcers on his forearms caused by jiggers, insects that had burrowed under his skin to lay their eggs. The eggs were now hatching into larvæ beneath his epidermis.

The house at Hindhead was not yet completed, so Conan Doyle and Louise, reunited once more with the children, who had been left in the care of Louise's mother, rented a furnished house, Grayswood Beeches, just outside the nearby small town of Haslemere. A fortnight later, he went to Southsea until the first week in July: Stavert's researches have shown that this was not just a social and cricket-playing visit. He also bought a house, South View Lodge, which was being rented by Arthur Vernon Ford who, having borrowed money from his father to set up a medical practice, was finding it hard going and was now in financial trouble. Once again, Conan Doyle's generosity and loyalty to those close to him came to the fore, providing Ford with the security and confidence he needed to succeed.

During this time, Conan Doyle finished his novel *Uncle Bernac*, which Horace Cox, the proprietor of *Queen* magazine, had commissioned and which Conan Doyle had begun in Egypt. It was another story based on French Napoleonic history, and set in 1805, to be first serialised and then, somewhat rewritten, published as a novel in the spring of 1897. He had found it hard to write: no doubt having been on the move for months, and having such distractions as camel rides to war on the side, had not helped. The story is weak, the multifarious characters opaque and, once again, only included for effect. Napoleon is well described, perhaps because he was as Conan Doyle said, a distillation of twenty books read in the research, but the story as a whole was a failure and he admitted as much.

In January 1897, the Conan Doyles moved to a small hotel called Moorlands in Hindhead, from which Conan Doyle could oversee the building of his house and into which they moved in the late summer or early autumn. They named the house Undershaw because it stood beneath a grove of trees, 'shaw' being the Anglo-Saxon for a small copse or wood.

Undershaw was built on a small ridge below the level of the main London-to-Portsmouth highway, close to the crossroads in the centre of the hamlet. Approached by a long bush- and tree-lined drive, the building stood with a tennis court and stables in four acres of grounds facing south, the garden sloping downhill to woodland, the view stretching far away over the sylvan Surrey countryside. It was constructed of red brick under a tiled roof in which were set gabled dormer windows. As it was sheltered from the wind, Ball designed the building with an abundance of windows. The drawing room was wood-panelled with a high shelf around the walls to accommodate Conan Doyle's souvenirs of his travels, and there was a vast billiard room. Stained-glass windows in the hall contained the Doyle family's coats of arms – bar one. Despite having been helped over the provenance of the shields by Sir Arthur Vicars, the Ulster King-at-Arms and a distant relative of Mary Doyle's, Conan Doyle omitted to include his mother's emblem and had rapidly to fit the arms of the Foleys of Lismore into the window over the main staircase. To help Louise, who was by now suffering badly from arthritis, the door handles in the house were of a sort that did not require turning, and a generator was installed to provide electric lighting which was, in rural areas, still a rarity.

The family's furniture, which had been put in storage when they gave up the South Norwood house, was brought to Hindhead, including some pieces Conan Doyle had inherited from his grandfather and Uncle Richard. The dining-room table was the most treasured. It had belonged to John Doyle and had stood in the house at Cambridge Terrace: round it, he had entertained all the great writers, artists and politicians of his day.

In next to no time, Conan Doyle was living the carefree life of a sporting country gentleman. The stables close to the house were occupied by four stallions and two saddle-mares: of the former, Brigadier was Conan Doyle's favourite. The two mares were used not only for riding but also to pull a newly purchased landau in which Louise was taken for drives around the wooded countryside, Conan Doyle often travelling by her side.

The house was an ideal home and the family settled comfortably into it. To be nearer her daughter, Louise's mother moved into The Cottage, a nearby property. In his autobiography, Conan Doyle refers to this period of his life as 'An Interlude of Peace'. All seemed well on the surface, but there was turmoil ahead.

'The most remarkable experiences in a man's life,' Conan Doyle once wrote, 'are those in which he feels most, and they are precisely the ones upon which he is least disposed to talk.' The experience he was least disposed to discuss in 1897 was Jean Leckie.

Conan Doyle met Jean Leckie on 15 March 1897. Where and how he was introduced to her is not known, but the exact date is: he celebrated the anniversary of it for the remainder of his life. He was thirty-seven, she twenty-four. It was love at first sight. Almost immediately, they became the core of each other's existence and remained deeply in love for the rest of their lives, hardly ever quarrelling.

The daughter of wealthy Scots parents, Mr and Mrs James Blyth Leckie of The Glebe House, Blackheath, Jean was descended from an ancient Scottish family. A pretty and dignified young woman, she had curly, dark golden hair, wide green eyes, a slender neck and an alabaster complexion. Feminine and slim, she was demur, discreet and softly spoken, widely read with a sharp intellect. She was also an accomplished horsewoman who rode to hounds, an excellent mezzo-soprano who had trained for the opera in Dresden, and an adroit and witty conversationalist. In short, she was as ideal a companion for a famous author as Louise had been for a provincial town general practitioner. The difference was that where Louise merely followed Conan Doyle, Jean possessed the self-confidence to live beside him, exert an influence over him and take an active part in his intellectual life. She was also a good deal harder, more headstrong and determined, more inflexible than Louise.

Conan Doyle had his faults – he could be intransigent, unforgiving and quick-tempered – but, for all that, he was a man of honour and this placed him in a terrible dilemma. He had a deep affection for Louise and felt responsible for her not just as his wife but also because of her illness. She plainly had not long to live but he would not – he could not – let her down, cast her off into a sanatorium: perhaps thoughts of his father's fate tugged at the strings of his guilt. Although he was passionately in love with Jean, he was still fiercely loyal to Louise and, from the start of their relationship, he informed Jean that he would neither leave nor divorce Louise. Furthermore, he would neither hurt her nor be unfaithful to her. Astonishingly, Jean seems to have accepted this without any attempt to try to sway him.

The code of honour Mary Doyle had imparted to her son held good, even in such trying circumstances. Conan Doyle could have cast it aside. Other writers had. H.G. Wells maintained a string of mistresses and several illegitimate children. Charles Dickens had had a mistress and a bastard. No one in the literary world would have censured him. The public may have looked askance at him but his situation would have mitigated on his behalf. Yet Conan Doyle would not behave dishonourably.

Being torn between affection and love, duty and desire, affected his health. An added complication was his enforced sexual abstinence. Louise was simply not strong enough to make love but, that aside, medical opinion forbade sexual union with tuberculosis sufferers as part of the cure. The hot-blooded Conan Doyle, man of action and letters, was now celibate and, as far as is known, was to remain so for almost a decade. It seems highly unlikely he ever sought to relieve his sexual frustration, as many repressed Victorian men did, by visiting the fashionable brothels of London. To have done so would have been to betray both the women in his life and lower his own self-imposed standards of gentlemanly conduct.

The strain started to tell. Gradually, over the years of his abstinence, he changed physically. His shoulders stiffened and his eyes narrowed, signs of his pent-up frustration which manifested itself in a certain harshness, an unyielding arrogance, a deliberate and self-centred crustiness.

His soul in turmoil, he nevertheless had to keep up the pretence of the loving husband at home. On days when she felt sufficiently strong, he took Louise out in the landau around the rim of the nearby circular valley called the Devil's Punchbowl, or up on to the heathland a few kilometres to the north. The role he was forced into playing sorely tried him. Writing to his mother in December 1899, he said, 'I have lived for six years in a sick room and, oh, how weary of it I am: Dear Touie: It has tried me more than her – and she never dreams of it and I am very glad.'

The strain touched his relationship with his children who, in some respects, had a difficult childhood. On account of Louise's illness, much of their time was spent with relatives. Mary was only four when Powell had diagnosed tuberculosis, Kingsley a babe in arms, so they had never really known their mother as anything but an invalid.

There is no doubt that Conan Doyle loved his children. Kingsley, a handsome, well-built child with fair hair, was his favourite. When they were younger, the children had been an integral part of his life. Mary had once crawled over his desk whilst he was working and had torn the manuscript of *The Refugees* but he had not minded. He taught Kingsley to play cricket and to box, hoping to instil in him his own sense of manly virtue. At a Christmas party in 1892, he had terrified Mary and other youngsters by appearing suddenly dressed as a dragon covered in luminous paint. Now, under the pressure of his dual existence, he was remote, threateningly larger than life and unpredictable. He was often away from home and, when he returned, lived in the world of his imagination. When he was writing in his study at Undershaw, the children were ordered to be quiet, which shows the strain he was under and the fact that their being present impinged upon his creativity. Once, he had been able to write anywhere – in a crowded room, in a surgery waiting for patients, in a rolling cabin on an Arctic whaler. Now, he needed tranquillity to concentrate his mind.

Both children admired and respected their father but their respect was based as much on dread as devotion. Conan Doyle gave them his love but he was also short-tempered with and critical of them in these strained years. They were not allowed to speak out of turn, had to be punctual and well behaved, seen and not heard. Conversely, they were allowed a liberty forbidden to many children, such as being permitted to go barefoot about the house and garden. They were also encouraged by their father to follow any sport they wished. Mary became an excellent shot with a rifle and, in their teens, the children were allowed to wander the countryside at will and even go on holiday to Seaview, near Ryde on the Isle of Wight, without parental supervision.

To keep his mind occupied, Conan Doyle maintained a very full social life, keeping his thoughts and frustrations well out of sight. Living near to London, to which he had easy access through a mainline railway station in Haslemere, four kilometres away, he attended literary societies, went up to town for lunch in his club, took on a busy public speaking commitment and played sport, particularly cricket. Signing on with a riding school in Knightsbridge, he took riding lessons in Hyde Park. He was never lax in taking any opportunity to get away from Undershaw and his wife's sick room for a day or two. That being said, when the urge took him, he invited guests to Undershaw for informal weekend parties, often at short notice. Whether Louise felt up to it or not seems not to have been a consideration.

Jean lived in London, where she shared an apartment with two lady friends, but, at first, he did not meet her that often. There were long periods when he did not see her at all, keeping in touch only by letter. It seems as if they both preferred their relationship to continue in this way, devoid of any temptation and a need for constant parting. However, as the years passed, it does seem that they met more frequently.

In Jean's absence, Conan Doyle tried to share in her world and joined a local fox-hunt, the Chiddingfold Hunt, which had its kennels eight kilometres from Undershaw and hunted the area to the north of Hindhead. Ultimately, he did not approve of hunting for sport, writing in his autobiography, 'I cannot persuade myself that we are justified in taking life as a pleasure. To shoot for the pot must be right, since man must feed, and to kill creatures which live upon others (the hunting of foxes, for example) must also be right, since to slay one is to save many: but the rearing of birds in order to kill them, and the shooting of such sensitive and inoffensive animals as hares and deer, cannot, I think, be justified.' He did go on to admit that he shot a good deal before coming to this conclusion, his attitude well ahead of his time. He also questioned the effect hunting had on the character of the participants, pondering 'whether it does not blunt our better feelings, harden our sympathies, brutalize our natures'. He excused fishing from his argument on the grounds that fish were cold-blooded and not of a higher order. Nor does he appear to have been completely approving of the blood sport of fox-hunting as is shown by a short story, 'The King of the Foxes': at the end of a hunt, the fox turns on the pursuing hounds and is found not to be a fox but a Siberian wolf which sets about savaging its tormentors. As if riding to hounds were not enough, he made another and somewhat more bizarre attempt to share Jean's life by trying to master the banjo. It was hardly an appropriate instrument on which to accompany his operatically trained mezzo-soprano love and his attempt soon fell by the wayside, but only on account of Conan Doyle's utter lack of musical ability.

His sexual frustrations were also sublimated by going away with friends, sometimes just for a weekend's fishing, sometimes for longer spells. In March 1898, he met H.G. Wells and his wife, Jane, who were visiting the novelist George Gissing in Siena. Conan Doyle was travelling through Italy in the company of his brother-in-law, E.W. Hornung. They all formed a group and spent a month together.

Wells recorded that they undertook 'tramps in the Campagna, in the Alban Hills, along the Via Clodia, and so forth, merry meals with the good red wine of Velletri or Grotto Ferrata'. At the same time, Conan Doyle was appointed a Cavaliere of the Crown of Italy, an honorary knighthood given in recognition of his literary achievements, although he kept quiet about it and the fact was only widely discovered after his death.

His difficult domestic situation did not mean that he ignored his relatives. When Innes fell in love with a Miss Dora Hamilton, Conan Doyle went to Exeter to vet her family and he kept an eye on his younger brother in other ways. In 1897, he contacted Kitchener, reminding him of their meeting in Wadi Halfa and requesting that Innes be put in command of a battery. This was not an exercising of undue influence, for advancement in the army, up until the First World War, still relied in part on patronage and who one knew. Conan Doyle was also to contact Sir Edward Ward, the Secretary of State for War, bringing Innes to his attention.

By 1899, whether owing to his elder brother's influence or not, Innes was a captain in the Royal Horse Artillery, posted to Umballa in India, in charge of his own battery. Even so far away, Conan Doyle kept helping his younger brother, who frequently wrote to thank Conan Doyle for the blank cheques, telling him, 'I will let you know how I fill them up.' To keep up with his fellow officers and the all-important social regimental life upon which advancement depended, Innes played polo, which was then, as now, a sport of the well-to-do, the cost of which his salary could not support. Conan Doyle helped out, as a letter from Innes was to show. 'I cannot thank you enough, old chap, for the £100 cheque,' he wrote. 'I had bought a fine charger just before it came, and he cost me 1,300 rupees.'

With Innes settled in his posting, Conan Doyle decided to send Lottie out for a holiday with him. It was not unusual for young ladies to go out to India, chaperoned by a spinster companion or a relative, and Conan Doyle felt she deserved a break. For many years, she had looked after the children and nursed Louise with unstinting selflessness, and she was growing tired. Conan Doyle wrote to Innes, 'I don't know what I shall do when Lottie is gone as well as you', yet he did not change his mind. Lottie embarked aboard the SS *Egypt* at the end of September 1899, bound for Bombay. Conan Doyle saw her off at Tilbury docks in London. 'My heart,' she wrote back to him, 'was too full to say much, but I felt a lot. I hate leaving you and am already looking forward to spring when I return.' Yet she did not return. As was quite common in bride-starved India, she fell in love with and married Captain Leslie Oldham of the Royal Engineers. Despite ordering her mother never to mention her financial affairs to Conan Doyle, she, like Innes, started periodically to receive blank cheques after her wedding.

One by one, his other sisters were leaving home, too. In 1898 Ida became engaged to Nelson Foley, a distant relative from Lismore. Dodo was wed in 1899 to Charles Cyril Angell, son of the vicar of Kirby Lonsdale, near Masongill, and a Cambridge-educated clergyman himself. He was a deacon when they married, and curate of the parish of Dalston, just south of Carlisle. Upon their wedding, Conan Doyle settled an allowance upon Dodo and was later to lend Angell sufficient money to start a private school, Hindhead School, not far from Undershaw.

On the literary front, in the autumn of 1898, Conan Doyle wrote a novel quite unlike any of his previous work. It was a domestic story, *A Duet with an Occasional Chorus*, usually referred to just as *A Duet*, about the courtship and marriage of a middle-class suburban couple, Frank and Maud Crosse. In effect, it was an everyday chronicle of late Victorian life, a novel of social manners that was moving, humorous and profoundly realistic. Written with a light touch, it had a poignant sentimentality about it, a wistfulness that hints at the early days of Conan Doyle's own courtship of and marriage to Louise. It was not autobiographical and yet it had a deep sense of personal experience underlying it. One has the feeling that Conan Doyle was in some way coming to terms with his own past as Louise's death drew inexorably nearer.

The book always had a special place in his heart. He had the manuscript bound and gave it to Jean. His motivation for such an action is hard to appreciate. Perhaps, by giving the book to Jean, he was somehow forging a link between his past with Louise and his planned future with her. Maybe the book was written as a foretaste of the life he hoped to live with Jean after Louise's death. Where he found the inspiration for the story is also in doubt. The narrative seems to refer to his life with Louise and yet Conan Doyle confided to his mother that it was born straight from his love for Jean which had, he declared, 'kept my soul and my emotions alive'.

Around this time, Conan Doyle took stock of his life, stepping back and looking pensively at himself. Much of his earlier naïveté was gone. In its place was a man with a complex personal nature. He wrote of the hero in the novel, 'Strength, virility, emotional force, power of deep feeling – these are traits which have to be paid for. There was sometimes just a touch of the savage, or at least there were indications of the possibility of a touch of the savage in Frank Crosse. His intense love of the open air and of physical exercise was a sign of it. He left upon women the impression, not altogether unwelcome, that there were unexplored recesses of his nature to which the most intimate of them had never penetrated. In those dark corners of the spirit either a saint or a sinner might be lurking, and there was a pleasurable excitement in peering into them, and wondering which it was. No woman ever found him dull. Perhaps it would have been better for him if they had, for his impulsive nature had never been content with a chill friendship.' Yet, if the truth be known, this passage was really Conan Doyle writing a self-critique, for one can see how the image of Frank is that which Conan Doyle would have liked to project of himself. How he described Frank was how Conan Doyle hoped Jean saw him.

Considering it the best book he had written, Conan Doyle refused large offers for the serial rights. The story would suffer, he felt, from being truncated. It was published as a novel in March 1899, but it was not successful. H.G. and Jane Wells praised it but the critics said it was sentimental and even mawkish. Some even accused it of being in bad taste. Booksellers did not buy it in quantity and Conan Doyle's readers dismissed it because it was not what they had grown to expect of him. The publisher, Grant Richards, had ordered a substantial print run of between 12,500 to 15,000 copies, at Conan Doyle's suggestion; he thought it would be a great success and beyond the censure of the critics. When sales failed to materialise, Conan Doyle blamed the reviewers but was upset that he had suggested a large run, writing to Richards, 'I hate that a young man entering business should lose by me.' He must have felt similarly upset a few years later. Dodo wrote two novels under the pseudonym of H. Ripley Cromarsh, *The Episodes of Marge: Memoirs of a Humble Adventuress* in 1903, and *The Secret of the Moor Cottage*, four years on. When the former was published by Grant Richards, Conan Doyle contributed towards its publication, but when the book failed to sell he was asked to purchase half the edition to prevent the publisher losing money.

Conan Doyle had never been fond of the critics but he was now, in his present mental state, unusually sensitive to their criticism. He accused the reviewers of the novel of being disparaging, destructive rather than constructive in their articles, and he questioned their intellectual integrity. Few of their articles would be pasted into his scrapbooks: Conan Doyle never retained copies of any material that was not favourable to him. He was seldom self-critical and believed that, to whatever he turned his hand, he was beyond reproach or criticism. This self-delusion did not help his temperament.

The criticisms of *A Duet* only exacerbated his current mood. He was always on edge, quick to look for and take offence, uneasy and sometimes belligerent. He was unnecessarily irked by adverse criticism, blowing real and imaginary insults out of proportion. This resulted in his becoming embroiled in literary feuds, the first substantial squabble being with Hall Caine who had, Conan Doyle considered, tastelessly self-advertised his new novel, *The Christian*. Caine was a clever self-promoter. Before he published a book, he puffed it hard in interviews, giving readers an idea of the background to it and generally hyping or talking it up. Conan Doyle stated that this was a violation of professional literary etiquette, which he hoped the Authors' Society might one day punish. 'What he [Hall Caine] has never seemed to realise,' he wrote in the *Daily Chronicle* on 7 August 1897, 'is that in every high profession – be it law, medicine, the Army, or literature – there are certain unwritten laws – a gentlemanly etiquette which is binding upon all, but most binding upon those who have a claim to stand among the leaders of the profession.' Quite what Conan Doyle would make of today's publishing industry is anybody's guess, but one is tempted to think he would have made the most of it himself. He may publicly have condemned Caine but, whilst he did not involve himself with promotional campaigns for his books until later in his life, he was still not above plugging his own work when he found the opportunity.

Far more justified was his vehement attack on William Robertson Nicoll, the editor of the *Bookman*. Nicoll had knocked *Uncle Bernac* in June 1897, remarking unfairly that Conan Doyle's research was flawed. The comment had rankled but Conan Doyle had more or less ignored it. However, on 6 April 1899, Nicoll laid into *A Duet* in the *British Weekly*, writing under the pseudonym of Paternoster Row. Three weeks later, he slammed the book in the *Daily Sketch* under the pseudonym of O.O. As if that were not enough, he went on to write a number of other pseudonymous reviews of the same novel in other popular publications.

When Conan Doyle found out that all the critics were one person, he was deservedly infuriated and wrote to the *Daily Chronicle* on 16 May, tersely pointing out that 'the publications of reviews upon the same book by the same reviewer in many different periodicals, so that what to the uninitiated might seem to be a general burst of praise or blame may really when analysed prove to be the work of a single individual', was unacceptable. His letter amazed the public, which had never realised that such a practice went on.

All the while, Conan Doyle was maintaining his output of short fiction, a substantial amount of which was horror stories. He wrote in the genre for most of his life, but literary history has tended to overlook this aspect of his work, which has been overshadowed by Sherlock Holmes and Conan Doyle's historical fiction. This is, in fact, an injustice, for his horror stories often come up to the standard of Edgar Allan Poe, H.G. Wells, E.F. Benson or M.R. James, and have stood the test of time, the amalgamation of medical information and the gothic qualities of the settings still thrilling, even today. In early 1898, he started to write a series of stories for the *Strand Magazine* known as *Round the Fire Stories*. Seventeen of these stories were collected in a single volume under the same title in 1908, the preface stating that they were 'concerned with the grotesque and with the terrible – such tales as might well be read "round the fire" upon a winter's night'.

Amongst such stories was 'The Story of the Beetle Hunter', in which two noblemen live together in a country house filled with thousands of dead beetles in display cases. Through this macabre setting one of the men nocturnally lurks, seeking to murder the other with a hammer. In 'The Sealed Room', an implausible but eerie yarn, a young man searches for his missing father, who still writes letters to him. Eventually, he discovers his father's corpse in a sealed room, he having long since killed himself but arranging for letters to continue to be mailed after his death. In 'The Brown Hand', Conan Doyle's main character is an investigator for the Society for Psychical Research sent to look into a ghost haunting his uncle, an eminent surgeon. The spirit is restless because its amputated stump of an arm lacks a hand, which the surgeon has kept as an exhibit, that it must possess in order to be complete and find peace in the hereafter. The subject of 'The Japanned Box' revealed echoes of Conan Doyle's own family life. Sir John Bollamore, a chronic alcoholic, keeps the dying words of his wife, imploring him to stop drinking, on a recording cylinder, replaying them at night to fill his house with her plea. Conan Doyle's description of the drunken knight is sympathetic: 'He was a man who was fighting a ceaseless battle, holding at arm's length, from morning to night, a horrible adversary, who was for ever trying to close with him – an adversary which would destroy him body and soul could it but fix its claws once more upon him.' Sympathetic he may have been as a doctor but, as a son, Conan Doyle kept quiet about his father's dipsomania, for alcoholism was at the time widely regarded as a character fault that could be inherited.

As well as prose, Conan Doyle also wrote poetry, with which he had been toying from his childhood, first encouraged by Francis Cassidy at Stonyhurst. His first book of verse, *Songs of Action*, was published in 1898: subsequent collections were *Songs of the Road* in 1911 and *The Guards Came Through* in 1919. His poetry was not in the least literary. It was more the verse of the common man, sub-Kiplingesque narrative ballads, superficial odes, comical verse and semi-doggerel. The comical poems are the best and one of these, 'Bendy's Sermon', is a minor classic, based upon the true story of a Nottinghamshire prizefighter called Bendigo who sees the light, converts to Christianity and becomes a preacher. At one of his meetings, he is heckled by five rowdies including 'Jack Ball the fighting gunsmith, Joe Murphy from the Mews,/ And Iky Moss, the bettin' boss, the Champion of the Jews'. Bendy begs Jesus to give him patience to ignore the taunts but, in the end, 'He vaulted from the pulpit like a tiger from a den,/ They say it was a lovely sight to see him floor his men'. As these lines show, Conan Doyle was more a competent light poetaster than a poet.

Yet there was one poem in which Conan Doyle was intensely serious. It was called 'The Inner Room'. In it, he assessed the different facets of his own make-up. When he wrote the poem is uncertain, but it was penned prior to 1898, as it was included in the first collection and it can reasonably be argued that he wrote it at or about the time he first met Jean. The emotions the poem addresses are those that he must have had to come to terms with when falling in love with her, facing the future as a man of two parts and two affections. His realisation of his love for Jean showed to him the many facets of his own inner being – the rooms of his soul – which, in many ways, echoed the many parts of his outward, adventurous and full-living personality. Many of the poems accompanying it were, from their subject matter and style, clearly written over the span of not more than eighteen months. Whilst some were written much earlier, such as 'The Song of the Bow', others, like 'Master', 'A Hunting Morning' and 'With the Chiddingfolds', which are three of eight hunting-related poems, clearly refer to his most recent life, thus also setting 'The Inner Room' in an approximate time frame.

The poem is fascinating, for it lays bare the powers he believed were in him, eternally fighting to get the upper hand on his soul. It begins:

> It is mine – the little chamber,
>   Mine alone.
> I had it from my forebears
>   Years agone.

Yet within its walls I see
A most motley company.
And they one and all claim me
As their own.

There is one part of him that is a soldier, 'Bluff and keen;/ Single-minded, heavy-fisted,/ Rude of mien'. He is balanced by a priest 'still schism-whole' who 'loves the censer-reek and organ-roll', a doubter and a black-souled man who 'has thoughts he dare not say/ Half avowed'. Other less tangible characters hover in the shadows. At the end of the poem, Conan Doyle resigns himself to what he is, saying that '. . . if each shall have his day,/ I shall swing and I shall sway/ In the same old weary way/ As before'. After poems about fox-hunts, point-to-point cross-country horse-racing, and Corporal Dick's army career fighting the fuzzy-wuzzies in the Sudan, 'The Inner Room' is a sobering, moving and unique piece.

As the old century ended and the new began, Conan Doyle's spiritual life was in chaos. The various controlling forces were in permanent conflict. In his autobiography, he wrote of the time, 'my soul was often troubled within me . . . I felt that I was born for something else, and yet I was not clear what that something might be'. He dipped his toe in a number of religions, testing their waters but finding them cold or lukewarm. He gave rationalism a try but felt it was nihilistic. He was fairly sure of the veracity of psychic phenomena but could not understand, interpret or assimilate them. 'In every direction I reached out,' he wrote, 'but never yet with any absolute satisfaction. I should have been relieved from all my troubles could I have given heartfelt adhesion to any form of orthodoxy – but my reason always barred the way.'

For the better part of a decade he was to be depressed, frustrated, miserable and torn between the two women in his life, shackled to Louise by his duty but chained to Jean by his deep but unrequited and unconsummated love. His future looked bleak, but there was an event unfolding on the international stage which would allow him some release from the torment.

10

Sir Arthur Conan Doyle: Patriot

The Boer (or South African) War was fought over the matter of supremacy in southern Africa with Britain and British colonialists on one side and Boer Dutch settlers in the Transvaal and the Orange Free State on the other. President Kruger, the Boer leader, wanted the British out of South Africa whilst Joseph Chamberlain, the British Secretary of State for the Colonies, was determined they should remain. Gold and diamonds were at the centre of it. On 10 October 1899, after a plethora of inconclusive peace conferences, Kruger issued an ultimatum which Britain rejected. War was declared. The British government thought the war would be over in three months. They were wrong.

The Boers struck at once, laying siege to Mafeking, Kimberley and Ladysmith. By November, over 10,000 British troops were pinned down. There were less than 50,000 Boers, as opposed to 250,000 British soldiers, at the height of the war, but they were mobile, bush-wise, well equipped and crafty. The British, on the other hand, were inappropriately trained, had inadequate equipment and insufficient supplies. Even their boots were unsuitable for the tropics and disintegrated in the dry veldt heat. What was more, the Boers fought a modern guerrilla and trench war whilst the British still maintained at first the traditional thin red line.

Conan Doyle was only too aware of the British army's disadvantage. In August 1898, he had attended manoeuvres on Salisbury Plain and had observed formal infantry advances such as were used at the Battle of Waterloo. Military thinking was locked in a time warp and he was appalled.

Before the war started, Conan Doyle had expressed an interest in pacifism. He had even spoken at a public meeting in Hindhead in January 1899, in support of Tsar Nicholas II's peace conference aimed at arms limitation between the European powers and the establishment of an international peace tribunal. George Bernard Shaw, also now a Hindhead resident, attended the meeting and actually agreed with him. Conan Doyle was very wary of Shaw. In his autobiography, he recorded an anecdote about attending a charity function at Hindhead where the guests were treated to an amateur group performance of a part of Shakespeare's As You Like It, of which Shaw quite unjustifiably wrote a scathing review in a local paper. Conan Doyle was furious and commented that it showed that the adoption by the world of vegetarianism would not bring unkind words and actions to an end, by which he was having a sly dig at Shaw's much-flaunted dietary foibles. He allowed that 'Shaw is a genial creature to meet, and I am prepared to believe that there is a human kindly side to his nature', but added that he thought it had yet to have a public airing.

With the declaration of war, Conan Doyle abandoned any thought of pacifism. He was a patriot and saw it as his duty to defend his country. He believed that the Boers had some right to be belligerent because their land had been swamped by gold prospectors and he expressed 'a deep respect for the Boers and some fear of their skill at arms, their inaccessible situation, and their sturdy Teutonic tenacity', but they were the enemy nevertheless and he had to side with king and country.

At first, the British suffered badly. In 'Black Week', 10–17 December, they lost three major battles, outwitted by the Boers' camouflaged trenches and use of barbed wire. The British commander-in-chief, General Redvers Buller, outsmarted by the Boer general, Louis Botha, was dismissed, to be replaced by Lord Roberts with Lord Kitchener as his second-in-command. Volunteers were called for. It was inevitable that Conan Doyle should want to join up.

It was not the first time he had taken steps to visit a war. In 1878, he had volunteered to go as a medical dresser to Turkey for the war with Russia whilst, in 1881, he had toyed with becoming a military surgeon. In 1892, he had applied for the post of war correspondent when it looked as if the English and French might come to blows over Egypt. He got the job but the war did not materialise; and, of course, he had failed to see any of the fighting in the Sudan in 1896. Now, at the age of forty, he believed this would be his last chance. He had, however, another reason for going. With war fever gripping Britain, he could not concentrate on his fiction. He had therefore decided to write a first-hand account of the war.

His mother, who was against the war, was aghast at his decision and tried to talk him out of it. In a forthright letter, which she addressed to her 'own dearest and very naughty son', she wrote, 'How dare you! What do you mean by it? Why, your very height and breadth would make you a simple and sure target!' Fighting for justice, she declared, was acceptable, but this was not a war of principles. It was nothing more than a scramble for 'that awful gold'. His first duty, she berated him, was to his family, then, knowing she had to be more persuasive, she continued, 'and is not your life . . . of more value, even to your country – at home? Think of the pleasure and solace your writings afford to thousands.' She ended by reminding him that she already had one son in the army: no doubt she was afraid Innes would be sent to South Africa and she did not want to risk losing both her boys at once.

Conan Doyle ignored her. He did not always agree with her and they could at times quarrel heatedly when they met but, ultimately, she usually won. On this occasion, she did not. It was probably the only time in his life he disobeyed his mother's wish over a matter of true gravity. In his reply, he stated, 'I learned patriotism from my mother, so you must not blame me.' It was, he told her, his duty to volunteer. He had said as much in a letter to the *Times*, advocating the drafting of all men who could ride and shoot, attributes he believed (quite rightly) would be much needed in the African theatre of war.

When his enlistment forms for the Middlesex Yeomanry, in which he had friends, received no answer, Conan Doyle travelled to the Hounslow recruitment centre and queued to be interviewed. On the forms, he had lied about his military experience in the Sudan in order to stand a better chance of acceptance. 'Two white lies,' he wrote, 'are permitted to a gentleman, to screen a woman or to get into a fight when the fight is a rightful one.' The recruiting colonel, who seemed to have had absolutely no idea as to who he was, peremptorily rejected him as too old and too fat, although there was not a cubic centimetre of spare flesh on his entire body. Fate was on his side, however. A few days later, John Langman, a philanthropist sending out a hundred-bed field hospital to the front line, asked him to be the senior physician, under Robert O'Callaghan as surgeon-in-chief, and supervise the management of the unit with Langman's son, Archie, who was a friend and a lieutenant in the Middlesex Yeomanry. Two Harley Street surgeons, H.J. Scharlieb and Charles Gibbs, completed the medical staff. Conan Doyle immediately accepted, paying his own way and receiving no salary. He set about interviewing for orderlies, camp cooks and nurses, and dragooned his own butler, Cleeve, into the expedition, paying his salary. As they were going to the front line, the War Office insisted they have a military officer in their complement and assigned an alcoholic Irish doctor named Drury to the hospital. He was of little use, Conan Doyle recording that his one aim in life was 'to leave the service and to "marry a rich widow with a cough"'.

Louise, giving Conan Doyle her blessing in this venture, went to Naples with the children for her health. Jean, no doubt fearfully, also approved. Whilst waiting for the departure date, Conan Doyle began experimenting with a means of dropping bullets on to troops in trenches, devising a simple pendulum sight to assess trajectory. When he submitted the prototype to the War Office for assessment, they ignored the idea. Undeterred, he wrote to the *Times* about his invention but the Secretary of State for War declined to consider it, which galled him. He thought it might have worked and should not have been dismissed in such a cavalier fashion. He gave up the experimental trials, however, after nearly killing a man on the heath at Frensham Ponds, a nearby beauty spot.

After being inspected by the Duke of Cambridge, who criticised their lack of military bearing, ill-fitting khaki uniforms with plain buttons and bush hats adorned with a small sprig of feathers, the field hospital unit departed from London on the P & O liner *Oriental*, on 28 February 1900. His mother, still very angry with her son, came down from Masongill to see him off. Jean also came but could not bear to say goodbye so she stayed on the dock, hidden in the crowds. They arrived in Cape Town on 21 March to discover that Ladysmith had been relieved and Roberts had reached Bloemfontein.

Whilst waiting to head up-country, Conan Doyle and Archie Langman went to a Boer prisoner-of-war camp on Cape Town racecourse where Conan Doyle handed out some money to the prisoners from a fund he had been given in London to use to charitable ends in the war. It must be said that the charity benefactors had most likely intended the money to be used on British colonialists rather than on the enemy but, for Conan Doyle, a man in need was a man in need, regardless of which side of the political divide he stood.

Once having seen the Boers, he wrote, 'they were certainly a shaggy, dirty, unkempt crowd but with the bearing of free men. There were a few cruel or brutal faces, some of them half caste, but most were good honest fellows and the general effect was formidable.' Even in the face of the enemy, Conan Doyle's natural sense of fair play and justice came to the fore. They might be the enemy but this did not preclude them from having their own share of honour and chivalry, or prevent him from being a magnanimous and generous victor.

Five days later, they sailed for East London, there to entrain for the front. News from the fighting was good. The British were making advances. Conan Doyle was in raptures. 'There were nights of that journey,' he recorded, 'which I shall never forget – the great train roaring through the darkness, the fires beside the line, the dark groups silhouetted against the flames, the shouts of "Who are you?" and the crash of voices as our mates cried back, "The Camerons," for this famous regiment was our companion . . . Wonderful is the atmosphere of war.' The regiment was, in fact, the Cameronians, otherwise known as the Scottish Rifles. His detractors have argued that, with such writing, he glorified war, but this is not quite true. He revelled in the spirit of comradeship, the excitement and the bravado. For him, war was an adventure, a chivalrous and honourable exploit: if he had not been a writer or a doctor, he would have been a soldier like his brother. He was soon to discover it was a bloody, unpleasant business.

Bloemfontein, when they reached it on 2 April, was a bustling town of 4000. The Boer capital of the Orange Free State, it was a pretty place of red-brick, tin-roofed houses, spacious wooden bungalows fronted by tidy gardens and native shanties. There was also a market square, an imposing English Club, the grand offices of a British insurance company, the Railway Bureau and the Ionic-columned Raadzaal, the Boer Orange Free State parliament building. The population consisted of black Africans who had welcomed the British upon their taking of the town, and white colonials and Boers with whom the British officers openly fraternised as a matter of political policy: it was the aim of the British to be as accommodating and friendly with the civilians as possible and many Boer municipal officials remained in their jobs. The abundance of comely white girls sparked off a wave of partying and entertainment and a British military band played every evening in the market square. In addition to the residents, there was also a population of British headquarters staff officers and war correspondents who issued their own bilingual daily newspaper, the *Friend*. Around the town, the veldt was crowded with the bivouacs of thousands of British troops, increasing the town's peacetime population tenfold. Not surprisingly, food and other essentials were in short supply as the railway serving the town was a single track line and could not cater for the demand made upon it. The weather was oppressive and thundery as the wet season had broken.

The medical equipment having been sent on a later train, Conan Doyle reported he had time to kill before getting down to doctoring and so he left the town on horseback to look for Boers but, mercifully, found none. He should have known this hunt for the enemy would be fruitless. The Boer forces had disappeared like morning mist on 13 March. Conan Doyle, however, liked to show off his readiness for action and bravado. The next day, in a similar vein of braggadocio, he wrote to Louise that he was sunburnt, dirty and wearing a pith helmet with a pink undershirt. The latter was medical issue, pink to match smeared blood. 'Ah,' he wrote, 'if you could have seen the men! I mean the troops. A whole brigade passed us today, such splendid chaps, bearded and fierce, picturesque brigands, my word!' At last, he was living the stuff of real adventures. He was no longer a writer but a doctor once more, a man of action. This action was soon to be the greatest test of his medical skills he had ever had to face.

The equipment arrived, all fifty tons of it, and the hospital was set up in the pavilion of the Bloemfontein Ramblers' Cricket Club, at one end of which was a stage set for a production of HMS Pinafore. Ward tents were erected on the playing field which was enclosed by a corrugated iron fence. It was not long before the hospital, now with 160 beds, was full beyond capacity.

Roberts had captured the town but not the water supply thirty kilometres away at Sannah's Post. The Boer commander of the Free State Army, Vecht-Generaal Christian De Wet, held that and he switched off the pumps. The troops occupying the settlement, restricted to half a bottle of drinking water each *per diem*, disobeyed orders and turned to rely for extra water upon watering holes, rainwater and the nearby Modder River, contaminated with effluent from a Boer camp upstream at Paardeberg Drift, and the corpses of horses, oxen and men. On top of that, the soldiers' basic sense of hygiene was at best rudimentary and even the most elementary sanitation provision in the army camps was neglected. By the time the Langman unit arrived, there was an epidemic of typhoid well under way, only a small proportion of the troops having been inoculated despite the fact that, in the wet season, the disease was endemic in Bloemfontein. The civilian 500-bed Volks' Hospital contained 1,700 patients and the Raadzaal was converted into a sanatorium. Conan Doyle and his companions were inundated and their morale plunged. It was not long before O'Callaghan realised he could not face this and he left for London. Some of the orderlies absented themselves and Drury disappeared down the neck of a bottle of scotch.

Conan Doyle stuck in there and took charge. For three months he, Scharlieb and Gibbs tended the sick and dying, living 'in the midst of death – and death in its vilest, filthiest form'. They were ill equipped for the number of patients they treated. The pavilion stage became the latrine but most could not get to it. The beds and floor were soaked in excrement. Outside, the tents stood in a field of grass, mud and human ordure. The air was thick with flies, crawling into mouths and drinking from the eyes of the semi-conscious. Even though they had been inoculated, a number of the Langman staff fell ill. Twelve were badly infected, five more collapsed and three died. Amongst the troops, five thousand died. Conan Doyle wrote, 'Our hospital was no worse off than the others, and as there were so many of them the general condition of the town was very bad. Coffins were out of the question, and the men were lowered in their brown blankets into shallow graves at the average rate of sixty a day . . . You could smell Bloemfontein long before you could see it.'

The adventure had turned into a nightmare. Conan Doyle was horrified by the squalor, the sordid death of brave men, the iniquities of war and the vision he now saw of the true, shabby basement of man's inhumanity.

Even in the midst of the mud and filth, Conan Doyle could not be rid of Sherlock Holmes. An artist called Mortimer Menpes arrived at the height of the epidemic to draw sketches of the famous author in his hospital for the *Illustrated London News* and wanted to know which was his favourite Sherlock Holmes tale. Conan Doyle, his mind on other matters, said it was the one about the snake but he could not remember the title. Menpes' sketches were suppressed at the request of the censor and only published after the epidemic was well and truly over.

After some weeks, the Boers were driven from the water supply and conditions improved, so Conan Doyle and Archie Langman left to visit the front line which was heading for Pretoria, the British Army now adapting to Boer tactics. He was present when Brandfort fell and came under heavy artillery fire at Vet River, seeing the chaotic and bloodier – as opposed to dysenteric – side of warfare. Still, he did not lose his enthusiasm for the thrill of it all and his respect for the ordinary trooper held, although he disliked military life with its smutty jokes, bickering and, in Brandfort, looting. The sight of burned British mailbags, captured by the Boers, angered him. De Wet had put them to the torch, which Conan Doyle considered 'one of his less sportsmanlike actions'. After a week, they returned to what he called the 'Café Enterique, Boulevard des Microbes, which is our town address'. Once more back in Bloemfontein, he came down with a fever that was to recur for the next decade. Possibly, he contracted a mild dose of typhoid, even though he had been immunised before leaving Britain.

When Pretoria was captured in early June, the British misguidedly thought the war was all but over and Conan Doyle, believing his task was done, decided to return home, eager to get on with his history of the war. There has been some criticism levelled at him for walking out before the job was over but, in truth, there was little left for him to do. The worst of the epidemic was over, the fighting had moved on, and the whole hospital unit was soon to be disbanded and heading back for Blighty.

Before departing, he visited the newly conquered Boer capital and interviewed Lord Roberts and other staff officers for his book, of which he had already penned a substantial amount. Writing to his mother, he informed her, 'I have my history done within four chapters of the end, unless the end of the war is unduly prolonged. I may hope to have it nearly done before I reach England.' He was disappointed by some of the staff officers he met. They were aloof and precious and Kitchener, he concluded in his autobiography, was 'inhuman in his cool accuracy. "Regret to report great dynamite explosion. Forty Kaffirs killed," was the report of one officer. "Do you need more dynamite?" was the answering telegram from Lord Kitchener.' Where he got this anecdote from is not known, for it is not a first-hand account as he did not meet Kitchener in Pretoria: presumably, the story came to him from an officer on Kitchener's staff. He also gave Roberts a first-hand report of the work of the Langman hospital unit which had been accused in the press of negligence and ineffectiveness during the typhoid outbreak. Conan Doyle refuted the charges, to Roberts' satisfaction, but found his meeting frustrating, for His Lordship was distant and remote. He further wrote to the British Medical Journal concerning the epidemic, criticising the lack of immunisation and declaring that it should be made compulsory. The truth is that the typhoid epidemic was an unmitigated disaster which the hospital had not handled well, despite the efforts of the doctors. They were simply neither equipped to deal with nor up to the enormity of the task they faced.

Whilst in Pretoria, he travelled eastwards to Waterval-Boven, where British forces had recently relieved a Boer prisoner-of-war camp in which Conan Doyle was shown an escape tunnel dug with spoons by British troops. He had his photograph taken in the tunnel entrance, captioned it 'Getting out of a hole, like the British Empire', and mailed it to friends. On his way back to Bloemfontein, he visited a gold mine in Johannesburg, then, on 6 July, a relief doctor arrived. Freed from his responsibilities, he returned to Cape Town and stayed at the Mount Nelson Hotel before setting sail on 11 July aboard the SS *Briton*, bound for home. He took with him a wealth of experiences and a souvenir Boer brass howitzer shell-case.

During the voyage, Conan Doyle spent a good deal of his time writing, although he also had an enjoyable voyage because the passenger list contained a large number of aristocrats, journalists and military personnel with whom he mingled freely, gleaning more information for his book. He also became friendly with Bertram Fletcher Robinson, the nephew of Sir John Robinson, who was a war correspondent for the *Daily Express*, whom he had already met at the fighting. By early August, he was back at Undershaw with Louise and the children, who had returned from Naples. Life reverted to normal. Later in the month, he played cricket for the MCC at Lord's, Jean coming to watch the game and sparking a family quarrel: he was henceforth frequently to use his attendance at cricket matches as a diversion or cover for meeting her.

Few people knew of Conan Doyle's romance, although his mother was aware of it from the very start. Most men would have kept very quiet about such a thing, especially where their mother was concerned, but his relationship with Mary Doyle was very close and special. She was, in her own way, approving and had met and accepted Jean, even giving her a family heirloom, a bracelet that had belonged to his aunt Annette. Her pragmatism was not surprising: after the life she had lived with a spouse who was unable to take part in a marriage, she would have understood her son's dilemma and would have wanted him to be happy. Quite possibly, she had sought such happiness herself with Waller and was in no position to moralise. She also supported Jean when she had doubts about her relationship with her son, as a letter he sent to Mary Doyle on 27 September 1900 proves. 'I loved your letter to-day . . .' he wrote to Mary. 'It is sweet to me to think of J. with your sweet motherly arms around her. The dear soul gets these fits of depression (it is her artistic nature), and then her remorse is terrible and she writes, poor soul, as if she had done some awful thing. I never love her more than at such moments. Dearest, I don't know how to thank you for all your goodness to us.'

Other members of the family also accepted Jean. Lottie corresponded with her and Conan Doyle had informed Innes of his love prior to going to South Africa. Connie and E.W. Hornung, however, took a different view. They knew about Jean but disapproved of Conan Doyle's liaison with her. What finally tipped the balance of their disapproval was seeing her at the cricket match at Lord's, walking around the pavilion arm in arm with him.

With this public display of their relationship, Conan Doyle came under censorious attack from both the Hornungs who thought his behaviour to be beyond the social pale. He recounted his sister and brother-in-law's attitude to his mother: 'Willie's tone was that of an attorney dissecting a case, instead of a brother standing by a brother in need. Among other remarks he said that I attached too much importance to whether the relations were platonic or not – he could not see that "that made much difference". I said "the difference between guilt and innocence" . . . When have I failed in loyalty to any member of my family? And when before have I appealed to them?' From Conan Doyle's point of view, Hornung's critical aloofness went beyond just a lack of brotherly understanding. He was the head of the family and, he believed, should be given support not censure, especially in the light of the fact that he was behaving honourably over the whole affair. The crux of the matter was that, if Conan Doyle decided this course for himself, it was the right one and the rest of the family had better fall in line behind it. The rift lasted for some while. Mary Doyle tried to pour oil on troubled family waters but was not too successful, as a letter from her son shows. 'I have,' he told her, 'written a polite note to Connie, which, between ourselves, is more than she deserves. And I don't feel better by contemplating the fact that William is half Mongol, half Slav, or whatever the mixture is.' In due course, as such things do, the storm passed and Hornung's Balkan ancestry was not to be raised again.

Whether or not Louise, who was now housebound, knew of or sensed the situation is hard to say. Shortly before she died, she told her daughter not to be upset if her father remarried, for she wanted him to be happy, but this is not to say she suspected it: such a comment would be natural coming from a loving wife.

The war behind him, Conan Doyle was now about to embark upon another venture, into politics. Both the Conservatives and the Liberals had asked for his support and both parties believed he would make an ideal candidate in the forthcoming general election of October 1900. He had a high public profile, was popular and considered honourable. Even before he went to South Africa, several newspapers had pondered his entry into politics. Now that he was back, the speculation grew.

Why he decided to take the political plunge is obscure but, within weeks of returning from Cape Town, he was writing to his mother, 'What is to be gained? A full and varied and perhaps useful life. The assurance that come what may I have at least tested my fate, and done my duty as a Citizen. The participation in many interesting scenes. What is against it? I shall be bored by dinners, deputations, functions, etc. I shall have less freedom . . .' Clearly, part of his motivation was a sense of duty and a desire to help the common good, but he might also have been seeking a new kind of fame for himself, looking for a new role that could promote him further in society. He may well have harboured altruistic feelings, but he was also a master of self-promotion, a man always ready to grasp any opportunity to get on.

The general election hung on three main issues – Home Rule for Ireland, the future of the Empire and free trade. Conan Doyle was against Home Rule and free trade but believed in the Empire, which he saw as a fine thing, for Englishman and native alike, where British democracy, sound administration and the values of white man's civilisation should be exercised for the common good, whether or not the locals wanted them. Yet, for all the issues, the election – known as 'The Khaki Election' – was dominated by the South African war and, although Conan Doyle was a Liberal Unionist, he wanted the Conservatives to remain in power to see the war through. Adopting this stance was not a turning of his coat, for the Liberal Unionists had by now joined the Conservatives, the main body of the Liberal Party opposing the war.

Conan Doyle was offered a number of safe constituencies in which to stand but he rejected them. If he was going to enter the fray and win then he wanted a noble victory. His first choice was to fight the Scottish constituency of Stirling, held by the Liberal leader Sir Henry Campbell-Bannerman, whom he disliked intensely, but, as this was not possible, he stood instead for Central Edinburgh. It was not going to be easy, for the constituency was a famously radical stronghold.

With characteristic fervour, Conan Doyle went to political battle, addressing the hustings and fielding hecklers, some of whom addressed him as Sherlock Holmes. According to the press, he took this in his stride, but his own opinion of the hecklers was that they were an odious and objectionable lot who strengthened his resolve and taught him how to exercise political patience. As his campaign progressed, it looked as if he stood a chance of winning, even though his opponent was a younger man, George Mackenzie Brown, a rich publisher and the son of the former leader of the Canadian Liberal Party. Several prominent local citizens supported Conan Doyle, Joseph Bell amongst them; he spoke for him at a meeting in the Literary Institute, saying that if he turned out to be anything like as good a Member of Parliament as he had been a dresser in his free teaching clinics at the Royal Infirmary, then the constituency would be fortunate.

Regardless of such endorsement from one of Edinburgh's famous residents, Conan Doyle did not fare too well in the hustings, for he made the mistake of stressing national rather than local issues. The war was the central nail in his plank and he seemed disinterested or ill-informed on the matters that concerned the constituency electorate. He could still have won. The voters trusted him and believed in his honesty: and he was, after all, a local laddie made good. Yet dirty tricks were afoot. The day before the election, three hundred handbills were posted across the town, laying out for all to see Conan Doyle's Catholic Irish background. He was accused of being a subversive Jesuit and against the Scottish Kirk and Covenant. The Eddie Tullochs were still about, only this one was a Scottish evangelical zealot from Dunfermline called Jacob Plimmer, who operated as the Dunfermline Protestant Defence Organisation. Conan Doyle lost the election the following day but only by a few hundred votes, reducing the Liberal majority by fifteen hundred.

After the results were announced, Conan Doyle, angered by the handbills and the lack of sportsmanship, wrote a defensive letter to the *Scotsman* in which he decried the underhandedness of the campaign, declared he was not a Catholic and outlined his religious beliefs as 'broadly tolerant, founded upon a Reverent Theism, rather than upon the special teaching of any particular sect. The process of religious thought in the future, and the best one for the happiness of the human race, lies, in my opinion, in the various creeds directing their attention to those things which they have in common instead of eternally accentuating the things which hold them apart . . .'

In hindsight, it is just as well he lost the election. Politics were not that important to him. He was an individual, too honest and guileless for the role. It would have been vexing for him to tow the party line and his literary career would have stagnated under the pressure of parliamentary responsibility. At the time, however, he was very disappointed and cross at not being taken for what he was by the electorate, annoyed he had lost a fight in which he had fought fair but the opponent had fought dirty. To the honourable author, this was shoddy practice indeed.

The election over, he returned to the matter of his book, *The Great Boer War*, subtitled (as the war was not yet over) 'An Interim History of the Boer War'. It was long, with five hundred pages of narrative, accounts of the fighting, maps, military statistics, casualty data, in-depth analysis, historical and political background and, finally, an assessment of the future. It was also issued in subsequent editions to keep abreast of events. When outlining arguments, Conan Doyle dealt impartially with both Boer and British viewpoints to such an extent than the Boer press in South Africa praised it. Proud of his non-partisan stand, he even sent copies of the book to Boer prisoners-of-war held in camps in Ceylon and St Helena. A letter he received back read, 'To the Camp Commandant. I am authorised by the officers of Hut No. 4 to convey to you and to the author, Conan Doyle Esq., our heartfelt thanks for the work, "Great Boer War", which is a very interesting addition to our library. We are, dear Sir, Respectfully yours, G.C. Amenur, Librarian.' The book sold thirty thousand copies in the first eight weeks, all the royalties going to military charities.

Through writing the book, and visiting South Africa, Conan Doyle had come to the correct opinion that the British Army was antiquated and in need of immediate and drastic reform. He saw it as his responsibility to draw public attention to the situation and had published an article in the *Cornhill Magazine* headed 'Some Military Lessons of the War', which he used again in the book. The press supported his conclusions but the military powers that be kicked up a storm. Here was a novelist chappie, with a few months at the front under his belt, dictating to them. Conan Doyle knew he was treading on military toes and admitted that perhaps he 'should have expressed my views in a more subdued way, but my feelings had been aroused by the conviction that the lives of our men, and even the honour of our country, had been jeopardized by the conservatism of the military'.

His main criticisms were that cavalry was outdated, artillery should be camouflaged and batteries diversified across the terrain as the Boers' guns had been, to devastating effect, it was better to have small numbers of highly-trained troops than large numbers of half-trained ones, rifle drill was more important than parade drill, and officers should not wear distinctive uniforms that made them targets. He also suggested, 'Above all, let us have done with the fuss and feathers, the gold lace, and the frippery! Let us have done also with the tailoring, the too-luxurious habits of the mess, the unnecessary extravagance which makes it so hard for a poor man to accept a commission!'

The army top brass was hopping mad. It had other detractors and critics, but Conan Doyle was the one with the highest public profile. When he pronounced, people took heed, and the army, whilst disregarding his opinions, had at least to acknowledge them. What he was suggesting was common sense. In due time, his ideas were acted upon, although this was not put down to him. He was one of the first gadflies to bite the complacent military and goad it into long-overdue change.

The book also suggested the founding of a civilian military reserve filled with trained citizens ready to play their part in time of war, thereby negating conscription and the hurried half-training of combatants. In response, the army countered with the suggestion that a part-time volunteer army might be a good idea. The Territorial Army had existed since 1859 and it was mooted that this might be considerably expanded: and it was, owing to Conan Doyle's pressure.

Having seen the efficacy of the marksmanship of Boer farmers, he also suggested establishing nationwide rifle clubs in which there should be 'no red tape, no uniform, no swagger – a broad-brimmed looped hat with a badge, and no other distinction. I am convinced that there are half-a-million men to be had on those terms.' Lord Roberts, who was himself behind army reform, supported the concept.

Conan Doyle, who considered it a gentleman's duty to set up such clubs, and more worthwhile to aim at targets than shoot pheasants, organised one at Undershaw. Buying the weapons and ammunition himself, and building a miniature range, he called it the Undershaw Rifle Club. Members wore broad-brimmed bush-type hats turned up at one side and adorned with a metal badge. Wooden targets were set up at random in the heather of the hillside below the house and the riflemen were allowed no sighting shots in the drive for realism. Twice a week, 130 club members from all walks of life shot at Undershaw and, by 1906, there was a national federation of rifle clubs in existence with Lord Roberts as president. In the same year, Conan Doyle was elected a life member of the National Rifle Association to which he donated a silver statuette as a trophy. A casting of a bearded, elderly and resolute-looking member of the Undershaw Rifle Club, it is still annually competed for over a thousand yards, with two sighting shots and ten to place. With it goes a prize of £40.

Roberts, with a few other enlightened senior army officers, paid more than lip service to Conan Doyle's book. In 1902, they forced into being a Royal Commission which found that the army was incompetent, inefficient, ill prepared for modern warfare, under-trained and poorly equipped. The regular issue Lee Enfield rifle was criticised, uniforms were badly made and inappropriate (in the beige-coloured veldt of South Africa, some troops had been issued with scarlet tunics), medical provision was sub-standard and the quality of the food was low. Things were to change.

Since the start of the Boer War, and more so as it progressed, the

British had come under considerable international condemnation. As the fighting dragged on, the outnumbered Boers relied entirely upon guerrilla tactics, sabotaging supply lines and derailing trains. Conan Doyle's solution to this, as he wrote in the *Times*, was a truck of 'Boer irreconcilables' hitched to every locomotive: to the critics who attacked him, his reply was 'Our first duty is to our own soldiers'.

The British responded to the guerrillas with a scorched earth policy. Kitchener ordered that all farms be burned, all crops destroyed and all livestock slain or utilised. Boer women and children were captured and placed in concentration camps for, it was officially stated, their own safety. The Boers were incensed and stirred up considerable anti-British feeling in the European press. Rumours of looting, rape and the use of soft-nosed, impact-expansion dum-dum ammunition were widespread. Adding fuel to the fire of controversy was the humanist and editor of the *Review of Reviews*, William Stead, for whom Conan Doyle had written over the years and with whom he was friends through their shared interest in spiritualism. He founded a weekly, *War against War*, and published two pamphlets, 'Shall I Slay My Brother Boer?' and 'Methods of Barbarism', in which he attacked the scorched earth policy and the civilian concentration camps.

The public largely tended to ignore Stead's publications and paid no heed to what foreigners thought of British policies, but Conan Doyle did and considered it his duty to set the facts straight. Approaching Reginald Smith, who was the co-proprietor of the publishers Smith, Elder & Co., he proposed to write a pamphlet countering foreign criticism. Smith agreed to print and publish it free of charge as a non-profit-making paperback retailing for sixpence. George Newnes distributed it.

On 9 January 1902, Conan Doyle started writing 'The War in South Africa: Its Causes and Conduct'. It was completed on 17 January and came in at sixty thousand words. In the *Times*, he appealed for funds to translate it. Over £1,000 was received in a week: Edward VII was said to have contributed £500. In ten weeks, 300,000 had sold and a fund was set up to handle the proceeds. In Europe and North America, it was distributed free, and it was translated into German, French, Dutch, Hungarian, Italian, Russian, Spanish, Portuguese, the Scandinavian languages, Braille and Welsh. A special preface for the Norwegian edition was held up by blizzards and had to be sent by heliograph.

Typically, Conan Doyle wrote the truth (if not the whole truth), even when it was not in the British interest. He criticised the British concentration camps as cruel but said they were better than leaving

Boer families to starve, and he added that, in their camps, the Boers treated British prisoners badly, torturing and executing black Africans found aiding them. He justified the scorched earth policy by saying the Boers often used the farmsteads as sniping points. It was, therefore, their own responsibility that civilian homes had been used as strategic bases and that they were, as a result, legitimate military objectives. He quoted not only official British military sources but also the Boers themselves, denying that the claimed widespread looting and raping or the use of dum-dum bullets had occurred, although in truth there had been instances of all three crimes, the soldiers perpetrating them being severely punished by their officers.

The publication, regarded as a pamphlet but far too long to be one, was a considerable propaganda success, Conan Doyle noting that it produced a 'rapid and marked change in the tone of the whole Continental press, which may have been a coincidence but was certainly a pleasing one', although he had no delusions as to how efficacious it might have been. Writing in *The Times*, he said, 'We expected no wholesale conversions. But at least we could be sure that the plea of ignorance could no longer be used.' How much impact the pamphlet had on overseas opinion is hard to gauge, for it actually had some adverse effects. Some humanists considered he had glossed over important British failings, had covered up some of Kitchener's inhuman tactical decisions and, in the Shakespearean sense, protested too much. On account of being issued free, it was considered to be official propaganda, and Conan Doyle was regarded by many, quite erroneously, as being an official British spokesman, which had not been his intention. Another aspect of the government's handling of war came under his critical eye. He was surprised to what extent politicians had ignored the potential power of publicity as a medium for stating a propaganda message, and he pondered how much an official organ could have accomplished when he, as a single individual operating alone, had achieved so much.

He was paid nothing for the pamphlet which, in due course, made a considerable financial surplus. He proposed that the profits be used to set up a scholarship for poor South Africans – black, British or Boer – to attend his old university. One thousand pounds was given to the university and, according to Conan Doyle, a bursary of £40, drawn from the investment of the capital, was offered, for he received a letter from a Zulu student applicant expressing the hope of winning it. Nothing, however, seems to have come of the idea, for the university archives show no record of the bursary having ever been awarded. The balance of the profits of the publication were eventually donated to, amongst others, the Civilian Rifleman's Movement, the joint forces' Union Jack Club, famine relief in India, a fund for distressed Boers, and the cause of nursing in Japan.

With his contribution to the pamphlet completed, Conan Doyle went on holiday in April to visit his sister Ida and her husband, Nelson, who was a wealthy industrialist, who were living in solitary splendour in a mansion on the tiny islet of Gaiola, north of Naples. From there, he went south to Sicily, north to Venice and then overland to the Italian lakes and Switzerland.

Just before he departed, he received notice that Edward VII was to make him a knight bachelor. Conan Doyle was in two minds about accepting the honour. In principle, he did not agree with honorifics, which might be one of the reasons for his having kept quiet about receiving his Italian decoration in 1898. He was being knighted for, as he saw it, simply doing his duty, for which he deserved no recognition. His most meaningful award, he later declared, was a silver bowl purchased by public subscription and presented to him after the Boer War, engraved 'To Arthur Conan Doyle, who, at a great crisis, in word and deed, served his country'. He told his mother that the title he most valued was Doctor. She was incensed that he should consider refusing a title and only won the argument when, after a good few letters had passed between them, she pointed out that a refusal would insult the monarch. In this, she was supported by other family members. Both Louise and Jean said he should accept. Mary Doyle was relieved that her view had prevailed: with her love of history and heraldry, her pride in her son and family, and her determination that he should succeed, a knighthood was the crowning honour.

His knighthood was conferred upon him on 24 October 1902 at Buckingham Palace. Conan Doyle was caustic about the ceremonial arrangements. Candidates for investiture were, as he put it, herded into wooden pens rather like cattle at a market. His discomfort was, however, alleviated by his meeting Oliver Lodge, who was also being knighted, in the same pen. At the King's personal insistence, he was also designated Deputy Lord Lieutenant of Surrey. This, too, was an honour he did not want, and he complained that the ceremonial uniform he had to wear on official functions, which he had to purchase himself, was too expensive and elaborate, with gold epaulettes and a bicorn hat. It made him look, he announced, like a monkey on a stick.

One outcome of his knighthood did amuse him. Shortly afterwards, he received the bill for goods he had ordered, duly made out to Sir

Sherlock Holmes. On complaining to the merchant sending the bill, Conan Doyle discovered that he was the victim of a practical joke. The clerks sending out the invoices had fooled one of their number into thinking that, when a man was knighted, he changed his name, and they convinced the youth that Conan Doyle had changed his to Sir Sherlock Holmes. Normally peeved at being confused with his detective, he just laughed the incident off.

He had been more or less obliged to accept his knighthood. To have refused it would, as his mother pointed out, have been a snub to the King and would not have stood him in good social stead. Yet he still managed to make his thoughts known. In 'The Adventure of the Three Garridebs', Sherlock Holmes himself refused a knighthood shortly after the end of the Boer War.

This was possible because Holmes was not dead after all.

11

The Resurrection of Sherlock Holmes

In 1896, Conan Doyle wrote of Sherlock Holmes, 'I have had such an overdose of him that I feel towards him as I do towards pâté de foie gras, of which I once ate too much, so that the name of it gives me a sickly feeling to this day.'

For years, ignoring the pleas and even occasional threats of readers, the nagging of editors and the offers of near-bribes by publishers, he had resisted writing anything more of Sherlock Holmes but, in late 1897, he had decided to write a Holmes play to mollify them all and to help pay for the building costs of Undershaw, which had gone over budget. The play, he stressed firmly, was not a resurrection.

At first, he approached Herbert Beerbohm Tree, who liked the script but demanded he be allowed to play Sherlock Holmes in a way to which Conan Doyle could not agree. A.P. Watt submitted the play to an American impresario, Charles Frohman, who was visiting London in July 1898. He and Conan Doyle met and instantly took to each other. When Frohman bid for the rights, his offer was accepted and, with Conan Doyle's agreement, the part of Sherlock Holmes was offered to the American actor William Gillette. When Gillette read the script he saw it had great potential but felt it needed more work, and cabled Conan Doyle to ask if he could be given permission to do a rewrite that included Sherlock Holmes getting married to the heroine. Conan Doyle replied, 'You may marry or murder or do what you like with him.' With such a response, Gillette promptly rewrote the play, although not without trauma. In November, he had his manuscript copy in his dressing room in a theatre in San Francisco when the building burned down. Gillette sequestered himself away for a fortnight and wrote another version.

The play was a five-act drama based loosely upon 'A Scandal in Bohemia' and 'The Adventure of the Final Problem', with snippets from some of the other stories thrown in. The play ends with Sherlock Holmes marrying and Moriarty under lock and key.

The following May, Gillette travelled to England and visited Conan Doyle at Undershaw. The person the latter saw standing before him appeared just as he had always imagined Sherlock Holmes, were he real. The actor was exceedingly good-looking, tall, with sharp features and an air of authority about him. In addition, Gillette's character fitted the part. He was an eccentric, often reticent, coolly detached, sardonic and rational with a dry, mocking sense of humour. He was not a misogynist but his wife had recently died and he was no longer interested in women.

Entitled simply *Sherlock Holmes*, the play opened at the Star Theatre in Buffalo, in upstate New York, on 23 October 1899. It moved on to Syracuse then Rochester before transferring to New York City, where it opened on 6 November. The New York run over, it toured for more than a year across the USA, then, after a few performances in Liverpool, opened at the Lyceum Theatre in London on 9 September 1901.

Although the critics were hard on it, the public was less demanding and it played to good houses from the start, the audience cheering when Sherlock Holmes did things they recognised from the stories, such as taking his shag tobacco out of a Persian slipper. Gillette was considered a superb Holmes and the play ran for six months before touring Britain. Subsequently, a French translation was a box-office hit in Paris.

On 30 January 1902, a royal command performance was staged for King Edward VII and Queen Alexandra, both of whom had just come out of mourning for Queen Victoria. The King, who was a great admirer of the stories – it was said Sherlock Holmes was the only fiction he read to the end – was so taken by the play that, in the interval, he requested that Gillette visit the royal box. Once there, he kept the actor talking for so long the audience grew restless and started to become fractious. At the end of the performance, Gillette and Conan Doyle stepped before the curtain to a standing ovation. The play also made theatrical history, for, the next year, the part of the page-boy was played by a fourteen-year-old child actor called Charles Spencer Chaplin. It was his first stage role.

Gillette went on playing Sherlock Holmes for thirty years, becoming the personification of the character, the benchmark against which the future detective would be measured. Frederick Dorr Steele based his

Conan Doyle, not long after arriving in South Africa.

The staff of the Langman hospital, Bloemfontein: Conan Doyle is second left in the back row.

Conan Doyle at Waterval-Boven, in the entrance to the PoW tunnel.

Left: Arthur Conan Doyle: a portrait taken in 1901 and used as his official election photograph when standing for Parliament.

Right: Jean Leckie, Conan Doyle's second wife.

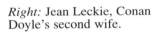

Left: George Edalji. (*Fotomas*)

Oscar Slater. (*Fotomas*)

The marriage of Sir Arthur Conan Doyle and Jean Leckie
at St. Margaret's, Westminster, 18 September, 1907.

Pietri Dorando finishing the Marathon
in the Olympic Games, 1908: Conan
Doyle, on the right, encourages him on.
(News International Group)

Conan Doyle at the wheel of number
23, a green Dietrich-Lorraine
landaulette, in the Prince Henry Tour.

Sir Arthur Conan Doyle, Private number 184343, the Crowborough Company of the 6th Royal Sussex Regiment, 1914.

Conan Doyle at the Italian Front, 1916.

Conan Doyle, in his custom-made uniform, 1916: by his side are his sons, Denis and Adrian.

The Conan Doyles with Harry Houdini below the boardwalk at Atlantic City, 1922.

The Conan Doyle family en route for America aboard the liner, *SS Olympic*, 1923: from left to right – Denis, Lady Jean, Jean, Sir Arthur and Adrian.

Above: Hollywood, 1923: Conan Doyle with Jean, Mary Pickford and Douglas Fairbanks.

Right: Conan Doyle (seated) with his secretary, Major Wood, one of the possible models for Dr. Watson.

Below: Conan Doyle playing billiards at Windlesham. (Wheeler, Fisk-Moore Ltd)

Bignell House, in the New Forest: to the right is Jean's croquet lawn. Conan Doyle's study, where his ghost was exorcised, is on the left. (Martin Booth)

Sir Arthur Conan Doyle, in the garden at Bignell House, 1929.

American illustrations on Gillette and, after Sidney Paget died, other illustrators followed suit. In the years to come, casting managers and film directors would take their lead. Gillette also brought more to the legend than his looks and acting ability. Sherlock Holmes's famous curly meerschaum pipe was his invention. He found it difficult to speak his lines with an ordinary pipe in his mouth, but the curl of the stem of the idiosyncratic meerschaum took the bowl beneath the line of his lips and permitted clearer enunciation.

From the start, Gillette was so associated with the part that he became the subject of music-hall skits such as 'Sheerluck Jones or Why D'Gillette Him Off?' in 1901 and 'Surelock Holmes' the next year. He was caricatured in magazines and even took part in a spoof, *The Painful Predicament of Sherlock Holmes*. A satirical postcard was produced by the post- and greetings card publisher Raphael Tuck, painted by the famous artist of cats, Louis Wain. It depicted Gillette as a Sherlock Holmes cat wearing a dressing gown, smoking a pipe and grasping a pistol in its tail. These parodies of Gillette were not, however, the first to appear about Holmes. In the winter of 1893, a revue called *Under the Clock* contained a sketch that took a rise out of Holmes and Watson, and included Watson frequently remarking, 'Oh! Sherlock, you wonderful man!' The same winter, a playwright called Charles Rogers put on his *Sherlock Holmes, Private Detective* whilst, for thirty issues of the famous halfpenny weekly, *Comic Cuts*, 'The Adventures of Chubb-Lock Holmes' was featured. In 1900, the first Holmes film was made. Entitled *Sherlock Holmes Baffled*, it ran for forty-nine seconds and took the form of a sort of fairground peep-show.

A play was not going to satisfy demand for the detective. If anything, it whetted the public appetite for more stories. Conan Doyle, who had long turned a deaf ear to the clamour, was still under pressure to produce. The time to write about Sherlock Holmes again was nigh. He knew it and consciously if reluctantly accepted it. He was also having to swallow the fact that Holmes was a successful literary creation and perhaps deserving of the acclaim after all. Another factor mitigating in Holmes's favour was that, if Conan Doyle had killed him off to avoid the pressure of deadlines, he was now more free. His reputation was made and he could take his time. He had settled into a comfortable house, Louise's illness was in temporary remission and he had had his thrilling adventure in South Africa. It was time to knuckle down to a bit more writing and Holmes seemed the appropriate direction to take. What was more, as Conan Doyle knew only too well, the detective was certain to earn money. All he needed was a good story.

Since returning from South Africa, he had kept in touch with Bertram Fletcher Robinson who, as well as being a successful journalist, was interested in folklore. In March 1901, they met up for a brief golfing holiday to Cromer, in Norfolk, golf being yet another sport Conan Doyle enjoyed, although his handicap was never below ten. For four days, they stayed at the Royal Links Hotel, playing on the course there and going sailing. Conan Doyle was worn out from his electioneering in Edinburgh, writing his book on the Boer War and a recent bout of the fever he had brought back with him from Bloemfontein.

Robinson was a Devonian who had been born and raised in Ipplepen, four kilometres from Torquay, and educated at Newton College in Newton Abbot before going up to Jesus College, Cambridge. Whilst walking the links and in the 19th hole, he regaled Conan Doyle with folk stories of Devon, mentioning the legends of spectral hounds that were said to roam Dartmoor.

Wild-dog legends abound in British folklore. Dartmoor itself has the Yeth or Wisht Hounds, which wander the moors searching for the souls of unbaptised infants. They are portrayed as ghostly black hounds with red eyes. To see them is to sign your own death warrant. Their huntsman is Satan, who supposedly resides in the ancient hill-fort of Dewerstone Rock near Shaugh Prior, the base of which is guarded by a massive hell-hound. Cranmere Pool, in the north-west quadrant of the moor, long infamous as a deadly quicksand, was where damned spirits went to drown in the peaty quagmire.

The Dartmoor hounds are not just generally related to the moor. One is associated with the Cabell family of Brook Manor, two kilometres from Buckfastleigh. The story goes that, in 1677, Sir Richard Cabell rode a black mare across Dartmoor at the bidding of a hound in response to a pact he made with the Devil. An alternative local story, and one more feasible, states that Cabell mistreated his wife who, fleeing over the moor, was chased by him. When he caught up with her, he stabbed her and her pet dog to death, to be haunted for ever after by the dog.

These stories caught Conan Doyle's imagination. He knew of the wildness of Dartmoor, having visited it during his time with Budd, not to mention publishing a photographic essay on the area in 1882, and thought it worthwhile setting a horror story there. He wrote from Cromer to his mother to tell her he was going to collaborate with Robinson on 'a real creeper' which, at first, was not intended to be a Sherlock Holmes story.

After fulfilling a speaking engagement in Edinburgh, Conan Doyle went to Dartmoor with Robinson towards the end of the month, taking rooms in the Duchy Hotel at Princetown, close to the famous prison, the governor, doctor and chaplain of which called on him to meet Sherlock Holmes, which did not amuse him. Basing themselves here and at Ipplepen, they took trips out on to the moor, either on foot or by pony and trap, visiting Brook Manor, the great ruined Bronze Age settlement of Grimspound, and Fox Tor Mires, a notorious bog three kilometres south-east of Princetown, said to be the resting place of a number of escaping convicts and close to more Bronze Age settlements, and Child's Tomb, a famous kistvaen to which the legend of Child the Hunter was attached. With such stimuli, the story quickly took form. Conan Doyle considered inventing a new hero for it, then realised he had one. It was Sherlock Holmes. Within a few days was born one of the most famous stories in English literature, *The Hound of the Baskervilles*.

In the story, Grimspound (not Grimspound Bog as many would have it: there is no such place) and Fox Tor Mires metamorphosed into Grimpen Mire. The name Baskerville was borrowed from the driver of their pony and trap who was employed by Robinson at Park Hill, his home at Ipplepen. In recognition, Robinson later presented him with a copy of the book, inscribed, 'To Harry Baskerville, with apologies for using the name'. Despite this dedication, there has been another suggestion for the source of the name and the story. It refers to a family called Baskerville which lived in the Welsh borders, and married into a local family to which the tradition of a hellhound, the Black Hound of Hergest, was attributed. Dr James Mortimer, who brings the mystery to Sherlock Holmes, is loosely based upon Robinson, Stapleton was based on Dodo's husband, Cyril, and the description of Baskerville Hall has echoes of Stonyhurst, both having a Yew Alley.

The idea of co-writing the story was dropped early on. The honourable Conan Doyle wanted Robinson to share the credit but Greenhough Smith refused to oblige him. A Sherlock Holmes story had to appear under just one name and that had to be Sir Arthur Conan Doyle. Despite this editorial decision, Conan Doyle acknowledged his source for the story in both the serialisation and the subsequent book. It is also thought he saw that Robinson received some payment for his origination.

One can imagine the pleasure George Newnes and Greenhough Smith must have felt at receiving a new Sherlock Holmes tale. The public were just as ecstatic. When the first episode was published in August 1901, the queue outside the magazine's offices reached right round the building. Long lines formed outside bookstalls and there were even bribes offered for pre-publication copies. Circulation of the *Strand Magazine* rose overnight by thirty thousand copies and the magazine had to go to an unprecedented seventh printing. The novel appeared immediately after the serialisation ended in April 1902.

The story was an instant success both in Britain and the USA. It was well reviewed not so much for its characters and plot but for its convincingly eerie and foreboding atmosphere, its specific and accurate descriptions of the Dartmoor terrain. Conan Doyle allowed himself some licence in these descriptions. Distances were exaggerated and he implied there was a greater covering of forest than has ever been the case. The result was a gothic thriller in the tradition of Charlotte and Emily Brontë, a worthy successor to Thomas Hardy's darker novels set on the heaths and moorland of Dorset.

As in the case of the play, Conan Doyle made it clear Sherlock Holmes had not been raised from the dead but that this was just another story from his casebook, previously untold. This disappointed both the publishers and the readers, for it meant that the author was under no sense of commitment to continue with his detective hero. The story was treated as a one-off but it also made Conan Doyle a bestselling author again, with a chance to earn big money. It was not long before the offers came in. *Collier's Weekly*, the American magazine, offered $25,000 for six new Sherlock Holmes stories whilst Greenhough Smith offered £100 per thousand words. The money was superb, but it carried a catch. None of the tales was to be retrospective. Sherlock Holmes had to be alive.

A.P. Watt fielded the offers and the author accepted with a terse postcard which read, 'Very well. A.C.D.' Such brevity became more common as Conan Doyle got older but is not an indication of curtness or arrogance: his private postbag increased considerably over the years and he simply did not have the time to reply at length to many of his correspondents. The sums were the highest ever paid to an author up to that time, but Conan Doyle knew they were being given to him not as a serious historical novelist but as a popular literary entertainer, and he had to accept that fact with the cheques. He resigned himself to the work with a distinctly cynical turn of mind. His attitude was that if someone was fool enough to pay such advances then he would accept them.

The new stories appeared in *Collier's Weekly* in the USA from September 1903 and in the *Strand Magazine* from October, and were collected in a volume entitled *The Return of Sherlock Holmes* the next year. The first story, 'The Adventure of the Empty House', was an instant blockbuster when it appeared. In Britain, customers crowded railway newsagents' stands, queued outside shops and elbowed each other to get a copy. Newnes had artfully hyped the story ahead of publication – not that he had needed to – by advertising in the magazine that it was on its way and even posting bills around London heralding its coming. On release, he could not print the copies fast enough.

From the start of the series, Conan Doyle had to explain how Sherlock Holmes had escaped death. It was Jean who suggested the solution to the dilemma. Holmes was an expert at *baritsu*, a form of Japanese unarmed combat. Using *baritsu* techniques, he broke free from Moriarty, then climbed the cliff above the path upon which they had fought in order to escape from Moriarty's henchmen. He had, however, wanted everyone to think he was dead so that Moriarty's compatriots would not seek him out. For two years, he travelled the world, stopping in Tibet, where he met the Head Lama (originally spelt 'Llama', which made the story famous amongst typographers), Persia, Mecca in Arabia and France. He also met the Khalifa in Khartoum. Finally, on hearing that all Moriarty's men were dead bar one, he felt he could surface once more and turned up in time to help Watson with a murder he was investigating.

Many readers felt this was not on. Sherlock Holmes would never run away like this. Indeed, some thought he had been engaged in work so secret that this story and the worldwide travelling were just a cover-up. Yet they all accepted it. The most important thing was that he had survived and was back. Conveniently, so was Watson, who was in mourning for, it is assumed, his wife. Thus freed once more into bachelordom, he moved into 221B Baker Street, the lease on which Holmes's brother, Mycroft, had retained, leaving the place untouched. In one short story, the past was rewritten and Sherlock Holmes and Watson were back in business.

The stories were not, however, set in the present day but in the years 1894–8, which allowed Conan Doyle to play the nostalgia card and keep the stories in an age that was not yet disturbed by war, changing politics and the mood of the new century.

The historical problem overcome, another more perennial one arose in terms of working out suitable new storylines. Before writing, Conan Doyle spoke to Greenhough Smith, Newnes, his mother, Jean and E.W. Hornung, from whom he was to borrow a few ideas used in the Raffles stories. To find some solitude in which to think, he even planned to go to Long Island and stay in a secluded house there whilst working on new narratives, perhaps having Holmes take on a case or two in the USA, a plan his American publishers avidly supported.

In the end, however, he did not go; nor did Sherlock Holmes. Conan

Doyle stayed in England and worked over the old themes instead. Revenge and blackmail were revisited, along with the avoidance of scandal, the importance of propriety and all the old Victorian values so familiar in the previous tales. International affairs and the problems of society were supplanted by Holmes taking on cases involving people seeking to prevent the exposure of their secrets. Conan Doyle's own predicament must have given him some inspiration, for over half the stories in *The Return of Sherlock Holmes* have characters keeping secret a love affair.

This was not the only similarity between the stories and their author's private life. In 'The Adventure of the Empty House', Ronald Adair is killed by a dum-dum-type bullet fired from an air-gun. It was the sort of bullet that had been occasionally used by British troops in the Boer War, in contravention of orders and international law. 'The Adventure of the Three Students' evinces Conan Doyle's student life, the school in 'The Adventure of the Priory School' is not unlike Hodder, and the house in 'The Adventure of the Norwood Builder' bears more than a passing resemblance to 12 Tennison Road. Two gentlemen approach Sherlock Holmes in 'The Adventure of the Second Stain' to ask him to find an important document that would cause a war in Europe: it contains accusations of British atrocities in South Africa. The use of a whaling trip and a murder with a harpoon drew upon Conan Doyle's voyage on the *Hope* and resulted in an irate letter from Captain John Gray to the *Strand Magazine*. As has been mentioned, alcoholism was to feature prominently in 'The Adventure of the Abbey Grange'. 'The Adventure of the Missing Three-Quarter' is even closer to Conan Doyle's life at the time of writing. It concerns a right-wing three-quarter rugby player of considerable renown who goes missing, only to be found hiding in a cottage in the woods with his wife, whom no one knew existed, dead of consumption: their love affair and marriage had been kept secret so as not to jeopardise the rugby player's inheritance.

Even though the stories were not written under the same pressure as the earlier ones, Conan Doyle still made glaring errors in them. A dum-dum bullet could not be fired from an air-gun and, in 'The Adventure of the Priory School', he made a mistake that many readers picked up, namely that Sherlock Holmes could not have told what direction a bicycle was going in by looking at its tyre prints. Conan Doyle actually took a cycle out to test the fact and found to his chagrin that Sherlock Holmes – or, rather, his creator – was indeed wrong.

Mistakes or not, the public lapped them up. The *Strand Magazine* sold over half a million copies of each edition. Queues formed monthly and it was said that public libraries opened their reading rooms into the evening to accommodate those who had missed buying a copy. Sherlock Holmes's international appeal increased, too. During the years of his absence in Tibet and elsewhere, people continued to think of him as a real person. There were rumours about what had happened to him after he went over the falls and there was even a report in the *Cape Town Times* in 1896 that he had arrived with Watson in South Africa. Letters were still sent to him care of Scotland Yard. Now, with his renaissance, Conan Doyle started to receive a veritable avalanche of correspondence from all over the world. In France, it was claimed, Holmes's methods were part of official police practice, whilst in Germany a new word was coined, *sherlockieren*, meaning to track down or deduce. Kaiser Wilhelm II liked the stories so much it was said he had a set of the books especially bound to match the decor of the royal yacht, whilst Tsar Nicholas II and the Tsarina were also professed Holmes admirers.

Such fame produced more apocryphal tales. One has a woman writing to Sherlock Holmes to tell him that she had mislaid a motor horn, some golf balls, a brush, a boot-jack and a dictionary, all in one week. What was the explanation? Sherlock Holmes allegedly replied, 'Nothing simpler, my dear lady. It is clear that your neighbour keeps a goat.' Another story, which Conan Doyle was apparently wont to tell, concerned a joke in which Holmes goes to heaven. St Peter meets him at the gate with a quandary. The angels cannot identify Adam amongst all the other men. What is to be done? Holmes orders all the men to strip and there, plain as day, stands Adam. When St Peter asks Holmes how he deduced the correct person, the great detective points to Adam's anatomy and indicates that he is lacking a navel. Problem solved, my dear St Peter.

As a result of the rebirth of Sherlock Holmes, Conan Doyle was now a very wealthy man, but he was not profligate with his money. He could not afford to be, for living the life of a country gentleman required a substantial income. Nevertheless, he still held by his credo of trying to experience as much as he could of life. In 1902, he made a balloon ascent from Crystal Palace in South London, landing at Sevenoaks in Kent, forty kilometres away, going up to an altitude of six thousand feet. In an interview he gave to P.G. Wodehouse the following year, for a publication called *V.C.*, he admitted that he had been scared stiff and that it was a long time before he felt confident enough to let go of the ropes, although, he added, he hoped soon to try a parachute jump. Wodehouse and Conan Doyle played cricket

together, Wodehouse avowing he was greatly influenced by Conan
Doyle, whom he venerated for the rest of his life.

Sport still occupied an important place in Conan Doyle's life. He
was most serious about his cricket and, at the age of forty-nine,
took seven wickets for fifty-one in a match between the MCC and
the Cambridgeshire county team, his best career performance playing
at Lord's. It was around this time that he acquired a new sporting
pastime. It was motoring, and he was one of the earliest motorists in
Britain. Without apparently having ever driven a car, he went by train
to Birmingham. For the journey, he dressed in the 'uniform' of the new
motorist, which was a long coat, goggles and a peaked cap, causing an
old lady to mistake him as a railway platform porter. In Birmingham,
he took delivery of a brand-new, ten horse-power Wolseley, which he
promptly drove all the way back to Hindhead, a distance of some 275
kilometres, over unmade roads hardly changed in a century. Although
he hoped he would in the future be doing most of the driving himself, he
took the precaution of sending his coachman, Holden, ahead of him to
Birmingham for several weeks' driving lessons, just in case. Inevitably,
he had some accidents, in one of which the car startled a horse which
reared and emptied its cartload of turnips on to him and his passenger
who, at the time, happened to be his mother. A more serious accident
occurred when he was driving with Innes, who had returned to England
to teach at a military staff college. Conan Doyle lost control of the car
as he drove in through the gates of Undershaw. The vehicle veered up a
steep bank by the side of the drive and toppled over, throwing Innes clear
but trapping Conan Doyle. Only the steering wheel and column saved
him from being instantly crushed. In a few moments, before he could
wriggle free, the steering wheel broke and Conan Doyle was pinned to
the gravel drive across his back and shoulders, just below his neck. He
lay there for some minutes, waiting for his spine to be severed at any
moment. Luckily, a crowd gathered and Holden organised a party of
men to lift the one-ton car off his employer.

His escape from injury was probably due to his physical strength
and level of fitness. Years playing sport had paid off, but he might also
have been spared because he had taken a course of muscle development
given by Eugene Sandow, the famous strongman, a friend of his who was
said to be able to lift up an elephant and to whose book, *The Construction
and Reconstruction of the Human Body*, Conan Doyle wrote a foreword
in 1907.

Undeterred, it was not long before he purchased a second,
twenty horse-power car and a motorcycle. He was soon speeding

along the high road. In September 1905, he was caught and fined for speeding, which prompted a vitriolic attack in the form of a letter to the *Daily Mail*, complaining about police unfairness and questioning their ability to judge speed. He observed that 'it is dangerous to drive at any speed upon a lonely country road, but that it is safe elsewhere, for it is only on the lonely roads that traps are set'. His opinion had remained constant twenty-four years later when one of his sons was fined for speeding. On that occasion, he wrote to the *Sussex County Herald* to draw attention to the fact that his son had been fined £5 for speeding on a clear road where he posed no danger to anyone, with no moral guilt involved, but a man appearing before the same magistrate on the same day had been fined only £2 on his thirteenth conviction of gross cruelty to a horse. The horse torturer was also not charged costs as his son was. 'How can anyone excuse such judgements as these,' he asked, 'and is it a wonder that many of the younger generation look upon the administration of the law with contempt?' As so often before, Conan Doyle was well ahead of his time.

His being a man of the future showed in more than his complaints about the state of law and order. In 1906, he built an electrically powered monorail balanced by a gyroscope which ran through the grounds of Undershaw. Ever ready to test a new gadget, he also purchased a motorised bicycle called an auto-wheel.

Not all his money was spent on speed and fripperies. He also took out a range of investments, believing that 'a man should know all sides of life, and he has missed a very essential side if he has not played his part in commerce'. For thirty years, he was a director of Raphael Tuck, the picture post- and Christmas card firm which, ironically, had sent up Sherlock Holmes with the Gillette cat card. He was also a long-standing chairman of Besson's, the brass musical instrument company, and invested in a motorcycle manufacturer. Some of his ventures were exceptionally speculative. He put money into a gold mine that produced no gold and a coalmine in Kent which produced coal that would not burn. In the latter case, he descended more than a thousand feet down the mine shaft to see his investment in its natural state, but the coal turned out to be so incombustible that, at a shareholders' meeting, the meal had to be prepared over an alternative fuel.

In the spirit of adventure, he also became involved, in August 1905, with the Grosvenor Recovery Syndicate. This was a company of treasure hunters set up to find and exploit the wreck of an East Indiaman, the *Grosvenor*, which sank off South Africa in 1782. Her cargo was supposed to be the spoils of the sack of Delhi, including a large number of maharajahs' jewels and a substantial amount of bullion. The crew were said to have come ashore from the wreck with a good deal of the cargo, which they then buried, drawing up a map of which the syndicate purported to own either a copy or the original. Previous attempts to locate the treasure had failed and the Grosvenor Recovery Syndicate was no more successful. It was wound up in 1911 but resurfaced in 1921 as the Grosvenor Bullion Syndicate.

With characteristic generosity, Conan Doyle also gave away large sums of money. Apart from writing books without charge or royalty, in order to support causes in which he believed, he continued to support members of his family, friends and even strangers. Just as he had, all those years ago, presented his watch to the impoverished Herr Gleiwitz, and more recently bought South View Lodge for Arthur Vernon Ford, so now he gave £500 to help a man divorce his alcoholic wife for the sake of their children, and surrendered a pair of brand-new golf shoes to a tramp with holes in his boots. He frequently gave lifts in his car and, on one occasion, took a female tramp who was ill twenty-five kilometres out of his way to her sister's house. As more than one person observed, Conan Doyle was more of a Christian, not being one, than many who professed to the faith. What is more, he never advertised his generosity, so the examples that have become known are probably only a few of very many.

His literary output was not restricted to Sherlock Holmes. He started writing more Brigadier Gerard tales for the *Strand Magazine* as well as assorted adventure and horror short stories. One of the latter, 'The Leather Funnel', has attracted interest over the years, for it concerns psychometry, the power of telling an object's past by touching or being close to it.

The main character in the story is an occultist called Lionel Dacre, who lives on Avenue de Wagram in Paris, where Michael Conan had been residing when Conan Doyle visited him in 1876. There has been a suggestion that Dacre is based on the infamous Aleister Crowley, but this is not so: although Crowley was to become labelled by the press 'the wickedest man in the world', he could not have been the model for Conan Doyle's character, for, at the time the story was written, Crowley was only in his late twenties and his evil reputation not yet widely established.

Dacre, a man whose experiments into the unknown 'have passed all the bounds of civilisation and decorum', hands a leather funnel to a guest as part of a psychometric test. The guest sleeps next to it and has a nightmare in which he sees a woman strapped spread-eagle across a torture table. Just as the funnel is about to be inserted into her, he wakes up. It would seem that the woman was about to suffer water torture, having her stomach forced full with liquid, but this is not made clear in the story although it is mentioned that the funnel bears teeth marks. The ambiguity of the description has been seen by many to suggest a fascination on Conan Doyle's part with sexual perversion, the linking of sex with death in a darker side to his character. Whether there is any truth in this assumption cannot be ascertained, although bearing in mind his self-imposed celibacy at the time of writing, it might be more a case of sexual frustration, rather than perversion, influencing the story. What can be said is that the story is chilling and justifiably considered a minor classic in the genre.

As if this wide range of work were not enough, he also commenced writing *Sir Nigel*, first planned fifteen years before and using many of the same characters as appeared in *The White Company*. By December, it was in print in its first serialised episode in the *Strand Magazine*, in which it ran until the following December when Smith, Elder and Co. published it as a novel. Conan Doyle was not in favour of serialising it but, as he told an interviewer, with serialisation he could earn four times as much as from a single-volume publication. As the American serial rights sold for $25,000, one can appreciate his point.

A prequel to *The White Company*, the novel attempted to show the workings of the code of chivalry rather than simply transport readers into the fourteenth century as the previous novel had done, but it contained some fundamental continuity flaws. The inaccurate chronology is the most obvious: *Sir Nigel* ends in 1356 with the wedding of Sir Nigel to his wife but, in *The White Company*, which starts in 1366, Nigel and his wife already have a twenty-year-old daughter.

The experiences Conan Doyle had had in South Africa afforded him a new outlook on warfare, which became evident in his handling of battles. As well as his personal experiences, he may have added other private touches to the book. Sir Nigel's grandmother, Dame Ermyntrude, was based upon Mary Doyle. The English part of the narrative, which moves to the Channel Islands and France, was set in the landscape near Hindhead and dealt with a quarrel between the monastery of Waverley (based upon Waverley Abbey to the south-east of Farnham) and Sir Nigel's family, the Lorings, culminating in the tenants on the monastic lands being evicted, much as the Doyles were in Ireland. In response, Sir Nigel attacked the monks' property just as Irish landowners had resisted the taking of their own lands. The fighting took place in the village of Tilford, upon the village green on which Conan Doyle sometimes played cricket, and on Hankley Common, between Hindhead and Waverley Abbey, over which he frequently rode.

When he completed *Sir Nigel*, Conan Doyle wrote to his mother, 'Dei Gratia, finished! 132,000 words. My absolute top!' In his autobiography, he notes that the novel 'represents my high-water mark in literature', but he was disappointed by the critical response it was given, adding that it 'received no particular recognition from critics or public'. This was not strictly accurate. The novel was a Christmas bestseller and it received wide and appreciative criticism, but not of the sort he wanted. It was praised, as was *The White Company*, as an adventure story, whereas he had wanted the research, the moral lesson and the political analysis to be appreciated.

Despite his failure to win the seat of Central Edinburgh, Conan Doyle decided to stand again in the general election of January 1906. This time, he stood for the constituency of the Border Burghs on the tariff reform ticket. The Border Burghs were the small towns of Galashiels, Hawick and Selkirk. He had agreed to stand as far back as 1903, accepting the prospective parliamentary candidacy for his party. In this election, the parties were split between the free trade (Liberals) and tariff reform (Conservatives/Unionists) platforms. His acceptance has to be put down to a personal approach by Joseph Chamberlain, now retired from politics owing to ill-health, to whom, in a manner of speaking, he was in debt. They held many opinions in common on the subject of South Africa and the Empire, and it had been Chamberlain who had been instrumental in proposing Conan Doyle for his knighthood.

He went into the election with the ground well prepared. For three years, he had nursed the constituency, visiting it, pressing the flesh, speaking at local functions and allowing some of his stories to appear in local newspapers. He even captained an MCC cricket team to play a local match and took part in the 'common riding' of the bounds of Hawick common land on horseback, which he disliked as it involved a section taken at a gallop over rough ground. He worked hard cultivating the constituents and understanding the issues involved in tariff reform.

As an old-fashioned politician, Conan Doyle was loyal to his party leader, Arthur Balfour, who took over as Prime Minister in 1902 from Lord Salisbury, his uncle. It was the wrong horse to back. Balfour was out of step with the times and the public were no longer against the open trade markets with which tariff reforms would do away by building up a favoured trading status for the colonies, thereby protecting the Empire by making it into a trading bloc.

At the hustings, he was canny enough this time around to address local issues. Innes helped with his campaign and was taken aback by how well his brother spoke at election meetings. Conan Doyle abhorred the personal indignities thrown at him and despised the fact that honest questions were few and far between, both his supporters and his opponents indulging 'in cries and counter-cries with rival songs and slogans, so that as I approached the building it sounded like feeding-time at the Zoo. My heart often sank within me as I listened to the uproar, and I would ask myself what on earth I meant by placing myself in such a position.' As at Edinburgh, dealing with the rowdies tested his temper as well as his resolve and gave him valuable experience, for there was to be a time in his later life when he would need it.

Only once, it seems, his temper snapped. As he was waiting for a train to London, a supporter approached him with a 'familiar greeting and squeezed my right hand until my signet ring nearly cut me. It opened the sluice and out came a torrent of whaler language which I had hoped that I had long ago forgotten.' Such a short-tempered reaction was to become a trait of his in later years when he grew somewhat brusque with well-intentioned but, as he saw it, over-familiar acquaintances. His son, Adrian, remembered that he could be very sharp with anyone who took such liberties as to address him by his given name, uninvited.

Once again, he had no chance of winning the election, even though the local woollen industry had been undermined by cheap German imports. The concept of free trade was close to the heart of the intransigently conservative Scots. He was beaten by 3,133 votes to 2,444. His opponent, Thomas Shaw, had ignored the constituency and left all the canvassing to an assistant. Conan Doyle was peeved by this but took his defeat stoically. In the nation as a whole, Balfour was soundly rejected by a landslide victory that brought in Sir Henry Campbell-Bannerman as the Liberal Prime Minister.

After the election, Conan Doyle was lampooned in *Punch* as a strange animal, 'The Coneydoil or Shurlacombs'. 'This big friendly Creature,' the caption went, 'is very shrood and saggacious. If he finds a footprint he can tell you what coloured hair it has and whether it is a libbral or a conservative – which is very clever I think. He plays all games and always makes a hundred. He likes to run through the 'Strand' with his tail in parts – all of them strong and healthy – then he collects it all together and it runs for a long time by itself.'

In his autobiography, Conan Doyle wrote that politics was not for

him and that, after his defeat, he thought some other sort of public
service might be more to his liking. 'One likes to feel,' he wrote, 'that
one has some small practical influence upon the affairs of one's time.'
He might not have secured a seat in the House of Commons but he
moved in spheres of influence, being on good and often friendly terms
with such people as Chamberlain, Balfour, Lloyd George and Winston
Churchill.

On account of Louise's frail health, he no longer did as much
entertaining at Undershaw as before. It was, he finally realised, too
great a strain on her. There was one occasion, however, when he did
open the house to a party of French VIPs. In August 1905, the French
main fleet sailed into Portsmouth on a courtesy visit to celebrate the
signing of the Entente Cordiale. Joseph Caillaux, the French Minister
for Foreign Affairs, who was travelling on the flagship, was asked who
he and the staff officers accompanying him would like to meet during
their stay. Along with a list of dignitaries was Conan Doyle. He was
hugely flattered and, inviting them to Undershaw, put on a grand
reception for them.

For all his fame and fortune, not all was well. Louise's health was
failing and there were many occasions when he wished she were dead,
for her own sake and for his. The tuberculosis remission periods were
growing shorter and farther apart and she was in considerable pain from
her arthritis. He looked after her but he also felt guilty. And so he should.
He had neglected her, not in a material sense, for he had provided her
with all she needed and the best medical assistance possible, but in
his mind he had abandoned her. He was also worried. Jean was being
astonishingly philosophical in waiting for him to become her husband
but, the longer the situation went on, the more likely he believed it
was that she might grow tired of it and leave him for a younger,
more available man, even though she frequently assured him of her
constancy.

Suddenly, in the spring of 1906, Louise's health quickly deteriorated.
She died on 4 July aged forty-nine and was buried in Hindhead.

With her passing, Conan Doyle's guilt increased. He started to sleep
badly and his own health declined, although he was suffering from
no medical condition. His ability to work left him and he grew very
depressed.

Two months after her death, he went to Scotland, primarily to distract
himself from his predicament, and, whilst staying at an inn near Dunbar,
he was invited to visit Arthur Balfour, who lived just a few miles away
at Whittingehame. They had first met at the Beaconsfield home of Lord

Burnham, proprietor of the *Daily Telegraph*, who, by chance, lived in the house built by Waller's ancestor, the pragmatic royalist poet. On that occasion, Balfour had unwittingly opened the door of a Turkish bath to find the creator of Sherlock Holmes sweating it out before him in a bundle of towels.

The house party at Whittingehame revived his spirits and somewhat dispelled his gloom. It was, he realised, now time to move on in life and get involved in new directions.

One of the first of these concerned George Edalji, a solicitor of Parsee extraction.

12

The Pony Molester,
an Upholsterer's Hammer and Other Injustices

From the earliest days of Sherlock Holmes, Conan Doyle was frequently asked to solve crimes or mysteries, even being sent clues to assist him, and he collected newspaper cuttings of crimes that interested him. On occasion, he responded to pleas for help whilst, on others, he took an interest of his own volition.

As a doctor, he possessed many of the attributes of a good detective. His memory was exceptional, his powers of observation finely sharpened, and his ability to assimilate and co-ordinate random information superb. Writing the Sherlock Holmes stories had sharpened his deductive skills, although he was always quick to point out that in these the solution came before the mystery unfolded or the crime was committed, at least on paper.

In the main, he was requested to look into disappearances. One case centred on a man who had withdrawn his entire bank balance and vanished from a London hotel during the evening. His relatives asked Conan Doyle if he could help. Assuming the bank withdrawal to have been deliberate, he guessed that the man had left the hotel at around eleven o'clock, mixing with the throngs of theatre audiences. He would not have fled so late if he was staying in London, so he must have left the capital and, at that time of night, by train from a major terminus where he could hide in the crowds. The overnight express for Scotland left Euston at midnight, so Conan Doyle suggested they look for their missing man in Edinburgh or Glasgow. He was correct.

THE DOCTOR, THE DETECTIVE AND ARTHUR CONAN DOYLE

The case, he noted, was 'to show that the general lines of reasoning advocated by Holmes have a real practical application to life'.

He was also involved in cases of theft, including the 1901 loss of the family jewels belonging to the Marquess of Anglesey, valued at the time at £150,000. Six years later, he was called in on another jewellery theft case connected to his family when a diamond badge, a diamond star and five collars mounted with gemstones, in essence the Irish crown jewels, were stolen from a safe in a tower in Dublin Castle, where they were under the protection of his mother's relative, Sir Arthur Vicars. There was, he felt, little he could do towards solving the case, and he did not become involved. This was just as well, for the scandal was considerable and might have rubbed off on him. Vicars, as Ulster King-of-Arms, had a coterie of men called Heralds around him. His deputy, Francis Shackleton, brother of the explorer, was a confidant of the Duke of Argyll, Edward VII's brother-in-law, and a member of a high-society homosexual ring in London and Dublin. In due course, the whole matter became so sticky that the police abandoned the case, the Heralds resigned and Vicars was removed from his post and ruined whilst Shackleton died in poverty in 1925.

Not all the requests were domestic. In 1913, a noble Polish family was to tell him he could set his own terms if he went to Warsaw to study the case of one of their number charged with murder. Conan Doyle was tempted to go but had to turn the opportunity down.

His interest in crime led to his being made a member of the Crimes Club in 1904. It was formed the previous year to debate famous criminal cases, and included amongst its members Bertram Fletcher Robinson and A.E.W. Mason, who was now writing his own series of detective stories about a police detective called Inspector Hanaud. At the meetings, the evidence of real unsolved crimes was available for study, with real criminals occasionally coming in to lecture on specific criminality.

By this time, Conan Doyle had occasionally started to write about true crime, although not in a sensationalist manner. The *Strand Magazine* had published a series of articles on the history of crime in 1901 entitled 'Strange Studies from Life', in which he wrote, 'In the study of criminal psychology one is forced to the conclusion that the most dangerous of all types of mind is that of the inordinately selfish man. He is a man who has lost his sense of proportion. His own will and his own interest have blotted out for him the duty which he owes to the community . . . The player who makes the mistake of selfishness may have a terrible forfeit to pay – but the unaccountable thing in the rules is that some, who are only spectators of his game, may have to help him in the paying.' Despite such a statement, Conan Doyle was uninterested in criminal psychology. As far as he was concerned, life was black and white. The innocent had to be delivered from injustice and the guilty locked away. It was his opinion that hardened criminals should be given life sentences and that was an end to it.

Justice and injustice were at the core of Conan Doyle's thinking. Sherlock Holmes saw that justice was done or injustice prevented and that was his role, too. All his life Conan Doyle fought injustice, from his days in a back street in Portsmouth onwards, and, because of his gentlemanly code of honour, he was never reticent in speaking out against it. An injustice uncovered enraged him. As Eden Phillpotts was to remark, 'Any rank instance of injustice instantly won a swift response from Conan Doyle and, without one selfish thought of fear, he would sanctify his whole great resources to fighting what he felt to be wrong or reversing any verdict that he deemed unjust.' At times, Conan Doyle could get very hot under the collar. His temper was roused by injustice and, although the outburst might be short, it was nevertheless violent. One of his acquaintances declared, 'I would rather face a pistol at five paces, than face the blaze of anger, or the cold contempt in Doyle's eyes, had I done that which gave him just cause to think me a liar, a cad, or a traitor to his or my country.' It was not only acquaintances who were in awe of Conan Doyle. Anyone dissenting from his viewpoint was likely to come under fire. In 1915, Innes wrote to argue in favour of conscription, of which Conan Doyle disapproved. His letter began familiarly enough with 'Dear Old Boy', but continued, 'I have written so many letters to you about compulsory service and torn them up that I can't remember what I have said and what I have not. I always feel like a rabbit in front of a boa constrictor when I try to put any opinions before you. I never dare to say to you that I don't agree at all and yet that is substantially the case about this . . .' At the time, Innes was an assistant adjutant-general on the Western Front.

On two famous occasions, Conan Doyle took up the call to arms to fight for what he deemed to be cases of injustice brought about by an ineffectual application of the law. The first concerned George Edalji.

Towards the end of 1906, in an edition of the *Umpire*, primarily a sporting magazine which also included general news items, he came upon an article entitled 'Edalji Protests His Innocence'. The sincerity of the piece caught his eye, although he had unknowingly already been approached by Edalji. Alfred Wood, Conan Doyle's secretary, had opened the correspondence but had set it aside as one of those matters his employer might be interested in when his spirits were higher. Conan Doyle was, at the time, in mourning for Louise.

The case was a curious one. The Edalji family lived in Great Wyrley, north-west of Birmingham. Edalji senior, the Reverend Shapurji Edalji, was a Parsee convert to the Church of England and a vicar married to an Englishwoman by whom he had three children including a son, George, born in 1876. The family suffered a good deal of racial intolerance: the locals referred to Reverend Edalji as a nigger and the family was subjected to campaigns of abuse, practical jokes and poisoned pen letters, a servant confessing to the latter in 1888. Then, in 1892, the letters started up again and ran for three years. They were in a different hand from the previous missives. Without evidence, Captain George Anson, the local chief constable, accused the sixteen-year-old George, by now an exemplary pupil at Walsall Grammar School, of writing them himself. The letters stopped.

In 1903, a bizarre twist occurred in the saga of abuse. A number of sheep, cows and horses in the area were mutilated, their stomachs cut open in the middle of the night. Anonymous letters accused George Edalji, now twenty-seven years old and employed as a solicitor in Birmingham, although he still lived with his parents. He was arrested in August and charged with disembowelling a pony in a field a few hundred yards from his parents' house. Granted a search warrant, the police found four blood-stained razors, a pair of muddy boots, muddied trousers and a damp, stained coat in the Edaljis' house. The razor stains were later found to be rust and the mud shown not to match the soil in the pony's field. Notwithstanding all this, the police prosecuted. A calligraphic expert declared that Edalji had written the anonymous accusatory letters. Ominously, the expert was Thomas Gurrin, whose testimony had already imprisoned one innocent man, Adolf Beck, seven years before.

Reverend Edalji swore that his son's alibi was solid, but his word as a priest was dismissed. The police altered their evidence to fit their case. The public was outraged and the whole affair was blown up into a racial issue, the mutilations of the animals being seen as a religious cult activity. George was sentenced to seven years' hard labour, which he served at Lewes in Sussex and, later, at Portland in Dorset, where he broke stones in the quarry. That the attacks on animals continued after Edalji was put away was discounted; the attacks said to be perpetrated by other members of the same cult.

This was not the end of the matter. A judge, R. D. Yelverton, organised a 10,000-signature petition, many of the signatories being barristers and solicitors, presenting it to the Home Office. After serving three years, Edalji was unexpectedly released from prison without compensation, explanation or a pardon. Having lost his law career, he pleaded his side of the story in the periodical *Truth*, other papers taking it up and exposing the farce of the investigation and trial.

When Conan Doyle read about it, he was convinced, writing, 'the unmistakable accent of truth forced itself upon my attention, and I realized that I was in the presence of an appalling tragedy, and that I was called upon to do what I could to set it right'. From December 1906 to August 1907, he investigated the matter in detail. For inspiration and guidance, he studied the documentation that the Crime Club had amassed referring to the Adolph Beck case, which had been reopened. Beck had been released as innocent of his crime in 1901 but rearrested in 1904, and was only saved from a second stretch of imprisonment by virtue of the guilty criminal being uncovered as a result of a joint Crime Club/*Daily Mail* newspaper investigation.

Satisfied that he was familiar with all the details, Conan Doyle met Edalji early in January 1907. Immediately, he saw a flaw in the police case. It was blatantly obvious to him. Edalji, apart from being a man of slight and almost weedy stature, was severely myopic with a pronounced squint. There was no way he could have crossed a field in darkness, then manhandled and maimed a pony. After closely questioning him, Conan Doyle visited the Staffordshire police and examined their evidence. This done, he set to work with his pen. His first in-depth article was published in the *Daily Telegraph* on 11 and 12 January. It summarised the case and drew the deduction that Edalji was innocent. This was followed up with a large number of letters to the press. He was stirring the pot. The *Daily Chronicle* published an editorial on the matter which could not have pleased him, for its central point was that, at last, Sherlock Holmes was having a real adventure. 'It is a tribute to the force,' the editorial read, 'with which he has impressed the personality of his hero upon the reader's mind that one instinctively merges the creator in his creation, and thinks of this special investigation as the work of the great Sherlock. So far as the story goes at present, nobody who makes this identification will be disappointed.' Next, knowing the influence his Boer War pamphlet had exercised, he published an 18,000-word booklet on 20 January, 'The Story of Mr George Edalji', in which he condemned Edalji's persecution and attacked police prejudice and inefficacy.

Believing Edalji to be innocent, Conan Doyle then set out to try to discover who was guilty. His suspicions fell upon two brothers, Royden and Wallace Sharpe. The former had been expelled from

Walsall Grammar School (where he was a contemporary of Edalji), had a reputation for forging letters, had been accused of ripping up railway carriage seats, had been a butcher's apprentice, and had gone away to sea on a cattle boat on which he learnt to handle livestock, his absence at sea coinciding with the cessation of the anonymous letters to the Edalji family. Furthermore, he was a racist, had a grudge against Edalji and was considered easily capable of cruelty to animals. In his booklet, Conan Doyle did not name the Sharpes because the police had warned him he would be prosecuted for libel if he did, so he called them by a pseudonym. When it was presented to them, officialdom would not accept any of this research and declared there would be no further opening of the investigation to consider the Sharpes' involvement.

Edalji became an instant national *cause célèbre*. An Edalji Committee was instituted with Conan Doyle and Jerome K. Jerome amongst its members, demanding to know why no pardon had been issued. The Home Secretary was forced to instigate a commission which published its findings in May. These stated that Edalji was innocent of the pony attack but guilty of writing the letters, thus still denying Edalji any compensation because he had perverted the course of justice. A pardon, but no payment, was forthcoming. Conan Doyle was livid and wrote in his autobiography, 'The sad fact is that officialdom in England stands solid together, and that when you are forced to attack it, you need not expect justice.' He had good reason to think this: one of the three-man commission members was Sir Albert de Rutzen, chief magistrate of the Metropolitan Police Courts but also a second cousin of Captain George Anson. Four years on, with a new Home Secretary in office, Conan Doyle attempted to get Edalji a retrial but was unsuccessful. The ruckus he had caused, however, did bring into question the efficiency of the law and led to the establishment of the Court of Criminal Appeal in 1907.

In recent years, some doubt has been cast on the Edalji affair. Research suggests that George was not all he seemed to be. Whilst he was almost certainly innocent of the pony molestation, there were rumours that he had misappropriated his clients' money and was not gentle and self-effacing but the owner of a devious and vicious mind. Whether or not Conan Doyle came to know of this evidence has yet to come to light. It may well be that he had rushed to Edalji's defence so quickly, jumping into the cause with more indignation that prudence, that he had failed to see any other side to him. It appears, however, that at the time he was ignorant of Edalji's possibly dubious background, for, on 18 September 1907, he was one of the guests at the wedding reception of Sir Arthur Conan Doyle and Miss Jean Leckie.

The wedding ceremony, in St Margaret's Church, Westminster, was a private family affair but it was reported around the world. The *Buenos Aires Standard* ran the headline 'Sherlock Holmes Quietly Married'.

Innes was the best man and Cyril Angell conducted the ceremony with his and Dodo's five-year-old son as page-boy. All the Doyle family, including his children by Louise, both now well into their teens, were present save Lottie. At the reception in the Hotel Metropole, Conan Doyle, aged forty-eight, carried his bride up the steps to avoid her tripping over her train. The guest list of 250 included Jerome K. Jerome, J.M. Barrie, George Newnes and Bram Stoker. It was the beginning of what Conan Doyle had sought for so long, a happy and fulfilling marriage with a soul mate as well as a wife. It was to last for twenty-three years with hardly a harsh word to disrupt it.

Conan Doyle's new marriage may have been blissful, but many were not, and he was only too conscious of the fact. His first marriage apart, in which the misery was caused not by disharmony but disease, he had memories of his parents' life together, from which his mother had never sought release through divorce: it would have been impossible in any case because of the strictures of the divorce legislation.

The law in England, ratified in 1857, was biased in favour of the husband, who could obtain a divorce on the simple grounds of unfaithfulness whereas the wife had to prove several years' desertion before she could petition. Physical abuse and cruelty were slim defences. In his autobiography, Conan Doyle remarked that he could not 'understand why England should lag behind every other Protestant country in the world, and even behind Scotland, so that unions which are obviously disgusting and degrading are maintained in this country while they can be dissolved in our Colonies or abroad'. He determined to do something about it and joined the Divorce Law Reform Union, founded in 1906 with the express aim of addressing the woman's rights. The union sought equal divorce rights for men and women, extending the grounds for divorce from unfaithfulness and desertion to insanity, chronic alcoholism, cruelty and the lengthy imprisonment of a spouse. A number of leading literary figures were involved in the society, including Thomas Hardy. Conan Doyle was elected president of the union in 1909 and remained in office for a decade.

The entire issue struck a painful chord in Conan Doyle. He could remember well the problems that had arisen in his own life as a result of Charles's drinking, and he knew first-hand of the effects a miserable marriage had upon any children brought up in an atmosphere of marital discord. His memories were sharply focused in a letter he published in the *Morning Post* in 1913. 'The wail of the helpless child,' he wrote, 'who is brought up in an atmosphere of drunkenness, cruelty, and brutality, which the law enforces as its unchangeable environment, is the most powerful voice which can be raised against our present dispensation.' Whilst there is no suggestion at all of Charles having been cruel or brutal to either his wife or children, Conan Doyle must have seen such barbarities carried out in the crowded tenements of his childhood Edinburgh.

In true style, he wrote a publication, *Divorce Law Reform*, in 1909 which was instrumental in having a Royal Commission of Inquiry sworn in. In November 1912, the commission published its deliberations which agreed in the main with his proposals, but the time was not politically ripe for initiating them. The Church also opposed the recommendations, stating quite bluntly that Conan Doyle was a meddling busybody who lacked Christian belief and did not appreciate the moral and religious basis of existing divorce legislation. It was a grossly unfair aspersion but typical of the established Church of England's bigotry. Matters were delayed until 1923, whilst the actual divorce law reform in its entirety did not enter the statute books until after Conan Doyle's death.

This was not the only occasion in the years immediately before the First World War on which Conan Doyle entered into religious controversy. In 1910, he addressed what he saw as an injustice against Roman Catholicism, despite his antipathy towards Rome. He believed the wording of the Coronation Oath made deprecatory reference to Roman Catholics, and he tried to have it altered for the crowning of King George V: he had, in fact, addressed the matter before the coronation of his predecessor, Edward VII, but to no avail. In a letter to *The Times* in May, he suggested that 'all creeds should receive the same courteous and respectful treatment so long as their adherents are members of the common Empire. To bring these mediaeval rancours to an end would indeed be an auspicious opening of a new reign.' The wording was changed, although his was not the only voice raised in protest against this iniquity.

His other religious controversy was anti-Catholic. Later in his life, he made vitriolic attacks on two fronts. The first was his concern that it was immoral and degrading for celibate priests to hear the confessions of young women which might contain sexual admissions. The second was his utterly scathing criticism of the way young girls were recruited into convents where, he maintained, they lived sorrowful, repressed existences in contradiction of their original ideals. In these two battles against injustice, his protests failed.

Conan Doyle may have fought for the cause of women but he was utterly against suffragettes and the cause of suffrage unless the women were taxpayers in their own right. It was, he thought, pointless to let them have the vote. It was a husband's role, he considered, to look after his wife as best he could and, if he succeeded, there was no need for female emancipation. It was not that he was prejudiced against women. He had shown he was not biased by his dedication to divorce law reform and his personal code of honour which had seen him stand by Louise through years of illness. An anecdote in support of his attitude to women was told by his son, Adrian, who as a teenager commented on a certain woman as being ugly. Conan Doyle was furious and told him that no woman was ugly, that every woman was beautiful but that some were more beautiful than others. In Conan Doyle's opinion, men had traditional roles to play as protective husbands and women had their part to play as succouring wives tending the family. The explanation for his support of women in the divorce court but not on the stage of human rights lies in the fact that he saw himself as a chivalrous protector of women who, in a soured marriage, could be physically abused and mentally scarred by an errant spouse but, where suffrage was concerned, women were to his mind not at risk and so he saw no need to champion them. The suffragettes were not behaving as women should and, as a consequence, qualified for neither sympathy nor assistance. Where the suffragettes were concerned, it was more a case of his not wanting to see the social status quo change, and his chivalrous code of honour was set aside in response to their arguments. When they started destroying property and became more militant, his remarks became withering and he was outspoken in his attack on their methods which, he also pointed out were, in his opinion, doing their own cause and argument harm. For his unequivocal plain speaking, he had sulphuric acid poured through his letterbox along with a large amount of almost equally caustic correspondence.

In addition to his chivalrous regard for women, Conan Doyle maintained two other principles in life which he believed made the gentleman. The first was his belief that one had to be utterly truthful where business and money were concerned: a man's word was his bond and his cheques, presented on demand, did not bounce. The second was his firm conviction that a gentleman owed a debt of consideration and courtesy to those lower down the social ladder than himself. Adrian Conan Doyle recalled receiving from his father what he termed 'a white blast of fury' when Conan Doyle found out that his son had been discourteous to a servant. This attitude of what might today be interpreted as social superiority was not born of snobbery but founded in the traditional gentlemanly principle that those who were better off had a duty of responsibility towards those who depended upon them and upon whom they, in turn, depended. It was, in other words, a stable master-and-servant relationship by which English society was governed.

His code of personal morality demanded that he seek to right any injustices he saw levelled at the lower orders. His attitude is well summed up by a letter he wrote in 1900 to a trade journal, the *Grocers' Assistant*, which states, 'The matter of shorter hours for shop assistants is one in which I take the deepest interest, believing that in a country which has no compulsory military service physique and well being of members of the class to which you allude can only be guaranteed by a universal adoption of short hours and frequent holidays.' Twenty years on, he actively engaged himself on behalf of chambermaids at the Metropole Hotel in Brighton who were being forced to take wage cuts or be dismissed.

The second noted criminal case in which Conan Doyle involved himself was that of Oscar Slater. At first, he was loath to have anything to do with the matter but, after reading a report of the case in April 1910, and having been contacted by Slater's lawyers, who admired what he had done for Edalji, he came to believe that a severe miscarriage of justice had once more occurred.

This was no racially motivated pony slashing. It was a murder case. Oscar Slater had been found guilty, on little more than circumstantial evidence, of murdering eighty-two-year-old Miss Marion Gilchrist on 21 December 1908.

· The victim had lived in a first-floor flat at 15 Queen's Terrace, West Princes Street, Glasgow. She was said to be a reclusive old lady who received few visitors and was looked after by a young maidservant, Helen Lambie. On the evening in question, the maid left the house as was her custom, to buy her mistress a newspaper. Miss Gilchrist then locked the door, which was fitted with several locks, for the old lady was very security-conscious on account of possessing £3,000 worth of jewellery. Shortly after the maid left, the downstairs neighbour, Arthur Adams, heard three knocks on his ceiling which signalled that Miss Gilchrist wanted help. These were followed by a thud. Adams went upstairs. The door of the building giving on to the street was open but the apartment door was shut.

The maid returned and she and Adams went upstairs, passing a man descending on the way. Adams, who was poor-sighted, thought he was respectably dressed. Helen Lambie described him as being about five foot six inches tall, dark and clean-shaven, wearing a light grey overcoat and a dark cap. A fourteen-year-old, Mary Barrowman, later attested to meeting a man leaving the building, but she said he was wearing a fawn coat, brown boots and a round hat. When Adams and the maid entered Miss Gilchrist's flat, they found her bludgeoned to death. Her personal papers, including her recently changed will which was kept in a wooden box, had been rifled, but only a crescent-shaped diamond brooch was missing.

The police bungled the case from the start. They failed thoroughly to search the building and look for a motive amongst the victim's relatives. There was public outcry at the brutality of the murder and they wanted a quick arrest. Five days later, they announced that they were searching for Oscar Slater, who had attempted to sell a pawn ticket for a diamond brooch.

Slater was an ideal scapegoat. A German Jew from Silesia, whose real name was Joseph Leschziner, he was known to the police as an illegal gambling-den operator. He had only lived in Glasgow for six weeks, just a street or two from Miss Gilchrist. Five days after the murder, Slater and his young French mistress boarded the liner *Lusitania* in Liverpool, bound for New York, booking their berth under false names. His photograph was shown to the maid and Mary Barrowman, who agreed he was the man they had seen. The police telegraphed New York, Slater was arrested when the liner docked, and the witnesses were sent to America to identify him. In his possession, the New York police found a small upholsterer's hammer which, it was claimed, was the murder weapon. Slater waved aside extradition and agreed to return of his own volition to prove his innocence. He thought this would be easy as the pawn ticket was for a brooch he had put into hock well before the murder.

The trial, in May 1909, was a stitch-up. The police knew the pawned brooch was not Miss Gilchrist's and the prosecution case, handled by Lord Advocate Ure, was full of holes, but a dozen witnesses testified to seeing Slater in the proximity of Queen's Terrace on the night of the murder. Slater's alibi was refused and he was forbidden to take the stand. The judge's summing up painted Slater as a debauched man who lived off the immoral earnings of prostitutes, which was irrelevant and, in any case, hearsay. The jury, prejudiced against him, found him guilty on a majority vote and he was sentenced to death.

Slater, who was a petty criminal and possibly a pimp, spent three weeks in the condemned cell but, on 25 May, two days before his execution, his sentence was commuted to imprisonment with hard labour for life. Slater's lawyer had waited until the clamour of the trial subsided, then organised a petition of twenty thousand signatures. The commuting of the sentence, the many inconsistencies in the prosecution case and the general sense that Slater was being framed aroused Conan Doyle's curiosity. 'I went into the matter,' he wrote, 'most reluctantly, but when I glanced at the facts, I saw that it was an even worse case than the Edalji one, and that this unhappy man had in all probability no more to do with the murder for which he had been condemned than I had.'

Conan Doyle did not like Slater. He was a member of the criminal underclass but, that notwithstanding, he was innocent and still deserved justice. With his usual thoroughness, Conan Doyle read through the transcripts of the trial and, after assessing these and corresponding with the prosecution witnesses, he published a booklet, 'The Case of Oscar Slater', in August 1912. In it, he drew attention to the flimsy prosecution case, the contradictory evidence of the witnesses and the date of the pawning of the brooch which Slater had used to raise money for the voyage to America. He also explained how Slater and his mistress had used false names to give Slater's wife the slip, but that they had used their real names when booking into a hotel in Liverpool, prior to embarking on the *Lusitania*. He went on to show that the upholsterer's tack hammer was too light to inflict the wounds from which Miss Gilchrist had died, and that it was too long to be a concealed weapon. If he had been carrying it from the scene of the crime, the witnesses would have noticed it. He added that there was no blood on it or on Slater's clothing. From the crime scene evidence report, he deduced that the murderer had been more interested in the victim's documents than her jewellery, and that the theft of the brooch was a red herring. The victim, he concluded, must have known her killer.

The booklet sold only because it bore Conan Doyle's name. The public generally had little interest in the innocence of a low life. Yet it did create enough of a stir to raise a question in Parliament and demands for a retrial. A commission of inquiry was appointed in 1914. It met *in camera* but some new evidence was presented to it. Slater's alibi was upheld by a grocer called MacBrayne. A Glasgow detective, Lieutenant John Trench, confirmed that the maid had actually named the murderer to Miss Gilchrist's niece, Miss Birrell, but that his superiors had told him to suppress it. Both women denied this. Trench was disgraced, sacked from the police and stripped of his pension. In spite of the new evidence, the commission members still decided not to overrule the sentence. It was a hollow victory, Conan Doyle not achieving all he wanted, at least for the time being.

As if national injustices were not enough, Conan Doyle took on some that were foreign, most notably his attack on the situation in the Belgian Congo.

During the nineteenth-century dismemberment of Africa by white colonialists, the International Association of the Congo had been founded by the Belgian King Leopold II, the Congress of Berlin handing over the administration of the Congo to him in 1885. He declared it the Congo Free State. It was in effect neither free nor a state but a private estate belonging to the King of the Belgians, who owned and exploited it. Roger Casement, appointed British consul in the capital of Boma, began to be concerned about the ill-treatment, mutilations, executions and forced labour of disenfranchised natives employed in the rubber industry. He drew the situation to the attention of the British government and, in 1904, founded the Congo Reform Association with Edmund Dene Morel, a journalist and African shipping line agent in Liverpool, as secretary, Lord Beauchamp as president and with the support of Evelyn Baring, now the first Earl of Cromer, as well as over a hundred Members of Parliament. It was agreed by Parliament that a report should be published based upon Casement's findings. This was duly done and sent to all the other European nations, including Belgium. King Leopold, faced with no other alternative, sent out a commission to look into the accusations. They carried out a thorough whitewash and, in 1908, the King passed the administration of the Congo Free State to the Belgian government, which made no real effort to address the iniquities.

The Congo Reform Association wrote to many influential writers for their support, amongst them Joseph Conrad and Conan Doyle, who thought the evidence so atrocious he had to do something. After meeting Morel in the summer of 1909, he put his back to the wheel and, as always in such cases, went into a Sherlock Holmesian retreat in his study, drinking coffee to keep himself going through long hours of reading. His son was to mention how, on such occasions when he got the bit between his teeth, he would not remove his slippers or leave the house for days on end. The whole building would fall silent with family and servants creeping about like mice. Trays of food left by his door went uneaten. On one occasion, he was so engrossed that his son noticed him wearing odd shoes.

The result of his endeavours was 'The Crime of the Congo', 45,000 words long and written in eight days, the effort sustained 'by a burning indignation, which is the best of all driving power'.

The treatise written, the entreaties began. Conan Doyle wrote to the papers, including a circular to sixty American publications, and to influential politicians and leaders ranging from Kaiser Wilhelm II to President Theodore Roosevelt, whom he was to meet the following year when he was in London, returning from one of his wildlife slaughtering safaris in Africa. Copies of the book were mailed to a large number of power-brokers on both sides of the Atlantic, and Conan Doyle went on a three-month national lecture tour on the subject. The book received international notice although it was criticised for its strong language which he defended by stating, 'There are times when violence is a duty.' It was graphically illustrated with pictures of mutilated natives. Conan Doyle once more accepted no payment.

He was not as successful as in some of the national cases in which he was involved. The Congo was far away and an international political problem. The American government, having no holdings in Africa and not wanting any after the intiquities of the slave trade, were lukewarm about the problem. Roosevelt wrote to Conan Doyle that his motto was 'Never draw unless you intend to shoot'. The European colonial powers were also loath to intervene. It was one thing to be indignant but altogether another to get involved.

Conan Doyle, now regarded as social crusader *par excellence*, was praised for his humanitarian zeal but, although other forces were also at work, he had his impact. By 1913, with a new Belgian monarch on the throne, reforms in the Belgian Congo were in place and what Conan Doyle had rather histrionically termed 'the sack of a country, the spoilation of a nation, the greatest crime in all history' was considerably lessened, although Belgian atrocities continued to occur for the next forty-five years.

His crusading for the Congo prevented him from accepting an invitation at which he would, as a sportsman, have otherwise leapt. In December 1909, he was asked to referee the world heavyweight boxing championship bout between Jim Jeffries and Jack Johnson which was to be staged in America the following July. Initially, he was all for going until friends explained that the fight was more than a boxing match. Jeffries was white and Johnson was black. The two fighters' managers had been at odds as to who might be an impartial referee, and the only person they could amicably agree upon was Conan Doyle. The race card was going to be as important as the match programme. After a week of indecision, he reluctantly declined on the grounds that the Congo was more important.

Boxing was a professional sport and, although he would dearly have loved to have refereed a world-class fight, Conan Doyle generally decried the professionalism that was creeping into sport. It was felt at the special Olympic Games held in Athens in 1906 and, later, at the regular Games in London in 1908, that some sportsmen, especially those from the USA, were entering as amateurs when they were, in fact, professionals. Conan Doyle, it goes without saying, added his voice to the clamour. To him, this was a matter of unfair competition, an injustice to be commented upon. Sport should be played for its own sake, not for personal or national aggrandisement. Professionalism was contrary to sportsmanship in his book.

At the 1908 Games, Conan Doyle was at the very centre of the controversy. He was on the field as a special correspondent for the *Daily Mail* covering the marathon. The first runner into the stadium was the Italian Pietri Dorando, who was close to collapsing from fatigue. Some spectators, Conan Doyle amongst their number, guided and helped the exhausted and confused runner to the finishing line. For being so aided, Dorando was disqualified, the gold medal going to an American. There was a public outcry. The Italian had not requested assistance so he could hardly be accused of unsportsmanlike behaviour. It is likely that he was hardly aware of the help he was given. Queen Alexandra, being so annoyed at the injustice, had a special gold cup cast, awarding it to Dorando herself. Conan Doyle, in the meantime, opened a subscription list for Dorando in the *Daily Mail* which collected sufficient money for him to open a bakery in his home town in Italy. There were those who believed that Conan Doyle felt guilty for having steered the runner in the direction of the finishing tape and that his fund-raising efforts were aimed at assuaging his guilt as well as morally supporting the Italian. Whatever the truth of the matter, it was yet another instance of injustice to which Conan Doyle addressed his energies and influence.

In the next Olympics, held in Stockholm in 1912, the British team performed abysmally and Conan Doyle was put in charge of the national committee preparing the team for the 1916 Games in Berlin. He threw himself into the task, bringing the various in-fighting factions on the Olympic committee to the table and pressing upon them the need for cohesion and co-operation in raising the money required for the team.

He was, of course, never to see his efforts bear fruit: an international contest of a different sort occupied Europe in 1916.

The same year, 1912, Conan Doyle took up the cudgel against injustice in an unlikely fight with George Bernard Shaw. On the night of 14 April, the *Titanic* sank. Amongst those passengers who died was William Stead, Conan Doyle's friend and the pacifist by whom he had been so angered during the Boer War. The press made much of the captain's bravery and the courage of the ship's orchestra which had kept playing as the vessel went down, but the papers also made up a good deal of what they reported. They needed good copy and, in the absence of hard facts, fabricated stories to fill the pages. A month later, in the *Daily News and Leader*, George Bernard Shaw published an article headed 'Some Unmentioned Morals', which begged the question as to why such a disaster prompted such 'an explosion of outrageous romantic lying'. He said, amongst other things, that the concept of 'Women and children first' was flawed and impractical as they needed men to row and steer the lifeboats, and the captain was hardly heroic when it was his fault the ship hit an iceberg at full speed in the first place.

Conan Doyle was furious and, a week later, published a response to Shaw, supporting the captain's heroism and accusing Shaw of shamelessness. Shaw's letter, he asserted, was 'written professedly in the interests of truth, and accuses every one around of lying. Yet I can never remember any production which contained so much that was false within the same compass.' Then, one by one, he attacked Shaw's arguments, illustrating how he had twisted the facts to suit his purpose and ending, 'it is a pitiful sight to see a man of undoubted genius using his gifts in order to misrepresent and decry his own people'.

Two days later, Shaw answered. He was more than a match for Conan Doyle in such an argument and skilfully destroyed every accusation levelled at him. Taking umbrage at being called a liar, albeit in not quite so many words, he proclaimed Conan Doyle had made a 'romantic and warm-hearted protest' but went on to say that the *Titanic*'s captain had not, as Conan Doyle had put it, 'made a terrible mistake' but had been negligent. Conan Doyle curtly closed the exchange by denying that he had accused Shaw of lying, ending his short letter, 'The worst I think or say of Mr Shaw is that his many brilliant gifts do not include the power of weighing evidence; nor has he that quality – call it good taste, humanity, or what you will – which prevents a man from needlessly hurting the feelings of others.' Shaw had perhaps won the logical argument but the nation stood behind Conan Doyle and those who could no longer answer for themselves, whom he was always ready to champion.

Not only humans received the benefit of Conan Doyle's desire to see justice served. On 22 April 1913, at the Mark Cross petty sessions in East Sussex, he stood in court on behalf of his own collie dog, Roy. A farmer claimed that the dog had killed one of his sheep. Conan Doyle put up a spirited defence, with witnesses, arguing that the dog was too old to chase sheep, that it had never chased sheep found near its home and that it suffered from a disease that prevented it from eating anything hard. A vet gave supporting evidence of the disease, a bailiff near Undershaw announced that the dog had never worried his sheep, and Conan Doyle's chauffeur assured the court that the dog had never gone after sheep on the road. At that point, the magistrate dismissed the case. Another underdog had received justice because of Sir Arthur Conan Doyle.

About the same time, birds became another beneficiary of his crusading. He was a prime activist behind the movement to ban the fashionable use of exotic birds' feathers in women's couture. This led to the Plumage (Prohibition) Bill placed before the House of Commons early in 1914, although the fashion lobby were to greatly reduce its effectiveness through a series of sweeping amendments.

Behind all his crusading there lay more than just Conan Doyle's desire to see fair play and the maintenance of honour and chivalry. There was a feeling that he did not want change, that his real aim was to ensure the survival of the old-fashioned virtues of courtesy, consideration and doing what was right. He was a conventionalist for whom change, just for the sake of it, was anathema. It had to have purpose and reason behind it. Yet with the virtues came the old-fashioned prejudices which he could not overcome.

His attitude towards change can be summed up in his reaction to the new directions in which art was moving. When, in 1910, an exhibition of Post-Impressionists was mounted at the Grafton Gallery, he went along to view it. Gauguin, Cézanne and Matisse were, he thought, appalling. Many of the critics agreed with him but that was not the point. To Conan Doyle, they were not bad because they lacked artistic merit: they were bad because they were different. He had considered the Pre-Raphaelites and Impressionists to be odd but the Post-Impressionists and the Italian Futurists, with their concept of movement in painting, seemed utterly deviant.

Although always ready to improve the world around him, eager to take on any new challenge or try out any new invention – motor cars and the wireless fascinated him – he was still conservative at heart. It was not that he was an old-fashioned humbug. In some respects, he was even in favour of the newly formed Labour Party, which he believed could be a winner if it could retain its integrity, although he would not support it, admitting it had faults: he was wary of the power the trade unions exercised over it. He agreed with some socialist views, as he illustrated in his autobiography: 'Our marriage laws, our land laws, the cheapening of justice and many other things have long called out for reform, and if the old parties will not do it then we must seek some new one which will.' Nevertheless, he was not so enamoured of socialism than he wanted to vote it into power.

In his diary for July 1912, commenting upon the state of modern art, Conan Doyle wrote that one of the characteristics of the present age was a wave of artistic and intellectual insanity which he saw breaking out in various forms in various places. If it stopped where it was, he suggested, it would be only a curious phenomenon but, if it was an on-going movement, it would be sure to herald vast human changes.

He could not have guessed what vast and terrible changes were on their way as the result of a far worse insanity.

13

New Worlds, Lost Worlds

Once married, the Conan Doyles started life afresh and moved into a house called Windlesham in the small town of Crowborough on the edge of the Ashdown Forest in Sussex, to which town Jean's parents had moved from Blackheath. In addition, because of his commitments in London, Conan Doyle also rented a flat at 15 Buckingham Palace Mansions.

On the outskirts of the town, the house stood in extensive grounds off a quiet lane. It was not in some ways as grand a property as Undershaw but it was still an imposing building to which they added over the years, with a somewhat baronial staircase to the right of which his secretary had an office. The main reception rooms overlooked the gardens with a vast billiard room next to the dining room which reached across the entire width of the house and could be converted into a ballroom if needed. Conan Doyle's study was on the first floor in the south-west corner of the house, from which he had sweeping views over the Sussex Downs. Every room was filled with books. Callers claimed it was like visiting a library. The grounds were not in good order when they moved in but Jean was a keen gardener who set about bringing them into shape, planting a rose garden and arboreal walks, several shrubberies and a kitchen garden. A small wooden structure, less than a gazebo but more than a shed, stood in the gardens, providing a sanctuary for Conan Doyle, who worked or read there, being joined in the late afternoon by Jean who took tea with him.

His new wife changed Conan Doyle's life. Gone were the pressures of looking after Louise, whom he respected but did not in the end love, the years of sexual frustration and marital subterfuge. Writing comparatively little in the first few years of his marriage, he shared the gardening with Jean, played sport and entertained lavishly, often on a much more formal scale than had happened at Undershaw, his wife proving to be an excellent hostess. In 1912, the British Medical Association even held their annual conference at Windlesham, the billiard room being turned into a convention centre. Jean also protected him, fielded unwanted visitors, arranged his day-to-day affairs with Alfred Wood and ran the household which now included eight servants. Conan Doyle returned to being his former genial self. Even, it is said, his moustache changed from being bristlingly military to droopingly casual. His hair began to grey but he was no less active and neither looked nor behaved like a man in his middle age. His health was good, bar one minor illness. In January 1909, he suffered a painful bout of the intestinal trouble he had picked up in Bloemfontein which led to an intestinal blockage requiring surgery which was carried out at Windlesham on January 10. Within a week, he was fit again.

It was not long before their marriage was blessed with children. Denis Percy Stewart Conan Doyle was born in March 1909. In the family fashion, he drew his names from forebears, Denis after Sir Denis Pack and Percy from the Percys of Ballintemple. He was followed in November 1910 by Adrian Malcolm (Adrian was Jean's choice, Malcolm her brother's name) and Lena Jean Annette in December 1912. She was named after her maternal grandmother, Selina Leckie, her mother and Annette, her father's sister and also his aunt. At the age of six, however, she chose to be called Billie.

These children had an altogether different upbringing from that of Mary and Kingsley. Their parents were very close, very much in love and involved in each other and their children's lives. Conan Doyle was no longer the strict authoritarian but an approachable, affable father who rarely lost his temper with them. He told them stories, just as his mother had done to him, took them on walks on which they hunted for Stone Age implements that were to be found on the downland, invented games for them to play and encouraged them to experience all that came their way. His sons were later to say of him that he was the best pal they had ever known.

Adrian remembered into adulthood his own puerile crimes such as crashing Conan Doyle's car into a tree, accidentally shooting the gardener and inventing a matchbox gun which set light to the billiard room. None of these pleased his father, who was thunderous in his reprimands but who still had, behind his anger, a certain laughter in his eyes. Yet, regardless of his approachability, the children always knew where the limit lay with their father and they were careful never to step over it.

This pleasant life was encapsulated in a book written in 1923 and entitled *Three of Them: A Reminiscence*. In the book, which consists of a number of essays on how the children grew up and what Conan Doyle did to keep them entertained, the children are known by their family nicknames of Laddie (Denis), Dimples (Adrian) and Billie. It is, by modern standards, a somewhat sugary and sentimental volume, but it serves an important literary purpose, for it sheds a new light on Conan Doyle's private life of which he was otherwise protective and unforthcoming.

Although he lessened his output as a writer for a few years, his fame continued to grow. He was no longer just a writer and the creator of Sherlock Holmes but a figure of national standing. People approached him to endorse their goods, which he found amusing but refused to do, although the name Sherlock Holmes appeared on a number of commercial items from board and card games to, not surprisingly, tobacco products. His postbag was enormous and he received far more invitations than he could accept. In addition, Sherlock Holmes's postbag grew no smaller, and he was constantly bombarded with mysteries to solve, cases to ponder and crimes to crack. From time to time, he was also tested by correspondents seeking to find out just how clever he (or Sherlock Holmes) was. Some of these tests took the form of practical jokes or fictitious cases and cryptic codes in need of solving, but a few were far more ingenious to the point of being worryingly devious. On one occasion, as Conan Doyle was about to enter a billiard competition, he was given a small box containing a cube of green cue chalk. For a while, he used it until it wore away, then suddenly crumbled. It had been carefully hollowed out and contained a note reading, 'From Arsene Lupin to Sherlock Holmes'. Conan Doyle commented in his autobiography, 'Imagine the state of mind of the joker who took such trouble to accomplish such a result.' Imagine, indeed. If a fan bent on testing him would go to such lengths, one has to consider what a serious-minded crank or enemy could achieve. In the years running up to the outbreak of the First World War, Conan Doyle received a number of death threats, most likely borne out of his stand on the Irish political situation and female emancipation. He was all for brushing these aside but, in 1912, they became so worrying he was temporarily given a police escort. Fame was not all a pleasant social whirl of parties and literary meetings.

Following his marriage, Conan Doyle's writing tended more towards the theatre, for which he wrote and produced plays based upon some of his own books. He recalls of the time, 'My work for a few years after my marriage ran largely in the direction of drama, and if it was not lucrative it at least provided us with a good deal of amusement and excitement.' None of his productions lit up the sky over the West End of London, but they appealed to contemporary audiences who particularly enjoyed costume dramas with clear-cut characters and direct plots.

One play, *Brigadier Gerard*, based upon the character of the stories, had in fact been performed in the spring of 1906, before Louise's death, with Lewis Waller, the matinee idol, cast in the title role. When he attended a rehearsal at the Imperial Theatre where the play was to run, Conan Doyle, always a stickler for authenticity, was incensed to see that the soldiers appeared on stage in pristine uniforms, although they were supposed to have just gone through Napoleon's final campaign. Regardless of the cost of the uniforms, he demanded they be muddied up and torn to look realistic.

Three years later, on 16 June 1909, Lewis Waller produced *The Fires of Fate*, at the Lyric Theatre. It was loosely based upon *The Tragedy of the Korosko*, Waller cast in the role of Colonel Egerton, a somewhat altered Colonel Cochrane Cochrane, who had been given only a short time to live and went on a cruise on the Nile in charge of a group of tourists. Again, authenticity was enhanced by the dervishes beating the captured tourists so realistically that Conan Doyle wrote of an officer friend of Innes who had to be restrained from climbing on to the stage to defend the victims. As did *Brigadier Gerard* before it, the play fared reasonably well.

Spurred on by these moderate successes, Conan Doyle, ever a man to try his hand at anything new, decided to have a go as an impresario. In February 1910, he staged *The House of Temperley*, which he had initially begun writing in 1894. The play revolved around the complex life of Sir Charles Temperley, an incorrigible gambler who has to risk the last of his fortune on a boxing match. To say the least, the play was ambitious, incorporating forty-three acting parts and seven complete changes of set. The cost of the production was in excess of £2,000, which is why Conan Doyle had to produce it himself, for no theatre manager or owner would accept such a risk. It was also a case of his believing that he knew best and that the play was sure to be a box-office hit.

To stage the play, he took out a lease on the Adelphi Theatre, the salaries of the cast and crew plus the rent coming to £600 a week. The Regency sets were utterly authentic to the smallest degree, many of the props were antiques, and the bare-knuckle fights, supervised by a military boxing instructor called Frank Binnison, real. In his autobiography, Conan Doyle recorded that 'Rex Davies, who played Gloucester Dick, assured me that he lost a tooth and broke both a finger and a rib during his engagement.' The opening night was 11 February 1910 and the play was well reviewed. Yet, for all its innovative fight scenes and accurate sets, it closed in just over twelve weeks of an intended six-month run. The fights were too violent and the story too masculine to appeal to women and, as most men went to the theatre with their wives or girlfriends, the audience was limited. The final blow came on 6 May with the death of King Edward VII which threw the capital into mourning and closed many a production.

The darkening of the stage landed Conan Doyle in financial trouble. He had invested a lot of money in the play and he had somehow to recoup it. There seemed to be only one person he could fall back on to help – Sherlock Holmes. For a week, he closeted himself away and then, within a fortnight, went into rehearsal with some of the cast from *The House of Temperley*. The new play was *The Speckled Band*. H.A. Saintsbury, who had been cast as Sherlock Holmes in the play Gillette had written, took on the role of the great detective which, in future years, he was to return to over a thousand times. The Shakespearean actor Lyn Harding was cast as Dr Rylott, the villain. In the published story, this had been spelt Roylott, probably a typesetting error or a slip of the author's pen, for it must be remembered that he had in mind Arnold Rylott, the Leicestershire cricketer, when naming the character. Harding wanted to built up his part and protested vigorously that his lines should be rewritten but Conan Doyle was adamant. J.M. Barrie, who was a friend to both of them, was called in as referee and agreed with the actor. Conan Doyle conceded and the play opened on 4 June.

With authenticity once again the aim, a real snake was used in the title part. Not being able to use a poisonous snake, Conan Doyle reverted to a small python which he recorded in his autobiography was 'the pride of my heart', and he was furious when a theatre critic remarked in a review, 'The crisis of the play was produced by the appearance of a palpably artificial serpent.' It had, it seems, not occurred to the producer or anyone else that snakes spend 95 per cent of their lives dozing. Conan Doyle wrote of the several snakes they had available for the part that none of them were true thespians and that they were 'inclined either to hang down from the hole in the wall like inanimate bell-pulls, or else to turn back through the hole and get even with the stage carpenter who pinched their tails in order to make them more lively'. Eventually, the living snake was replaced by a much more lively rubber one. Thanks to Harding's performance, the play was a success and saved Conan Doyle's financial bacon. It also taught him not to risk financing another production. He later cautioned a friend, Horace Annesley Vachell, who had a play on at the Haymarket Theatre, not to give up novels for plays and never to back anything on the stage with his own hard cash.

The early closing of *The House of Temperley* was not the only reason Conan Doyle's fingers were burnt in the theatre. He also lost about £8,000 through being represented by a theatrical agent, Addison Bright, who falsely accounted income and royalties. He did succeed in recouping the money from Bright's executors after the agent killed himself, but the experience made him wary. In late 1908, he wrote to his next theatrical agent, Arthur Hardy, to let him know that, henceforth, he was going to handle *The Fires of Fate* and *The House of Temperley* himself. 'I have,' he declared, 'found the openings, so why should I continue to use your agency? It really forms a needless complication. I may say that in the case of "Brigadier Gerard" also, it was I who approached Waller and managed the whole thing, so that I have always felt the payment of commission an unnecessary thing.'

Although actively involved in matters theatrical, he did not abandon book writing. *Through the Magic Door* was published to good notices. It started life as a series of articles dealing with his literary interests, favourite authors and books he possessed and loved which had influenced him. The readership was intended to be young people who were just setting out on a lifetime of reading. A rumour went around, however, that Lloyd George purchased a copy in the belief that it was an adventure story.

In addition, Conan Doyle continued to write short fiction, a fair number of the stories verging on the genre of horror or the supernatural. His imagination was, as ever, stimulated by subjects beyond the everyday. 'The Silver Mirror', published in 1908, was told by a man who finds he is being haunted when, looking into an ancient silvered mirror, he sees that the eyes gazing back at him are not his own but those of a beautiful woman. Becoming obsessed by these, he continues to stare at the mirror until the picture changes into the scene of Darnley's murder of Rizzio, Mary Queen of Scots' lover, in Holyrood Palace. Another tale was 'The Terror of Blue John Gap', written in 1909 and published the following year. The narrator of the tale visits a chasm in the Peak District of Derbyshire into which sheep have disappeared, the surrounding rocks being smeared with blood. He finds the massive spoor of a bear-like creature with which he later comes face to face, discovering that it is an unknown species, which seems to reflect his own subconscious fears. Not long afterwards, Conan Doyle also published a series of stories, *The Last Galley*, set in ancient historical times, but that year was to see him produce a much more important piece of work, his first novel since *Sir Nigel*. It was to become his most famous story apart from the Sherlock Holmes tales. Entitled *The Lost World*, it was published in 1912 and was the first appearance of a new character, Professor Challenger.

From time to time, some of Conan Doyle's stories verged upon science fiction, but it was not until now that he turned fully towards the genre and proved, as in so many things, to have a marked talent for it. Where his initial stimulus for the plot came from is hard to say. It may have had its origin in one of two Mediterranean cruises he and Jean took in the years immediately after their marriage. They visited the Greek islands, Egypt and Turkey. In Constantinople, on their honeymoon, they obtained permission to attend the sacred Night of Power ritual in the Mosque of Sophia, and Sultan Abdul Hamid awarded Conan Doyle the Order of the Medjide, Jean being given the second-class order of the Niehan-i-Chafahat: the Sultan, it would appear, was a Sherlock Holmes fan. During one of these cruises, Conan Doyle believed he saw what he described as a young ichthyosaurus swimming in the Aegean Sea, describing it as 'about 4 feet long, with thin neck and tail, and four marked side-flippers'. It was most likely a school of dolphins, but it could have set his mind to work. There again, the idea may have come from his new fascination with palaeontology, which had already produced the Derbyshire sheep-eating beast. He had found a number of iguanadon fossils and the tooth of an ichthyosaurus in a quarry near Crowborough, and had several casts of dinosaur footprints in his study, incongruous additions to his eclectic collection of items such as a mud-encrusted cricket bat with which he had scored his first century at Lord's, Greek coins, pieces of Roman glass and pottery, sporting trophies, Egyptian statuettes and a large chunk of ambergris. Like every creative writer, he had a mania for acquiring memorabilia or items that might serve as images or stimuli for his fiction. Another source of inspiration for the novel was the eminent zoologist, Sir Edwin Ray Lankester, director of natural history at the British Museum, with whom he was friendly. Lankester, to whom Conan Doyle alluded in the novel, gave suggestions for twists in the story and Conan Doyle relied for his research in part on Lankester's book, *Extinct Animals*. Further research included studying Lieutenant-Colonel P.H. Fawcett's accounts of his expeditions in Mato Grosso do Sol in Brazil, in the area of the Guaporé River system, and the Ricardo Franco Hills in the Serra dos Parecis, and reading H.W. Bates's important work, *The Naturalist on the River Amazon*, published in 1863. Also, in 1910, Conan Doyle sent an outline of his story to Roger Casement, who was leaving for a diplomatic assignment in Peru where he was instructed to look into the treatment of native labour by the Peruvian Amazon Rubber Company, asking him to send back any information that might be of use. A final and seminal influence was Sir Charles Wyville Thomson's scientific expedition on HMS *Challenger*, from which he drew the name of his enigmatic hero.

Professor George Edward Challenger was as complex a character as Sherlock Holmes. He was unorthodox, eccentric, ill-mannered, doctrinaire, arrogant and coarse, yet he was also a pioneer scientist and explorer, as fully developed and as fascinating as the detective. He was, in all probability, based upon Professor William Rutherford, Conan Doyle's physiology lecturer at Edinburgh who, in later life, lost his reason for some time and provided the idea of the brilliant but mad professor. Challenger's capricious temper, bursts of energy and fantasising owe more than a passing debt to Budd, but his love of adventure and controversy are pure Conan Doyle.

Also of a large and powerful build, Challenger reflected other aspects of his creator, to such an extent that, when the *New York Tribune* carried the first episode of the serialisation in March 1912, the author posed as his own hero on the cover, dressed in suitable clothing, a wig and a false beard. His portrait was also used for Challenger in the *Strand Magazine* and a major publicity campaign was mounted around it.

The story goes that Conan Doyle, delighted by his disguise, put it on and visited the Hornungs at West Grinstead Park where they lived on the estate of E.W.'s brother, Sir Pitt Hornung. Making the most of E.W.'s short-sightedness, he presented himself as a German doctor, a friend of Hornung's famous author brother-in-law. Hornung warmly welcomed him in. Conan Doyle chattered volubly in German for some minutes before Hornung realised he was being duped, at which point he was furious and turned him out of the house.

The plot of *The Lost World* concerns an expedition led by Challenger to discover a plateau in the Amazon basin on which, it was said, prehistoric animals had survived. With over 70 per cent of South America still unmapped, the premise had a distinct ring of feasibility about it. Accompanying him was a scientific opponent, Professor Summerlee, who frequently quarrelled with Challenger, providing a comic sub-plot and relief from the tension of the main story, John Roxton, an explorer and fighter for natives' rights, and a young journalist, Edward Dunn Malone, who is the narrator. Summerlee bore similarities to Christison, Roxton was more firmly based upon Roger Casement, and Malone was modelled on Edmund Dene Morel. They reach the plateau to discover a prehistoric world of dinosaurs and pterodactyls in which a society of ape-men are ruling a tribe of Amazonian Indians whom the explorers save by driving the ape-men out. The story ends with a neat, ironic twist, for Malone went on the expedition in order to win the hand of his love who would not consider his proposal of marriage until he had proved himself a man. He does, and returns to her house in suburban South London to propose only to find she has not waited and has married a solicitor's clerk. It could well be that Conan Doyle was exorcising the fears he had entertained over his years as husband-in-waiting to Jean.

With *The Lost World*, he was on to another winner. The plot was tight and controlled, the descriptions of the jungle and plateau masterful. The tension was maintained throughout the book, the humour was effective and the transformation of the jungle from a paradise to a hell on earth superbly contrived. His imagination was given full rein and the description of the pterodactyl rookery, the creatures' red eyes and umbrella-like wings, their yellow eggs and the stink of their guano, could not be bettered, lingering in the mind of every reader. The prehistoric world came alive with the calls of iguanadons, the swish of branches, the sound of primeval footsteps and a huge, unidentified amphibian face peering through the undergrowth.

The author's imagination did not do all the work, however. As usual, in his hunt for realism, although he used Fawcett and Bates for some of his descriptions, he also relied upon newspaper reports of other parts of Brazil. The story has no defined setting but the most likely candidate for its location is southern Venezuela, on the border with Brazil and Guyana, for here there are over a hundred *tepuis*, or table-like mountains, in the proximity of Mount Roraima, most of them unexplored to this day. Scientists who have entered this remote and highly inaccessible region have reported finding large numbers of unique species including small, saurian-looking reptiles. As in the story, the sheer sides of the *tepuis* act as environmental barriers, and it may well be that, ape-men and cavemen apart, there actually exists a corner of Conan Doyle's imagination brought alive in the last wilderness on earth.

There are flaws to the story. The plateau is too small to support such a plethora of prehistoric creatures as Conan Doyle inhabits it with, and the practicalities of life for both ape- and caveman are badly thought out. Greenhough Smith, when he read the manuscript, pointed out that the balloon fashioned by the explorers from animal hides could not have flown, although Conan Doyle countered the criticism with a defence that he attested came from his research. The gas used to lift the craft was volcanic lovogen, proven by Professor T.E.S. Tube, FRS, to be 35,371 times less dense than hydrogen.

The novel was intended for a wide readership. Conan Doyle told Greenhough Smith that his ambition was to 'do for the boys' book what Sherlock Holmes did for the detective tale' and he dedicated it with a verse:

> *I have wrought my simple plan,*
> *If I bring one hour of joy,*
> *To the boy who's half a man*
> *Or the man who's half a boy.*

To add appeal and the semblance of reality, he produced faked photographs, maps and diagrams to accompany the serialisation. In October 1912, Hodder and Stoughton published the story as a novel. The reviews were highly praising and Conan Doyle, although somewhat miffed that the critics had not commented upon his sardonic humour, knew that he had another successful character on his hands whom he could, as with Sherlock Holmes, run to further stories.

The publication led to a somewhat enduring spoof in 1914 when an American newspaper published a highly plausible story about the University of Pennsylvania sending an expedition up the Amazon to find Conan Doyle's dinosaur plateau. The facts were lifted and twisted from a real expedition then currently being made under the leadership of Dr William Curtis Farabee. The spurious expedition was led by a 'Dr Farrable' and the publication date of the article was 1 April, but it fooled many Conan Doyle fans and at least one of his biographers.

With inevitable changes to suit the silver screen, the story was filmed and released as a sixty-five-minute silent film in 1925. It had been in production for several years and made cinematic history for its special effects, mastered by Willis O'Brien. Other versions, not to mention a sequel, appeared in 1960 and 1993, and the story was also to be the starting point for *King Kong* and, to a lesser extent, *One Million BC*, *Two Lost Worlds* and the *Planet of the Apes* series of films. The special effects in the former were also the responsibility of O'Brien, who admitted he had cut his cinematic teeth on *The Lost World*.

With the success of the story assured, Conan Doyle immediately set about writing another Challenger story. Entitled *The Poison Belt*, it used the same characters but was much more serious. Published in 1913, it is about a gas that poisons the world, although Challenger and the others survive it by breathing pure oxygen in a sealed room in his house, which is patently the study at Windlesham. The story lacked the ripping-yarn adventure elements of *The Lost World*, yet it was important because in it Conan Doyle not only expressed, through Challenger, his meditations on mortality but also showed how he had picked up a new stylistic technique. As a result of his involvement with the theatre, he had learnt to write more tersely, more dramatically and with a certain direct punchiness that was to be much imitated in the future and set a trend in English fiction. The long-winded descriptions of the nineteenth century were, through Conan Doyle, transformed into the concise, exact diction of the twentieth, with direct speech becoming far more realistic. Also loosely imitated was Austin, Challenger's manservant, who was the foundation for P.G. Wodehouse's famous butler, Jeeves.

Other authors may have been imitating Conan Doyle, or accepting his influence, but he was accused of more than mere imitation. Paul Souday, a critic for the French publication *Le Temps*, charged that Conan Doyle was guilty of plagiarism after noticing a similarity between *The Poison Belt* and a story called *La Force mystérieuse* by a French writer, J.H. Rosny. Conan Doyle avoided the charge by being able to prove that he had delivered his manuscript to Greenhough Smith six months before Rosny's story appeared. It was not, however, the only occasion on which he was accused of plagiarism, which is not surprising when one considers how wide he cast his net in searching for plots for his stories, especially for Sherlock Holmes.

Challenger was to usurp Sherlock Holmes for a while, but Conan Doyle did not abandon his detective, although the next collection, *His Last Bow*, did not appear until late in 1917, containing stories that were first published between August 1908 and September 1917 and including, at last, 'The Adventure of the Cardboard Box'.

It was a disparate lot. 'The Adventure of Wisteria Lodge' concerned a Latin American dictator, 'The Adventure of the Red Circle' was about a secret society, 'The Disappearance of Lady Frances Carfax' was inspired by a real event in Lausanne, whilst 'The Adventure of the Devil's Foot' had its roots in a 1906 report about people in Paris being killed by poisonous fumes given off by a tropical plant. The story was set in Cornwall, where

Sherlock Holmes had gone on his doctor's orders, just as Conan Doyle had some time after his intestinal operation, staying at a hotel near Mullion on the Lizard where he took to studying the Cornish language: there was never a time in his life when Conan Doyle was not in the process of studying something.

In the middle of the short stories came a new Sherlock Holmes novel, The Valley of Fear. Written over the winter of 1913/14, it was serialised in the Strand Magazine and published in book form in 1915. The narrative started at Birlstone Manor, which Conan Doyle based on Groombridge Place, north of Crowborough. The story then flashed back twenty years to describe a secret society called the Scowrers operating in the mining communities of Pennsylvania. For his society, he borrowed details of an Irish-American secret fraternity known as the Molly Maguires, drawing his facts from an 1877 publication, The Molly Maguires and the Detectives, written by Allan J. Pinkerton, the famous founder of Pinkerton's National Detective Agency, set up in Chicago in 1850. By taking the story to America, Conan Doyle wooed his transatlantic readers, but his British followers wanted to be back home in Baker Street, not wandering about in industrial America.

For some critics, the first part of the story was on a par with the best of the Sherlock Holmes stories but, whilst the style of the writing was as superb as anything Conan Doyle had ever turned out, the flashback was considered too long, putting a brake on the pace of the story even though it was fascinating in its own right. The consensus of opinion was that the premise of the plot was gripping, but the structure was weak.

Despite his continuing success and happy private life, storm clouds were looming over which Conan Doyle had no control. His ardent reading of the newspapers, his contacts in high places and his general awareness of the state of the world were all telling him that war with Germany was on the way. He found it hard to comprehend that Germany should be behaving so belligerently towards a country with which it had such close ties, and he could not believe that the Germans might actually want war. They were surrounded by enemies, with France on one side and Russia on the other: surely, he considered, they would neither want to attack nor dare take on the British Empire. Yet the indications were otherwise.

As early as 1906, he had been concerned with the defence of his country. In a letter to The Times, he advocated the mobilisation of car owners, always believing that ordinary citizens should be involved in the defence of their homeland. In February 1910, he published a letter in the Daily Express proposing the establishment of a civilian militia cycle cavalry comprising bicycles fitted with rifle clips and ammunition saddlebags which could supplant the horse. Regardless of this, he continued to foster Anglo-German relations. When Edward VII died in 1910, he covered the state funeral for the *Daily Mail* writing, '[the] troop of Kings who escorted their dead peer, with the noble Kaiser riding at their head. England has lost something of her old kindliness if she does not take him back into her heart to-day.' The article was republished as a pamphlet and it was said that when, some years later, Conan Doyle came upon a copy, he added a full stop after 'peer', deleting the rest.

The following year, he took part with Jean in the Prince Henry Tour, a motor rally instigated by the German prince. Set to coincide with the coronation of King George V, it commenced in Hamburg, went by way of Cologne to Bremerhaven, then crossed by sea to Southampton to tour through Britain before ending in London. Each car carried an observer from the opposing country, all the observers being military officers. Conan Doyle's entry was number twenty-three, a green Dietrich-Lorraine landaulette which he piloted for nearly four thousand kilometres although, on the northward leg from Harrogate to Newcastle, it broke down and he had to be towed to the next checkpoint. The whole tour took three weeks and was won by the British, who received an ivory trophy at a dinner at the Royal Automobile Club. It was ironically entitled 'Peace' and consisted of a woman holding a dove.

During the rally, Conan Doyle came to appreciate the enmity that was seething between the Germans and the British. Sporting camaraderie had gone by the way and he wrote, 'I came away from it with sinister forebodings.' It was, in retrospect, generally believed that the Germans had used the event as an overt means of espionage, gathering information about Britain *en route*. All their observers carried and liberally used cameras. On the other hand, so did the British.

From the attitude of the Germans, Conan Doyle now knew that war was inescapable, and he started to prepare for it, reading as much German war literature as he could get and being shocked by the sabre-rattling of General von Bernhardt's book *Germany and the Next War*. Once he was certain in his mind of how the future was shaping up, he advised those companies in which he held shares to pull their money out of Germany and wrote an article, published in early 1913 in the *Fortnightly Review*, provocatively entitled 'Great Britain and the Next War'. One of his intentions in the piece, which was reprinted as a pamphlet just before war broke out, was to warn of the threat posed by airships and submarines. The gist of the Sherlock Holmes story 'The Adventure of the Bruce Partington Plans', published in 1908 and concerning the theft of some blueprints for a submarine design by a German spy, was coming true.

Airships, he believed, were ideal espionage machines, capable of observing enemy territory from an altitude beyond the reach of guns, but he did not otherwise regard them as a threat. Aerial bombing was beyond his imagination. He considered submarines to be a greater danger. They could blockade Britain, cutting off vital food imports and impeding troop transportation overseas. He suggested increasing national food production, levelling a tariff on imports, building submarine cargo vessels and constructing a tunnel under the English Channel whereby troops could move to Europe and food come into Britain unhindered by maritime interference. The tunnel had been in his mind for some time and he had studied its viability in some detail. It would, he estimated, take three years to construct at a depth of sixty metres below the sea bed. Consisting of a two-way railway tunnel that would cost £5,000,000, it would increase trade, bring in tourists and beat any naval blockade. A parliamentary commission was appointed to look into the feasibility of a tunnel but the debate to discuss it in the House of Commons was overtaken by history. It was tabled for 29 June 1914, the day after Archduke Ferdinand was assassinated in Sarajevo.

In February 1914, as war drew ever nearer, Conan Doyle wrote 'Danger! Being the Log of Captain John Sirius'. A short story, it was published in the *Strand Magazine* in July and was about a small nation called Norland at war with Britain, the latter being under blockade. Norland has only eight submarines, but it cripples British merchant shipping and causes a nationwide famine. When Greenhough Smith came to edit it, Conan Doyle asked him to submit it to some naval strategists for their opinions, and these were published with the story in the magazine. One senior naval officer commented, 'I do not myself think that any civilised nation will torpedo unarmed and defenceless merchant ships', whilst another responded that the story was improbably Jules Verne-like. Conan Doyle was angry at what he regarded as their lack of comprehension, but it seems, with the hindsight of history, that whilst the British may have paid him no heed, the Germans did. On 18 February 1915, when the Germans announced a submarine blockade, a neutral American journalist reported interviewing senior German officials who said they had thought of the idea through reading Conan Doyle's articles. The next year, the German Admiral Eduard von Capelle, second only to von Tirpitz in the German naval command, stated during a speech in the Reichstag that 'The German people can thank the British Admiralty for disregarding the warning given them in 1913 by Sir Arthur Conan Doyle on the coming shape of U-boat warfare.' How much of von Capelle's statement was the truth and how much propaganda, to make Britain think one of her famous subjects had thought of the idea and unwittingly tipped off the enemy, can only be surmised. Whatever the truth, Conan Doyle was considerably shocked and immediately held a press conference at which he announced, 'I need hardly say that it is very painful for me to think that anything I have written should be turned against my own country. The object of the story ['Danger!'] was to warn the public of a possible danger which I saw overhanging this country and to show it how to avoid that danger.'

This was not all. In the papers, he also – unthinkingly – blew the whistle on the lack of defensive provision for the Royal Navy at its main sea anchorages at, amongst other places, Scapa Flow. Churchill, as First Sea Lord at the Admiralty, had already recognised this deficiency, as had the rest of the naval top brass, but they kept quiet about it. It may well be that naval strategists were playing down the threat of submarine warfare for the same reason: they did not relish the information reaching German ears. Fortunately, the Germans did not exploit this naval Achilles' heel although, in October 1939, a German U-boat did infiltrate Scapa Flow to sink the battleship HMS *Royal Oak*, with considerable loss of life.

As Britain slipped inexorably towards war, Conan Doyle and Jean were invited by the Canadian government to tour Canada by train as official guests, visiting national parks. The children were left with their nanny and Lily Loder-Symonds, a close friend of Jean's who had been a bridesmaid at their wedding and who had now fallen on hard times. She lived at Windlesham as an assistant to the nanny and cabled frequently throughout the trip with news of the children. They crossed to New York aboard the *Olympic*, the sister ship of the *Titanic*. It was the very latest and most luxurious liner in the world, and the first to sport a swimming pool, but neither of them used it. The crossing was very rough and they arrived in New York at the height of a massive summer thunderstorm.

They were met by a famous New York police officer, William J. Burns, often referred to as the Sherlock Holmes of America, founder of the William J. Burns National Detective Agency. He had visited Windlesham the year before and Conan Doyle liked him, admiring his professional deductive skills with which he had solved several difficult and highly public crimes. Taking rooms in the Plaza Hotel on Central

Park, they remained in New York for six days. Conan Doyle got himself into a bit of trouble. To the journalists who besieged him with questions about women getting the vote, he replied that if militant suffragettes kept on disrupting London they would get lynched. The headlines for 28 May read, 'Sherlock's Here: Expects Lynching of "Wild Women"' and 'Conan Doyle says: Let the militants die of starvation'. No sooner had the papers hit the sidewalk than he had to set about putting the record straight and his comments in context. He was also questioned about the Irish situation, to which he replied saying he now supported Home Rule, but he went on to forecast serious trouble amounting to civil war in Northern Ireland if Home Rule were forced upon the population there.

During their stay in the city, they lunched with the mayor and were dined in honour at the Pilgrim Club, which was dedicated to Anglo-American friendship. With friends, they went to Coney Island and sampled most of the rides, the press running the headline 'Lady Doyle finds Coney Island fascinating, but Sherlock fails to solve hot dog mystery'. Even more of a celebrity in America than he was in Britain, Conan Doyle was fêted wherever he went. When he entered a dance-hall on Coney Island, the band instantly switched to the British national anthem, all the dancers stopping to applaud him. He also attended a World Series baseball game between the New York Yankees and the Philadelphia Athletics at which he expressed his dislike for sporting professionalism when he was informed the players earned up to £1,500 a season.

William J. Burns and the senior officers of the New York Police Department arranged for him to go to The Tombs and Sing Sing prison, where he was locked in a cell and sat in the electric chair, which he described as 'a very ordinary, stout, cane-bottomed seat, with a good many sinister wires dangling round it'. Later, when a journalist enquired what he had thought of the chair, he replied, 'It was the most restful time I have had since I arrived in New York, for it was the only chance I had to get away from the reporters.' Yet he was also critical of Sing Sing, which was overcrowded and out of date. In his record of the North American tour, *Western Wanderings*, serialised in the *Cornhill Magazine*, he wrote that the prison should be demolished and that it had made him feel humbled in the face of the 'human suffering which you cannot relieve', although he felt no sympathy for the convicts, suggesting 'when a man has thrice been convicted of a penal offence he should forever be segregated from the community in a permanent seclusion'. Even in the matter of penal servitude, he was eighty years ahead of his time and the present-day American 'three strikes and you're out' system of punishment.

From New York, he and Jean headed north up the Hudson River by train to Canada for the official segment of their trip, travelling through the Adirondack Mountains and visiting Lakes George and Champlain on the way. They arrived in Montreal on 3 June and started to head west on the Grand Trunk Railroad, which laid on the company president's private car, complete with living room, dining room, bedroom and private bathroom. En route, they visited most of the major cities and the Great Lakes, and crossed the prairies, which impressed Conan Doyle with their huge vistas, to the Rocky Mountains, where they stopped in the Jasper National Park while he relaxed, riding and fishing and taking in the air of the mountains of which he had dreamed since his boyhood.

From Jasper, they headed down to Vancouver in British Columbia where Conan Doyle expressed his distaste at seeing a large number of Sikhs awaiting clearance through immigration. That Indians were coming to Canada to work as labourers, making up a considerable shortfall in manpower that was desperately needed to help the region grow, did not occur to him, and he remarked that the Germans must have chartered their ship for them, in order to 'promote discord among the races under the British flag'. Such xenophobia as he had given vent to earlier in his life, and had suppressed or exorcised over the years, resurfaced as a result of the patriotic fervour he was incubating for the war. His racial intolerance also showed again when, in Sault Ste. Marie, he visited an American Indian school, describing the pupils as 'mutinous little devils. Not that their actions were anything but demure and sedate, but red mutiny smouldered in their eyes. All the wrongs of their people seemed printed upon their cast-iron visages.' His stereotypical image of the plains Indians was not a little tinged by his reading of western adventure novels, although at least he appreciated the reason for their attitude.

The Conan Doyles arrived back in Britain in July. On 4 August, war was declared with Germany. Spy mania promptly gripped the country. A German agent was apprehended in London where his cover as a moneylender was blown: he had set himself up in business in Sherwood Street, off Piccadilly Circus, operating under the name of Sherlock Holmes. William Gillette was arrested in possession of a plan of the British Embassy in Paris, which he used as a stage prop, and had to ask the police to check his bona fides with Conan Doyle.

Within a short while of war being declared, Conan Doyle offered his services to his country. 'I am fifty five,' he wrote to the War Office, 'but I am very strong and hardy, and can make my voice audible at great distances, which is very useful at drill', adding that he had not practised medicine for many years but he could certainly tend the wounded in battle. Not surprisingly, he was politely rejected. He may still have seen war as a glorious adventure and wanted to partake in it, but this is to simplify his thoughts, for he was under no illusion. Even if he had not actually tended battlefield casualties, Bloemfontein had shown him what it was really like. Certainly, to him, war was indeed an adventure, and it was glorious if the cause was noble, but it was also squalid, demeaning and dangerous, and he had no delusions of grandeur when he applied to be drafted. It was the patriot in him who wrote to the War Office, not the thrill-seeking author who went off to Cape Town fourteen years before. He was now a realist, as he has shown in his autobiography, in which he laments that the war 'was all so evidently preventable, and yet it was so madly impossible to prevent it'.

On 4 August, Conan Doyle chaired a meeting in Crowborough and set about organising a civil defence unit which he named the Civilian Reserve. His concept was that every village or town in Britain should organise a local partisan force to repel invasion and thereby release the Territorial Army and military reservists for active service. As usual, he wrote to the papers about his idea and the *Times* published his letter. Subsequently, over 1,200 towns and villages contacted him and he and Alfred Wood worked long hours drawing up, printing out and mailing guidance documents and rules for the reserve. After several weeks, however, the Home Office ordered all groups to disband as there was to be an official government organisation created. Once more, it seems, Conan Doyle's enthusiasm got the better of him but spurred the authorities into action.

The volunteer civil defence force was reconstructed, ultimately numbering over 200,000 men who were mostly too old for active service. Conan Doyle's unit was named the Crowborough Company. He was not the commanding officer but enlisted in it as Private Sir Arthur Conan Doyle, No. 184343, 4th Battalion, The Sixth Royal Sussex Volunteer Regiment. Remaining with the unit for the duration of the war, he was offered the commander's role but refused it. He said that being a private gave a better example to the men around him, showing them that, regardless of status, everyone was equal in the fight to preserve their country and the Empire. His lowly rank was the cause of some wry humour. When the unit was inspected by a new brigade adjutant, the officer saw Conan Doyle's South African War medal, which he proudly wore on his uniform on parade, and remarked, 'You have seen service, my man', with which Conan Doyle concurred. After the inspection, the adjutant was somewhat nonplussed to discover who 'his man' really was.

Conan Doyle's duties were not too onerous. He had to patrol the town, drill, go on local exercises and shoot. 'It was quite usual [he wrote] for us to march from Crowborough to Frant, with our rifles and equipment, to drill for a long hour in a heavy marshy field, and then to march back, singing all the way. It would be a good 14 miles apart from the drill.' He loved it. When not training and keeping fit, his unit took turn guarding German prisoners-of-war who were sent out from Lewes prison as labour details on farms and at roadworks.

The war was not all that distant. Crowborough was only thirty kilometres from the coast and, on a still day, the guns on the Western Front could be clearly heard, like far-off thunder. Jean established a home for Belgian refugees in a house she rented in the town, whilst Conan Doyle turned over a part of Windlesham as an officers' mess for Canadian soldiers living in a nearby tented camp, for a hundred of whom he held a weekly dinner. To contribute to the war effort, the family cut their weekly rations by a quarter. Mary, Conan Doyle's daughter by Louise, worked on an assembly line making artillery shells in a factory run by Vickers, spending her evenings working as a cook and skivvy in an army canteen. Kingsley joined up to serve his country.

Once the war got into its stride, Conan Doyle's imagination started to address military problems in earnest, and his output of correspondence to both contacts in high places and the press increased considerably. Again, because of his fame, attention was paid to him, but it must be said that, in many of these instances, he was not alone.

One of his ideas was a device to counter mines laid to sink shipping. It consisted of 'some sort of steel trident or fork which could be projected into the water in front of the bows of a vessel to explode a contact mine before the prow actually touched it'. The idea was not taken up, for the navy had invented the paravane to cut the anchorage lines on mines. After three British cruisers were sunk in the first few weeks of war, with the loss of 1,400 lives, he suggested the issuing of inflatable rubber belts to sailors. This idea was accepted and the government put into production a quarter of a million life-saving rubber collars, the forerunners of the life-vests found on all modern passenger vessels and aircraft. When HMS *Formidable* was sunk off Plymouth on 31 December 1914, Conan Doyle proposed the building of collapsible, inflatable rubber boats. Ships, he pointed out, were replaceable but sailors were not. The navy replied that such boats could become a hindrance in battle but conceded the need to increase lifeboat capacity. Instead of inflatable boats, they produced large numbers of Carley floats, a sort of self-launching platform-cum-lifeboat to which sailors could cling until rescued.

As the trench warfare of the Western Front ground to an impasse, and the body count rose alarmingly, Conan Doyle mooted the issuing of infantry body armour, protecting at least the head and upper torso. The idea was not, in fact, his own, even though it might have been influenced by his love of the knights of old: it was similar to one of the scatter-brained ideas Budd had formulated along with his magnetic shell deflector. In a letter to the *Times* on 27 July 1915, he wrote that he had championed the concept of body armour for twenty-five years, citing in support of his argument the famous Australian outlaw, Ned Kelly, who had made a viable and effective suit of armour to defend himself against the police. To further prove his case, he had a number of plates of armour made by a local blacksmith which he himself tested in the garden at Windlesham although not, it must be admitted, whilst he or anyone else was wearing them. Bullets were more deadly than gelseminum. The principle of body armour, which he kept promoting for over a year, was ignored by the War Office but steel helmets were extensively issued and it is fair to say he was one of the main instigators behind the widespread use of helmets by soldiers.

One of the twists in modern warfare that upset Conan Doyle was the fulfilment of his submarine prophecy. He felt the military had ignored the warnings he had given, which he firmly believed would be proved accurate, and it was not many months after war was declared that merchant ships started to be torpedoed, just as he had forecast. When the *Lusitania* was sunk on 7 May 1915, he was particularly saddened. Amongst the 1,198 who lost their lives was his friend Charles Frohman.

Whereas Conan Doyle was not overly successful in selling some of his ideas, he was far more effective as a writer of propaganda. He lectured widely on the causes and progress of the war, illustrating his talks with officially provided photographs, and was so good at it he was subsequently invited to be the director of the Home Office propaganda unit, but he turned the offer down, preferring to be his own man so that he could speak his mind when he wanted. Never a party man in peacetime politics, he was not going to be a government mouthpiece in time of war. As a propagandist scribe, he was in good company, for the propaganda machine employed a number of famous writers, including John Buchan, who was, in many ways, a superior but less conspicuous operator, being deputy director of the Ministry of Information. As well as accepting contributions from Conan Doyle, the unit also used Thomas Hardy, G.K. Chesterton, Arnold Bennett and John Galsworthy. The secret service also used authors. John Buchan was a major in military intelligence in 1916 whilst Somerset Maugham and A.E.W. Mason were wartime spies. When Mason was sent to Mexico to spy on the German embassy in Mexico City and study German mercantile shipping movements in Veracruz, the cover he chose was as a lepidopterist. He later admitted he had taken the idea from Stapleton in *The Hound of the Baskervilles*.

In 1915, Conan Doyle – as he put it – 'managed to establish a secret correspondence with the British prisoners at Magdeburg'. He was sent a report informing him that Allied prisoners-of-war were forbidden to read anything other than German newspapers. Aware that this was unfair and likely to undermine morale, he sent one of his books to one of Lily Loder-Symond's brothers who was held at Magdeburg, piercing letters in the text with a pin so as to spell out the real news of the war. Aware that the book might be censored, he added an innocuous-looking letter saying that the story was a bit slow at first but picked up after the third chapter, in which the pin-pricks started. For some months, he carried on this subterfuge, only to stop when he discovered that his information was erroneous and the prisoners were actually allowed to read British newspapers which were sent to them by the Red Cross.

His war effort was not restricted to lecturing and sending coded messages to PoWs. 'All sorts of queer jobs,' he reported, 'came to me as to many others in the war. I was, of course, prepared always to do absolutely anything which was suggested.' He wrote a large number of jingoistic, patriotic pamphlets, starting, within three weeks of the outbreak of war, with 'To Arms', a thirty-two-pager with a preface by the eminent barrister and head of the Press Bureau, Frederick Smith, the future first Earl of Birkenhead. The pamphlet justified the British cause, criticised those who shirked their responsibilities and attacked Germany for its long-standing anti-British belligerence and invasion of Belgium. A month later, he wrote 'The World War Conspiracy' with which he intended 'to enlighten the British public of the vital issues involved in this great European War'. Unlike 'To Arms', which cost one penny, the pamphlet was free, and readers were requested to pass it on to friends. With 'Great Britain and the New War' plus a body of journalism containing such articles as 'The Great German Plot' and 'A Policy of Murder', the pamphlets were published as a book, *The German War*, in December.

It was not long before Conan Doyle's patriotism became further inflamed by reports of German atrocities, some of them true but many of them invented by government propaganda. His view of the Germans, already low, dipped still lower. In the *New York Times*, he spoke out against the indiscriminate German laying of mines in open water, the aerial bombing from Zeppelin airships of unfortified towns with no military objectives, such as Yarmouth and Scarborough, and the slaughter of Belgian and French civilians. In their treatment of prisoners-of-war the Germans were, he wrote in the *Times* in April 1915, 'European Red Indians who torture their prisoners'. However, whilst condemning Germany, he advocated retaliation in like form, justifying the bombing of German cities. Britain had no Zeppelins so he suggested building aerodromes in eastern France so aircraft could do the job. He defended his remarks by saying, 'there are times when clean-handedness becomes a vicarious virtue by which other people suffer'. He did not leave it at that but argued that Britain should warn Germany of reprisals for the next airship raid on London. 'The Hun,' he argued in the *Times* in January 1916, 'is only formidable when he thinks that he can be frightful with impunity. "Blood and Iron" is his doctrine so long as it is his iron and someone else's blood.' As he had suggested in the Boer War with trains, so he now advised German officers be carried on British hospital ships as hostages against torpedoes and German PoWs be stationed all over London on nights when Zeppelin raids were anticipated. The shooting by firing squad of the British nurse Edith Cavell, the assassination of Captain Fryatt and the aerial bombing of field hospitals on the Western Front incensed him. He demanded an eye for an eye and wrote, 'Why are we so mealy-mouthed with these barbarians, who are sensitive to no appeal save that of fear? Why do we not officially state that every man, up to the Kaiser, shall be tried for his life in return for the murder of our prisoners?' Such nationalistic sentiments caused Ferdinand Hansen, a German-American writer, to remark after the war on the 'all-red-eyed patriotism of Sir Arthur Conan Doyle'. This in no way hurt his feelings.

Not all Conan Doyle's letters to the press were directly addressed to the problems of war. He recommended the official use of advertising hoardings to combat drunkenness, with such slogans as 'The sober workman fights for Britain – the drunk workman fights for Germany'. He was against compulsory enlistment but he was in favour of recruitment committees which he said should draw up lists not only of local men willing to fight but also a register of those who were unwilling which, he decreed, should be publicly posted to shame them. He complained about prostitution and the 'vile women who at present prey upon and poison our soldiers in London', lamenting the fact that London museums had been closed for the duration but brothels had been kept open. He expressed the fear that young men from the colonies, visiting the centre of their Empire for the first time, would take home with them not a knowledge of the civilisation that had fostered them but a dose of the clap. Prostitutes, he opined, should be interned as unpatriotic, for they were spreading venereal disease amongst personnel on active service.

Just as he had done with the Boer War, Conan Doyle started to write a history of the conflict. It was to turn into one of his most exhaustive and ambitious projects. First published in six volumes starting in 1916, it was entitled, *The British Campaign in France and Flanders*, and after the war was brought out in a single volume. His sources of information were impeccable. More than fifteen generals, including Douglas Haig, the commander of the First Army, gave him access to their personal diaries and papers. He sent questionnaires to many of his correspondents, who replied to him in the most uninhibited fashion. Innes, by now a senior staff officer, also provided him with information, as did the *Daily Chronicle* newspaper to which he frequently contributed. Not satisfied with official sources, he also recorded conversations with junior officers, noted tittle-tattle he picked up in London clubs, and read the foreign press.

The War Office, on the other hand, did not assist him, and the commander-in-chief of the British Expeditionary Force, Field Marshal John French, who at first endorsed his work, turned against it on reading the proofs of the first volume. His private secretary wrote to Conan Doyle, telling him that the Military Censor regarded the book as inappropriate for publication at the time and the French refused to have the volume dedicated to him.

Overall, the book is interesting and a valuable addition to the corpus of war studies, but it is by no means perfect. Conan Doyle was too trusting in believing everything he was told and the generals are often exonerated of any responsibility for the disasters of the conflict for which they were frequently uniquely liable. Nevertheless, he did not try to cover up the horrors of the fighting. His writing on the Battle of Passchendale, for example, one of the greatest military catastrophes of the whole war, pulled no punches. 'For four days and nights, the men were in shell-holes without shelter from the rain and the biting cold winds, and without protection from the German fire. At 6pm on the evening of October 13th., the 66th., and also the 49th. fell in to move up the line and make an attack at dawn. So dark was the night and so heavy the rain that it took them eleven hours of groping and wading to reach the tapes which marked the lines of assembly. Then worn out with fatigue, wet to the skin, terribly cold, hungry, and with weapons that were often choked with mud, they went with hardly a pause into the open to face infantry who were supposed to be second to none in Europe . . .' The ignominy of war was not mitigated, but then neither was the fortitude of the troops. He still regarded war, for all its misery, as an adjunct of a defunct chivalry, although he was not out of touch with the cruelty of modern warfare. He was condemnatory of the German use of chemical weapons but he regarded it not as inhuman but as ignoble and unfair. He wrote, 'the Germans, foiled in fair fighting, stole away a few miles of ground by the arts of the murderer . . . the poisoning of Langemarck will be recorded as an incident by which warfare was degraded'.

When it was finished, he believed the book to be the major work of his life, and although it was highly readable, but it did not sell well. The first volumes fared satisfactorily, but the war was still in progress then and the public wanted information. Once the Armistice was signed, people lost interest in the war and the book became, in his own words, an 'undeserved literary disappointment'.

Conan Doyle did not spend all his war years marching around Crowborough, guarding prisoner-of-war work parties and writing. In 1916, he engineered a trip to the Western Front. He had wanted to visit it all along, to see the fighting personally and add to his knowledge for his book. At last, the suggestion was made that he should go to the Italian front line. After the retreat from Trentino in May, the Italians had come under fierce criticism and wanted an independent observer to visit them and assess the truth. Thomas Legh, the second Baron Newton and controller of prisoners-of-war at the Foreign Office, put Conan Doyle's name forward and he accepted the request on the condition he could visit the British and French fronts as well, to be able to use them as a comparison. He was supposed to wear uniform to visit the trenches but, as he was only a volunteer regiment private, he went as the Deputy-Lieutenant of Surrey, ordering his tailor to run him up 'a wondrous khaki garb which was something between that of a Colonel and a Brigadier, with silver roses instead of stars or crowns upon the shoulder-straps'. To add some authenticity to this comic opera attire, he pinned his South African War medal ribbon to it. At the same time, he had matching uniforms made for his two sons, aged five and seven, including officers' peaked caps such as Conan Doyle had to finish off his ensemble.

Crossing to France on a Royal Navy destroyer, he first visited the British front where he was given a conducted tour, but was more than likely shown only what it was thought wise to let him see. It was deemed inadvisable to allow him to observe the real horror of the primary forward trenches, for there was no way of preventing him from publishing his thoughts on what he was confronted with: the last thing Field Marshal John French wanted was a writer of Conan Doyle's stature firing off his fusillades in the press like a loose cannon. At this juncture in the war, the public was fairly ill informed about the dreadful situation at the front, the ineptitude of the general staff and the overall military stalemate. Above all, national morale had to be maintained, and it was felt that Conan Doyle might compromise it with his truthfulness.

Visiting troops in rearguard trenches and holding stations, he pronounced the British Tommy to be the salt of the earth and, in fact, did blame the recent defeats and deadlock on the incompetence of officers in the field, poor strategic planning and inadequate equipment. The soldiers cheered his remarks and gathered round for his autograph. When he came upon German dead, he glanced compassionately at them and passed on. Coming upon a work party of conscientious objectors, he labelled them 'half-mad cranks whose absurd consciences prevented them from barring the way to the devil', although he went on to say he was glad their forced labour was turning them into real men.

In the rear trenches, he met Innes, who was Assistant Adjutant-General of the 24th Division. During his absence on active service, Innes's Danish wife, Clara, whom he had married in 1911, and their son, John, moved into Windlesham. Conan Doyle visited the dereliction of Ypres, succeeded in meeting Alfred Wood, now a major serving with the Fifth Sussex Territorials in civil administration, and caught up with his own son, Kingsley.

After being educated at Eton, Kingsley had gone overseas to Lausanne and Hanover, in much the same way as his father had gone to Feldkirch. In 1911, he entered the medical school of St Mary's Hospital, to follow in his father's footsteps as a doctor. At the outbreak of war, having completed three and a half years of a five-year course, he joined up and was, by the time his father visited him, an acting captain and medical officer with the First Hampshire Regiment.

From Flanders, Conan Doyle went by train to Udine by way of Padova and Venice. At Padova, he talked with the Italian headquarters staff and, at Udine, visited the trenches. Driving to Monfalcone, his open car came under artillery fire but he survived unscathed. All the while, he took copious notes, hoping to make the British public more sympathetic to what he termed the uncharismatic Italian troops. From Italy, he went to Paris, which he found depressingly lifeless. There he had a meeting with the elderly French statesman Georges Clemenceau, with whom he was not impressed, and heard of Lord Kitchener's death aboard HMS *Hampshire*, sunk by a mine off the Orkneys. The meeting with Clemenceau was arranged by Robert Donald, editor of the *Daily Chronicle*, who travelled with Conan Doyle to the French front at Argonne where the latter noticed that the French troops wore wound stripes. He passed the idea on to the War Office in London which started issuing them to British soldiers. Upon his return to Windlesham, he wrote three articles on his visit to the fronts for Donald, subsequently gathering them together in a small book, *A Visit to Three Fronts*, published later in the year.

This was not his only visit to the war. In 1918, the Australian High Command invited him to visit Péronne, on the River Somme east of Amiens, where Anzac forces were positioned. He found them 'rough, valiant, sporting but rude-handed', their character underlain by 'a reckless dare-devilry'. He was with the Anzacs for a part of the Battle of St Quentin, coming under a fierce artillery barrage which did not seem to shake him unduly, thus gaining him the admiration of the troops to whom he gave a speech, praising their courage and fighting abilities but warning them, in the face of their dare-devilry, to keep a sense of proportion. He must have believed that his advice was pertinent and may have found it difficult to keep such a sense himself, for the war he saw here was far from the glory of chivalrous combat. At Péronne, he came face to face with the real fighting. The Australian lines, he wrote, were 'a tangle of mutilated horses, their necks rising and sinking. Beside them a man with his hand blown off was staggering away, the blood gushing from his upturned sleeve . . . Beside the horses lay a shattered man, drenched crimson from head to foot, with two great glazed eyes looking upward through a mask of blood.'

Whilst at Argonne in 1916, a French general had enquired if Sherlock Holmes was serving with the British Army. Conan Doyle was quick to remind the general that Sherlock Holmes was too old for active service but, in fact, he had not missed out on the war. When the next collection of short stories, *His Last Bow*, was published in 1917, the title story, the first Sherlock Holmes tale for four years and one not narrated by Watson, was subtitled 'The War Service of Sherlock

Holmes' upon publication in the *Strand Magazine*. It was set on the eve of war and had Holmes foiling a German spy named Von Bork. Conan Doyle was keen to show that Holmes was as patriotic as his creator, and to answer those many readers who had written to him to ask with what the detective was now engaged. As the title suggests, it was intended to be the last Sherlock Holmes case, and his espionage escapade, being the final story in the book, had him going off into retirement to breed bees, although without the standard textbook on the subject, *Practical Handbook of Bee Culture*, which Von Bork had unwittingly gone off with in place of a dossier of British naval codes.

Conan Doyle may have been fiercely patriotic throughout the war but there was one period when his patriotism fell temporarily by the wayside, although not dishonourably. It was again a matter of seeing justice done and it concerned Sir Roger Casement, knighted in 1911 for his consular work. Casement was an Irishman with his roots going back as far as the Doyles'; like them, he had French ancestors. Unlike the Doyle family, however, his ancestors moved from southern Ireland to Ulster early in the eighteenth century, embracing the Protestant religion and becoming, by the time of his birth in 1864, a part of the Ulster establishment. Yet Casement had read widely about Irish history and became an Irish patriot. Despite being a British diplomat, he was clandestinely in touch with the Irish nationalists even before accepting his knighthood.

He and Conan Doyle had met in 1910, shortly before Casement left for Peru, and they kept in correspondence. Sometime around 1911 or 1912, probably partially as a result of Casement's influence, Conan Doyle changed his mind about the Irish question. Until then, he had not been in favour of a completely autonomous Ireland but, swayed by Casement's argument, he began to believe in the principle of Home Rule, although when, at the outbreak of war, the 'Sinn Feiners', the separatist antecedents of the IRA, violently opposed Britain and sided with Germany, he was scathing of them and took every opportunity to denounce them. This no doubt led to some of the death threats he received, although it must be added that he was just as caustic about the Unionists' preparedness to use violence against Home Rule. In short, he was in favour of Home Rule in Ireland if it meant the country staying loyal and within the Empire, considering this a better alternative to continued civil strife.

Shortly after war was declared, Casement had a secret meeting with Sinn Fein leaders in Dublin and New York, calling upon them to rise up against the British and thereby ally themselves to Germany, on the assumption that if they were not for Britain, they must be with the Germans. In support of the Irish nationalists, he published a number of inflammatory pamphlets denouncing British imperialism in Ireland, demanding independence and decrying the organising of Irish volunteers to fight with the British forces in Flanders. He travelled to Berlin, visited Irish prisoners-of-war to try to persuade them to change sides, form an expatriate army to invade Ireland and drive the British out. This done, he then entered into secret negotiations with Germany to ensure that, if Germany won the war, Ireland would be given its sovereignty.

Although his homosexual private life embarrassed them, the Germans were quite in accord with his plans and arranged for him to return to Ireland by submarine to take part in the Easter Rising in Dublin in 1916. He did not join the rebellion, however. No sooner was he landed on the west coast of Ireland, in the company of two Sinn Fein leaders, than he was challenged by a policeman, arrested, identified and shipped off to London. He was incarcerated in the Tower of London, charged with treason, sent to trial towards the end of June, 1916 found guilty and sentenced to death.

Conan Doyle believed that Casement had lost his reason, describing him in his autobiography as 'a fine man afflicted with mania'. 'He was,' he wrote in the *Daily Chronicle* in 1914, when Casement was in Berlin, 'a man of fine character, and that he should in the full possession of his senses act as a traitor to the country which had employed and honoured him is inconceivable to anyone who knew him . . . He was a sick man, however, worn by tropical hardships, and he complained of pains in his head.' Recalling Casement's humanitarian work in the Congo and Peru, he considered him to be a true Irish patriot who had behaved treasonably because of his mental collapse of which his homosexuality was but a symptom. He also thought that if Casement were executed, the British government would be making not only a martyr for the Irish separatists but also a propaganda coup for the Germans.

Because he presumed Casement was insane and therefore not being justly treated, Conan Doyle wrote and organised a petition to Herbert Asquith, the Prime Minister. In it, he stated that Casement was guilty as tried but should not be executed. He had, he outlined, 'for many years been exposed to severe strain during his honourable career of public service, that he had endured several tropical fevers . . . [and that] some allowance may be made in his case for an abnormal physical and mental state'. He went on to argue that the execution 'would be helpful to German policy' and could be used 'as a weapon against us in the United States and other neutral countries . . . Magnanimity upon the part of the British government,' he concluded, 'would soothe the bitter feelings in Ireland and make a favourable impression throughout the Empire and abroad.' The petition was signed by a wide range of influential people. Through his literary connections, Conan Doyle gained the support of Arnold Bennett, G.K. Chesterton, John Galsworthy, John Drinkwater, Israel Zangwill, Jerome K. Jerome and John Masefield. George Bernard Shaw organised his own petition. Only H.G. Wells and Rudyard Kipling refused to sign either.

On top of the petition, Conan Doyle paid £700 towards Casement's legal defence, nearly half the total amount, but Casement was ungrateful and scorned him for his motives, which further convinced him that the traitor had lost his sanity. Even when he learnt of Casement's pornographic homosexual diaries, discovered by the police in his house in Dublin, he did not waver in his support. He was disgusted by the revelations they contained but went on to state, quite rightly, that they bore no relevance to the charge of treason. When the British government sent transcripts of the diaries to President Wilson and the Pope, bolstering their political determination for the death sentence, a number of the signatories to the petitions withdrew their support but Conan Doyle did not. Instead, he attempted to have Casement classified as a prisoner-of-war. All the petitioning and arguments went unheeded and Casement was executed in Pentonville Prison in London on 3 August 1916. After the execution Conan Doyle, who was still well connected in high places, continued to maintain that it was wrong but the government ostensibly failed to grasp his argument.

His sympathy for Casement was not extended to Edmund Dene Morel, who was also in prison. In the run-up to war, he had campaigned vigorously for appeasement or political accommodation with Germany. When the conflict commenced, he joined with Ramsay MacDonald, the Labour Member of Parliament for Leicester, to form the Union of Democratic Control, a pacifist organisation which blamed all the combatant nations for the war and pressed for reconciliation and an armistice. Conan Doyle was horrified on the grounds that the UDC opposed reprisals for German atrocities. Morel, as UDC secretary, published a number of pamphlets in 1917 which led to him being accused of treason and put on trial. He was sentenced to six months in prison and Conan Doyle never contacted him again.

In his autobiography, Conan Doyle summed up the war years as being 'the physical climax of my life as it must be of the life of every living man and woman. Each was caught as a separate chip and swept into the fearsome whirlpool, where we all gyrated for four years, some sinking for ever, some washed up all twisted and bent, and all of us showing in our souls and bodies some mark of the terrible forces which had controlled us for so long.' The opening line has often been used to criticise Conan Doyle, but it has usually been taken in isolation, out of context, and this is unfair. The implication drawn from it, that he found the war to be a thrilling and exciting adventure, is justifiable, yet, as the remainder of the quotation shows only too well, it was no longer the experience of the young, eager, idealistic and chivalrous Conan Doyle, but that of a man experienced in the horror that had started in the typhoid ward in Bloemfontein and ended with the soldier with his hand blown off at Péronne.

With the fighting over, Conan Doyle knew that the world would never be the same again. Unlike any before it, the war had deeply affected every single person and changed society across Europe. The post-war world was also in a state of flux. Technology was moving ahead fast, boosted by the war. Away to the east, communism was establishing itself after the Russian Revolution of 1917, something he found incomprehensible and strangely terrifying but which he believed would not be long-lasting. This new world was alien to him but he was not unduly concerned. He had by now a new set of beliefs and a new crusade upon which to march.

14

Into the Ether

Towards the end of 1916, Conan Doyle publicly announced his conversion to spiritualism, although he preferred to call it psychic religion. It was to be the main driving force to which he dedicated the rest of his life. In it, he finally found a rational doctrine which, he believed, offered physical proof that the human personality could survive death, and for it he risked everything – his talent, his fortune and his reputation. For such dedication, he has to be admired, for he was not a mindless extremist but a man with a solid belief and a determination to crusade for something he had been studying for much of his adult life.

The forces that turned him to spiritualism are complex. They might even be said to be hereditary. Richard Doyle had become interested in it, having been friendly with the spiritualist writer Frederick Marryat who, as Captain Marryat, was the author of *Children of the New Forest*, and his spiritualist novelist daughter, Florence. Charles Doyle, as his sketchbook-cum-diary showed, was fascinated with ghosts and spirits, elves and the netherworld, not seen merely through the bottom of a bottle but also in his lucid imagination.

His forebears aside, Conan Doyle had long been concerned with the conflict of science and religion, and had just as long sought proof of the central design of creation, the meaning to existence that included a role for humanity. Science had failed to give a cogent solution to the puzzle but the psyche, in the form of the imagination with which he was so familiar as a writer, did. In the creative process there came together the inner man and his contact with the outer world, proof to him that there was a spirit. He was able to rationalise this, come to terms with it as he could with no other religion, bound as they were by dogma and ritual.

One of the important staging posts along his spiritual path came when he read Myers's book, *Human Personality and Its Survival of Bodily Death*, published in 1903, two years after the author's death in Italy. The premise of the book was that human personality was made up not just of physical and mental material elements but also of a supernatural personality that could exist independently outside the body. This concept fascinated and excited Conan Doyle. He attended more seances, looking for tangible proof for the phenomena he experienced, which he was gradually convinced, over time, emanated from beyond the grave, produced by some force or power that science had yet to understand or examine.

Through the years of mediums being debunked and the criticisms of rationalists, Conan Doyle remained questioning. There were, he acknowledged, some charlatans, but there were also, he maintained, many genuine mediums, such as the American, Mrs Piper, who was subject to a detailed investigation by the Society for Psychical Research. If mediums cheated on occasion, he reasoned, they only did so in order not to disappoint their clients, whose needs had to be addressed, and one cheating medium did not mean that others were not the real thing. This was the view he held to for the rest of his life. What Conan Doyle was searching for himself was proof of the post-mortem survival of the human personality, proven by communication with the dead.

For over thirty years, he pondered the possibility of there being life beyond death, his researches characteristically thorough and so convoluted and involved that they have led to a body of literature concerned specifically with this aspect of his life.

His spiritualist information came from a wide variety of sources. He continued to read extensively, received reports of mediums' activities, attended seances and talked with people who had communicated with the dead. One of these was the eminent barrister Edward Marshall Hall, with whom he become friendly in about 1910, and whose spiritualist conviction arose as a result of a medium informing him of a letter he had received from someone who was dead. The letter was from his brother in South Africa who had died whilst the letter was on the mail-boat. To Conan Doyle, this type of happening was proof of the ability of the human soul to pass over the divide of the grave.

The dilemma of the finality of death kept haunting him. For years, until 1914, his views hardly altered. John Dickson Carr, having had the opportunity to read Conan Doyle's papers, stated that, writing in his commonplace book over many years, he kept harking back to the question of whether or not death was the true finality. Carr came to the conclusion that, some time between 1905 and 1913, Conan Doyle came to terms with his feelings concerning psychic messages. Until this revelation, he just could not accept that such phenomena as a table moving could have any great import. Now he drew the analogy that one does not judge the validity of a telephone message from the ringing of the telephone bell, or the importance of a visitor by their knock on the door. With the coming of war, his beliefs were to move on further.

In the war years, and those immediately after it, the spiritualist movement expanded manyfold. The loss of life on such an unprecedented scale had many thousands of bereaved eager to try to come to terms with or assimilate the death of loved ones. In addition, the wartime press had carried stories of unexplained phenomena, such as the Angels of Mons and ghostly apparitions appearing in the trenches of Flanders, whilst families reported seeing the faces of the dead appearing in their homes or in military cemeteries. With such a national outpouring of emotion and the failure of Christianity to intellectualise or set into context the horror of modern warfare in respect of its teaching, spiritualism offered an attractive and immediate alternative. Whilst not undermining Christian belief, it consoled the bereft with the concept of a life after death in a better place and provided a supposed means of communication with the dead who could contact the living and put their minds at rest. Needless to say, mediums appeared by the hundreds to cash in on the market.

There was not a family in Britain that had not lost a close relative in the war, and Conan Doyle's family was no different from any other. Jean's brother, Malcolm, serving as a military doctor, was killed in the retreat from Mons in August 1914, not three weeks into the war. Conan Doyle's nephew, Oscar Horning, was killed in the trenches in 1915 along with Leslie Oldham, Lottie's husband. Both Innes and Kingsley survived the war, although the latter was badly wounded in the Battle of the Somme in 1916 and invalided out of the army. He enrolled once more in the medical school of St Mary's Hospital but he was much weakened by his injuries and succumbed to the terrible post-war pan-European influenza epidemic, dying of pneumonia on 28 October 1918. The same epidemic killed Innes four months later.

The further the war progressed, the more convinced Conan Doyle was by spiritualism. It must be said that he was not converted to it by the war, as were tens of thousands of others, for he was already well on the way to conversion before the fighting started, but it certainly helped to tip the balance of his belief. With so much death and grief around, he came into contact with many more psychic experiences than in peacetime, which all combined to persuade him.

In September 1915, Sir Oliver Lodge's son, Raymond, was killed near Ypres. Shortly afterwards, a medium called Mrs Leonard brought messages from Raymond to Lodge and his wife, each one containing specific and intimate information of which it was thought the medium had to be ignorant. This so impressed Lodge that he wrote of his experiences in a book entitled *Raymond; or Life and Death, with Examples of the Evidence for Survival of Memory and Affection after Death.* Published in 1916, it was a watershed in spiritualist writing and remains one of the most important texts on the subject, for Lodge, being a scientist, looked at it with if not dispassionate attachment then certainly a degree of objectivity.

The book had a considerable impact upon Conan Doyle, and it may well have been one deciding factor in his conversion, although, more than likely, it simply gave him more conviction, for he had already undergone a few experiences of his own and reached a decision.

Lily Loder-Symonds was a dedicated spiritualist who could perform automatic writing: in other words, the dead supposedly dictated their messages to her and she wrote them down either whilst in a trance-like state or simply by allowing herself to be a conscious vehicle. Three of her brothers were killed at the Battle of Ypres and she received spirit letters from them. Conan Doyle was, at first, sceptical. All the details of the battle the letters described could easily have come from newspaper reports. His interest changed markedly when a message came through from Malcolm Leckie concerning a conversation he had had with Conan Doyle some years before. There was, he considered, no way Lily could have known of it, and he therefore decided that spiritualism was real and that it was his role in life to dedicate himself to its furtherance. From this, one can see that he was not being impetuous. His was not conversion by flash of lightning but by what he saw as reasoned thinking, research conducted over many years and a final piece of supposedly incontrovertible proof with which he could not intellectually argue.

When this occurred is unknown, but it must have happened between September 1915 and the end of the following January. In the September issue of the *International Psychic Gazette*, an article appeared seeking advice from the famous for those grieving for lost relatives and friends. Conan Doyle's remark was blunt. 'I fear,' he wrote, 'I can say nothing worth saying. Time only is the healer.' Then, in late January, Lily died and her automatic writing ended. By November 1916, he was a committed spiritualist with a firm belief in the world of the hereafter. In the 4 November edition of the psychic magazine *Light*, he laid his convictions on the line. They were cautiously presented but they nevertheless proved that he had fully accepted the principles of spiritualism.

His caution was greatly diminished the following April by a dream from which he awoke with the word 'Piave' impinged upon his mind. It was not unknown to him, for he had crossed the River Piave on his way to the Italian front, yet he now believed it was so important that he harboured it in his thoughts for six months, then gave a sealed envelope to the Society for Psychical Research in November, demanding that it not be opened until he requested it. A year later, in the autumn of 1918, he asked for it to be read. By now, the river was famous as the site of a major battle between the Italians and the Germans which he claimed was the decisive engagement of the war.

By now, Conan Doyle's spiritualism was a matter not of finding proof but of maintaining, strengthening and propounding belief. He did not suspend all his disbelief, for he was still fascinated by the scientific basis of the religion, much as a Christian archaeologist might want to find proof positive of Christ's crucifixion, and engrossed in the phenomenality of it, but what was central to his whole being was his faith and its offered explanation of the deeper existence of man.

In October 1917, he gave his first public lecture on spiritualism to the London Spiritualist Alliance, sharing the platform with Lodge. He was now committed and, in true fashion, was quite forthcoming in his declaration of his faith. He started to write about it, too. *The New Revelation* appeared in 1918 to be followed by *The Vital Message* the next year. Both books laid the facts on the line, as Conan Doyle saw them. Death, he surmised, was not the end of human existence, for there was a world beyond the grave which paralleled the physical world and was within communicable reach. He summarised the history of spiritualism and criticised the Bible, particularly the Old Testament, which he regarded as a literary document of little religious value, concentrating as it did on Christ's death as central to the faith, rather than his life, although he was later to admit, as many spiritualists and Theosophists have since, that Christ was himself a man with considerable psychic power and energy, which he greatly admired. He also outlined his interpretation of the spirit body, which was essentially that of the human from which it derived but without any infirmities or flaws. The spirit life, he contended, was one of perfection, of beautiful people in beautiful surroundings thinking beautiful thoughts, which was all very well for members of the intelligentsia like Conan Doyle but not a little inappropriate for the majority of the population, and this sentimental view of the after-life was to lead to ridicule.

The books were straightforwardly candid and aimed at the ordinary reader. The critics reacted with reticence whilst the spiritualist community was somewhat taken aback and worried by such a high-profile admission of belief. It was thought tactically better to go softly forward, spreading the word as quietly and unspectacularly as possible to avoid sensationalism that attracted criticism and mockery. Conan Doyle was of another mind. In his usual way, once he got the bit between his teeth there was no stopping him. He had seen the light and was determined, with all his usual naïve dynamism, to spread the word, gain converts and extend the crusade. Nothing would deter him, nor was he the least bit apprehensive for either himself or his reputation. What was more, he spoke as he always did in the certainty that what he was espousing was unequivocally and unarguably right, unafraid of both disparagement and derision. As for the public, they regarded his admission of his belief with a mixture of censure and incredulity, finding it hard to come to terms with the fact that the conservative, level-headed creator of the astute, logical Sherlock Holmes, devotee of justice and a man of learning and science, could fall for such, as they saw it, dubious claptrap. Some believed he was losing his senses, some thought he was sick whilst others, who could accept neither of those presumptions, believed the whole thing to be a publicity drive in support of a forthcoming book or serial.

Conan Doyle did not convert alone. Jean fully supported his decision to go public, regardless of the consequences. Like her husband, she had had her own doubts at first. Spiritualism had seemed little more than poppycock to her and, like many others, she could not understand in the early days of their marriage her husband's abiding interest in it. Furthermore, Lily Loder-Symonds's automatic writing sessions at Windlesham alarmed and scared her. Gradually, however, his persuasion started to convince her until, when spirit messages were received from her brother, she was comforted by them and accepted her husband's arguments. After Lily died, her last doubts vanished and, around 1921, she discovered that she shared her friend's facility for automatic writing.

In this, Conan Doyle encouraged her. It was not just a matter of her realising a skill, for it brought them even closer together. To discover that his wife had psychic powers was of immense importance to him. At first, she was reluctant to practise but, with his urging, she slowly began to collect snippets of information from deceased relatives and came to believe that these did not emanate from her own subconscious but from the ether, and it was not long before she found the facility to speak when in a trance. With husband and wife both committed spiritualists, it was no surprise to learn that the children also became involved and seances were regularly held in the nursery at Windlesham.

Once he went public with his belief, Conan Doyle set about promoting it in earnest. This meant not only publishing and writing but travelling and lecturing; soon he became the most ferocious and evangelistic propagandist the cause could claim.

His lectures took two forms, the photographic and the philosophical. The former consisted of a magic lantern slide show of recorded phenomena including apports and spirit photographs. Once the audience, which in those days generally believed in the veracity of the camera and considered that it could never lie, was curious and interested, the second lecture kicked in. In this, he presented the moral and ethical basis for his new religion. The photographic lecture was constantly updated as new proof arrived, but his philosophical talk remained essentially static until his death. Once he was convinced, there was no need for further intellectual justification.

Through his powerful oratory and fame, he was in a matter of months the most important spiritualist speaker in Britain, a mouthpiece for the movement. He saw himself as a spiritualist missionary going out into the jungle of ecclesiastical dogma and atheism, on the lookout for souls to save. His audiences, on the other hand, were in many cases of a different opinion. They did not attend his lectures to be persuaded of the spirit life but to see the creator of Sherlock Holmes. For this reason, his lectures were popular, and he could easily fill a provincial theatre, the takings at the door going to the cause after he had extracted his expenses. He almost never sought payment from his missions. He was also aware of the audiences' motivations and did not mind them. If Sherlock Holmes brought them in, so be it. They may have been coming to see the author, but they heard the evangelist, and it must be said that after his visit to a town, the local spiritualists and mediums did experience an increase in business.

In his study at Windlesham, he had a map pinned on the wall. Upon it, he placed a marker for every town visited. Through 1918 and '19, he lectured across the British Isles and, by the second summer, reckoned that he had spoken to over fifty thousand people. It was exhausting work, for he not only had to maintain his diary of events and organise meetings, but he had to keep up his output of spiritualist writings, arrange and attend seances, meet and sometimes investigate mediums, travel widely and, at every venue, talk to local journalists and present a rousing ninety-minute lecture. Nothing would break his dedication and zeal. In October 1918, he received a telegram from his daughter Mary informing him of Kingsley's death, but even this did not persuade him to cancel his lecture engagements. His audience needed him and, he told Mary, Kingsley would have approved. By 1920, this was the set pattern for the remainder of his life.

Kingsley's death was a terrible blow. He had survived the war only to die within weeks of the Armistice. Within a few hours of his passing, however, Conan Doyle contacted him. On 7 September 1919, Kingsley once more communicated with his father through a Welsh medium, Evan Powell, for whom Conan Doyle had a strong regard, for Powell never sought payment for his seances. Kingsley informed his father that he was content in the after-life. As he spoke, Conan Doyle said that he felt Kingsley's hand upon his head, his lips brushing his forehead. It was, he wrote, the supreme moment of his spiritual experience and, for the remainder of his life, he was sure that he was in touch with his son as well as Innes and other relatives.

In addition to preaching and teaching persuasively, he also fought belligerently. His enemy was not just a sceptical public but also the established Church. He criticised both Roman Catholicism and Anglicanism, claiming that they were losing their power because of their 'windy words and dogmatic assertions' preached by a mediocre clergy. This invariably produced the expected backlash. In 1919, the Bishop of London was outspoken in his attack on both Conan Doyle and Lodge for seeking to contact the dead. It all smacked of witchcraft. When the church was not on the offensive, others took up the cudgel. One of these was Joseph McCabe, a rationalist thinker who saw it as his mission to expose the fraud of spiritualism. In March 1921, he threw down the gauntlet of a public debate. He and Conan Doyle duly met at the Queen's Hall in London. By now, Conan Doyle was famous as a spiritualist proselyte and the debate was a sell-out. Ticket touts even operated at the door. The debate was keen, both men presenting their arguments with composure. At the end, there was rousing applause, and it was generally felt that Conan Doyle had won the contest.

One of the battlefields for the spiritualist cause was in the newspapers. Stunts were organised by editors to try to debunk spiritualism. In 1919, James Douglas, the *Sunday Express* editor, offered £500 to any spiritualist or medium who could prove beyond doubt communication with someone recently dead. A jury of professional magicians and illusionists, several clergymen, and a number of scientists was appointed. Seances were held but no one claimed the prize purse. No money was paid out and Conan Doyle expressed concern that such demonstrations were disadvantageous to the cause because they belittled it and reduced spiritualism to the level of a fairground stall, which, for many people, was just what it was, an entertaining diversion.

As a lifelong writer of letters to editors, Conan Doyle was well aware of the power of the printed word and he used this to its fullest extent, for he was sure that one of the only things holding spiritualism back was its misrepresentation due to its poor press. It was only when a fraud was unearthed that the cause made headlines. This negative press, unbalanced by a the lack of positive one, irked him. It also included him. On account of his fame, he was widely reported, but he was also vilified and ridiculed at every opportunity. In 1920, the *Daily Express* reported a dinner at which he spoke under the headline 'Wine and Spirits'. He was incensed and penned a sharp letter to R.D. Blumenfeld, the editor and a friend. He in turn apologised for the slight, to which Conan Doyle replied, 'the cause is very sacred to me. "Wine and Spirits" was to me like "Holy Wafers and Penny Buns" to a Catholic. And so cheap. But all reasonable criticism I love and find beneficial.'

One group that vehemently attacked spiritualism was magicians. They claimed to see through the mediums, asserting that they used similar trickery themselves in their acts. There was no magic, only illusion. On occasion, magicians actually attended seances, unmasking the medium in mid-phenomenon. Conan Doyle was tricked by one in 1919, although knowledge of it only came out some years later in an article published in the magazine *John Bull*, headed 'How Conan Doyle Was Tricked'.

A journalist, Sidney Moseley, had invited Conan Doyle and others to attend a demonstration by a medium. Everyone present put an article in a black velvet bag before the demonstration began, this bag being locked in an iron box. Conan Doyle's contribution was Kingsley's ring. The medium, who was dressed in black with a veil, sat with the box on her lap and, one by one, reeled off a list of the contents. When she got to the ring she described it perfectly, even down to the worn initials engraved on it. The article explained how a magician called P.T. Selbit had been working in collaboration with the supposed medium. The box had been substituted for another identical one, and had then been opened in another room, the medium being given information on the contents by means of a thin wire connected to earphones hidden under the veil.

When the article was published, Conan Doyle was furious, but the trick was repeated for him at the magazine's offices and he was obliged to admit that he had been duped, although it did not so much as send a shiver through the rock of his belief. His attitude was that, on this occasion, he had been had by someone deliberately falsifying a fake seance. Yet this did not, in his mind, detract from real seances. Magic in fairgrounds and the theatre was one thing, true spiritualism was quite another.

Famous though he was as a spiritualist, Conan Doyle still received letters addressed to himself and Sherlock Holmes, asking for advice on missing persons and assorted crimes. He did not ignore these but saw them as grist to spiritualism's mill. In 1920, he published an article, 'A New Light on Old Crimes', in which he outlined how unsolved crimes had been cracked by mediums and psychometry. In time, he met an Australian psychometrist who had traced a missing man from touching his boot, which experience convinced Conan Doyle that psychometry had great possibilities. In this, he may have been correct, up to a point. Some police forces in both Europe and America call in a psychometrist on exceedingly baffling cases, even today. The difference is that it is their imagination which is being used, not necessarily their psychometric abilities: the services of crime novelists have also been called upon to give a new line of thought to investigations.

By early 1920, Conan Doyle had come to appreciate that the only way spiritualism would advance, in the current climate of acrimony and distrust, was by a concerted, ceaseless and dynamic publicity campaign which should not be targeted just at the British Isles. The word had to go overseas.

The first trip was to Australia and New Zealand, undertaken between September 1920 and February 1921, at the invitation of Australian spiritualists. The whole family went, the children thoroughly enjoying the voyage during which Conan Doyle gave his lectures to the ship's passengers. At Adelaide, his photographic lecture was a massive success. The audience was spellbound and the local press astonished. In Melbourne, he attended a seance with Charles Bailey, a famous Australian medium who specialised in apports. That he had several times been caught cheating in the past did not concern Conan Doyle, who thought he should be given the benefit of the doubt and an opportunity to prove himself genuine. In Sydney, he was fêted by the Press Club but, at one of his lectures, he was heckled by anti-witchcraft agitators.

The tour was not all spiritualism. When not lecturing, Conan Doyle and the family indulged themselves, visiting tourist sites and attending sporting fixtures. Near Brisbane, they were given a tour around the Redbank Plains Apiary, Australia's biggest bee farm, which made him think of what he had consigned Sherlock Holmes to in his retirement by making him an apiarist.

As with his lecture tours in Britain, Conan Doyle received income from every venue but, after deducting expenses, paid the balance over to the cause: this being said, he usually took his wife, children, secretary and a maid with him on these overseas trips, which were a very good expenses-paid holiday on the side for all but him.

He also wrote a book about this antipodean tour, the first of four describing his trips overseas in the furtherance of spiritualism. A curious blend of travel writing and spiritualist exhortation, it was published in 1921 under the title *The Wanderings of a Spiritualist*. The travel aspect of the book is highly readable and still fascinating, but the spiritualism is heavy going.

On the journey home to England, the family visited the battlefields of France, stopping off in Paris where Conan Doyle met the astronomer Camille Flammarion, gave a spiritualist lecture at the Institut Métaphysique and went to a private seance with the medium Eva C.

Eva Carrière, whose real name was Marthe Béraud, was a very celebrated medium of whom Conan Doyle had known since 1906. Her fame lay in her ability to produce ectoplasm, a semi-luminescent vapour or slightly glutinous substance which streamed or oozed out of the orifices of a medium's body to form vague shapes in mid-air. These could take on various configurations, including that of spirit faces. Eva C.'s credentials were good, for she had been thoroughly investigated by Dr Charles Richet, Professor of Physiology at the University of Paris, whom she appears to have satisfactorily hoodwinked. The German psychic investigator Baron von Schrenck-Notzing photographed her extruding ectoplasm, copies of which photographs had astonished Conan Doyle, who included them in his photographic lecture. She had also been investigated by Dr Gustave Geley of the Institut Métaphysique, a fellow spiritualist and friend of Conan Doyle, who had seen and photographed ectoplasm seeping out of the top of her head, her mouth, fingertips, nipples and vagina. He described it as being protoplasmic and either a paste-like substance or a tangle of thin membranes. It was silky to the touch and inflexible when membranous but it hardened when twisted into a cord. Conan Doyle was convinced that ectoplasm was the stuff of spirits which needed some substance in which to materialise and that ghosts formed themselves from a certain variety of it. It was his belief that, once the medium had extruded the stuff, it took on the shape the spirit required by moulding it through the medium's subconscious.

At their seance, Eva C. obligingly produced ectoplasm. Conan Doyle was gripped by it and wrote, 'The ectoplasm which I saw upon Eva, the much-abused medium, took the form of a six-inch streak of gelatinous material across the lower portion of the front of the dress. Speaking as a medical man I should say that it was more like a section of the umbilical cord than anything else, but it was wider and softer. I was permitted to touch it and I felt it thrill and contract between my fingers. It seemed to be breaking through the cloth and to be half embedded in it.' This was an electrifying appearance of ectoplasm which gripped him, and it was by no means his last experience of the substance. In his *The History of Spiritualism*, he wrote that he had personally seen ectoplasm many times, prognosticating that 'several different forms of plasma with different activities will be discovered, the whole forming a separate science of the future which may well be called Plasmology'. In this he was, not for the first time, uncannily accurate, but his vision could extend no further than declaring the plasma to be of supernatural importance or interest.

It was whilst he was in Australia that word reached him of his mother's death. She was eighty-three and had been ill for a while, but this had not deterred him from his vital spiritualist mission. Around 1917, Mary Doyle had left Waller and Masongill to move into Bowshot Cottage, close to West Grinstead Park where Connie and E.W. Hornung lived. Conan Doyle had offered her a home at or near Windlesham, but she declined his offer. In the light of their lifetime closeness, one has to question her decision, and it seems that it was in no small part coloured by her antipathy towards his psychic work. She refused to have anything to do with it and it was the cause of some friction between them. This aside, it did nothing to diminish their relationship, and when he heard of her death, Conan Doyle was very distressed that he had not been with her at her passing and had been absent from her funeral. One funeral he did attend, before reaching Britain, was Hornung's. He died in France of influenza on 22 March 1921 and was buried at St Jean de Luz.

Spiritualism did positive harm to Conan Doyle's reputation but something else did far more damage to it. Even his friends, who made allowances for his tinkering with spooks in the name of his quest for religious fulfilment, could not understand what it was in him that made him fall for fairies.

It all began in May 1920, when the editor of *Light*, the spiritualist periodical, told Conan Doyle of the existence of some alleged photographs of fairies. He then contacted Edward L. Gardner, a Theosophist who deemed fairies, pixies and goblins to exist. He, in turn, was in touch with a family called Wright who lived at 31 Lynwood Crescent, Cottingley, a village halfway between Bradford and Keighley in Yorkshire. Elsie Wright, the then fifteen-year-old daughter of the family, and her then eleven-year-old cousin, Frances Griffiths, had apparently photographed fairies flitting around a stream near their home in July 1917.

Both girls were enraptured by fairies, painting portraits of them and furnishing their imaginations with them just as any child might; and Elsie's father was an amateur photographer with his own darkroom. Borrowing his camera, the girls photographed three fairies and a pixie. No deceit was intended and the photographs, not meant for publication, were destined just for the family album. Frances mailed a copy of one to a friend in South Africa with a letter in which she mentioned in passing, 'I am sending two photographs, one of me in a bathing costume in our back yard, Uncle Jack took that, while the other is me with some fairies. Elsie took that one.'

Two years later, Elsie's mother, who had started going to meetings of the Theosophical Society in Bradford, happened to mention that she had a few photographs of fairies and prints were given to the society. These were in turn sent to Gardner, who instantly saw them as proof of his theory that fairies, a sub-human species lower down the evolutionary tree from mankind, were for real. He had the photographs reproduced and distributed them far and wide.

In June 1920, Conan Doyle and Gardner met. Gardner, keen to enlist a supporter and as convinced about fairies as Conan Doyle was about ectoplasm, assured him that the photographs were not fakes and that experts had been unable to fault them. Conan Doyle took a set of the photographs and showed them to spiritualist friends. Lodge dismissed them as fakes. Conan Doyle was annoyed, refusing to accept that two little girls could be so devious, yet even he had his doubts. In a letter to Gardner, he wrote, 'I let Kenneth Styles who is a fairy authority see the prints. He was suspicious. "If my surmises are correct," he writes, "one at least is a most patent fraud and I can almost tell you the studio it came from . . . the coiffeurs of the ladies are much too Parisienne."' The fairies were, it seems, dressed in the latest Paris fashions.

Determined to discover the truth, Conan Doyle took the photographs to the London offices of Kodak in Kingsway. Their experts could find no proof of the superimposition of the fairy images but they did admit that they could reproduce the negatives themselves if required. This was not what he wanted to hear so he turned a deaf ear and prepared to leave for Australia.

In the meantime, Gardner visited Cottingley to meet the girls. They gave him more details about the fairies and showed him the camera they had used. Gardner, also willing only to hear what he wanted to hear, believed them, although he did return to the village with his own camera and a set of marked plates in order to take his own fairy photos. The weather was bad when he arrived so he left the camera with the girls, who duly provided him with three more pictures. These new fairies were also not a little fashion-conscious, and even had the latest bob-cut hairstyles, but Gardner was blind to their sartorial taste. He immediately contacted Conan Doyle who replied, 'My heart was gladdened when out here in Australia I had your note and the three wonderful prints which are confirmatory of our published results . . . When fairies are admitted other psychic phenomena will find a more easy acceptance.' He was well and truly suckered.

For the Christmas issue of the *Strand Magazine*, he wrote an article about the fairies, publishing the photographs. He had in fact been commissioned to write an article on fairy lore in the summer, and it might well have been that he came into contact with Gardner through his research. The issue quickly sold out. To protect the Wrights' privacy, he had used pseudonyms, but the press soon uncovered the truth and, on his return from Australia, he was roundly scorned by the tabloids and pilloried by the broadsheets for his credulity. One magazine laconically summed up the matter with the statement, 'For the true explanation of the fairy photographs what is wanted is not a knowledge of occult phenomena but a knowledge of children.' It was not long before Conan Doyle became the butt of jokes, the most memorable one declaring him to be the first member of the audience to clap his hands on request to revive Tinkerbell, the fairy in J.M. Barrie's play, *Peter Pan*.

Yet it was all water off the spiritualist duck's back. Conan Doyle was now accustomed to such vituperation. Three months later, he wrote another fairy article for the *Strand Magazine*, accompanied by more photographs. He went on to write a book, *The Coming of the Fairies*, which appeared in 1922 and was reissued with even more photographs in 1928. Neither edition sold well.

In time, the controversy passed. Conan Doyle continued to receive a fairy postbag from believers but most people forgot the matter. Gardner disappeared from public view after declaring fairies to be a genus of

lepidoptera and the natural spirits in charge of plant growth. The two
girls continued to avow the validity of the photographs until well into
old age, when they finally admitted to faking them. It was all a childish
bit of fun which got out of hand.

Conan Doyle never lost either his interest or his belief in fairies. The
reason why has long been an enigma. It might be argued that, just as he
may have inherited his fascination for spiritualism and the supernatural
from his father and uncle, so might he also have acquired his curiosity
in fairy folk. This hypothesis, the fact that he had been brought up in
a family where fairies and spirit figures appeared in his relatives' artistic
work and, presumably, were a common topic of conversation, may be
valid, up to a point. Yet it must also be considered that, when a child
becomes an adult, and that adult is highly educated and possessing
of an active mind, it usually develops its own opinions and does not
cling to infantile parental influences.

There is, however, an additional and darker interpretation. Charles
Doyle was committed to an asylum because he heard voices in his head.
Conan Doyle lived in the shadow of his father's madness, dreading the
thought that this madness, for all its attached artistic genius, might
be transmitted to him. After all, Charles Doyle – not to mention his
brother, Uncle Richard – were both believers in fairies. It occurred to
Conan Doyle that, if he could prove that fairies were real, and if he
could further prove that spiritualism was genuine, then he might be
able to assuage his fear. The fairies were equated in his mind with the
voices his father had been locked up for hearing. In other words, in
Conan Doyle's mind, if fairies and spirits existed, his father was not
mad and he was not likely to go insane.

The truth is that he wanted to believe in them so he did. And he
would brook no opposition. If he stated that fairies lived in dells by
streams in Yorkshire then he was right and there was no argument
to be countenanced about it. Once his mind was set, his opinion or
interpretation was, infallibly, correct.

Anything that smacked of another world, another sphere of supernatural existence, was acceptable to him and, so far as he was
concerned, fairies were an adjunct of the spirit world. He wanted
the largely materialistically-minded public to believe in them because,
by doing so, they would acknowledge the unexplained mysteries of
human existence embodied in spiritualism. He discussed with John
Lamond, his first biographer, why mankind was so cocksure that
it was the only inhabitant of what he termed 'this material plane'.
There were many wonders in the world which science had not yet

uncovered, and he gave the recent invention of the radio as an example of a technological advance that had shown how little men knew of their physical world. The colloquial phrase used by wireless engineers, that radio signals were 'sent through the ether', was a common term used by spiritualists to describe the medium through which ghosts travelled. If 'disembodied' voices could travel through the air on radio waves then, he reasoned, what prevented spirit voices from using the same means and fairies from existing in another yet-to-be-examined or accessed plane? It might have been the unsophisticated dialectic of a man searching for a truth he wanted to find at all costs, but it has to be admitted that it has a curious if warped reasoning to it, and one can only wonder how much Conan Doyle would see his theories justified by the advent of television.

As for being taken in by the two girls, he simply could not accept that they would lie. His own children, he reasoned, would never have been so deceitful, so why should they? Apart from that, he could see no reason for them to lie. They had no motive, received no monetary gain from the photographs and, in time, became bored with the attention the media focused upon them. As he saw it, they were not even in it for the fame. That they stuck by their story also suggested to him that they were telling the truth. His own simple honesty precluded any situation where others could be lying without any rational motive.

Another reason why he believed in the Cottingley fairies was his own interest in spirit photography, of which he had probably the most comprehensive collection in the world. Spirit photography, a popular craze in the last quarter of the nineteenth century when photography was in its infancy and most people were ignorant of the technology, provided a golden opportunity for pranksters. Photographic plates were easily doctored in the darkroom to make faces float in mid-air or disembodied hands point at sitters. So many fakes were produced that, by 1910, most people rejected them. Conan Doyle was dismissive of most but not all. He could, he said, quickly tell a fake when he saw it, but he had also come across a few genuine examples. As with the fairies, he was loath to accept widespread fraud, even after participating in an experiment conducted by James Douglas in 1921 in which a newspaper photographer showed exactly how such a picture was contrived.

Throughout 1921, Conan Doyle wrote in defence of spirit photography in the press and published a book the following year, *The Case for Spirit Photography*. In it, he stood by William Hope, whom he had known since 1918, who had photographed many spirits, including some taken at night using a magnesium flare. That Hope had been caught cheating in January 1922 by Harry Price, a member of the Society for Psychical Research noted for his exposure of fraudsters, did not deter Conan Doyle one jot. He rubbished the trap into which Hope had fallen, Price having secretly marked the photographic plates he gave Hope with X-rays only to find that two of them had been substituted. Conan Doyle's rejoinder was that X-ray markings could be removed if plates were over-exposed.

In his autobiography, Conan Doyle gives a list of his psychic experiences which includes holding hands that have materialised out of thin air, scenting 'the peculiar ozone-like smell of ectoplasm', observing 'heavy articles swimming in the air, untouched by human hand' and the faces of dead people appearing on unexposed photographic plates. That most of what he experienced was the stock-in-trade of every duplicitous medium in the game is ignored, for he refused to discredit such explanations because they did not fit in with his credo.

From April to July 1922, the family were abroad again, this time in North America. The ship had hardly docked before the press corps was aboard, asking awkward spiritualist questions. Amongst other things, they wanted to know if and what spirits ate, whether or not they smoked cigars and drank alcohol and if they had sex, a subject that had regularly confused spiritualists. The following day, the newspapers pulled no punches with the headlines 'Do Spooks Marry?' and 'High Jinks in the Beyond'. One journalist on the tour wanted to know if there were spirit golf courses in the hereafter, to which Conan Doyle replied that he had no reason to believe there were, but the headline still ran 'Doyle says they play golf in Heaven'. The *New York Times* editorial declared that he was now a pathetic and even laughable figure who should be pitied for his gullibility.

Despite this initial mockery, his first lecture in Carnegie Hall was before an audience of 3,500, the leading New York papers reporting favourably on it. In all, he gave seven lectures in New York, the photographic first half of each causing people to scream or shout out, demanding communication with relatives killed in the war in Europe. Mass hysteria built up. Women fainted or wandered about the auditorium weeping.

As well as lecturing in the metropolis, he also attended seances, investigating mediums. At one, several reporters set him up and tried to trick him with a figure dressed up as Mary Doyle. Conan Doyle immediately smelt a rat but said nothing so as not to hurt peoples' feelings. His silence was construed as his being taken in, and he was resoundingly smeared in the next morning's editions, although the fake mediums were later arrested and charged with deception.

From New York, the Conan Doyles travelled to Boston, New Haven, where he lectured at Yale University, Washington DC, Philadelphia, Buffalo, Chicago, Atlantic City and Toledo, where Conan Doyle visited Ada Bessinett, a famous medium he had already met in England and through whom he had purportedly had contact with his mother. As in Australia, the family took in the sights along the way, paying their respects at the grave of Oliver Wendell Holmes and going to Fordham, where Edgar Allan Poe had lived in poverty in a small shingle cottage.

In Washington, he attended a performance by the mentalist Julius Zancig. This he believed also proved psychic phenomena. Zancig's act was simple but ingenious. He would sit blindfolded on a stage whilst his wife worked her way through the audience, taking objects from people at random which Zancig then identified. There was no magic involved. It was done by an elaborate code, which Conan Doyle allowed might have been the case, although he preferred to think that most of the show was conducted by telepathy.

It was on this trip to the USA that he stopped off on several occasions to visit a Hungarian Jew called Ehrich Weiss, otherwise known as Harry Houdini. He had started his life in show business as a trapeze artist at the age of eight but was now, at forty-eight, a world-renowned magician and escapologist. As a magician, he was fascinated by the art of illusion in the pursuit of knowledge, as a result of which he attended seances, although he was not a spiritualist. On the contrary, he considered all mediums to be confidence tricksters and was ever keen to denounce them. He knew most of their techniques and was able to prove how even quite complex apports were conducted. With little effort, he showed how spirit messages upon blank slates were made by the substitution of the slate, how luminous cheesecloth could be made to appear like ghosts or ectoplasm, and how spirit hands were fashioned out of paraffin wax. In addition to spiritualist mediums, he also attacked fortune-tellers, palmists and astrologers, but he had a weakness. Like Conan Doyle, he had been very close to his mother and after her death had been keen to contact her if possible.

Conan Doyle had met Houdini before. In 1920, he had gone to Portsmouth to see one of Houdini's escapological shows and was most impressed not only by his performance but also by his muscular control, which was part of the secret of his escaping from straitjackets and the like. After the show, he was taken backstage to meet Houdini with whom he spoke for several hours. He believed Houdini's powers were partly spiritualistic. Houdini, who knew otherwise, was circumspect on the matter and held his tongue. Later, Conan Doyle told him that he should come out and admit his supernatural powers, but Houdini rightly stated that he was not a spiritualist but an illusionist. He even offered to show Conan Doyle how some of his tricks were performed, but the latter refused the invitation. He already knew what he believed and that was all there was to it. Houdini was to write to a friend that he thought it unsurprising that Conan Doyle believed in spirits when he was so impressed by a showman's magic act.

A few days after their meeting in Portsmouth, Houdini called on the Conan Doyles at Windlesham, putting on a show for the children. Afterwards, Conan Doyle and Jean recounted their spiritualistic experiences to which Houdini avidly listened, and they talked long into the night. Houdini did not make any disparaging remarks, out of respectful deference to his host, but he found it incomprehensible that someone with Conan Doyle's powers of deduction and logical thought, so well displayed in the Sherlock Holmes tales, could be so utterly credulous.

Despite their different viewpoints, they were for a while good friends who corresponded and sent each other news articles on spiritualism and related subjects they thought to be of interest. When Conan Doyle visited Houdini's home in New York, he was most impressed by his considerable library of illusionist and spiritualist books and documents which, after Houdini's death, were considered so important they were presented to the Library of Congress.

In June 1922, Harry Houdini and his wife called on the Conan Doyles where they were staying at the Ambassador Hotel in Atlantic City. Together, they sat on the beach below the boardwalk and, whilst the children played, talked about spiritualism. Houdini put on a little show by staying an inordinate length of time under water in the hotel swimming pool; then, on the afternoon of 17 June, Jean reciprocated with a show of her own. At her suggestion, a special seance was held in the Conan Doyles' hotel room.

What occurred was an automatic writing session during which Jean suggested they try to contact Houdini's mother. Impressed by her sincerity, Houdini agreed. He later wrote that he put his whole being into the seance, for he wanted to believe and he admitted that he would have become a spiritualist if the evidence of spirit existence was incontrovertible.

The sitters at the seance were Houdini, Conan Doyle and Jean, who claimed she had seen Houdini's mother in a vision, carrying a crucifix. This was hardly likely as Houdini's mother was a devout Jewess, but nothing was said. The seance got under way and Jean received a message which she wrote down exactly as it came to her. It began, 'Oh, my darling, thank God, thank God, at last I'm through – I've tried, oh, so often – now I am happy. Why, of course I want to talk to my boy – my own beloved boy – Friends, thank you, with all my heart for this . . .' It rambled on in a similar vein, saying very little of any import, addressing Conan Doyle as Sir Arthur and lamenting, 'If only the world new [sic] this great truth', meaning spiritualism. It looked genuine and it might have fooled the average sitter, but not the ever-vigilant and sceptical Houdini. Two facts did not fit. The first, perhaps of little consequence, was that 17 June was Houdini's mother's birthday, yet she made no reference to it. The second was more crucial. The message 'came through' in English but Houdini's Jewish mother had only ever spoken Yiddish fluently and she always wrote in German. Furthermore, as Houdini knew full well, it was always believed that the dead communicated in their own language: in other words, a Chinese spirit spoke in Chinese even if the medium was Dutch. Houdini was not impressed, but Conan Doyle dismissed the anomaly by saying that spirits often became more educated in the after-life. He was eager to get Houdini on the side of spiritualism. With him on board, the movement would have had another very powerful advocate. Jean clearly shared this opinion, which accounts for Houdini's mother's remark about the 'great truth' which she followed up with the words, 'how different life would be for men and women – Go on let nothing stop you – great will be your reward hereafter'.

After the seance, Houdini returned to New York to struggle with his principles. He knew that he had been conned but he did not wish to ruin the Conan Doyles by letting it be known what a farce the seance had been. On the other hand, he was determined not to let spiritualists get away with their chicanery. As a stopgap he decided, for the time being, to say nothing and, when the Conan Doyles set sail for England on 24 June, he saw them off. Four months later, he published a piece in the *New York Sun* deriding spiritualism. At the same time, he wrote to Conan Doyle stating that the seance had been a sham and giving his reasons. Thereafter, their friendship understandably cooled somewhat.

The following year, Conan Doyle and his family returned to the USA and Canada for a five-month-long tour starting in New York on 3 April 1923. Jean gave a broadcast on national radio to an estimated half a million listeners whilst her husband lectured again in Carnegie

Hall, to similar exhibitions of hysteria, one photograph in particular exciting the audience. It was taken by a medium called Mrs Deane at the Cenotaph in Whitehall on 11 November 1922, during the annual remembrance service for the war dead. It clearly showed spirit faces hovering over the crowds. The dead of the Great War, it seemed, had come to pay their respects to themselves and their fallen comrades. Conan Doyle believed the picture genuine until, two years later, the *Daily Sketch* took one of its own and explained how it was done.

Another exercise in exposing spiritualism occurred whilst Conan Doyle was in the USA. In December 1922, *Scientific American* magazine established a competition for anyone who could produce and authenticate a psychic phenomenon. Two prizes were on offer, $2,500 for a spirit photograph with another $2,500 for a physical manifestation, both having to occur under scrupulous test conditions. A committee of doctors and a psychology professor was appointed. The last committee member was Houdini, who had instigated the competition in the first place. Before he left on his trip, Conan Doyle was invited by letter to suggest the names of genuine mediums who could be used to achieve the photograph and apport, but he declined to name any, suggesting instead that an impartial researcher be sent to England to find an appropriate medium for himself. J. Malcolm Bird, an associate editor of the magazine, sailed for England where Conan Doyle met him, took him to seances and befriended him. Bird went on to Berlin and Paris, then returned to England to sail with the Doyle family for New York in late March.

During Conan Doyle's tour the committee, in which he stated he had no faith, looked into a number of mediums. One after another, Houdini and the doctors discredited them. Of those appearing before the committee, one was a man called Nino Pecoraro, who had astonished Conan Doyle by producing psychic manifestations whilst bound to a chair. In front of the committee, he could achieve nothing. Houdini had been the one to tie him up.

After the committee disbanded, Houdini became a fervent anti-spiritualist. He lectured widely against it, warning of the harm and cruelty it inflicted by giving false hope. Conan Doyle and he remained in contact until 1924, when Houdini published a book entitled *A Magician among the Spirits*. With this, their friendship ended. Houdini wrote in the book that he treasured Conan Doyle's friendship, acknowledging that he had a brilliant mind except with regard to his religious beliefs. The gist of what he was saying was similar to a comment made in his anti-spiritualist lectures, that Conan Doyle, who always invented an excuse for any medium's shortcomings, was a deluded man of integrity. Despite this, when Houdini tragically died in 1926 as a result of a stunt going wrong, Conan Doyle was genuinely dismayed.

Even after his death, Houdini hounded the spiritualists. Shortly before he died, he arranged a secret ten-word code which he gave to his wife saying that, if there was life after death, he would communicate this to her within ten years. Mediums, set the challenge, strove to contact him. Many claimed they got through to him on the other side but none of them successfully reproduced the code.

In the second week of April 1923, Conan Doyle set off from New York on his longest and most gruelling lecture tour yet. Over five months, he and his family travelled well in excess of 50,000 kilometres, speaking to an estimated 250,000 people. He visited Hydesville, where spiritualism began, then headed for all the major cities of North America, aiming to go to as many as he could in which he had not previously spoken. He was welcomed everywhere, even in Salt Lake City, where the Mormons had taken a dim view of his portrayal of them in *A Study in Scarlet*, which he now agreed did them an injustice. As on his previous trip, many came to hear him as the creator of Sherlock Holmes, not as a spiritualist guru.

Travelling west, the family went to San Diego, then up the coast to Los Angeles, where they visited Hollywood, watching a film being shot in a studio. Conan Doyle was introduced to Mary Pickford and her husband, Douglas Fairbanks, dining with them at their lavish home, Pickfair; to Jackie Coogan, the nine-year-old child star of the day, he reportedly told 'a gruesome Sherlock Holmes tale'. He went to a seance organised by the Society of Advanced Psychic Research, at which his mother allegedly materialised, and another held by a psychiatrist, Dr Carl Wickland, one of the early exponents of electric shock therapy. He possessed a chair in his clinic into which patients were strapped and then given a charge of static electricity to, as the doctor put it, drive demoniac spirits from their bodies. Conan Doyle gave it a try, writing in the book of his trip, 'I sat on the platform, received a shock, and entirely sympathised with the spirits in their desire to quit.' For all his spookist seriousness, he still had a sense of humour.

For a few days, the family was a guest on Santa Catalina Island, thirty kilometres off Los Angeles, at the private estate of William Wrigley Jr, the chewing-gum baron. Conan Doyle might have been glad to accept Wrigley's hospitality, for he badly needed the rest, but he was exceedingly disapproving of the source of his host's immense wealth. 'There was,' he wrote of chewing gum, 'never so hopelessly undignified a custom. A man may drink and look a king among men, he may smoke and look a fine fellow and a sportsman, but the man, or, worse still, the woman, who chews becomes all animal at once.'

From Los Angeles, they travelled north to San Francisco, where spiritualism was widely scoffed at, then on to Portland and Seattle before crossing over the Canadian border to Vancouver. After Conan Doyle had finished lecturing there, they turned east, calling in for a brief respite at Jasper National Park before heading across the prairies for Winnipeg and home.

In free moments on both his American tours, Conan Doyle wrote up his two books, *Our American Adventure* and *Our Second American Adventure*. As in the old days, he wrote whenever he could and wherever he was, undisturbed by his surroundings. He still entertained high hopes for Anglo-American unity which was now all the more important, for he considered the USA an ideal launching pad for his new universal religion. In addition, he became something of an Americanophile, remarking how American hotels were superior to British ones and how, despite his love of cricket, he thought baseball would supplant it as Britain's national game. Cricket was, he considered, an anachronism, for post-war life was too hurried for a game that lasted several days. Baseball was a more modern and faster game.

Two months after his return from North America, in October 1923, the *Strand Magazine* began serialising *Memories and Adventures*, Conan Doyle's autobiography. Sixteen years before, in *Through the Magic Door*, he had considered the art of autobiography. 'It is [he wrote] the most difficult of all human compositions, calling for a mixture of tact, discretion, and frankness which make an almost impossible blend.' Certainly, in *Memories and Adventures*, he neither strove for nor achieved that impossible blend, and the book was by no means a complete, unrestrained autobiography. Being essentially by now a private person who shunned intimacy despite his fame, he omitted any details he wanted to suppress, especially of his early life. His inner thoughts and feelings were largely ignored and he avoided any sense of the intensely personal. What remained was a chronicle of events rather than an exposition of the man who had lived them.

For all its omissions, the book was honest, a sincere stocktaking in which he criticised some of his own books and admitted some of his mistakes but portrayed his life as a romantic adventure with a strong emphasis on his wartime exploits. His sense of excitement, chivalry and manly achievements was strongly in evidence, as was his old sense of humour. His introduction to a camel told of how 'it put its lips gently forward, with a far-away look in its eyes, and you have just time to say, "The pretty dear is going to kiss me," when two rows of frightful green teeth clash in front of you, and you give such a backward jump as you could never have hoped at your age to accomplish'. In mentioning Sir Moses Montefiore, the famous Jewish philanthropist and baronet, who was said to sink a bottle of port a night, he wrote, 'Like all bad habits, it overtook the sinner at last, and he was cut off at the age of 116.' Admittedly, Conan Doyle made mistakes – he misspelt the name 'Montefiori', and he got his lifespan wrong, for he died at 101 – but the joke still held good.

Apart from his missionary work, Conan Doyle did much more for spiritualism. He was, at one time or another, president of the British College of Psychic Science, the London Spiritualist Alliance and the Spiritualist Community, associate of the Marylebone Spiritualist Association, and acting president and chairman of the International Spiritualistic Congress held in Paris in 1925. He funded weekly meetings at the Aeolian Hall and, later, the Queen's Hall in London and, in 1926, financially assisted the Marylebone Spiritualist Association in booking the Albert Hall for an Armistice Day meeting at which he spoke to an audience of five thousand. He also agreed to underwrite the costs of the spiritualist magazine, *Light*.

Not content with figurehead roles, he and Jean opened a spiritualistic bookshop in the summer of 1925, the Psychic Bookshop. Situated in the ground floor and basement of Abbey House at 2 Victoria Street, close to Westminster Abbey, it not only sold books but also contained a small reference library and a modest museum. The idea of the shop was to create a spiritualist presence in central London, close to the Houses of Parliament and the fashionable residential districts around Westminster, catering to the administrators of the nation and the intelligentsia of the capital. Both husband and wife frequently came up to London to take turns at manning the till, organising the shelves, talking to customers or guiding visitors around the museum, which contained a variety of spiritualist relics, photographs and documents. Mary, Conan Doyle's spinster daughter, who was also a spiritualist, often served in the shop, which was supervised by a salaried manager. Not surprisingly, it never made a profit. Indeed, the spiritualist cause generally cost Conan Doyle a substantial sum of money, reckoned to be in the region of £250,000 at the time.

In retrospect, his greatest contribution to the movement, apart from his incessant lecturing, was his writing. He turned out a considerable number of spiritualist books and pamphlets, the majority of which he paid for himself. Any royalties were ploughed back into the cause and he also bankrolled the publication of books by other authors. His own two-volume study, *The History of Spiritualism*, published in 1926 and considered now to be the most important text on the subject, had great difficulty finding a publisher. Most editors were at the very least cautious, and it was only when Conan Doyle agreed to meet a substantial part of the production costs that Cassell finally accepted it.

Dedicated to Sir Oliver Lodge, it was an astonishingly substantial study which was written for the cognoscenti, not the general reading public, and it did not duck contentious issues such as the production of ectoplasm and the sex life of the dead. He actually co-wrote it with Leslie Curnow, a noted spiritualist scholar and researcher, whom he wanted to name as co-author, but the publishers refused. If the book were to sell at all, it had better have the undiluted Conan Doyle name on the cover. As was probably the case with Robinson and *The Hound of the Baskervilles*, he shared the royalties with Curnow and his descendents.

The cost of spiritualism to Conan Doyle was more than fiscal. Other spiritualists either begrudged him his status in the organisation or were concerned by his get-up-and-go zeal. Even Lodge had reservations, writing to a friend, 'I rather regret Doyle's decision – if it is a decision – to set up a Spiritualistic Church in London. But that I suppose is a natural outcome of his missionary activity. I suppose he regards himself as a sort of Wesley or Whitefield.' Many of his literary friends snubbed him, some resentful of his persistent spiritualist preaching. There were times when he could be a distinct bore. Those who remained in touch with him were careful to avoid entanglement in controversy with him, or on his behalf. Some derided or abandoned him. Eden Phillpotts wrote, 'I never met him again after he went over, lock, stock, and barrel, to the spiritualists, and my memory of him embraces no shadow of the interests he afterwards developed', and Jerome K. Jerome became one of his fiercest critics, actively denouncing both him and his beliefs.

Conan Doyle seems not to have been unduly worried by his loss of friends. What did concern him were those influential friends and acquaintances whom he knew to be spiritualistically inclined but who would not declare it. One of these was the statesman Arthur Balfour. He wrote asking him to come out of the closet and commit himself publicly to the movement. Balfour's reply was a masterly example of political expediency. 'Surely,' he wrote, 'my opinions upon this subject are already sufficiently well known.' Fortunately, for his political career, they had not been.

Other influential friends found Conan Doyle either an embarrassment, an enigma or a harmless but vociferous crackpot. In the mid-1920s, the Right Reverend Monsignor Richard Barry-Doyle, a second cousin, visited Windlesham to discuss the subject of a peerage, which it seems was a distinct possibility. There was, however, a string attached: the peerage would not be instituted unless Conan Doyle gave up spiritualism. No record has yet come to light on the conversation that must have passed between the two men, one a convinced spiritualist and the other a high-ranking Roman Catholic priest. The outcome was predictable. Conan Doyle, man of honour and principle, sacrificed the peerage for his beliefs. It was possibly the second time he lost a chance to be elevated to the House of Lords: his support for Roger Casement had, it is thought, cost him a baronetcy during the war.

In time, as memory of the First World War faded, so did the lure of spiritualism. The Roaring Twenties was the era of flapper girls and fun, not ghosts and gullibility. Jazz was the new music, Surrealism and Abstraction, Futurism and Constructivism were the new visual arts, and the new literature was that of D.H. Lawrence, E.M. Forster and Aldous Huxley, rich with cynicism, different mores and sexual vitality. The wave of artistic and intellectual insanity that Conan Doyle had so despised in 1912 was now a rip-tide. The new morality was contrary to the very core of his character. Young women were comparatively liberated and young men threw tradition to the winds. Where there had been decency there was now indecency, and where there had been respect there was now disrespect. To top it all, a socialist government came to power in 1924. The old order was breaking down, Conan Doyle becoming somewhat of an anachronistic outsider.

His sense of being left out of things was exacerbated by the failure of spiritualism. He was continually criticised and not infrequently satirised and parodied for his belief, his patience wearing thinner and his outward sense of humour waning as the years passed. He became irritable and petulant with anyone – and there were many – who criticised spiritualism and sought verification of its phenomena. This in turn led to him starting to prognosticate in a distinctly Nostradamus-like fashion.

In 1924, he wrote to Lodge that he had been amassing a number of dire predictions which he would not yet publish but intended to study further. Three years later, he informed Lodge that he had eighty-seven separate forecasts of doom but that these should be hushed up in case the predicted apocalypse did not occur. Either the gods might change their minds or humanity might alter and offset the catastrophe by, one presumes, overturning the new immoral order. He also wanted to avoid the press sensationalising the forecasts and thereby diminishing their effect. Clearly, he was not a little sensitive to the ridicule with which he knew he would be bombarded were he to publicise his auguries. He did, however, predict a second world war and admit privately in a letter to a friend that he believed that the world would end in a second Great Flood, the information having come to him from the spirit world. To avoid yet more mockery, he requested that the letter be suppressed in his lifetime. It was, but, within a fortnight of his death, the *Sunday Express* got hold of it, much to the discomfort of the family, who took out an injunction to prevent its further publication.

His spiritualist fanaticism, his loss of so many friends and his being out of kilter with modern times all suggest that Conan Doyle lived a narrow and perhaps unhappy life, but this is not so. He was utterly dedicated to but not obsessed with spiritualism to the exclusion of all else. His domestic life was very happy, he enjoyed the company of his family, and his love for Jean was as deep as ever. He indulged the children, was faintly amused – or bemused – by their penchant for jazz, and never missed a chance to try something new. Both his sons being keen motor-racing drivers and car owners, he was driven round Brooklands motor-racing circuit at 170kph at the age of seventy. He regretted never having learnt to fly, although he had, just once, taken a flight from Hendon aerodrome in May 1911, which he described as a not entirely pleasant experience. Continuing to play sports, he also took daily exercise, for physical fitness was important to him and he always kept himself trim and lean. His working day commencing at 6.30 a.m. and going through to 11.00 p.m., with an hour's nap in the afternoon, he mitigated these long hours in his study with brisk walks. Although he was terse with people he considered shallow, he was still essentially his old unpretentious self with an abiding and insatiable interest in everything that came his way.

Still interested in the *Grosvenor* treasure, he purchased a thousand shares in the Grosvenor Bullion Syndicate, the prospectus carrying a facsimile of a letter from him to the board, lending it some respectable credibility. His involvement was, however, somewhat maligned at the annual general meeting of 1923 by a fellow shareholder who requested that, as Conan Doyle was a spiritualist, he might enquire of the spirit of the wreck as to its location. The new syndicate, having as much luck as its predecessors, was broken up in 1929, the *Grosvenor* remaining untraced to this day.

As always, he kept up his barrage of letters to the press and not, as many have supposed, only on the subject of, or in defence of, spiritualism. His letters to editors were written in the late morning, after he had scanned the daily editions. His subjects, not all of which were serious, ranged from the opening hours of the British Empire Exhibition at Wembley to his proposal for a tunnel under the English Channel, which he was still advocating, the merits of baseball, the desirability of publicly blacklisting tax dodgers, the injustices of the Oscar Slater case, and apparent unaccountable changes in ocean depths.

At Windlesham, his own mail was still delivered by the sackload and he answered as much as he could himself. With his involvement in spiritualism, a fair percentage of it was abusive. One example was from Lord Alfred Douglas, one-time homosexual partner of Oscar Wilde whose father, Lord Queensberry, was the cause of Wilde being tried and sentenced to two years' hard labour in 1895. Douglas, a pious Roman Catholic convert, accused him of being 'a disgusting beast' deserving a horse whipping, whose 'blasphemous ravings' were sure to bring 'a dreadful judgement' raining down on him. Conan Doyle replied coolly, 'Sir, I was relieved to get your letter. It is only your approval which could in any way annoy me.' Accusations of blasphemy were common in his postbag. One letter, addressed simply to 'The Devil, London', was delivered to him at his flat in Buckingham Palace Mansions.

Conan Doyle claimed that his prediction of a second world war came from beyond the grave, but he had more down-to-earth fears which hinted at the coming conflict. Keeping up to date with current affairs, he watched with alarm as Germany started to rearm itself and rebuild its national pride and identity. A number of his friends and acquaintances in Germany, many of them spiritualists and not a few of those of Jewish background, wrote to voice their concerns. It required no crystal ball or muttering medium to show where Germany's rising anti-Semitic mood would lead.

Throughout his post-spiritualist conversion years, Greenhough Smith and the *Strand Magazine* stood behind him. They published some of his esoteric articles, but the editor wanted him to write more populist material. For a long time he refused, with the excuse that he had more important matters about which to write, but he had, in fact, been toying with introducing spiritualism as a theme into the life of one of his literary creations. At first, he wondered if Sherlock Holmes might not become a convert, but decided against it. The detective was too much of a rationalist and his creator was too much of a pragmatist. For all his dedication to the cause, he knew that Sherlock Holmes was a major source of income and therefore not something he should jeopardise or compromise for the sake of spiritualism.

Sherlock Holmes was unsuitable but there was one character whom he felt could be swayed. It was Professor George Edward Challenger, the erratic scientist. In October 1924, Conan Doyle wrote to Greenhough Smith, 'I have for years had a big psychic novel in me, which shall deal realistically with every phase of the question, pro and con. I waited, I knew it would come. Now it has come with a full head of steam and I can hardly hold onto my pen it goes so fast – about 12 or 15,000 words in three days.' The novel was *The Land of Mist*, which he initially called *The Psychic Adventures of Edward Malone*. The magazine serialised it before it was published as a book in 1926. Containing the same characters as *The Lost World* and *The Poison Belt*, the plot of what is a very poorly constructed narrative revolves around the conversions of the narrator Malone and Challenger, with whom Conan Doyle identified himself. The land of mist was not an Amazonian table mountain but the country beyond the veil of death. In the foreword, he announced that all the spiritualist events in the book were based on reality: certainly parts of the story were autobiographical. He wrote a number of real spiritualists into the story, just as he had written real people into his historical novels, for effect and to give the plots, as he thought, more depth. Even he is included in the guise of a character called Algernon Mailey. The story lacked any real direction, being too much a diatribe dressed up as fiction, and the public did not like it. Conan Doyle was too preachy and readers felt they were being moralised at and manipulated, which they were.

Through these years, Sherlock Holmes was not abandoned. The last Holmes collection, *The Case-Book of Sherlock Holmes*, appeared in 1927, containing twelve stories written between 1921 and 1927. It had been Conan Doyle's intention to stop writing Sherlock Holmes tales after *His Last Bow*, but there had been a resurgence of interest in the character as a result of the release of a number of Holmes films.

In the post-war years, a number of stage plays appeared based upon the Sherlock Holmes stories, but mass interest was spurred by the advent of cinema. Quite early on in cinematographical history, Conan Doyle had sold the film rights in Sherlock Holmes to a French company, Eclair. They shot one film in France in 1911, then eight more in Britain the following year. These were, of course, one-reel silent films. He then repurchased the rights and sold them on to the British Stoll Film Company which, in 1921, made a series of sixteen two-reelers under the collective title of *The Adventures of Sherlock Holmes*, directed by Maurice Elvey and starring Eille Norwood as Sherlock Holmes. One of the stories was retitled 'The Tiger of San Pedro', at the behest of the film company. Remarkably, all the films still exist in the archives of the British Film Institute, but there are no viewing copies.

Conan Doyle was very pleased with Norwood's portrayal of Holmes. 'He has [he wrote] the brooding eye which excites expectation and he has also a quite unrivalled power of disguise. My only criticism of the films is that they introduce telephones, motor cars and other luxuries of which the Victorian Holmes never dreamed.' In 1922, Elvey was temporarily dropped and a new director, George Ridgwell, was appointed to shoot another two-reeler series of fourteen under the title *The Further Adventures of Sherlock Holmes*, followed in 1923 by thirteen more films, *The Last Adventures of Sherlock Holmes*, directed by Elvey and Ridgwell, and stand-alone two-reeler versions of 'The Adventure of Charles Augustus Milverton' and *The Sign of Four*. With each reel being only fifteen minutes long, the films were much-abridged versions of the stories, but they were screened worldwide. Since then, Sherlock Holmes has gone on to be the most portrayed character in the history of the cinema.

Although Conan Doyle was still writing Sherlock Holmes stories, albeit intermittently, he was not doing it out of love for the character or literature in general. To some extent, he wrote to satisfy a continuing public demand but, first and foremost, Holmes was a source of much-needed and assured income. The spiritualist crusade was taking a heavy toll on Conan Doyle's pocket. Yet there may have been other reasons for his writing the stories. The more involved he was with spiritualism, the less popular he became, and it may be that he saw Sherlock Holmes as a way of redeeming himself in the eyes of a mocking public and an antagonistic press. It is certainly true that, no matter how publicly derided he was, his creation remained immensely popular. In 1924, Conan Doyle was requested, with many of the leading authors of the day, to write a microscopic Sherlock Holmes volume for inclusion in the library of Queen Mary's doll's-house, on display at the British Empire Exhibition. He obliged the royal command by writing an original story, 'How Watson Learned the Trick'.

The full-sized Sherlock Holmes stories were in some ways not up to the standard of their antecedents. They were shorter and, although still skilfully constructed, somehow lacked a certain sparkle. Conan Doyle did not put his heart and soul into them, for his energies were directed elsewhere and he had really had enough of the character. Already, he had twice tried to stop the series, only to be forced by public demand or pecuniary considerations to resurrect the character. The stories were not written, as they used to be, to please their author but to satisfy the demand of his readers. Sherlock Holmes had reached the end of his viable literary shelf-life, which is hardly surprising when one considers that the stories spanned nearly forty years.

Just as Conan Doyle was now a different person so, too, was Sherlock Holmes. No longer the detached, cool methodologist, he did not preach in the stories but he tended to philosophise a little too much and started to lose his presence on the page. Events were seen to control him rather than, as before, vice versa. The stories themselves were different from their predecessors, too. They were darker and made more use of horror. In 'The Adventure of the Sussex Vampire', there is a mentally deficient child from whom blood is apparently sucked, although not to kill but to save the child, who has been poisoned by curare. Mutilation is central to 'The Adventure of the Veiled Lodger', whilst deformity caused by a professor's self-experimentation with monkey glands is central to 'The Adventure of the Creeping Man'. Almost gratuitous violence appears in several of the tales, the dramatic impact of the plot is sometimes diluted, and the tested formula of Watson as narrator set aside in more than one story.

In 'The Adventure of the Three Gables', horror is abandoned to allow Sherlock Holmes to demonstrate his racist views where a Negro petty criminal called Steve Dixie is concerned: in a travesty of a portrayal of black Americans, Conan Doyle has the man address the detective as 'Masser Holmes'. The author also displays his own racial prejudices in describing Dixie as a savage and putting into Holmes's mouth the words, 'I've wanted to meet you for some time. I won't ask you to sit down for I don't like the smell of you . . .' The memory of Henry Highland Garnet's views had clearly faded with the passage of time.

The purists amongst his readers carped at the stories but, understandably, Conan Doyle liked them and declared that, if he had to name his top six Sherlock Holmes stories, two of the last dozen, 'The Adventure of the Illustrious Client' and 'The Adventure of the Lion's Mane', would be amongst them. In March, 1927, he had to do just that for the *Strand Magazine*, which organised a competition for readers to name Conan Doyle's favourite twelve Sherlock Holmes stories out of the forty-four published in book form to date. The first prize was £100 and a signed copy of *Memories and Adventures*. Conan Doyle gave Greenhough Smith a sealed envelope. The winner named ten out of the twelve. Conan Doyle's list consisted of 'The Adventures of the Speckled Band', 'the Dancing Men', 'the Final Problem', 'the Empty House', 'the Second Stain', 'the Devil's Foot', 'the Priory School', 'the Musgrave Ritual', 'the Reigate Squire' and 'the Red-Headed League', 'A Scandal in Bohemia' and 'The Five Orange Pips'.

In April 1927, the sixtieth and last Sherlock Holmes story was published in the *Strand Magazine*. It was entitled 'The Adventure of Shoscombe Old Place'. On completing it the previous December, Conan Doyle had written to Greenhough Smith, 'It's not of the first flight, and Sherlock, like his Author grows a little stiff in the joints, but it is the best I can do. Now farewell to him for ever!'

Not long afterwards, he announced in the press that he would write no more Sherlock Holmes material. There was some protest in response but it was muted. Not only was Conan Doyle done with his character but the public, it seemed, had also had enough of him, yet this was not the case. Sherlock Holmes's subsequent literary immortality has proven as much. Certainly, public interest waned in the author but not in the detective. Both at home and in the USA, Holmes's other big market, what people had had their fill of was Conan Doyle and his spiritualism. The critics were, for similar reasons, not over-generous with their remarks, which hurt him, but the truth was that he was also now facing some stiff opposition. The detective story, which he had done so much to place on the literary stage, was now an accepted and highly competitive genre.

Conan Doyle might have done with Sherlock Holmes but Holmes was not done with him. He continued to loom over his creator's life, swamping out most of his other literary work and burying his spiritualist writings. This annoyed Conan Doyle who, not eight weeks before his death, was to say to his last interviewer, 'To tell the truth I am rather tired of hearing myself described as the author of Sherlock Holmes. Why not, for a change, the author of *Rodney Stone*, or *The White Company*, or *Brigadier Gerard*, or of *The Lost World*? One would think I had written nothing but detective stories.'

He had a point but he could do nothing about it. Sherlock Holmes was and remains the epitome of the fictional detective, probably the best-known literary character of all time. His image, comprising his deerstalker hat, curling pipe and cape, is universally recognised. The books have been published in virtually every written language on earth, including Esperanto, Eskimo, Gaelic and, somewhat pointlessly, Pitman's shorthand. Discounting more than fifty silent films, there have been well over twenty major feature films of various stories (some of them not based upon Conan Doyle originals), five cinema versions of *The Hound of the Baskervilles* and one each of *A Study in Scarlet* and *The Sign of Four*. On top of these, there have been innumerable televisions films, drama series, stage and radio plays and productions, parodies, spoofs and even a ballet. Still today, tourists seek out 221B Baker Street.

Sherlock Holmes has become canonised. Even the body of stories is known to Sherlockians as the Sherlock Holmes Canon or, simply, the Canon. Some of his followers treat Sherlock Holmes, Watson, Lestrade and the rest as actual historical figures. This is not a recent trend. In 1902, both the *Cambridge Review* and the *Bookman* magazine in America analysed *The Hound of the Baskervilles* as if it were fact. Then, in 1911 or '12, scholarly studies got under way with an essay by a fellow and chaplain of Trinity College, Oxford, Reverend Ronald Knox, later to become a famous Roman Catholic scholar and monsignor. He sent a copy to Conan Doyle, who was astonished that anyone would care to study the Sherlock Holmes tales: they were, after all, not what he considered his important work. Not long afterwards, Knox's essay was the subject of an intellectual literary argument with Sydney Roberts, a professor of English at Cambridge University. A literary game commenced concerning the chronology of the lives of Sherlock Holmes and Watson. Others joined in. By 1933, a number of studies had been published, including *Sherlock Holmes and Dr Watson* by H.W. Bell and a biography, *The Private Life of Sherlock Holmes*, by Vincent Starrett. Sherlock Holmes clubs and societies were formed around the world, many still existing, their members playing 'The Game'. This assumes that Sherlock Holmes was a real person and Watson his biographer, with Conan Doyle either ignored or considered in a minor role, such as that of Watson's literary agent. The rules established, the stories are studied as if they are real historical events which occurred in real locations.

What Conan Doyle would have thought of such developments is anyone's guess. In all likelihood, he would have found it highly amusing and yet, at the same time, very galling that his other writing was being overlooked, smothered by such intense interest in just one small facet of his life's work.

Despite not quite hitting the usual standard of Sherlock Holmes stories, *The Case-Book of Sherlock Holmes* was still popular and sold well. What bombed was his other book of 1927, *Pheneas Speaks – Spirit Communication in a Home Circle*.

Pheneas was the Conan Doyles' spirit guide, purportedly an Arab philosopher who had lived in the third millennium BC Sumerian city of Ur in Mesopotamia, the ruins of which had been discovered in 1854 but not fully excavated until the British Museum launched an expedition there in 1918/19, digging in earnest beginning in 1922 and continuing every season until 1934. Pheneas, whose name was a corruption of the Biblical Jewish Phinehas and therefore not Arabic in root, started to appear at seances in Windlesham around the winter of 1921 or the spring of 1922. Thereafter, the group attending the family seances, consisting of Conan Doyle, Jean and the children, referred to themselves as the Pheneas Circle. Sceptics wondered if Pheneas, who was the harbinger of some of Conan Doyle's calamity prophecies, had suddenly appeared because of the British Museum digging into his ziggurat.

The first part of the book deals with spirit contact with Kingsley, Innes and other departed souls, all of whom speak of the pleasures of the after-life. The remainder concerns Pheneas, who acts as a go-between for a number of the spirits of former relatives and friends of Conan Doyle, some of whom expressed regret at having been spiritualist sceptics during life. Most of their messages were vague. E.W. Hornung announced, 'I am so glad to be here, Arthur, this is wonderful.' He added that he was engaged in a kind of literary activity beyond the grave, though its nature was not discussed. Conan Doyle's mother also sent a message through Pheneas to the effect that she wished she had trusted her son's spiritualist judgment when on earth.

Such messages do not seem all that interesting but, on the odd occasion, something more substantial came through, sometimes verbally and sometimes by means of automatic writing. On 2 September 1923, according to a letter Conan Doyle published in the New York Times, Oscar Wilde broke through the ether with an automatically written screed which Conan Doyle termed a script. In his letter, Conan Doyle explained why he believed it really was from the great playwright and wit. 'Wilde was [he wrote] a man with a very peculiar quality of thought and of expression. The latter may be parodied, but the former can hardly be copied in its fullness, for to do so would imply that the copyist had as great a brain as the original. Yet both in thought and in expression this script rings true. There are passages in it which Wilde in his best movements has never bettered . . . The other characteristic of Wilde was his freakish, paradoxical humour. This also is much in evidence in the script. "Being dead is the most boring experience in life, that is if one excepts being married or dining with a school-master!" . . . I defy any man of real critical instinct to read that script and doubt that it emanates from Wilde.' No real critic seems to have answered this challenge.

In 1925, at Pheneas's suggestion, the Conan Doyles purchased a house in the New Forest. Jean had long expressed a wish to own a quaint, thatched cottage by a stream, and her husband had been fond of the area since his doctoring days in Southsea. Bignell House, on the edge of Bignell Wood at Wittensford near Minstead, built in the reign of George I, fitted the bill exactly. The property was steeped in history and actually consisted of a two-storey cottage beside a Saxon barn. Conan Doyle substantially rebuilt the cottage, joining it on to the barn and installing an electric heating system driven by a generator: an electric pump provided water from a well and nearby stream which ran along the boundary of the garden, in which Jean laid out a miniature golf course and a croquet lawn, adding a number of garden gnomes and statuary to the shrubbery. A wicket gate led directly into the forest.

Both Conan Doyle and Jean used the house as a quiet retreat until August 1929, when sparks from the kitchen fire set light to the thatch. The whole family was in residence at the time and fled into the study to rescue what they could. Fortunately, all Conan Doyle's manuscripts were delivered from the flames, but the building was gutted. A few days later, he published a letter in the *Southern Daily Echo*, thanking all those who had assisted in helping to save what belongings they could from the house, including the one or two who 'showed a disposition to remove the goods even further'. Despite the disaster, he kept his sense of humour and immediately issued a commission to have the house rebuilt, but he was never to stay in it again.

On account of the Conan Doyles' spiritualism, Bignell House was long regarded with suspicion by the locals who, by and large, assiduously avoided it. In 1960, new owners – both of them also University of Edinburgh-trained doctors, the father of one of them having coincidentally been a contemporary and acquaintance of Conan Doyle when a student – discovered the house to be haunted. Noises were heard in the attic and the figure of a tall, old man with a moustache was seen in the house: it was clearly recognisable as Conan Doyle. The ghost said it was searching for a diary bound in red leather and held by a black elastic band. In the summer of 1961, an exorcism service was held and the haunting ceased. Shortly afterwards, it was discovered from a Doyle relative that Conan Doyle had indeed kept a secret diary bound in red leather which had gone missing.

For many years, Conan Doyle had continued, off and on, to lobby for justice in the case of Oscar Slater. Every time a new Secretary of State for Scotland came to office, he wrote to him to demand a judicial inquiry. His every letter drew much the same response. No inquiry was to be held, for the case had been settled satisfactorily in the eyes of the law. However, in the late 1920s, matters began to move again.

Slater, incarcerated in Peterhead Prison on the windswept, easternmost extremity of Scotland, succeeded in 1925 in smuggling out a

message to Conan Doyle by way of a released fellow convict, William
Gordon. In the message, Slater shed no new light on his conviction
but essentially pleaded his innocence, begged not to be forgotten and
requested that Conan Doyle make one last effort to free him. Slater
was unaware that Conan Doyle, who had not stayed in touch with
him, had not forgotten his case.

In response to Slater's plea, Conan Doyle girded his loins for another
attempt at overturning the conviction. He was not, as has often been
assumed, fighting Slater's corner alone, for a number of other prominent
men were also involved in the campaign, including Sir Herbert Stephen,
but he had the highest public profile.

As usual, his first salvo was a series of letters to the Secretary of
State for Scotland demanding a pardon, followed by more to influential
friends and the press. With public awareness increasing once more,
he gave a series of speeches and press interviews restating the details
of the case and outlining his reasons for believing there had been
a miscarriage of justice. The campaign gathered momentum when a
Glaswegian journalist, William Park, started to take an interest in what
was a local story and became absorbed in it. He delved deeply into the
background and was convinced of Slater's innocence. In July 1927,
he published a pamphlet, 'The Truth about Oscar Slater', for which
Conan Doyle wrote a foreword. The pamphlet was forthright and, for
its day, courageously outspoken. Park attacked the police handling of
the investigation, criticised the trial judge and openly accused Miss
Gilchrist's nephew of her murder.

The pamphlet stirred up the mud. A number of newspapers, seeing a
good story if nothing else and conscious that it could boost circulation,
took up the case, and several law journals, interested in the legal
implications, joined in. With the furore gathering pace, the *Empire
News* traced Helen Lambie, the maid, who had emigrated to the USA.
On 23 October, they published a statement from her in which she
declared that, when first interrogated by the police, she had named
the man she had seen leaving the building at the time of the murder.
He was, she claimed, a regular visitor of Miss Gilchrist's whom she had
seen on several previous occasions. The police, she said, had chosen
to ignore her. She added that, far from being the reclusive old lady
she had been made out to be in the trial, Miss Gilchrist quite often
entertained visitors, at which times the maid was told to make herself
scarce. The climax of the statement was Helen Lambie's insistence
that the police had made her identify Slater. Spurred on by such a
revelation, and not to be outdone by a competing newspaper, the

Daily News unearthed Mary Barrowman, the teenage girl bystander, whom they found living near Glasgow. She claimed that the police had virtually dictated her statement and that, before the trial, she had spent a considerable length of time with the Procurator-Fiscal, being coached as to what to say in court. She admitted that she had never been sure of the identity of the man leaving the building and added that she had been bribed with £100 to finger Slater with the crime. It then transpired that Helen Lambie had also been paid off with £40.

Within weeks, Slater was released on the pretence of having earned remission from his sentence for good behaviour. Upon gaining his freedom, he wrote to Conan Doyle, 'Sir Conan Doyle, you breaker of shackels [sic], you lover of truth for justice's sake, I thank you from the bottom of my heart for the goodness you have shown toward me. My heart is full and almost breaking with love and gratitude for you . . .'

Slater now possessing his liberty, Conan Doyle temporarily put aside his spiritualist writing to update 'The Case for Oscar Slater', a copy of which he then sent with a covering letter to every Member of Parliament. His intention was to press for a retrial, for, although he was free, Slater had not been given a pardon. As the verdict was so old, a special Act of Parliament had to be passed allowing the Scottish Court of Criminal Appeal to reopen the case. A preliminary hearing was held on 8 June 1928, the appeal date being set for 9 July in Edinburgh. The matter looked set for a satisfactory conclusion, but then Slater, on discovering that he was not to be allowed to give evidence, decided against proceeding. Conan Doyle was understandably livid. He had put a lot of energy into righting Slater's injustice, at the expense of spiritualism and his own writing, and he was damned if he would see this wasted. Fortunately, Slater was persuaded by his legal advisers to proceed with the appeal.

At the appeal hearing, Conan Doyle met Slater for the first time. He was covering the case on behalf of the *Sunday Pictorial*. Slater, who was virtually penniless, discovered that the government would not meet his legal costs, so Conan Doyle guaranteed £1,000 towards the three defence barristers' fees, the remainder of the money being raised by subscription in the Jewish community (Slater, it will be remembered, was a Jew). On the tenth day of the hearing, he was cleared of all charges on a face-saving technicality. It was claimed that the original trial judge had misdirected the jury. The verdict of murder was dismissed and Slater declared not guilty. He was awarded £6,000 compensation, which he accepted, but he still had to pay his costs. This he did, but with money from Conan Doyle and his Jewish supporters. The bill settled, he then refused to reimburse Conan Doyle's guarantee on the grounds that, the government having declined to meet the cost of a retrial, he should keep all his compensation.

Conan Doyle was disgusted and hurt. It was not a matter of the money but rather of integrity. He thought Slater was honour-bound to meet his obligation, and he also felt that he should offer a token of gratitude to William Park, who had really set the ball rolling with his pamphlet and newspaper features. When Slater sent Conan Doyle a silver cigar cutter as a sign of his gratitude, he immediately returned it. His thoughts were summed up in a letter to Slater which read, 'If you are indeed quite responsible for your actions, then you are the most ungrateful as well as the most foolish person whom I have ever known.' He subsequently allowed that Slater probably behaved dishonourably because of his long years of confinement. Yet he still did not forgive him.

Slater's was not the only case of injustice to fill Conan Doyle's time in 1928. On account of an ancient piece of anti-witchcraft legislation dating back to the reign of James I, mediums and those attending a seance were legally liable to prosecution and imprisonment. Furthermore, any supernatural society or association was unable by law to be the recipient of a legacy or deed of covenant. If the anti-witchcraft law was inapplicable in a case, the matter could be dealt with obliquely under the provisions of the Vagrancy Act of 1824.

The law was not often tested but, in 1928, a medium called Mrs Cantlon, employed by the London Spiritualist Alliance, of which Conan Doyle was president, was arrested and prosecuted. As in the Slater case, the police did not behave with much professional circumspection. The arrest resulted from entrapment. Two policewomen infiltrated a seance as clients and were the main witnesses for the prosecution. When it came to trial, the London Spiritualist Alliance lost the case and, although no fine was levied, they had to pay heavy costs. Conan Doyle, considering this unfair, wrote to The Times to complain about the persecution of spiritualists and embarked upon a course of action to have the laws repealed.

After this brief interlude fighting injustice, Conan Doyle returned to the spiritualist barricades with a five-month lecture tour of South Africa and the Rhodesias, the British African colonies of Kenya and Uganda and the British Protectorate of Tanganyika, formerly German East Africa, which Britain had come to administer after the Treaty of Versailles. He left with his family in November 1928 but against his doctor's orders. His circulation was poor ther*   347

and he occasionally felt dizzy, with a sporadic loss of feeling in his limbs.

The party sailed to Cape Town, staying in the Mount Nelson Hotel, where he had briefly stopped over in 1900. The local newspapers violently attacked him, especially those affiliated to the ultra-devout Dutch Reform Church. Undeterred, he conducted seances and gave a radio broadcast. From Cape Town, he set off for as many main towns as he could reach in the time allowed, the southern leg of the itinerary culminating in Johannesburg, where his lectures included one on the Cottingley fairies, which he still could not believe were a hoax. After a brief stopover in the city, the family moved on to Pretoria, then headed north.

Even today, the overland journey they embarked upon is a hard one. Despite the colonial infrastructure of roads and railways, the route Conan Doyle plotted out for them – and spiritualism – was ambitious and arduous. Leaving Pretoria, they went to Salisbury (now Harare) by way of the Great Zimbabwe ruins near Fort Victoria (now Masvingo), then on to the Matopo Hills, where he and Jean held a seance at the grave of Cecil Rhodes, who sent them a message in automatic writing. Moving on to Bulawayo, they travelled to Livingstone and the Victoria Falls before striking out across what is now Zambia, Malawi and Tanzania to Lake Victoria, where they crossed by boat to Kampala, the capital of Uganda, from where they then went on by train to Nairobi and, finally, Mombasa. The whole journey from Cape Town was well over twelve thousand kilometres.

Conan Doyle was nearly seventy years old yet still very active. He took every opportunity to be a tourist, was still insatiably curious and just as abrasive. When someone accused him of using Kingsley's death as a publicity gimmick for spiritualism, he chased after them with an umbrella. Near Bloemfontein, when he visited the Boer memorial to the thousands of women and children who had died in British concentration camps during the South African War, he declared it was a disgrace that the British had been blamed for the atrocity. His protestation was picked up by the Afrikaans press which vehemently attacked him. A hostile crowd gathered outside his hotel, but Conan Doyle and the family were not there at the time. The police suggested, for his own safety, that he might leave town by road to board his train a station or two down the line but, needless to say, he refused.

While he and Jean involved themselves in spiritualist matters, the children made the most of the opportunities Africa offered. Denis and Adrian indulged themselves with a spot of big-game hunting. On one occasion, this led to Adrian putting his life at great risk. He shot a large crocodile which had, the night before, killed a local native. As soon as it was hit, the reptile disappeared under the surface of the water. An African youth then waded out with a pole to try to hook the carcass, although the animal might well not have been dead. He seemed oblivious to the fact that where there was one crocodile there were almost certainly more. Conan Doyle called out for the youth not to bother but he was already in the water. Adrian, although terrified, joined him, for he knew that to shirk the responsibility of sharing the danger would put him in a bad light with his father, such was the respect and awe in which Conan Doyle was held by his children from whom he expected the same high standards of moral behaviour as those by which he governed himself.

By the time the tour was over, and the family on board ship bound for England, Conan Doyle was exhausted. The long train journeys, the strain of so many public speaking engagements, the excitement of travelling through the Dark Continent and the heat of the African summer had all adversely affected his health. His dizzy spells grew more frequent and it was clear to both his doctors and himself – for he had not forgotten his medical training – that his circulation was deteriorating and his heart not as strong as might have been wished.

Upon returning to Windlesham in March 1929, he finished his account of the tour, *Our African Winter*. The book dealt with not only the spiritualistic side of the trip but also the social, economic and political state of affairs as he saw them across British colonial sub-Saharan Africa. His attitude towards black Africans was patronising and paternalistic, but this is not to condemn him, for he was merely expressing the commonly held opinions of the time. He was against educating Africans because he thought, as did many others, that education would foster discontent which, in turn, would threaten social and colonial stability. In South Africa, he remarked upon the continuing rift between white settlers of British and Dutch extraction, the problems arising from Asian labour immigration, especially from the Indian subcontinent, and the vast outnumbering of white by black South Africans. He needed no spirit message from Pheneas to appreciate that, as he put it, 'The present rate of [population] increase is all against the whites. The danger is not immediate, but it is a very real one for the future. The only solution would seem to lie in greatly accelerated immigration.' Regardless of his proposed solution, he still made some protest about the manner in which he saw black Africans being ill treated. Wherever it arose, he still saw the glimmer of injustice and felt it needed addressing.

That summer in Windlesham, Conan Doyle made a recording for the Gramophone Co., Ltd, who owned the famous His Master's Voice label. Entitled 'Conan Doyle Speaking', it has him recounting the background to his writing of the Sherlock Holmes stories and why he converted to spiritualism. More or less at the same time, he was filmed at home for a short newsreel by Movietone News. As on the record, he spoke of his spiritualist convictions and Sherlock Holmes. These were the only occasions on which he was either recorded or filmed.

Before departing for Africa, and throughout the tour, he had been working on some new fiction, but it was not without motive. He knew he could once again use his status as a fiction writer to further his spiritualism. In 1929, a new collection of short stories, *The Maracot Deep and Other Stories*, was published, the contents leaning heavily towards science fiction.

The title story had its roots in the Atlantis legend and *The Lost World*. Indeed, it was subtitled 'The Lost World under the Sea'. The plot involved a diving bell that was severed from its chain to sink into a deep chasm on the seabed where the occupants were rescued by descendants of the lost world of Atlantis, to be guided into a submarine city governed by black dwarfs who had enslaved a taller white race. Obviously, his thoughts on racial supremacy in South Africa were getting another airing. In writing of Atlantean society, he exposed his own opinions of modern Britain. 'There was [he described] no longer the quiet and simple family life, nor the cultivation of the mind, but we had a glimpse of a people who were restless and shallow, rushing from one pursuit to another, grasping ever at pleasure, for ever missing it, and yet imagining always that in some more complex and unnatural form it might still be found.' All was not lost, however, for there remained in the sunken world a reformer 'of singular strength of mind and body, who gave a lead to all the others'. He was also gifted with the ability to communicate with spirits. It takes no great leap of the imagination to suggest on whom this reformer might have been based. At the end of the story, Professor Maracot, the leader of the diving-bell crew and physically not far removed from Sherlock Holmes, succeeds in reducing the mystical Lord of the Dark Face, who is threatening to destroy the city, to a 'semi-liquid heap of black and horrible putrescence'. He achieves this by means of meditative, concentrated prayer.

In two of the other stories in the book, Professor Challenger reappears, none the worse for his brush with spiritualism. 'The Disintegration Machine' is about a machine that can deconstruct matter, then move it through space to reconstruct it at another location. Conan Doyle saw such a possibility as evil and had the machine turn on its inventor. It is believed that he was one of the first writers of science fiction – if one can, for convenience, so temporarily classify him – to consider the possibility of the transference of matter. This would not have seemed so bizarre to him when one considers his belief in the spiritualistic production of ectoplasm. 'When the World Screamed' is about another invention made by Challenger, a sort of borehole-drilling machine which he drives deep into the earth to find that the planet is a living creature. The imagery was well ahead of its time, as was the modern idea of the earth as a dynamic ecosystem functioning as a vast, complex, integral organism. Just as he might have been the precursor for the transporter equipment on the *Star Trek* spaceships, so he was possibly the first fiction writer to conceive of the concept of the living planet. The fourth and final story seems to have been added simply to make up the required length of the manuscript. After three science fictionesque pieces came 'The Story of Spedegue's Dropper', about A.P. Lucas's freak bowling feat. It is quite out of place in the volume, which was, overall, weak. The plots were ill-thought-out and the characters cardboard. It looked as if, at last, the master might be losing his grip on his art.

Over the years, everyone had chided Conan Doyle for his spiritualism but, with most of them, he had won the fight, even if only on points. Now, in 1929, he faced an opponent altogether more formidable than any of the rationalists and medium-bashers of the past. He came into conflict with Father Herbert Thurston, the Jesuit priest who had been his contemporary at Stonyhurst.

In a pamphlet, 'Modern Spiritualism', Thurston gave no ground in his criticism of Conan Doyle. He stated categorically that spiritualism smacked of the Antichrist, Conan Doyle's style of writing showing him to be a dedicated but bitter old man. Conan Doyle's reaction was to bring out his own booklet, 'The Roman Catholic Church – A Rejoinder'. He systematically undermined Thurston's argument point by point, highlighted the priest's misunderstandings of the precepts of spiritualism, criticised his petty vindictiveness, and outlined his own opinions of Catholicism, its intolerant dogma and its history of narrow-minded inflexibility. He allowed, 'There is much that is sweet and beautiful in [Roman Catholicism]', but he quickly qualified this with 'there is [also] much which is vile and detestable. If some second reformation inside the Church itself were to preserve the one and destroy the other, it might still be a great agent for good in the world. It is however hardly likely to be so so long as it is the unresisting servant of the little junta of prelates in Italy.' After the better part of fifty-five years, he was still antagonistic towards a religion he felt had let him down.

Despite feeling increasingly ill, Conan Doyle undertook yet another, although not quite so adventurous, overseas trip in the cause of the spirits. In October, he was invited to Scandinavia. Lecturing on the way at The Hague, he moved on to Copenhagen, Stockholm and Oslo, giving radio interviews and receiving a generally friendly press. In Copenhagen, however, he woke in the night with searing chest pains. He must have known what they meant but he carried on with his commitments, most of the time in considerable pain. On his return, when his cross-Channel ferry docked at Dover on 10 November, he had to be carried ashore.

The diagnosis was angina, pains in the chest caused by a restricted blood flow to the heart muscles. He was ordered to rest but ignored the instruction and, the next day, travelled up to London to attend the Armistice Day Sunday spiritualist commemoration in the Albert Hall. In the cab going from the railway station to South Kensington, he suffered a violent attack but kept going. His speech to the assembly was halting and he found it hard to stay on his feet. Later that same Sunday, he spoke again at the Queen's Hall.

For the remainder of the winter, he suffered permanent ill-health and was not allowed to leave Windlesham. He even found going upstairs a trial, so his bed was moved into a downstairs room. Regardless of the pain and orders not to exert himself in the least, he continued to work. By Christmas, he was in good cheer but weak and forbidden any heavy Christmas dinner, having to make do with a bunch of grapes.

Much to his chagrin, his illness forced him to cancel all public engagements and, in January 1930, although not a result of his illness, he sadly felt obliged to resign from the Society for Psychical Research, of which he had been a member and staunch supporter for thirty-six years. He had of late been at odds with the society, which he thought had started to consider all mediums to be impostors. When the January issue of the society journal published a critical review of a recent book, *Modern Psychic Mysteries*, he could not restrain himself.

The reviewer, Theodore Besterman, was critical of the description of seances held in Millesimo Castle near Savona, west of Genova, the home of an Italian nobleman and spiritualist acquaintance of Conan Doyle. The article stated that the nobleman had taken insufficient precautions against fraud at his seances, thus maligning his spiritualist character and credentials. Conan Doyle was quick to come to his defence. With much regret, he resigned from the society, circulating his letter of resignation amongst the members, stating that he thought it inconceivable that a nobleman would cheat and that the society, by implying he had, was doing harm to its good reputation. Not satisfied to leave it at that, he then wrote a number of letters to the journal decrying the society's approach to its investigation of psychic occurrences.

By the spring, he felt a little more himself again. He continued to read on a wide range of subjects, studied the daily papers with his usual avidity, wrote letters to editors and, as a form of relaxation, started to paint and draw. One of the pictures he drew was entitled *The Old Horse*. It was more of a humorous cartoon than a picture, but it carried a serious message. In it, an ancient nag is seen pulling a cart labelled 'Life Work Carriage Co.', piled high with Conan Doyle's achievements. Behind it wends a road dotted with way stations, each of them a staging post in his own life – Edinburgh, Stonyhurst, his voyage on the *Hope*, his medical practice in Southsea, the Boer War . . . The last, just behind the cart, shows Conan Doyle himself lying on a chaise-longue with two bottles of medicine on a side table.

When he felt able, he went on day trips to London, visiting the bookshop in Victoria Street and taking a light luncheon at the Reform Club after which he would have a game of billards. Still a keen cricket fan, he followed the fortunes of the county cricket teams, but his playing days were well and truly over.

Owing to his ill-health, he was unable to assist in the production of what was called the Crowborough Edition of his literary work. It was a twenty-four-volume, 760-copy signed limited edition issue of all his works of fiction. It had been the intention of the publisher, Doubleday, Doran and Company in New York, to have him revise every book, write a preface to each and put them all into creative chronological order, but the task was beyond him and all he provided was a general introduction. What was to be his last book appeared in June 1930. Entitled *The Edge of the Unknown*, it was a collection of essays on spiritualism, all of which had been previously published in periodicals.

Also that month, it looked as if his continued agitation for justice for mediums under the law might be paying off. As a result of his correspondence with the Home Secretary, a meeting was convened for 1 July between the latter as representative of His Majesty's government and a selected group of spiritualist supporters. The idea was to draft a private member's bill to be put before Parliament as soon as was feasible, addressing anomalies in the witchcraft legislation and excluding spiritualist mediums from its scope. The meeting duly took place, Conan Doyle coming up to London to make a speech in support of the rescinding of the relevant Acts of Parliament. Yet the strain of his day in London was too much and he returned home very much weakened, although, three days later, he felt fit enough to write a letter to the editor of the *Daily Telegraph* about Winston Churchill's account of why he thought the British had failed to capture Constantinople during the First World War, Conan Doyle arguing that, in the long run, it had been a good thing that the military campaign had failed.

He knew he was dying but it did not concern him. He told a friend that he was content, at peace and happy, not bothered whether he stayed or went. Death held no fear for him. As a spiritualist, it was nothing to be afraid of, just a gateway in the passage of existence, a door through which one had to pass to a better place. He had written, just a day or so before, 'I have had many adventures. The greatest and most glorious of all awaits me now.'

On the night of 6 July, Conan Doyle suffered a heart attack. Aware that the door was opening for him, he expressed the wish not to die in bed, and was helped into an armchair facing the window, looking out over the Sussex countryside, resplendent in high summer. Seated there, surrounded by his family, he died at 8.30 on the morning of Monday, 7 July 1930. He was seventy-one.

On the last page of one of his many notebooks, probably written some time during 1926, he wrote, 'I desire to die as I have lived without clerical interference, and with the peace which comes from acting honestly up to one's own mental convictions.'

And so he did.

He was buried four days later in a grave in the garden at Windlesham, close to the little hut in which he had liked to work and where he and Jean had so often taken tea together. The funeral service for three hundred guests was held in the rose garden. There was reportedly little sign of mourning. The many spiritualists present did not assume he was dead but rather that he had simply passed over to the next plane. His literary friends were the ones who most keenly felt the loss. Although he had not wanted to be interfered with by clerics, the service was conducted by Reverend C. Drayton Thomas with Cyril Angell assisting. Upon his grave was placed a grave-board made of British oak bearing his name, date of birth and an epitaph.

His death was covered worldwide in the press, over the course of several days in the USA. The *Strand Magazine*, which had in so many ways made him, just as he had shaped its own fortunes, summed him up best in its memorial notice: 'He lived and enjoyed life to the full.'

On Sunday, 13 July, a spiritualist memorial service took place in the Albert Hall with a congregation of eight thousand. An empty chair was placed between Jean and Denis for Conan Doyle to sit in. A medium, Estelle Roberts, stated that she saw him enter the auditorium and sit in it, giving her a message which she passed on to Jean. She, however, had apparently already been in touch with her husband, within twenty-four hours of his death. In the days that followed, mediums worldwide reported messages coming in from him. In death, as in life, it seems he kept up his busy routine of correspondence.

A fortnight later, Jean announced in the press that her husband had positively communicated with her through a spirit photograph taken by William Hope, as well as by messages sent over the divide in automatic writing. Over the coming years, Jean heard voices in seances which she knew were Conan Doyle. In 1936, when she was suffering from cancer, he apparently diagnosed the problem before her doctors did, and he was known to advise other members of the family of happenings that were about to affect them. Jean died in 1940 and was buried next to Conan Doyle. After her passing, it is said that members of the family received messages from her as well.

In 1955, the family sold Windlesham. Conan Doyle and Jean were exhumed and their bodies taken for burial in the churchyard of the thirteenth-century Norman church at Minstead, in the New Forest, not far from Bignell House. Stories circulated about this reburial. One of Conan Doyle's biographers has actually claimed that the bodies were moved in secret, at night, hidden in a laundry van to put the press off the trail, but this tale is just a good yarn which might have made a very sound basis for a Sherlock Holmes story. The truth is that their remains were transferred by hearse for a simple ceremony attended by family and friends.

Conan Doyle, with Jean at his side, is buried on the south side of the churchyard, beneath a massive ancient oak tree which spreads over their grave. Upon his headstone are carved his name and, under that, the words 'Knight. Patriot, physician and man of letters' with the same epitaph as had been carved into the oak board at Windlesham: 'Steel true, blade straight'.

Bibliography

Book sources

The works of Sir Arthur Conan Doyle

Anon, *Confessions of an English Doctor*, George Routledge & Sons, London, 1904.

Ashley, Richard, *Cocaine: Its History, Uses and Effects*, St Martin's Press, New York, 1975.

Baker, Michael, *The Doyle Diary*, Paddington Press, London, 1978.

Baring-Gould, William S., *The Annotated Sherlock Holmes*, John Murray, London, 1968.

Berridge, Virginia, & Edwards, Griffith, *Opium and the People: Opiate Use in Nineteenth-Century England*, Yale University Press, New Haven and London, 1987.

Birkenhead, Lord, *Rudyard Kipling*, Weidenfeld and Nicolson, London, 1978.

Boar, Roger, & Blundell, Nigel, *The World's Greatest Unsolved Crimes*, Hamlyn, London, 1991.

Brown, Gerry, *The World's Greatest Mysteries*, Hamlyn, London, 1990.

Brown, Ivor, *Conan Doyle*, Hamish Hamilton, London, 1972.

Byck, Robert (ed), *Cocaine Papers by Sigmund Freud*, Stonehill Publishing Company, New York, 1974.

Carr, John Dickson, *The Life of Sir Arthur Conan Doyle*, John Murray, London, 1949.

Christopher, Milbourne, *Houdini: The Untold Story*, Cassell, London, 1969.

Connolly, Joseph, *Jerome K. Jerome: A Critical Biography*, Orbis, London, 1982.

Cooper, Joe, *The Case of the Cottingley Fairies*, Robert Hale, London, 1990.

Coren, Michael, *Conan Doyle*, Bloomsbury, London, 1995.

Cox, Don Richard, *Arthur Conan Doyle*, Frederick Ungar Publishing Co, New York, 1985.

Deacon, Richard, *A History of the British Secret Service*, Frederick Muller, London, 1969.

Doyle, Adrian Conan, *The True Conan Doyle*, John Murray, London, 1945.

Eagle, Dorothy, & Carnell, Hilary (eds), *The Oxford Literary Guide to the British Isles*, Oxford University Press, London, 1977.

Edwards, Owen Dudley, *The Quest for Sherlock Holmes*, Mainstream, Edinburgh, 1983.

Gibson, John Michael, & Green, Richard Lancelyn, *The Unknown Conan Doyle: Letters to the Press*, Secker & Warburg, London, 1986.

Gibson, John Michael, & Green, Richard Lancelyn, *The Unknown Conan Doyle: Essays on Photography*, Secker & Warburg, London, 1982.

Green, Richard Lancelyn (ed), *The Uncollected Sherlock Holmes*, Penguin Books, London, 1983.

Green, Richard Lancelyn, & Gibson, John Michael, *A Bibliography of A. Conan Doyle*, Clarendon Press, Oxford, 1983.

Hardwick, Michael & Mollie, *The Man Who Was Sherlock Holmes*, John Murray, London, 1964.

Higham, Charles, *The Adventures of Conan Doyle*, Hamish Hamilton, London, 1976.

Jones, Kelvin I., *Conan Doyle and the Spirits*, The Aquarian Press, Wellingborough, 1989.

Lamond, John, *Arthur Conan Doyle: A Memoir* (with an epilogue by Lady Conan Doyle), John Murray, London, 1931.

Lellenberg, Jon L. (ed), *The Quest for Arthur Conan Doyle*, Southern Illinois University Press, Carbondale and Edwardsville, 1987.

Mackenzie, Norman & Jeanne, *The Time Traveller – The Life of H.G. Wells*, Weidenfeld and Nicolson, London, 1973.

McAll, Dr. Kenneth, *Healing the Family Tree*, Sheldon Press, London, 1994.

Nordon, Pierre (trans. by Frances Partridge), *Conan Doyle*, John Murray, London, 1966.

Nown, Graham, *Elementary, My Dear Watson: Sherlock Holmes Centenary; His Life and Times*, Ward Lock, London, 1986.

Oriel, Harold (ed), *Sir Arthur Conan Doyle: Interviews and Recollections*, Macmillan, London, 1991.

Parssinen, Terry, *Secret Passion, Secret Remedies: Narcotic Drugs in British Society 1820–1930*, Manchester University Press, Manchester, 1983.

Pearsall, Ronald, *Conan Doyle: A Biographical Solution*, Weidenfeld and Nicolson, London, 1977.

Pearson, Hesketh, *Conan Doyle*, Methuen, London, 1943.

Pegg, John, *After Dark on Dartmoor*, John Pegg Publishing, Tunbridge Wells, 1984.

Pointer, Michael, *The Pictorial History of Sherlock Holmes*, Bison Books, London, 1991.

Pope-Hennessy, James, *Robert Louis Stevenson*, Cassell, London, 1989.

Rodin, Alvin E., & Key, Jack D., *Medical Casebook of Doctor Arthur Conan Doyle*, Robert E. Krieger Publishing, Florida, 1984.

Rosenberg, Samuel, *Naked Is the Best Disguise – The Death and Resurrection of Sherlock Holmes*, Arlington Books, London, 1975.
Sparrow, Gerald, *The Great Traitors*, John Long, London, 1965.
Stavert, Geoffrey, *A Study in Southsea – The Unrevealed Life of Doctor Arthur Conan Doyle*, Milestone Publications, Portsmouth, 1987.
Symons, Julian, *The Tell-Tale Heart – The Life and Works of Edgar Allan Poe*, Penguin Books, London, 1981.
Symons, Julian, *Portrait of an Artist – Conan Doyle*, Whizzard Press/André Deutsch, London, 1979.
Watson, Colin, *Snobbery with Violence – Crime Stories and Their Audience*, Eyre & Spottiswoode, London, 1971.
Weller, Philip, with Roden, Christopher, *The Life and Times of Sherlock Holmes*, Crescent Books, New York, 1992.

Miscellaneous other sources

Folklore Myths and Legends of Britain, Reader's Digest, London, 1973.
Out of This World: Mysteries of Mind, Space and Time, Macdonald, London, 1989.

Journalism

Independent (2 March 1996) – 'Where Sherlock Holmes feared to tread'.
Sunday Times (19 May 1996) – 'Begorra, c'est élémentaire, Miss Watson'.
Sunday Telegraph (4 February 1996) – 'The case of the treacherous mountain crossing'.
British Medical Journal, 1874, Volume 1 – J.A. Bell, 'The Use of Coca'.
British Medical Journal, 1876, Volume 1 – R. Christison, 'Observations on the effects of the leaves of Erthroxylon Coca'.
Alchemist, 1957, Volume 21 – W.R. Bett, 'Cocaine, divine plant of the Incas: Some pioneers and some addicts'.
The Dalesman (July 1975), Volume 37, No. 4 – W.R. Mitchell, 'The Mystery of Masongill House'.

Index

ACD indicates Arthur Conan Doyle